THE FUTURE OF ROME

How was the future of Rome, both near and distant in time, imagined by different populations living in the Roman Empire? It emerges from this collection of essays by a distinguished international team of scholars that Romans, Greeks, Jews and Christians had strikingly different answers to that question, revealing profound differences in their conceptions of history and historical time, the purpose of history and the meaning of written words and oral traditions. It is also argued that practically no one living under Rome's rule, including the Romans themselves, did *not* think about the question in one form or another.

JONATHAN J. PRICE is Lessing Professor of Ancient History at Tel Aviv University. He is the author of *Jerusalem Under Siege: The Collapse of the Jewish State, 66–70 C.E.* (1992), *Thucydides and Internal Conflict* (Cambridge, 2002), and dozens of articles on Greek and Roman historiography, the Jews under Roman rule, and epigraphy in Greek, Hebrew and Aramaic. He is the editor of the Jewish inscriptions for the *Corpus Inscriptionum Iudaeae/Palaestinae: A Multi-lingual corpus of the Inscriptions from Alexander to Muhammad* (CIIP) (5 volumes, 2010–2020).

KATELL BERTHELOT is a Centre National de la Recherche Scientifique (CNRS) Professor within the University of Aix-Marseille, working on the history of Judaism in the Hellenistic and Roman period. Her most recent book is *In Search of the Promised Land? The Hasmonean Dynasty Between Biblical Models and Hellenistic Diplomacy* (2018). She has received a Consolidator Grant from the European Research Council, to work on the political and religious challenge posed by the Roman Empire to the Jews (www.judaism-and-rome.org).

THE FUTURE OF ROME

Roman, Greek, Jewish and Christian Visions

EDITED BY

JONATHAN J. PRICE

Tel Aviv University

KATELL BERTHELOT

Centre National de la Recherche Scientifique

CAMBRIDGE
UNIVERSITY PRESS

University Printing House, Cambridge CB2 8BS, United Kingdom

One Liberty Plaza, 20th Floor, New York, NY 10006, USA

477 Williamstown Road, Port Melbourne, VIC 3207, Australia

314–321, 3rd Floor, Plot 3, Splendor Forum, Jasola District Centre,
New Delhi – 110025, India

79 Anson Road, #06-04/06, Singapore 079906

Cambridge University Press is part of the University of Cambridge.

It furthers the University's mission by disseminating knowledge in the pursuit of education, learning, and research at the highest international levels of excellence.

www.cambridge.org
Information on this title: http://www.cambridge.org/9781108494816
DOI: 10.1017/9781108860000

© Cambridge University Press 2020

This publication is in copyright. Subject to statutory exception and to the provisions of relevant collective licensing agreements, no reproduction of any part may take place without the written permission of Cambridge University Press.

First published 2020

A catalogue record for this publication is available from the British Library.

Library of Congress Cataloging-in-Publication Data
NAMES: Price, Jonathan J., author. | Berthelot, Katell, author.
TITLE: The Future of Rome : Roman, Greek, Jewish and Christian Visions / Edited by Jonathan J. Price (Tel-Aviv University), Katell Berthelot (Centre national de la recherche scientifique (CNRS), Paris).
DESCRIPTION: Cambridge; New York: Cambridge University Press, 2020. | "Cambridge University Press is part of the University of Cambridge." | Includes bibliographical references and index.
IDENTIFIERS: LCCN 2020015740 (print) | LCCN 2020015741 (ebook) | ISBN 9781108494816 (hardback) | ISBN 9781108860000 (ebook)
SUBJECTS: LCSH: Rome – Forecasting
CLASSIFICATION: LCC DG270 .F88 2020 (print) | LCC DG270 (ebook) | DDC 937–dc23
LC record available at https://lccn.loc.gov/2020015740
LC ebook record available at https://lccn.loc.gov/2020015741

ISBN 978-1-108-49481-6 Hardback

Cambridge University Press has no responsibility for the persistence or accuracy of URLs for external or third-party internet websites referred to in this publication and does not guarantee that any content on such websites is, or will remain, accurate or appropriate.

Contents

List of Contributors		*page* vii
Acknowledgments		viii
List of Abbreviations		ix

	Introduction	1
1.	Some Remarks on Cicero's Perception of the Future of Rome *Carlos Lévy*	17
2.	*Eclogue* 4 and the Futures of Rome *Brian W. Breed*	32
3.	*Imperium sine fine*: Rome's Future in Augustan Epic *Ayelet Haimson Lushkov*	47
4.	Posterity in the Arval *Acta* *Greg Woolf*	64
5.	The Future of Rome in Three Greek Historians of Rome *Jonathan J. Price*	85
6.	Philo on the Impermanence of Empires *Katell Berthelot*	112
7.	From Human Freedom to Divine Intervention: Agrippa II's Address on the Eve of the Jewish War *Samuele Rocca*	130
8.	Josephus, Caligula and the Future of Rome *Jonathan Davies*	155

9. "Will This One Never Be Brought Down?": Jewish Hopes for the Downfall of the Roman Empire 169
   Vered Noam

10. The Sibylline Oracles and Resistance to Rome 189
    Erich S. Gruen

11. Revelation 17.1–19.10: A Prophetic Vision of the Destruction of Rome 206
    Peter Oakes

12. Cicero and Vergil in the Catacombs: Pagan Messianism and Monarchic Propaganda in Constantine's *Oration to the Assembly of Saints* 227
    Marko Marinčič

13. The Future of Rome after 410 CE: The Latin Conceptions (410–480 CE) 245
    Hervé Inglebert

Appendix 259
Bibliography 274
Index Locorum 298
Index of Names and Places 311

Contributors

KATELL BERTHELOT, Professor at the Centre National de la Recherche Scientifique (CNRS) and Aix-Marseille University.

BRIAN W. BREED, Professor of Classics, University of Massachusetts Amherst.

JONATHAN DAVIES, Lecturer in Ancient Classics, Maynooth University.

HERVÉ INGLEBERT, Professor of Roman History, Université Paris Nanterre.

ERICH S. GRUEN, Wood Professor of History and Classics, Emeritus, University of California, Berkeley.

CARLOS LÉVY, Professor Emeritus, Sorbonne Paris University.

AYELET HAIMSON LUSHKOV, Associate Professor of Classics, The University of Texas at Austin.

MARKO MARINČIČ, Professor of Roman and Greek Literature, University of Ljubljana.

VERED NOAM, Professor in the Department of Jewish Philosophy and Talmud, Tel Aviv University.

PETER OAKES, Rylands Professor of Biblical Criticism and Exegesis, University of Manchester.

JONATHAN J. Price, The Lessing Professor of Ancient History, Tel Aviv University.

SAMUELE ROCCA, Ariel University.

GREG WOOLF, Professor of Classics and Director of the Institute of Classics, University of London.

Acknowledgments

The original conference from which this volume originated was funded by the Israel Academy of Sciences and Humanities; the Centre National de la Recherche Scientifique, Paris, in the framework of the research network Groupement de Recherche International (GDRI) on Judaism and Rome (JUDROME); and in Tel Aviv University by the President's Fund, Vice President Professor Raanan Rein, the Dean of Humanities, the School of History and the School of Jewish Studies. The editors thank all of these sources for their generosity. We would also like to thank Adrian Sackson for his attentive editing and Noam Rytwo for his labors in compiling the bibliography and indices; their conscientious attention to detail was exemplary. Finally, we would like to thank Michael Sharp at Cambridge University Press for his patient guidance in bringing this volume to a successful conclusion; it is certainly better because of his tactful involvement.

Abbreviations

CIL = Corpus Inscriptionum Latinarum (Mommsen et al.)
IGRR = Inscriptiones Graecae ad Res Romanas Pertinentes (Cagnat et al.)
ILS = Inscriptiones Latinae Selectae (Dessau)
SEG = Supplementum Epigraphicum Graecum (Chaniotis et al.)

Introduction

This volume brings together studies from diverse academic disciplines around a central, unifying question: how was the future of Rome, both near and distant in time, imagined by different populations living under the Roman Empire? The volume originates in a conference in Tel Aviv (2013), titled "The Future of Rome: Roman, Greek, Jewish and Christian Perspectives." Scholars of Greek and Roman history and literature, Jewish history and thought, and early Christian history and thought, were asked the question about the future of Rome in relation to the people and texts they study; thus it was refracted through contemporary but disparate (and not perforce mutually informative or interactive) literary and religious traditions. One of the remarkable results of the conference was the realization that practically no one living under Rome's rule, including the Romans themselves, did *not* think about the question in one form or another.

Such was the effect of the vast extent and power of Rome's empire, the antiquity and success of the city, with its explicit and implicit claim of universality and eternity, and its penetration into the lives of its subjects, that it imposed on basic aspects of human cognition and sentience, affecting people's individual and group identity, their self-understanding on a historical continuum and their concepts of historical time, their beliefs about the role of divine and supernatural factors in present personal circumstance and all history. Thinking about the future in any period will evoke such existential questions as one's sense of place and purpose; in the period extending from the Late Republic to Late Anquity, these questions frequently took the form of reaction to Rome, in a variety of forms.

It is important to state that the main question occupying the lecturers at the conference and the contributors to this volume (not an identical roster) is not what Jonas Grethlein has called in a recent book, "futures past."[1] This term concerns the historian's perspective, both the modern historian

---
[1] Grethlein 2013.

looking back with a long view at past events, and more interestingly, ancient historians' use of teleology, i.e. knowledge of outcomes, in constructing their narratives of past events. Grethlein is interested in separating the experience of the historical subjects, who did not know their future, from the construction of their experience by the historian armed with that knowledge. The *telos* in this sense lies within already-experienced historical time. By contrast, we are interested here in how historical subjects and writers conceived of the not-yet-experienced future of the Roman Empire, which was for them more or less equivalent to the future of humanity but also could have direct personal consequences. Thinking about the future of Rome could employ any number of means: logical speculation, reasoning from historical patterns, extrapolation from nature, exegetical reasoning, and application of religious belief. The question concerns all those who lived across the wide swath of the Empire (not just Romans and educated Greeks) and who tried to make sense of their lives on a historical continuum.

There existed in antiquity various concepts of time, but they divide into two main (but not mutually exclusive) types with variations, linear and cyclical. Aside from scholarship on time in Greek philosophy, the fundamental article by Arnaldo Momigliano, "Time in Ancient Historiography," and subsequent studies have focused on historical writing.[2] The present collection finds intersecting ideas about the future in a wide array of literary genres and cultures. François Hartog has written, in *Régimes d'historicité: Présentisme et expériences du temps* (Paris, 2012), that the pre-modern notion of lived-in time was undynamic, history serving as an undifferentiated resource for great ideas and actions informing the present. Thinking about the future is a habit of culture, and, for Hartog, defining one's present in terms of the future is a modern phenomenon (and after 1989, he says, we returned to a disorienting presentism). This characterization of the past, in which history is primarily *magister vitae*, is not the focus of analysis of most of the texts and thoughts in this volume. Rather, the analyses here focus on how the Romans and their subjects found patterns in historical time and used them to assess their present condition by peering into the future.

1 Romans

The Roman imperialistic notion of an unending future, which became a propagandistic theme of the Principate, first emerges in the late Republic.

---

[2] Momigliano 1977b. See also e.g. the two collections of essays edited by Alexandra Lanieri (2011 and 2016).

Cicero is our earliest surviving source for both the concept of Rome's eternity and an attempt to work out in Latin a concrete understanding of historical time. Historical immortality can be expressed in both linear and cyclical models of time. Carlos Lévy, in Chapter 1 (Some Remarks on Cicero's Perception of the Future of Rome), observes that while Cicero invokes the concept of eternal Rome, he shows "no deep reflexion on Rome's future." Cicero rather uses the concept of timelessness as a rhetorical and philosophical tool to work out the implications of Rome's exceptionalism. This was particularly pressing during Cicero's lifetime, "when the crisis of the Republic was so deep that even the incantatory evocation of the powerful empire and of prominent *exempla* was insufficient to mitigate it." *De Legibus* is an almost desperate last-ditch attempt to imagine the potential of Rome's greatness, but is based on what Lévy calls a "somewhat naïve teleology." Cicero's persistent, hopeful focus is on the grand elements of Rome and Romans that can be called immortal.

Translating the potentially immortal elements of Roman character and deeds into the immortality of Rome is presented most clearly in the *Pro Sestio*, where Cicero asks rhetorically, *quod si immortale retinetur, quis non intelligit immortalem hanc ciuitatem futuram*? ("If this example be preserved for ever, who can doubt that this State will be immortal?"). Immortality can be found in cyclical history as well: in his letters, Cicero evokes the theory of the mixed constitution in its Polybian form to wonder about Rome's future, elaborating on the exceptional qualities of Rome's geographical situation, legal and political system, and personal qualities of its people. But it is all phrased in the form of a condition: "If, for Cicero as much later for Descartes, the power of will is infinite, the concept of eternity of the *res publica* gets a new meaning. It produces the perfect adaptation of the Romans, and especially of the *maiores*, to the nature of things, and especially of political evolutions, but at the same time it depends on the ability of the citizens to want to maintain this privileged situation."

Vergil's Fourth *Eclogue*, marking the birth of a divine child and for-telling the imminence of peace in a new golden age, is another artifact of the struggle with hopes and doubts about the future in the catastrophic last years of the Republic. Brian Breed's Chapter 2 in this volume (*Eclogue* 4 and the Futures of Rome), a thoroughgoing analysis of that crucial poem, points to the ambiguity and uncertainty that arise from what are in fact multiple time-schemes underlying the poem. He learns from this that "Time does not fall easily into mutually exclusive periods with clear borders. Different ways of organizing time overlap and come into conflict, and Rome's future, its many possible futures, will develop through patterns and relationships that involve both division and continuity, and that expose tendencies toward both unification and fragmentation." The reason for uncertainty about the shape of the future derives from uncertainty about the present, and how to orient oneself from it: possibilities include but are not limited to the mythological metallic ages, the *fasti*, the human lifespan, the *saecula*, the *magnus annus*. Moreover, the golden age prophesied in the poem presents a difficult problem of interrpretation. Since Rome did not exist in the Hesiodic golden age, a new golden age represents not the return of a glorious Roman past but a new, unfamiliar era; the Romans had to decide what to carry from the old Rome into the hope-laden future. Thus the new golden age, by the terms of *Eclogue* 4, will coexist with elements of the iron, and universal peace will still be contingent on the matters of Rome and the suppression of its self-destructive tendencies.[3]

The universal harmony of a golden age, when established, will not be the same thing for all Romans. In fact, people will perforce experience it in radically different ways. To quote Breed's cogent conclusion:

> The association of the golden age with the rule of one man suggests that in or around 40 BC it was possible to imagine a future in which a fundamental change in the political culture at Rome could represent the basis for a claim that one period of time has ended and a new one has begun. But it equally offers the possibility of recognizing that lives will be differently impacted by any such change. For all that some will embrace change and adapt accordingly and others struggle to cope with the consequences, there will also be a choice to go on living in total or occasional disregard of the claims of a political authority to have altered the rhythms of life equally for all. So Vergil in the end is right about another thing. A change of eras will be as much a matter of interpretation, of recognizing patterns and balancing alternatives, in the political and social life of the Romans as it is in a literary text like *Eclogue* 4.

A different kind of multivalence attended the concept of Rome's eternity once the idea became a part of Augustan propaganda. The stability of the new regime and the early Principate, in retrospect, can make us forget that the confident assertions of the everlasting future of the city and Empire were expressions more of hope than solid facts (here the *telos* in the sense of

---

[3] That contingency may be seen as well in Horace *Odes* 3.30–6-9, in which the poet seeks to claim the eternity of his own poetic reputation by asserting that it will last so long as the *pontifex maximus* and the silent Vestal "climb the Capitol" in their annual rite. As Greg Woolf says in Chapter 4 (discussed pp. 6–7), "Horace's Ode evokes not just posterity but also eternity, the extension of the present conceived of endless iterations of the ritual cycle."

Grethlein's "futures past" is useful). In the first century, recent and even more distant history presented a situation of constant and rapid change: Rome's remarkable rise to world dominance, its rapid deterioration into internal chaos. The Augustan poets contended with the claim of a new unending historical era, but had to coordinate that with the evidence of their experience and learning. The actual term Roma Aeterna appears infrequently in Augustan literature.[4] As Philip Hardie has shown in some detail,[5] most of the Augustan poets' references to Rome's new stability and eternity are colored by an acknowledgment, either patent or implied, of the mutability of all things, a natural law to which even Rome is subject. The poetic accounts of early Rome bring out the dramatic contrast with present-day Rome. *Aeneid* Book 7 is rife with metamorphosis. Ovid's mention of Roma Aeterna in the *Fasti* is put into perspective by the role of Janus in the same poem, representing endless change.[6] The poets were reluctant or unable to harness themselves unambiguously to the theme of Rome's eternity stemming from its present restoration.

This ambiguity is explored by Ayelet Haimson Lushkov in Chapter 3 (*Imperium sine fine*: Rome's Future in Augustan Epic), which is a close comparative reading of a crucial concept from *Aeneid* 1 and the end of Ovid's *Metamorphoses*. The famous promise by Jupiter of *imperium sine fine* is explained straightforwardly: it "embodies ... the formal rejection of a narrative doubling back on itself, and celebrates instead the linear teleology of Augustan triumphalism: the Romans will never have run half the race, since theirs is a never-ending march to glory. To Venus' question – *quem finem?* – Jupiter's answer is a resounding 'none'." No actual limit, then, either temporal or geographical. The *imperium sine fine* is realized long after the epic poem itself ends in a grisly and unsatisfactory way with Turnus' death. Continuity implies necessary closures, so that the promise of Rome's future may also cause some anxiety in Vergil's readers: for Rome to be on the cusp of embodying Jupiter's promise, it had to pass through many violent endings, *inter alia* of Troy, Iulus' *imperium*, the kings, the Republic as it had been: what was the *imperium* that would extend endlessly into the future? Given the Romans' Trojan roots and historical memories such as the proposed transplantation to Veii opposed by Camillus, the Romans did not know even whether they would perpetually

---

[4] Cf. Tibullus 2.5.23; Ovid, *Fasti* 3.72. Actually, it is an expression that is used more in modern times than in antiquity. The phrase *Roma aeterna* does not appear on coins until the time of Hadrian (RIC II, 265a–d).
[5] Hardie 1994: 59–82.   [6] See also Newlands 1995: 7.

inhabit their imperial city (and cf. Horace's Epode 16, imagining Rome bereft after the civil war):

> The future imagined for Rome is one where not only the place itself but also its values have been abandoned, and that negative image functions protreptically to defend the city and ensure its proper and more glorious future. But choice of ends is also a choice of futures, and the contest between parallel futures is especially characteristic of the epic genre . . . .

The future of Rome is even more ambiguous in end of Ovid's *Metamorphoses*. We return here to Ovidian paradoxical juxtaposition of expressions of eternity beside finitude. The poem closes with the apotheosis of Julius Caesar, which Lushkov reads as a delicate intertextual play with the *Aeneid*, and then the poet's final assurances of his own poetic immortality being coterminous with Rome's. Caesar's deification is fulfillment of Helenus' prophecy, given voice by Ovid, of future Roman – and Julian – greatness. Essentially, this transition into a new era requires transitioning from historical time to mythical time: a cyclical return, but with no projected end. Yet the final scenes are preceded by the long discourse of Pythagoras expounding the constant flux of the universe, a law of constant change that must apply to Rome. "In the *Metamorphoses*, a poem which ends literally and figuratively with a decisive break in Rome's constitutional and religious growth, Rome's empire is *sine fine* in the sense that it is without a *telos*, which is not to say that it is without end." Thus Ovid's implied doubts about Rome's eternity affect even his own immortality as a poet.

It may be supposed that a notion of time extending indefinitely into the future was embodied in the Roman calendar, which erased distinctions between mythical and historical time and, after Caesar's reform, regularized and stabilized the year and brought order to ritual junctures.[7] This regularization allowed the Romans to relate to the future as static. Greg Woolf's explication of the Arval rituals and records, in Chapter 4 (Posterity in the Arval *Acta*), is based on a key insight, namely that ritual is a way of *suppressing* time, an attempt to flatten distinctions between past and future, so that the conception of time may not even contain proper linear motion: "the *Acta* construct a kind of continuous present in place of a sense of time flowing unidirectionally from past to future via the present. The implications for the future are clear. If change is always inconsequential and non-directional – Brownian motion more than entropy – then the future is

---

[7] Feeney 2007.

envisaged as essentially a prolongation of the present." The Arvals' purpose in publishing their proceedings was in fact to demonstrate the rituals' very timelessness, their (hoped-for) immunity to change, to ward off, almost talismanically, drastic and usually violent collapses, failures, and overturnings. The older cults of Rome, even those thought to predate the foundation of the city, served the same purpose, i.e. to establish the eternity of Rome by making the distant past and the infinite future an undifferentiated temporal space. Thus the function of commemorative time can be understood as "the recording of key events but in isolation, not as points on a sequence or moments in a narrative. Perhaps we might even see these dating conventions working actively to suppress any sense of history unrolling."

2 Greeks

The strongest interest in proofs of Rome's eternity – that is, Rome's breaking the historical law of the rise and fall of states with which Herodotus staked out his history – or at least the most serious attempts to grapple with the claim, are to be found in Greek writers, who, while within the intellectual and literary orbit of Rome, still endowed their writings with the enthusiasm of admiring non-natives explaining Rome to outsiders and skeptics. By the same token, the strongest assertions of Rome's certain demise – and the reasons for it – are conveyed in sectarian texts in languages other than Latin: Greek, Hebrew, Aramaic.

After Rome's victory in Pydna in 168 BCE, Greek historiography shifted its primary focus to Rome and universal history. The task of the historian is to narrate and explain, and Rome required explanation, not only its rise to domination but its continuing success and prognosis. Jonathan Price shows in Chapter 5 (The Future of Rome in Three Greek Historians of Rome), how Polybius, Dionysius of Halicarnassus, and Appian of Alexandria, while living in different eras, each used, as a means of analysis and explanation, the typological succession of four empires defining world history. These four empires were followed by a fifth, which in the Greek historians is Rome; the question was whether that fifth empire would be the last in the succession, or the succession would continue indefinitely. This 4+1 model, as later chapters in this volume bring out, was the basis for an apocalyptic vision in Judaism and Christianity, going back ultimately to the Book of Daniel. But the oriental origins of the model are irrelevant to the Greek historians' understanding of it: by Polybius' time it had migrated into Greek culture and was available for him to interpret. Polybius, as Price shows, is the hardest case, because of his notorious change of opinion about the shape and purpose of his history, reflecting (apparently) a change of opinion about Rome's fate: he seemed at first to think that Rome had overcome the inherent fatal flaws of other states and in fact had defeated the cycle of history, implying that the Roman Empire would last forever; but by the end of his *History*, near the end of the extra ten books he added after changing his mind, he marshals the 4+1 model to state as clearly as he could that Rome was subject to the same forces of decline as other states, and this fifth world empire would eventually come to end, giving way to a sixth, and so forth, *ad infinitum*.

Not so, however, Dionysius and Appian, who lived in different, less volatile ages (or at least in times when the volatility in certain provinces was felt less directly in Rome). Dionysius opens his work with the 4+1 model to justify his claim, in the manner of Thucydides, that his subject, Rome's origins and history, is the most worthwhile subject for the writer and reader of history. In his Preface he elaborates the implications of the model, and offers the climactic assessment that Rome "was ordained by fate to excel in the course of time all other cities, whether Greek or barbarian, not only in its size, but also in the majesty of its empire and in every other form of prosperity, and to be celebrated above them all as long as mortality shall endure." This seems to be Dionysius' genuine belief; at least the search for nuance and subterfuge in his writing have not been completely successful. It is certainly a plainer and less encumbered statement of Rome's immortality than anything found in Latin writers, even Aemelius Sura and Pompeius Trogus, whose use of the 4+1 model can be recovered from their fragmentary works.

The historian Appian lived at a time when the stability of the Roman Empire, despite a relatively brief violent transition between dynasties a hundred years previously, seemed secure and almost indisputable. Like Dionysius, Appian prefaces his *History* with the 4+1 succession of empires to demonstrate Rome's unprecedented greatness. Appian openly expresses confidence in Rome's continuing strength and domination; it had survived *stasis* by becoming stronger than before. Rome's endurance was a more prominent theme in Appian's time. In a similar manner, Aelius Aristides expressed the hope that Rome would be the last empire in history: "History records five empires, and may their numbers not increase."[8] Plutarch suggested that Rome, unlike all previous political entities, may have

---

[8] Aelius Aristides, *Panathenaic Oration* 234 (183–4).

defeated Fortune herself.[9] Yet doubt lingers: were *five books*, more than a fifth of the entire composition, really necessary to make the point of Rome's endurance – especially when those books are filled with ever more hideous examples of "the measureless ambition of men, their dreadful lust of power . . . "? The Romans had overcome internal division – but through military means; the second-century reader may have wondered whether the Romans had overcome innate human tendencies as well.

We see, then, that the concept of immortal Rome was used in a perhaps less critical or fraught manner in Greek literary sources, especially as the Principate proved its stability and resilience; the one who offers complications is Polybius, writing in the Republic. It may be added that, from the early Principate, ἀέναος Ῥώμη is occasionally invoked in Greek inscriptions from the provinces, such as in an oath to Tiberius from Cyprus and a foundation text from Akmonia,[10] without apparent hesitation about the literal meaning of the term. The untroubled invocation of immortal Rome shows the kind of devotion or loyalty to the central power that a local powerful figure would wish to demonstrate, both locally and to any Roman official who might see it.

3 Jews

Further from Rome, towards the periphery of the Empire, the idea of Rome's future demise was widespread and the reasons for it were more openly and explicitly stated. Most provincial authors did not write for the Roman rulers in Rome; Josephus is the obvious exception. For Philo, laboring in first-century Alexandria to understand the Hebrew Bible (in Greek) and Greek philosophy as a unified system of thought, the only thing of permanence is God's providence; earthly empires rise and fall according to the divine will, and according to a divine plan. This theological view of history, both past and future, is explicated in Chapter 6 (Philo on the Impermanence of Empires) by Katell Berthelot. She writes that:

> . . . from Philo's perspective, the only human community that shall endure against all the vicissitudes of life is that of Israel. The Roman Empire shall fade away, as all worldly powers do. Roman rule may last longer if emperors truly attempt to rule in a just way, and respect the right of Israel to live

---

[9] *On the Fortune of the Romans* 1, 2; see Chapter 6 by Berthelot in this volume.
[10] SEG 18.578, compare SEG 17.750 and *I. Salamine* 138; IGRR 4.661; see also possibly SEG 59.278 from Athens and SEG 49.1488 from Ephesus (undated).

according to its ancestral laws. It may come to an end sooner than most people think if the Romans behave unjustly and challenge God's providential care for Israel.

Thus it is not Philo's business to make predictions about when and how Rome will fall. That Rome will eventually fade away is stated unambiguously in *Quaestiones in Genesim*, but without the triumphalism that marks other Jewish writings of the first century, rather a sound philosophical certainty that God will eventually bring the perfect balance of justice to the world, and enact his "providential care for Israel." Unlike the Greek historians of Rome, Philo found little significance *per se* in the succession of previous empires; all fallen empires are examples of the same truth, namely that terrestrial powers are all impermanent; the better ones may last longer, as a reward for just rule, but inevitably come to end. In the *Legatio ad Gaium*, Philo subtly undermines the conventional claim that Rome ruled over the entire world. Yet he avoids not only Greek historiographical models, but also direct interaction with the prophetic texts like Daniel that inspired confidence in God's providence among other Jews in the period. Moreover, Philo's conviction about the existence of a divine historical plan, providing for the eternal existence only of Israel, gives a different, less important meaning to *Tyche* as a factor in history than do other writers of the early Principate, since in his theology, *Tyche* as a deliberate supernatural force guiding events must still be subordinate to God, and as a random force is contradicted by God's careful and deliberate orchestration. Even Rome's unquestioned dominance cannot be attributed to any other cause than the divine *logos*. Berthelot concludes: "It seems that for Philo, Roman rule was not the result of mere chance, insofar as God controls everything on earth, but simultaneously could not be described as a divine gift implying that divine providence worked on behalf of the Romans. In Philo's work, providence seems to be covenantal: God's providence either sustains the cosmos or benefits Israel . . . ."

Philo, in his avoidance of the Book of Daniel and apocalyptic visions in general, as well as the historical succession of empires, stands apart from most other streams of thought in first-century Judaism about Rome's future, especially after 70 CE. The idea of the succession of four world empires, with a final fifth entity bringing down the fourth, originated in the second chapter of the Book of Daniel, the 4+1 model in its original form. Four empires symbolized by regressively cheaper metals will succeed one another until an enigmatic stone will smash the fourth and endure forever. Jews interpreted the stone as the Messiah, and in the first century it was widely believed that the prophesy was being fulfilled and that a fifth eternal period of history was beginning or about to begin.

With a confident belief that acting in partnership with God they could bring about the demise of Rome, the Jews in Judaea rebelled against the Empire in 66 CE and again in 132 CE, each time with disastrous results that modified but did not subvert belief. Even establishment Jews like Josephus, who with his aristocratic colleagues were the first leaders of the rebellion against Rome in 66 CE, seem to have believed, for a time, in the imminent fulfillment of the prophecy. After the destruction of Jerusalem and the Temple, Josephus, as a believing Jew, still trusted the truth of biblical prophecy but adjusted his interpretation after defeat: the timing of its fulfillment is unknown and the task of Israel is to wait patiently for God to do his work without human initiative. This view is apparent throughout Josephus' writings, most explicitly in his statement that "Daniel also revealed to the king the meaning of the stone, but I have not thought it proper to relate this, since I am expected to write of what is past and done and not of what is to be" (*A.J.* 10.210). Yet already in his first published work, *The Jewish War*, Josephus inserted hints of his belief in God's plan for Israel's eventual triumph, and his conviction that Jews had to wait for its fulfillment. Samuele Rocca, in Chapter 7 (From Human Freedom to Divine Intervention: Agrippa II's Address on the Eve of the Jewish War), finds just such an encoded message in the grand speech in *B.J.* 2 that Josephus wrote for Agrippa II, discouraging his fellow Jews from going to war against Rome. Agrippa argues that Jewish redemption from their current form of enslavement will be brought about by God, as the Bible promises and past events testify. In the meantime, the Jews must accept that Rome's current rule was perforce sanctioned by God, and that rebelling against Rome would thus be rebellion against God himself. Yet the king suggests that just as God maintained the Roman Empire for the present time, in the future he will bring it down if the Jews maintain their loyalty to God's commandments and laws. "It is therefore necessary for the Jews to wait patiently for Divine salvation" (Rocca). Agrippa is shown to be saying that it is by discontinuing the war against the Romans that the Jews will bring about not only their own world sovereignty, but the salvation of all mankind.

A similar assessment of Josephus' theology and purpose as a historian emerges from Jonathan Davies' analysis in Chapter 8 (Josephus, Caligula and the Future of Rome) of Josephus' account of Caligula's reign and assassination in Books 18 and 19 of the *Jewish Antiquities*. This is, by Davies' account, one of the clearest pieces of textual evidence for Josephus' conviction that the Jewish God has absolute control over human history, has sanctioned Rome's present rule and will one day – at a time of his choosing – bring that rule to an end in pursuance of a plan, revealed by the prophets, for the ultimate redemption of Israel. Agrippa's speech and the account in *A.J.* of Caligula obviously are focalized differently, but the thought is the same. As Davies writes, "Beneath the diplomatic language and apologetic strategies, divine authority over the Roman superpower is a constant feature of Josephus' thought; the *Jewish War* brings this theme right up to the present, by illustrating how Rome's triumph over the Jews and the Flavians' rise to the purple were also sponsored by the divinity." The divinely ordained assassination of the emperor was not, naturally, the divinely planned end of Rome, but a sign of God's power to bring it about and a hint of his intention to do so. Caligula's crimes were such a perversion of justice that it was clear that the normal courses of correction were not sufficient: only God's intervention could restore order to the world, and that restoration was proof of God's detailed orchestration of events, in turn proving the prophets' cosmic view of the future of humanity to be brought about by God about whom Isaiah declared, "the whole earth is full of his glory."

For most Jews, then – so far as we can tell – there was no question that Rome would some day fall, by God's mighty hand. The question was whether the Jews themselves should take an active part. For, unlike Josephus, other Jews still insisted that the realization of the apocalypse demanded immediate action. The intense political–theological debate was played out around competing exegeses of biblical verses, as Vered Noam shows in Chapter 9 ("Will this one never be brought down?": Jewish Hopes for the Downfall of the Roman Empire). Noam draws attention not only to Daniel's prophecy as dealt with in rabbinic midrash, but also to Isaiah 10:33–34, predicting that "Lebanon by a mighty one will fall." Before the first Jewish rebellion, Lebanon was equated with Rome itself, whose fall would be brought about by God himself. This interpretation was an incentive to action on the part of many sects and groups. The sect at Qumran predicted Roman defeat in a soon-to-arrive messianic era at the hands of the Sons of Light (the Sons of Darkness included both the Romans and their supporters). But the same verse in Isaiah was interpreted by the opponents of war to mean that the temple – Lebanon – would be brought to end by the mighty Roman Empire (with God's sanction, without which it could not have happened).

This same verse remained the center of attention after the disastrous end of the war, in the context of the Jews' anguished internal deliberations to find meaning in the disaster and to know what to do next. Apocalyptic works such as 2 Baruch as well as rabbinic liturgy refashioned exegesis to assert divine revenge on Rome in an undefined messianic future. But others persisted in their militant belief that the temple's destruction was itself God's signal for immediate action; that belief was belied by the failure of the Bar Kochba revolt 132–135 CE, which had been supported by such spiritual leaders as Rabbi Akiva, who believed Bar Kochba to be the Messiah. After that, the rabbis of the Talmud taught that the same verse in Isaiah still predicted Rome's eventual downfall, but the time of it could not be known and should not be sought or calculated. Later, during Rome's wars with Persia, the rabbis taught that the prophecies of Rome's destruction – this time, relying variously on Jeremiah, Daniel, Obadiah, and pseudo-historical calculations – were being fulfilled, but they still counseled to let world powers do God's work: the Jews were to watch and wait. Thus the final exegetical stage was to take comfort in a glorious future at an unspecified time, as Noam concludes: "The eventual punishment of Rome is in divine hands alone, and will take place in an unknown future. God's determination, however, should grant comfort to Israel: 'therefore fear not, O Jacob my servant' – even if you see him rise to the skies, I will bring him down!"

But it was not just the Jews who were consumed by apocalyptic dreams of Rome's downfall, even imminent destruction, if Erich Gruen is right in Chapter 10 (The Sibylline Oracles and Resistance to Rome), his study of the Fourth and Fifth Sibylline oracles. These texts have conventionally been considered Jewish. If they are not, and the Jewish theme is just one piece of a "hodge-podge" of angry anti-Roman texts, as Gruen argues, then we learn that the devout wish for Rome's destined fiery destruction, and the belief in its imminent occurrence as indicated by current events, were widespread in the East. According to this reading of the fourth and fifth oracles, the visionary end of Rome was not sectarian or particularistic, rather, the imagined and wished-for and preached-for end of Rome was even more dramatic, astonishing, significant: violent dreams of a much wider swath of the populations living under Rome than understood so far. This shared "visionary end" incorporated the rather bizarre (to us) notion of Nero, the symbol of Rome's corruption and condign destruction, returning to the world to serve as the agent of the violent punishment. Gruen's crucial conclusion is as follows:

> The Sibyllines, in short, do not readily qualify as targeted resistance literature. Nor do they serve as expression of Jewish riposte simply or chiefly to

the loss of the Temple. The oracles look ahead to a distant divine intervention, but not one triggered by a particular event or by a single deed that sealed the future of Rome... The language belongs to the genre rather than to any special historical circumstances. Sibylline verses reflect a much broader experience of long-term perseverance under imperial power... Apocalyptic literature has a momentum of its own, independent of particular events, no matter how cataclysmic.

4 Christians

Oppressed people fantasize the destruction of their oppressor. Like the Jews, the early Christians, reading the same Bible, were in the grip of apocalyptic visions and convinced of the imminent end of Rome. Peter Oakes, in Chapter 11 (Revelation 17.1–19.10: A Prophetic Vision of the Destruction of Rome), shows that those explosive but enigmatic two-and-a-half chapters in Revelation, which have been subject to multiple interpretations, refer to Rome's awful crimes and its destruction as punishment. For "Babylon" in the passage is none other than Rome, excoriated for its violence, arrogance, and luxury. The prooftexts are again, naturally, found in the prophets – Isaiah, Jeremiah, Ezekiel, Amos, Daniel – but different verses from those at the heart of Jewish eschatological debates. Oakes also considers, but rejects, that Revelation calls for direct action against Rome by Christians, but he notes that "Revelation has been a key text for Christian groups in some political resistance movements such as those opposing apartheid in twentieth-century South Africa."

Yet, as Oakes writes, "almost nothing stays as it was." The Book of Revelation may have raised Christians' hopes, or provided them comfort, during the severe oppression through the third century. After Constantine, Rome became Christian and its success as an Empire equaled the success of Christianity. As Marko Marinčič writes in Chapter 12 (Cicero and Vergil in the Catacombs: Pagan Messianism and Monarchic Propaganda in Constantine's *Oration to the Assembly of Saints*), the idea of Rome's eternity, which became coterminous with Christianity's eternity, was revived: "apology could give place to triumphalistic propaganda." This takes us back *inter alia* to *Eclogue* 4. Using Lactantius as a foil – Lactantius, living under the oppressive Tetrarchy, rejected pagan authors because of their ignorance of divine truth; *Eclogue* 4, lacking divine revealed truth, foretold an earthly ruler who had no role in redemption – Constantine saw the world ruler in the *Eclogue* as Christ himself, the Virgo as Mary, Jupiter as God the Father, and himself as a Christian incarnation of Augustus. In

Introduction

fact, both Cicero, in his rational understanding of a Sibylline oracle, and Vergil in the *Eclogue* and elsewhere, are presented as having understood Christian truth before Christ's advent; the two pagan authors kept that knowledge secret so as not offend pagan religious authorities. But the code could be unlocked. The meaning of historical parallels became evident: Constantine takes the same role in ushering in the new messianic age as Augustus for the birth of the messiah; the Second Triumvirate was the precursor to the Tetrarchy, each defeated by sanctioned world rulers who were each a vindicator sanctioned by God:

> The position of Christianity in the empire had changed since the victory at the Milvian bridge, and apology could give place to triumphalistic propaganda. As an aspiring sole Augustus, Constantine had a much more favorable image of Vergil and the Augustan *imperium sine fine* than Lactantius would have had a few years earlier, during the persecutions and in the years immediately following them.

Thus, "With Constantine's ascension to power, the destruction of the pagan empire became superfluous, and a Christian empire of peace presented itself as a real possibility." The Christian view had metamorphosed from a fervent wish for the punishment of the harlot Rome to the triumphal assertion of its eternity.

That was the propagandistic view of the first Christian emperor based in the East: he had an interest similar to Augustus' in declaring Rome's eternity. As Hervé Inglebert shows in Chapter 13 (The Future of Rome after 410 CE: the Latin Conceptions (410–480 CE)), the Christians of the West, living through repeated crises and invasions in the fifth century CE, reverted to conflicting interpretations of prophetic promises, and variously calculated the end of Rome. Both the variety and the phases of these calculations are graphically represented in Inglebert's comparative tables in the Appendix, which chart the "regimes of historicity" (à la Hartog, see p.2 above) in relation to Rome, the Roman Empire, and the Christianization of the world during the fifth century CE. Western Christians' understanding of the future of "Rome" fluctuated dramatically throughout the vicissitudes of the turbulent fifth century. The challenge, as with all exegetical methods of prediction, was to fit events to texts. After 468 CE, "the last glimmer of hope for an imperial recovery finally vanished. Nevertheless, the cultural and Catholic Roman rites and customs survived the fall of its power in the West, which greatly benefited Justinian (I) fifty years later."

Writers across a wide spectrum of religions, cultures, and literatures spanning the vast territory and the long duration of the Roman Empire gave thought to the future of Rome. The idea of an eternal city and civilization was nurtured at the center of power and by provincial elites for whom the notion of unending domination served their interests. The Roman calendar and religious ritual flattened out time so that past and future were melded into a continuous present. Visions of Rome's violent end became radical and certain towards the periphery of the Empire. What was imagined to happen after Rome's destruction varied according to background, identity, and purpose: sectarians and other kinds of believers envisioned a different kind of eternity, whereas Greek historians drew on perceived laws of nature or historical patterns to extrapolate the future fall of Rome or posit its eternity by rational explanation of its exceptionalism. The idea of eternal Rome did not die, of course, with the end of its sovereignty. Mussolini's fascist ideology was based on an assertion of immortal Rome, and enthusiastic guides today invoke the idea when touring the ruins of the ancient city.

CHAPTER I

Some Remarks on Cicero's Perception of the Future of Rome

Carlos Lévy

Cicero is often perceived as someone who lived intensely in the present moment, as he did during the Catilinarian conspiracy, for example, or the outbreak of the civil war. He is also said to have had a knack for nostalgia. While in exile and during the civil war, he spent a great deal of time deploring his former glory. He is less known for his contemplation on Rome's future. Yet, as Girardet brilliantly demonstrates,[1] *De legibus* is one of the most powerful prefigurations of the Roman Empire. The texts we present and analyze here are for the most part less well known than his treatise on laws, which is of Platonic inspiration. Nonetheless they reveal the complexity of Cicero's concerns about the future of Rome. We need not insist here on Cicero's importance as both a major witness and actor in a century in which Rome became the foremost power in the Mediterranean world. This also happened to be the moment of a terrible crisis that led to a civil war that most Romans perceived as absolute *nefas*, that is to say, the abomination of desolation. Today, despite our powerful electronic means and many prestigious think-tanks, almost nobody – or perhaps nobody – was able to anticipate the so-called "Arab Spring" or the bloody civil war in Syria.

The problem lies in knowing what kind of idea of the future a man of extraordinary intelligence and exceptional political acumen could have had in Roman antiquity. In writing this paper, we have encountered two main difficulties:

1) Cicero's life was exceptionally long, rich, and complex. He himself was often hesitant and ambivalent,[2] and he sometimes hid his inconsistencies behind philosophical expressions and/or justified them as the result of Academic skepticism.

---

[1] Girardet 1983.
[2] See Harrer 1918; Michel 1960; Jal 1963; Rawson 1985; Wistrand 1979; Habitch 1990; Mitchell 1991; Narducci 2009; Lévy 2012; Nicgorski 2016.

2) Cicero engaged in forensic and political eloquence, philosophy, the art of letter writing, and even poetry, for which he had no particular gift. We thus need to carefully identify the genre of the text as well as the historical context of each case we examine.

Our main aim is to present some aspects of Cicero's perception of Rome's future and try to define the logic behind it.

1.1 A Methodology of Prevision: The Letter to Aulus Caecina

In October 46 BCE, Cicero sent a letter to his friend Aulus Caecina, who was in Sicily waiting for Caesar's permission to return to Rome.[3] Aulus was a son of the Caecina of Volaterrae, for whom Cicero had written *Pro Caecina* in 69 BCE. Fond of oratory himself, Aulus had been friendly towards Cicero while in exile.[4] It was therefore an *officium amicitiae* for the consul of 63 BCE to help his friend during a difficult situation of this kind. The Caecina family was renowned for its expertise in Etruscan divination. Aulus Caecina himself had written a book on a form of divination based on the observation of lightning – a treatise still read by Seneca and Pliny the Elder.[5] Caecina was said to have foretold the return of Cicero from exile, a prediction he based on the *Etrusca disciplina*.[6] It was a bit difficult for Cicero to openly criticize this kind of prognostication as he himself had been elected an augur in 53 BCE. A conservative politician, he felt it was important to keep the augural institution alive for the sake of the *res publica*.[7] Yet, at least towards the end of his life, he believed that proving that divination was not a forgery or a matter of chance was impossible, and, in the second book of *De diuinatione*, used Academic arguments to refute in a skeptical way the Stoic justification of divination.[8]

In our opinion, the most important element in Cicero's letter is his mention of a new and peculiar kind of divination, founded neither on the

---

[3] *Fam.* 6.6. Caecina wrote an offensive pamphlet (*criminosissimo libro*, Suet. *Iul.* 75.5) against Caesar, who, however, spared him after the battle of Thapsus, but did not allow him to return to Italy. On this episode, see Shackleton Bailey 1977: 2 and 399. On Caecina and divination, see Rawson 1985: 304–7.

[4] Seneca, *N.Q.* 2.56.1: *hoc apud Caecinam inuenio, facundum uirum et qui habuisset aliquando in eloquentia nomen, nisi illum Ciceronis umbra pressisset.*

[5] Cf. Seneca, *N.Q.* 2.49 and Pliny, *Nat. hist.* 1.2b.11.197.

[6] The *Etrusca disciplina* was contained in three kinds of books: *haruspicini, fulgurales, rituales* (*Diu.* 1.72). On this point, see Guillaumont 2006.

[7] On Cicero as an augur, see Guillaumont 1984.

[8] On the *De diuinatione*, see the excellent commentary of Kany-Turpin 2006 and Santangelo 2013: 10–32.

1. Cicero's Perception of the Future of Rome

observation of the sky nor on inspection of animal entrails, but rather on a knowledge of political philosophy and one's personal experience of political life. Clearly this part of the letter contains some subtle humor, which does not seem to be a key feature since its presence does not mean that Cicero is simply joking. In our opinion, his secularization of divination can be interpreted as another sign of the increasing rationalism of Roman society towards the end of the Republic, a phenomenon well described by Claudia Moatti in *La raison de Rome*.[9] Cicero wrote the letter about two years before completing *De diuinatione*, in which he harshly criticized the Stoics for integrating a defense of divination into their system.[10] Here two things should be emphasized. First, Cicero writes that his personal divination is so effective that it has never failed, even during the most troubling moments of war. He claims that he was able to foretell everything, but nobody trusted him. It would be easy to show how Cicero manipulated the past to demonstrate that though not a sage, he had been perfectly aware of how things would turn out. For example, he states that he had warned Pompey on multiple occasions not to ally himself with Caesar, a claim that is probably an exaggeration. Actually, his position before and during the war was far from being as clear and coherent as he later maintained. Yet despite such ambiguities, he felt that the science of the future was possible for anyone who studied philosophical theories and knew how to apply them:

> If you have not been misled by a certain scientific system of Etruscan lore bequeathed you by your illustrious and excellent father, neither shall I be misled by my own skill in divination, which I have acquired not only from the writings and precepts of the greatest philosophers and my extensive study, as you yourself know, of their teaching, but also from a wide experience in dealing with public affairs, and the many vicissitudes of my political life.[11]

The *sapientissimi uiri* whom he mentions without explicitly stating their names are Plato, Aristotle, and Polybius, creators of the philosophical theory of the cyclical rhythm of history, known as *anakyklôsis*.[12]

---

[9] Moatti 1997.   [10] On Cicero and divination, see Schofield 1986 and Beard 1986.
[11] *Fam.* 6.6.3–4: *Si te ratio quaedam <m>ira Tuscae disciplinae, quam a patre, nobilissimo atque optimo uiro, acceperas, non fefellit, ne nos quidem nostra divinatio fallet, quam cum sapientissimorum virorum moni[men]tis atque praeceptis plurimoque, ut tu scis, doctrinae studio tum magno etiam usu tractandae rei publicae magnaque nostrorum temporum varietate consecuti sumus. cui quidem divinationi hoc plus confidimus quod ea nos nihil in his tam obscuris rebus tamque perturbatis umquam omnino fefellit.* Translations in this chapter are, sometimes with some modifications, those of the Loeb Classical Library.
[12] On this concept, see Walbank 2002: 277–92.

Our second point is that in this letter, rational divination not only coexists with the traditional *Etrusca disciplina*, but also, in some way pretends to retain its traditional structure. Like Etruscan augurs but in a radically new manner, Cicero analyzes the signs of his divination according to two axes, that is, *duplici quadam uia*: "Now in noting these signs for the purposes of my prognostications, I follow a sort a double system, the source of half of which is Caesar himself; of the other half, a studied survey of the present political situation."[13] So, the first axis of this new style of divination is Caesar, his personality, his ambition, and his contradictions. The second is that of the nature and logic of political circumstances. The future is determined both by the ruler's psychology and by the situation he has to face. In his definition of the two kinds of divination, Cicero implicitly expresses the idea that religion must be considered an earlier and somewhat confused form of what philosophy will say in a far more scientific manner. All this can be compared to the circular Stoic conception of time.[14] Stoics did not deny the possibility of progress in knowledge, but they did assert that such progress would lie in the final realization of an initial adumbration rather than be a radical innovation. A good example of this kind of circularity can be found in Seneca's *Letter* 90,[15] which states that in the beginning of civilization, human beings were happy and careless, but this was a kind of spontaneous happiness without reflection. A long itinerary was necessary in order to access true wisdom, which can only be conscious.

This letter is an amazing example of a *pro domo* plea, based on a very personal reconstruction of the past. The idea that theory and experience enable man's understanding of the future is justified by a somewhat naive teleology:

> It would be intolerable to the nature of things and political circumstances (*rerum ... natura et ciuilium temporum*) and incompatible with existing logic or any change of logic that all men engaged in the same cause should not receive the same treatment and lot, and that honest men and good citizens, to whom no stigma of disgrace has been attached, should not return to a community which has readmitted so many found guilty of heinous crimes.[16]

---

[13] *Fam.* 6.6.8: *Notantur autem mihi ad divinandum signa duplici quadam via; quarum alteram duco e Caesare ipso, alteram e temporum civilium natura atque ratione.*

[14] See Goldschmidt 1969 who asserts that one of the main structures of Stoic doctrine is that of time as an essential factor of the relationship between human being and nature: at the higher level he/she has to conquer that which was initially given him/her by nature.

[15] On the Greek sources of *Letter* 90, see Zago 2012.   [16] *Fam.* 6.6.11.

1. Cicero's Perception of the Future of Rome

Here again Cicero affirms the belief that, despite the civil war and all kinds of violence, there is a rationality to history that sets a limit on erratic attitudes, at least in Rome. Opposing Maridien Schneider's thesis,[17] we do not believe that Cicero is representing himself as a haruspex inspecting the corpse of the Republic. His rationalization of prognostication, despite its references to traditional forms of divination, is based on a quite different form of *auctoritas*, that of philosophy. And it is on the basis of his philosophical beliefs that Cicero argues that at least some optimism regarding the Republic's future is permissible. Actually, neither in his letters nor in his treatises does he ever affirm that one of philosophy's tasks is to get rid of national traditions.[18] In his opinion, philosophy had above all to strip tradition of false dogmatic beliefs. His letter to Caecina is an excellent indicator of the multiple parameters that were present in his mind as he thought about the situation of Rome.

1.2 A Science of the Future?

Let us say a little bit more about this science of the future. In the first book of *De re publica*, Cicero develops a cyclical theory of the life of cities: "Periodical revolutions and circular courses followed by the constant changes and sequences in governmental forms."[19] From a philosophical point of view, there seems to be nothing new in this affirmation, which is the Roman expression of the Greek theory of *anakyklôsis*.[20] It is well known, however, that in contrast to his Greek predecessors, Cicero never asserted that there was a rigid order in the succession of constitutions. In §45 of Book 1, Scipio states that a monarchy, an oligarchy, or a democracy arise from tyranny. Some paragraphs later he affirms that everything depends on who kills the tyrant.[21] Nonetheless Cicero did not believe that history was governed by pure chance. In his opinion, its movement was cyclical, determined by a limited number of political forms, and capable of being theorized by the *ciuilium commutationum scientia*, an expression he uses in his famous letter to Lucceius, in which he asks the

---

[17] Schneider 2013, on the problem of the haruspices at the end of the Republic, see Santangelo 2013: 89–98.
[18] See Santangelo 2013: 107: "Human intelligence and industria are equally significant. There is no opposition between them and religion. In fact, the appropriate way to experience religion is to practise it both intelligently and diligently."
[19] *Rep.* 1.45.
[20] See note 12. The literature on *De re publica* is extensive. Particularly useful to this paper are Sharples 1986; Powell 1994; Schofield 1995; Atkins 2013; and Nicgorski 2016, esp. Chap. 4.
[21] *Rep.* 1.65.

historian to provide him with a somewhat adorned version of his consulate.[22] Despite all his rhetorical variations on the uncertainty of the era and the chaos of civil war, Cicero did not wholly abandon the idea that human societies were predictable entities. But, as he writes in *De Republica*,[23] having perfect knowledge of these periodic revolutions is a privilege reserved for the sage, who, according to Stoic doctrine, is a person even rarer than the phoenix. However, an exceptional politician who is not a sage may be able to foresee them and could at least try to modify the development of the situation. During the civil war, Cicero was generally less trenchant than he appears in his letter to Caecina. He actually tried to analyze all potential outcomes and define the proper attitude to adopt with as much rigor as he could muster, without, however, excluding the possibility that he might be wrong. A good example of this attitude lies in his letter to Torquatus, in which he writes:

> For it is inevitable that the Republic should be eternally harassed by the clash of arms, or some day see those arms laid aside and gain a new existence, or be utterly extinguished. If the sword is to be master, you have nothing to fear ... if the state ever breathes again ... then you will be permitted to enjoy both your position and your prosperity; and if there is to be ruin, absolute and universal ... there is always this consolation – a poor one, it is true, especially for a citizen and a man of your type, but one we cannot but accept – that no man should make a special grievance of what happens to all alike.[24]

Here he scrutinizes all the eventualities in a way that owes much to the Academic method of systematic division, the *diairesis*. Noteworthy too is that a complete disappearance of the *res publica* is not excluded from these eventualities.

However, despite all his uncertainty and conjectures about the immediate future, Cicero, even if he did undergo a period of deep discouragement, as we can see in his *Letters*, did not entirely give up his attachment to the cyclical evolution of history. Evidence of this exists in the surprise, disappointment, and indignation that he felt when seeing Caesar replaced by another tyrant. Delighted at first by the death of a man whom he admired from an intellectual point of view, but who represented to him both the *rex* of the Roman tradition and the tyrant of Greek philosophy, he noted, "Good God, the tyranny lives though the tyrant is dead!"[25] In the *ciuilium*

---

[22] *Fam.* 5.12 (from Antium, April or May 56 BCE). [23] *Rep.* 1.45.
[24] *Fam.* 6.2. This letter was written in Atticus' villa in Nomentum, about 20 April 45 BCE.
[25] *Att.* 14.9.2 (see also 11.9.2): *vivit tyrannis, tyrannus occidit*.

commutationum scientia, a murdered tyrant could be replaced by various kinds of political regimes, but his death meant the death of the regime that he embodied. Cicero lucidly predicted that the disintegration of the traditional institutions of the *res publica* would lead to tyranny. Yet, since he felt no respect for Antonius, it was very difficult for him to understand that the fall of tyranny could simply be an occasion for perpetuating tyranny, or even for the emergence of a new tyrant worse than the former one. The aristocracy that normally succeeded the death of the tyrant was merely a façade: "Two of them are the so-called consuls designate" (*duo quidem quasi designati consules*). Such repetition was impossible to imagine in either Polybius' or Cicero's own conception of history.

1.3 Roma aeterna

1.3.1 Some Words on the Rhetoric of Eternity

When we read Ciceronian texts, we always need to take into account his rhetorical background. Was the theme of eternity or at least that of the long duration of the *res publica* frequent in his rhetorical treatises and in his speeches? We might expect to find a great many such references in them, but that is not the case. Whenever Cicero speaks about the *imperium* and/or the *res publica*, he mentions their power and the fact that Rome rules the world, but he does not claim that his city is going to last forever. One of the most interesting of these statements can be found in the *Pro Rabirio perduellionis reo*, a highly political speech that Cicero delivered in 63 BCE, while he was consul. In this discourse, in which he defends Rabirius against the *populares* led by Caesar, he writes:

> And so, among the many reasons that lead us to think that the souls of good men are divine and immortal, the chief is that the spirits of our best and wisest men look forward with a gaze fixed on eternity. Therefore do I call to witness the souls of Gaius Marius and all other wise and good citizens, whom I believe to have left behind the life of men and passed to the holy and sacred estate of the gods, that I feel it my duty to contend no less in defense of their honor, their glory, and their memory than I would for the temples and shrines of my country.

Here the theme of eternity is applied to exceptional individuals, not to the city itself. Of course, the eternity of these men could be considered a factor in the eternity of the city, but this is not explicitly stated. The opposition between the narrow bounds within which nature has confined human lives and the infinite bounds of glory were certainly developed by Cicero in his now-lost *De Gloria*, which he wrote at the end of June 44 BCE.[26] Actually, in his discourses, Cicero refers to many aspects of the city as *sempiterni* or *aeterni*, as, for instance, when writing about the decision to recall him from exile,[27] when calling the Senate the most prestigious institution of the city,[28] when discussing glorious actions, such as the murder of Caesar, or when celebrating the memory of the greatest Roman *imperatores*.[29] To the best of our knowledge, the clearest transition from the immortal elements of the city to the immortality of the city itself can be found in the *Pro Sestio*, where Cicero says that if Rome retains eternal memory of his return from exile, the city itself will be immortal: "If this example be preserved for ever, who can doubt that this state will be immortal?" (*quod si immortale retinetur, quis non intelligit immortalem hanc ciuitatem futuram?*).[30] This affirmation is certainly somewhat bombastic, but perhaps with some indulgence we can suppose that what Cicero wants to say here is that the immortality of a city is based on its respect for the most essential ethical value, namely, justice. However, in this case, the eternity of Rome is a conditional affirmation, bound to Cicero's situation and the memory of this situation. Thus, we may say that we cannot find in Cicero's rhetoric any structure for a deep reflection on Rome's future, as we can find, for example, in the speeches that Thucydides attributes to Pericles. The theme of everlasting glory is a rhetorical topos, the presence of which cannot be considered original or significant in Cicero's speeches. When, in a fragment of a lost speech, he states that the borders of the Roman Empire cannot be found within the regions of the earth because they stretch to the sky,[31] he portrays Rome as approaching the realm of immortality. Yet we are still within the boundaries of rhetoric.

In the speeches, eternity only pertains to exceptional individuals. The thesis of Rome's eternity is, in fact, a philosophical construct that arises at a moment when the crisis of the Republic is so deep that even the

---

[26] On Cicero's variations on glory, see Sullivan 1941 and Achard 1981.
[27] On Cicero's post-exile rhetoric, see Narducci 2009: 233–43.
[28] *Sest.* 137 : *Ita magistratus annuos creaverunt ut consilium senatus rei publicae praeponerent sempiternum, deligerentur autem in id consilium ab universo populo aditusque in illum summum ordinem omnium civium industriae ac virtuti pateret.*
[29] On the rise of the theme of Rome's deification, see Cole 2013.   [30] *Sest.* 50.
[31] Cicero, "Orationum deperditarum fragmenta," in *Sch. Bob.* 172.4: *qui populi R. imperium non terrarum regionibus, sed caeli partibus terminavit*, Crawford 1994, *ad loc.*, stresses the fact that "here Cicero states that Pompey's achievements have expanded the limits of Roman power beyond earthly boundaries, thus inviting to a comparison, which is certainly not subtle, with Cicero's enclosure of Pompey himself within the walls of his own house."

1. Cicero's Perception of the Future of Rome

incantatory evocation of the powerful empire and prominent *exempla* are not enough to mitigate it.

1.3.2 Debet enim constituta sic esse ciuitas ut aeterna sit, Rep. III. 34: An Immanentist Election?

Gods are eternal but eternity does not necessarily mean deification.[32] By the term "immanentist election," we shall try to demonstrate that in Cicero's opinion, at least in his opinion as a philosopher, Rome did have a unique fate, but due only to an exceptional conjunction of natural elements. In Cicero's speeches, gods as protectors of the city are omnipresent. However, there is no tie between them and Rome that could be compared to the alliance between God and Israel. Nor is the universalist perspective of Genesis present in *De Re Publica*: Scipio notes that he will not go back to the first union of a man and a woman, but only to the creation of the political structures of the city.[33] In this case, Cicero seems to be stressing the difference between Lucretius and himself. At the beginning of Book 5 of *De Rerum Natura*, Lucretius offers a striking picture of the birth of humanity without any reference to the specific case of Rome. Stoicism, the theory of natural law, which is supposed to be the same everywhere, is presented in Book 3, but in the context of an antilogy, in which it is opposed to the thesis of man's fundamental egoism.[34] When Cicero writes in his treatise that the city's constitution will make her eternal, he does not ignore the fact that this goal is even greater than that of Plato in the *Republic*. The Greek philosopher actually states that despite all human effort, the Republic, whose concept he is elaborating, cannot be everlasting, since every human construction ultimately submits to disintegration.[35] Conversely, for Cicero, Rome is not the image of the best constitution, but rather that of its effective presence in history.[36] In order to present Rome as the only eternal city, Cicero bases his argument on the Polybian theory of the mixed constitution, which combines the three elementary forms of political constitution and is thus the only one capable of avoiding the corruption that threatens them if they are isolated.

---

[32] The Latin sentence from *Rep*. III. 34. in the section heading is not easy to translate. The verb *debet* generally expresses moral obligation. The translation by Walker Reyes in the Loeb Classical Library misses this nuance: "for a State ought to be so firmly founded that it will live for ever."
[33] *Rep*. 1.38.   [34] See Ferrary 1977.   [35] *Rep*. 546a.
[36] Berti 1963: 61: "In virtu di questa unità fra idea e storia, *ratio e res*, il metodo ciceroniano vuol essere un'esposizione filosofica e storica insieme, una filosofia intimamente sostanziata da analisi storiche ed una storia razionalizzata e ricondotta a un sistema di idee."

Moreover, Cicero also uses more specifically Roman elements. If, in brief, we try to bring together the different components of this immanentist election, we come up with the following:

- the advantages of Rome's geographical situation, which was not very far from the sea, but with a position more secure than that of a harbor and thanks to this distance, protected from the moral corruption that frequently befalls coastal cities;[37]
- the *prudentia* of its ancestors, who, despite the many differences among them, understood from the beginning that a city with such ambition could not be the creation of a single man, but was necessarily the realization of a long-term collective project: *nostra autem res publica non unius esset ingenio sed multorum nec una hominis uita, sed aliquot constituta.*[38] Although Cicero felt genuine respect for Caesar as an intellectual and warrior, he believed that the latter's project, founded on the idea of personal power, was at odds with the essential values of the city;
- a paradigmatic use of nature. Far from imitating Plato's eidetic construction of the Republic, Scipio chooses to describe Rome's evolution as that of a person: "I shall, however, find my task easier if I place before you a description of our Roman State at its birth, during its growth, at its maturity, and finally in its strong and healthy state."[39] Whereas the natural fate of a person is to die, that of Rome – at least the Rome of the *De re publica* – is said to be eternal. This is something of a contradiction, but Cicero's answer would be that within the law of nature exists a structural possibility – and only a possibility – that a city will become immortal, precisely because it respects the dynamics of nature.

A man too may deserve immortality – the immortality of his soul – as we can see in *Somnium*. But what could the eternity of a city be? This needs some explanation. Several lines of Book 2 have aroused many comments: "Yet you will be able to realize this more easily if you watch our commonwealth as it advances, and by a route which we may call nature's road, finally reaches the ideal condition."[40] This metaphorical interpretation is tempting but needs development since the metaphor here is the vector

---

[37] Rep. 2.10: *Qui potuit igitur divinius et utilitates conplecti maritimas Romulus et vitia vitare, quam quod urbem perennis amnis et aequabilis et in mare late influentis posuit in ripa?*

[38] Rep. 2.2: "our own commonwealth was based upon the genius, not of one man, but of many."

[39] Rep. 2.3: *Facilius autem, quod est propositum, consequar, si nostram rem publicam vobis et nascentem et crescentem et adultam et iam firmam atque robustam ostendero.*

[40] Rep. 2.30: *Atqui multo id facilius cognosces, inquit Africanus, si progredeintem rem publicam atque in optimum statum naturali quodam itinere et cursu venientem videris.* On this passage and the commentaries on the many difficulties it raises, see Ferrary 1984.

towards deeper philosophical meaning. Cicero certainly did not believe that the perfection of the *res publica* was the consequence of an itinerary specifically scheduled by nature. The political laws of nature were the same for all constitutions. From the point of view of nature, the coexistence of the three simple constitutions was necessary for avoiding violent revolutions. Only the balance among them could guarantee the permanence of the state. But Cicero does not present the relationship between these political structures of nature and the decisions of political actors as a simple one. A good case in point is his reflection on the creation of a tribunate. When observing: "Such a claim may have been unreasonable but the essential nature of the commonwealth often defeats reason" (*uincit ipsa rerum publicarum natura saepe rationem*),[41] he is saying that a reasonable politician, foreseeing the problems that Roman plebeian tribunes will lead to, would certainly disapprove of their creation. Nevertheless, this creation, problematic in itself, was a necessary element of the political balance that was inserted into the nature of the political structures. Nature defines the great directions that mankind must respect and diversify through specific initiatives. Right after speaking of the *res publica*'s natural evolution towards perfection, Cicero claims that all this has been possible thanks solely to the qualities of the Roman people (their political astuteness, their capacity to learn and to teach, their ability to integrate foreign traditions and improve on them).

An exceptional conjunction of geographical and anthropological circumstances, the capacity to feel nature's political laws and make original contributions to them – these are the main elements of what we have called "immanentist election."

1.4 The Status of Rome among Nations: Were the Romans Barbarians?

Cicero knew perfectly well that the perfect mixed constitution was a kind of philosophical speculation that would grant special status to the city that could reach it. At the same time, the main cultural and political division in the world of his day was the one separating Greeks from Barbarians. How could he simultaneously claim the eternity of Rome and accept a division in which Romans were integrated into the discriminated-against category of Barbarians? In our opinion, the answer has to be found in the evolution

---

[41] *Rep.* 2.57.

of Cicero's thought, which gradually became able to describe with special emphasis the place of Romans among people of other nations.

In his first treatise, *De inuentione*, which he wrote when he was quite young – a *puer aut adulescentulus*, in his own words – Cicero is so concerned with the difference between Greeks and Barbarians, with no intermediary category in between, that he redacted the handbook as if he were writing for a Greek audience. When, in §35 of Book I, he refers to the concepts needed to define someone, he lists nation first – adding *Graius an Barbarus*, as if mankind as a whole were divided into these two categories – then homeland, adding the words *Atheniensis an Lacedaemonius*. Though a young Roman, he does not seek to assume this identity, preferring to appear as a Greek-speaking Latin. Accordingly, his perception of Barbarians is very negative. In I.103, we find them listed between savage beings and the cruelest beasts. We could easily provide many other examples of this – at least rhetorical – contempt, which denies humanity to these nations. However, towards the end of his life, Cicero seems to have abandoned the duality of Greek and Barbarian. In *De divinatione*, for example, he relies on a tripartite division. When speaking about the attitude of nations towards divination, he tells his brother Quintus that divination is accepted by everyone, "Greeks, Barbarians, and even our ancestors."[42] In this sentence, Roman *maiores* appear in a category that is reducible neither to Greek nor Barbarian. Evidence exists that in the forty years between *De inuentione* and *De divinatione*, Cicero never ceased to wonder about the difference between Greeks and Barbarians. The most illuminating passage in this respect is probably *Rep.* 1.58, in which Scipio asks: "Did Romulus rule over Barbarians?" To which Laelius, a man who in Roman tradition was considered a model of wisdom, replies with extreme subtlety: "If, as the Greeks, we admit that men can be only Greeks or Barbarians, I fear that he had ruled only over Barbarians." Here we find a kind of dissociation of linguistic from ethical criterion, but this interesting answer prepares us above all for Scipio's remark, which places specific traits above generic perceptions of ethnic groups: *non quaerimus gentem, ingenia quaerimus* ("Yet for the purposes of our present subject we consider only character, not race").[43] Another example lies in the pathetic and famous reference to the tortures inflicted by Verres on Roman citizens, in which, as Cicero states, the protestation *ciuis Romanus sum*, which was respected even by Barbarians, became, in front of Verres, an aggravating condition.[44] In this kind of passage, we are tempted to substitute the

---

[42] *Div.* 1.84.   [43] *Rep.* 1.58.   [44] *Verr.* 2.5.147.

Romani nominis dignitas with Greeks in accordance with the traditional dipole: Greeks–Barbarians. More precisely, we notice the emergence of a triangle in which the *maiestas romana* is opposed to both the *leuitas* of the Greeks and the *crudelitas* of the Barbarians. The antithesis of Romans, the inhabitants of Massilia, are said to be *leuitate Graeci, crudelitate Barbari*.[45]

Merely a word on *Pro Flacco*. Cicero had no reason to feel a real interest in Jews, a tiny nation like so many others in the mosaic of the Near East. It has been argued, rightly, that as a lawyer, Cicero systematically resorted to xenophobic stereotypes.[46] It is also true that *Pro Flacco* must be read in its political context: Roman Jews were supporters of the *populares* and more specifically of Caesar, a political choice that Cicero could certainly not approve. Yet I wonder whether Cicero, obsessed by the idea of differentiating Romans from both Greeks and Barbarians, was not shocked to discover that there was another people that refused to be reduced to the category of Barbarians and that had a capital, Jerusalem, that he describes as a place to which a significant portion of the Roman *imperium*'s wealth had been brought by Jews. *Pro Flacco* is also his involuntary recognition of a mimetic rivalry as, in the discourse, he presents Judaic values as the exact contrary of Roman values.[47]

1.5 Will

Cicero thus tried to define the principles of a political science within the context of a meditation on the future of Rome. In his view, this would be a global science founded not only on the idea of the natural rationality of political change, but also on the determinism of geographical and climatic conditions and a knowledge of the psychology of the politicians. At the same time, however, Cicero reflected a great deal on the Latin notion of *uoluntas*, one of the main contributions of Roman thinkers to Occidental philosophy.[48] Historians of philosophy usually emphasize the role of Seneca or Augustine in the shaping of this notion, forgetting that most of the work was done by Cicero. In Book 5 of *De Re Publica*, he uses a powerful metaphor as he compares the Republic to a beautiful painting

---

[45] *Flac.* 24. On the relation between anti-judaism and political thought in Cicero, see Bernard 2000.
[46] On this point see Daugé 1981, Lévy 1984, Corbell 2002, May 2002, Ndiaye 2005.
[47] *Flac.* 69: *Stantibus Hierosolymis pacatisque Iudaeis tamen istorum religio sacrorum a splendore huius imperi, gravitate nominis nostri, maiorum institutis abhorrebat; nunc vero hoc magis, quod illa gens quid de nostro imperio sentiret ostendit armis quam cara dis immortalibus esset docuit, quod est victa, quod elocata, quod serva facta.*
[48] On this point, see Lévy 2007.

whose colors have faded with age, so that even its composition and general outlines have disappeared: "For it is through our own faults, not by any accident, that we retain only the form of the commonwealth, but have long since lost its substance."[49] With this metaphor, he stresses the Romans' responsibility for the disasters of the Republic but without using a precise vocabulary to state this. More precisely, his vocabulary is essentially ethical: *nostris enim uitiis*. However, the concept of *uoluntas* is present in one of the most interesting passages in *De re publica*:[50] "*and every state is such as its ruler's character and will make it.*" The general idea is clear. The state is not a fixed reality; it is the image of the people who govern it. However, French and English translations of this sentence generally ignore the disjunctive meaning of *aut*. They translate the sentence as if it contained *et* instead of *aut*. We, on the contrary, believe that the choice of *aut* is important. *Natura* and *uoluntas* are different entities, as we can see in *Rep.* 3.23, when Cicero writes: *etenim iustitiae non natura nec voluntas, sed inbecillitas mater est. Natura* designs the structural order of things, while *uoluntas* means the human capacity to get rid of nature's determinations. This is an idea that will be expressed again some years later: "*If you wish for the safety of those that are by nature citizens, but by will enemies.*"[51] The power of *voluntas* is so great that it can transform a citizen into a *hostis*, that is, an external enemy. At the same time, this raises a difficult question, for if Cicero, like Descartes much later, believes that the power of will is infinite, then the concept of the *res publica*'s eternity acquires new meaning. In doing so, will leads to the perfect adaptation of Romans – the *maiores* in particular – to the nature of things, and especially to political development, but at the same time it depends on the citizens' desire to maintain this privileged situation. Will can be the most precious auxiliary of nature or its fiercest opponent.

1.6 Conclusion

Cicero contributed significantly to the development of the concept of *Roma aeterna*, which, however, never appears in his works. Actually, the

---

[49] *Rep.* 5.2: *Nostra vero aetas cum rem publicam sicut picturam accepisset egregiam, sed iam evanescentem vetustate, non modo eam coloribus eisdem, quibus fuerat, renovare neglexit, se ne id quidem curavit, ut formam saltem eius et extrema tamquam liniamenta servaret ... Nostris enim vitiis, non casu aliquo, rem publicam verbo retinemus, re ipsa vero iam pridem amisimus.*
[50] *Rep.* 1.47: *talis est quaeque res publica, qualis eius aut natura aut uoluntas qui illam regit*, trans. Loeb modified.
[51] *Phil.* 8.13: *sin eos qui natura cives sunt, voluntate hostes saluos uelis.*

emergence of this expression was one of the results of the civil war, after which it became a key word for the Augustan cultural and political renovation of the *Urbs*. When discussing the year 403 BCE, Livy affirms with some anticipation that Rome will become blessed, invincible, and eternal, thanks to *Concordia*.[52] Meanwhile Tibullus, when speaking of the origins of the *Urbs*, states that Romulus has still not built an eternal city.[53] For Cicero the philosopher and politician, the main concept is that of the *res publica*; and within the *res publica*, he is deeply anxious about the destiny of the souls of prominent citizens. However, the idea that perfection in human affairs and especially politics is the result of both natural factors and the high capacities of the individual, creates a solid conceptual framework for the notion of Rome's exceptional destiny. By making this claim, Cicero defined a kind of secular eternity – if the expression of such made sense at this time. This concept was obviously the opposite of the Jewish idea of the transcendental election of Israel. The main weakness of this Ciceronian system is the variability – both synchronic and diachronic – of the will of politicians and the Roman people. Not all Roman politicians were sages or even probabilists, and Romans did not always have a good intuitive sense of what needed to be done. The emperors mitigated this weakness by proclaiming themselves gods. From a conceptual point of view, it was an ingenious solution for perpetuating an affirmation of Rome's eternity. Nevertheless, it would be a bit rash to claim that this was exactly the kind of decision that extended a bridge to the Jewish people.

---

[52] *AVC* 5.7.10: *beatam urbem Romanam et inuictam et aeternam.*
[53] Tibullus 2.5.23: *Romulus aeternae nondum formaverat urbis/moenia.*

CHAPTER 2

Eclogue 4 *and the Futures of Rome*

Brian W. Breed

Virgil's fourth *Eclogue* was written in or around 40 BC.[1] It honors the birth of a miraculous child and prophesies the salvation of Rome in his lifetime. In the fall of that year Rome was celebrating *concordia* between the triumvirs Octavian and Mark Antony, a hopeful moment in the midst of the larger civil crisis that would eventually see Octavian victorious over Antony and able to consolidate power in himself as Augustus, the first Roman emperor.[2] Such was Rome's future. Before there was an Augustus, before what Augustus would represent for Rome could be appreciated, *Eclogue* 4 is nevertheless a key Augustan text, important for the development of Augustan ideology.[3] That is to say, *Eclogue* 4 influenced how people might think about who Augustus was and how they could interpret messages the *princeps* broadcast about himself. The poem is, for example, a significant source of language for praise of the emperor and his rule.[4] Virgil himself made the connection. In the *Aeneid* he drew on his earlier poem so that Anchises could depict Augustus as the man under whose rule its prophecies would one day be fulfilled (6.791–95):

> hic vir, hic est, tibi quem promitti saepius audis,
> Augustus Caesar, divi genus, aurea condet
> saecula qui rursus Latio regnata per arva
> Saturno quondam, super et Garamantas et Indos
> proferet imperium.

---

[1] The dramatic date of the poem, established by Pollio's consulship in the year 40 BC, is consistent with datable historical references in the *Eclogues* and with the traditional dating of the collection to the period 42–39 BC. See recently Cucchiarelli 2012: 15–16, 238.
[2] On the poem in light of events at the time, see Du Quesnay 1977: 25–43; Osgood 2006: 193–200.
[3] A theme also explored by Geue 2013.
[4] Cf., e.g., *Aen.* 6.801–803, Hor. *CS* 57–60 (*iam . . . iam . . . iam*, 53–57; cf. *Ecl.* 4.4–7), followed later by Calp. Sic. 1.33–88 (Nero), Mart. 5.19 (Domitian), Claud. *In Ruf.* 1 (Honorius). Houghton 2014 and 2015 looks at panegyrical uses of *Ecl.* 4 in Renaissance Italy, while Hardie 2014: 93–126 tells the extended story of the return of the golden age as an enabling myth for different European imperialisms.

2. Eclogue 4 and the Futures of Rome

This is the man, this is he, the one you have often heard promised to you, Augustus Caesar, who will again found a golden age in Latium, across fields once ruled by Saturn, and he will extend his authority over the Garamantes and the Indians

Already in *Eclogue* 4, the refoundation of a golden age is associated with the rule of one man. This is seen, for example, where the poem's miraculous child is prophesied to "rule a pacified world" *pacatumque reget ... orbem* (17), supported by references to the return of Saturn's kingdom, *Saturnia regna* (6) and to the reign of Apollo (*tuus iam regnat Apollo*, 10), which represents the arrival of a new age brought on by the rule of a new, divine king.[5] The Augustan principate, which effectively restores monarchy to Rome, is not only a future that the poem prophesies, but also, as Andrew Wallace-Hadrill has argued, one that it helps to bring about by acclimating readers to the idea of Augustus as sole ruler.[6] This does not require crediting Virgil as an early adopter of Augustanism. *Eclogue* 4's contribution to the package of ideas assembled under the heading of "Augustus" is primarily a function of reception, and the future of the poem was largely out of Virgil's hands. Moreover, *Eclogue* 4's view of the future for Rome is, as this chapter explores, a complicated one that suggests deep skepticism about the universality of any imperial golden age.

In hindsight the urge to cast the events of the years before the establishment of Augustus' rule as the necessary prelude to the change from the republic to the principate will be powerful. In 40 BC, the true nature of that change would not be, could not be, apparent, but change between systems and between eras is a primary concern of *Eclogue* 4, which combines a number of different schemes for organizing time by dividing it into periods. Emerging from the transitional time between republic and empire, the poem should not be judged on how accurately it did or did not predict the future, though the history of interpretation of the poem as prophecy, whether of imperial rule or of a Christian Messiah, is a fascinating aspect of the text.[7] For the purposes of my argument, it is more important that *Eclogue* 4 speaks to consequences and complications of dividing time into divergent eras. One conclusion supported by the poem's multifarious time schemes is that time does not fall easily into mutually exclusive periods with clear borders. Different ways of organizing

---

[5] See Miller 2009: 254–60 on the "reign of Apollo" and various related configurations of divine rulers and world ages in the context of saecular speculation in the late 40s.
[6] Wallace-Hadrill 1982.
[7] For the Messianic eclogue tradition, see Ziolkowski and Putnam 2008: 487–503 and now Hadas 2013 specifically for the early Christian world.

time overlap and come into conflict, and Rome's future, its many possible futures, will develop through patterns and relationships that involve both division and continuity, and that expose tendencies toward both unification and fragmentation. Transitions between eras of time are thus not a fact that can simply be proclaimed, but they require interpretation, and this is true whether they occur in literary texts or in the life of a society. To see this at work, I first describe the different ways time is divided up and organized in *Eclogue* 4, whereby time is represented as both linear and cyclical and the future is seen as the result both of process and of disruption. I then turn to two comparisons, Horace's *Epode* 16 and *Eclogue* 1, to shed light on two crucial dynamics related to the future of Rome as seen from the environment of civil war that these texts all share. First, because of Rome's self-destructive tendencies, society must change in order to have a better future, but the necessary change can also look like a form of destruction. Rome's salvation might entail abandoning the city, or disregarding it in one way or another. Second, the result of a change of eras is ideally a world without divisions, but time itself and how people experience it is a source of continuing divisions. What for some will be a golden age will not be the same for all. In the end, *Eclogue* 4 contemplates the possibility of a new, peaceful era for Rome only in the awareness that any division between times is always subject to varied negotiation on the part of those who live through them.

2.1 Dividing Time in *Eclogue* 4

Among the systems and patterns for organizing time in *Eclogue* 4, the most prominent is the "ages of man," which describes the arrival by stages of not only social and technological progress but also simultaneous decline, symbolized by metallic "races" or "ages," gold, silver, bronze, and iron. This is a widely attested, and widely adapted myth, of Greek, specifically Hesiodic, and Near Eastern origins.[8] In *Eclogue* 4 it appears in the boiled-down form common at Rome, in which an idealized golden age gives way to the current, debased age of iron.[9] Virgil innovates on that premise with the idea that the one-time golden age can be restored.[10] In addition to this literary tradition, Virgil also associates Rome's position in history with

---

[8] Gatz 1967 remains the most comprehensive discussion.
[9] For recent accounts of the complications of the transition between golden age and iron age at Rome, see Perkell 2002 and Feeney 2007: 108–37. On the shift from Hesiodic "races" to Roman "ages," see Feeney 2007: 115–16, with further bibliography.
[10] Gatz 1967: 25, 87–103.

2. Eclogue 4 and the Futures of Rome

temporal patterns that are more the domain of learned experts. These include the procession of *saecula*, an Etruscan concept, the proper application of which was a topic of regular speculation in late republican Rome,[11] as well as the doctrine of a *magnus annus* or "great year," which was based on the vast scale of astronomy, specifically, the alignment of heavenly bodies, and elaborated in Stoic philosophy in the related form of the *periodos*, the temporal scale for a cosmic cycle of destruction and regeneration.[12] The two patterns are combined in the first lines of the poem's prophecy (4–5):

> Ultima Cumaei venit iam carminis aetas;
> magnus ab integro saeclorum nascitur ordo.

> The final age of the Cumaean prophecy has now come; the great series of eras is starting again from the beginning.

By invoking diverse systems, Virgil sites contemporary Rome both at the end of a sequence, that is to say, in the *ultima aetas*, the "final age," which would be the tenth in the Etruscan scheme,[13] and on the point of cyclical renewal inasmuch as *magnus ordo saeclorum*, "the great series of eras" is being reborn, that is to say, starting over, though in this scheme renewal might first require cataclysmic destruction. The same variation in ways of conceptualizing time, as linear sequence and as repetitive cycle, characterizes other points of reference for time in the poem. *te consule* (11), "in the year of your consulship," addressed to Asinius Pollio, consul for the year 40 BC, marks the date for the poem in the Roman way of denominating years by reference to the consuls, in a sequence stretching back to the foundation of the republic. Meanwhile the poem also exhibits similarities to a body of texts, the Oracula Sibyllina, steeped in systems of sequencing world history according to the cyclical rise and fall of civilizations, expressed from perspectives, Eastern and Jewish, opposed to Roman authority. In a different vein, an embodied way of reckoning time, brought in at the end of the poem, is as humble as it is universal, the ten long, tedious months of pregnancy: *matri longa decem tulerunt fastidia menses*, "ten months gave your mother long trouble" (61). This is a count

---

[11] See Weinstock 1971: 191–7.
[12] The *magnus annus* is the period of time it takes for the heavenly bodies to return to the same disposition in the sky and is related to, but not entirely the same as, the Stoic *periodos*, the time between destruction and rebirth of the cosmos; cf. Cic. *Rep.* 6.24, *ND* 2.41, 118; for Stoic *ecpyrosis*, cf. Sen. *Dial.* 6.26.6–7, Luc. *BC* 1.72–80.
[13] Cf. Serv. ad *Ecl.* 4.4, 10.

presided over by the Parcae, who in the guise of goddesses of childbirth are responsible for insuring that a baby is born at the proper time.[14] They are also responsible for a person's fate, and in this role they appear in lines 46–47, as weavers directing the flow of time from their spindles. A life's linear course provides the poem its possibly most essential timeline, in the form of the birth and maturation of the child, in relationship to which Virgil plots the arrivals of the various aspects of the new golden age, some in infancy, some in youth, and some in adulthood.

This multiplication of schemes for organizing time impacts the poem's prophetic stance toward the crisis confronting Rome and its solution. For Rome to achieve its promised deliverance time has to fall into different eras. And so the poem points to a future that is distinct from the present. The miraculous child will earn the honor of his fellow citizens and that "time will soon come" (*aderit iam tempus*, 48). With joy and anticipation the world looks to the "coming age" (*venturo ... saeclo*, 52). The poet hopes to live to see the day (*o mihi tum longae maneat pars ultima vitae*, 53). A present beset by the consequences of societal guilt, called *sceleris ... nostri*, "our crime" (13) and *priscae ... fraudis*, "ancient deceit" (31), has to be set apart from a future in which harmony reigns. But where the dividing line between times lies is not clear. In Hesiod's progression of the metallic races first one dies off, then another one is created. In Virgil by contrast, changes are mapped onto the story of the child's development, "with whom the iron race will first decline and a golden race arise in the whole world," *quo ferrea primum / desinet ac toto surget gens aurea mundo* (8–9), but there is not a moment where the change from gold to iron happens. Virgil's golden age and iron age are not mutually exclusive; they overlap and contaminate each other. For example, the continuation of warfare and violence might be a necessary step toward undoing the effects of societal guilt (31–36), but it exists simultaneously with a golden age that is also here now, in the form of the return of the kingdom of Saturn, the return of Justice, and the descent from heaven of a new generation announced in lines 4–7 (*iam ... iam ... iam*). In other words, the golden age seems to be simultaneously present, developing, and still to come, and without formal milestones marking the transitions, the recognition of where one era passes into another is a matter of interpretation. Even to know how the future will be the same and different requires in the first place knowing where we are at the present, and for that question the poem offers different answers,

---

[14] Varro apud Gell. *NA* 3.16.9–11.

2. Eclogue 4 and the Futures of Rome

depending on whether we orient ourselves according to the metallic ages, or the procession of *saecula*, or the *magnus annus*, or the consular *fasti*, or a human lifespan, or some other scheme.

On this point, Virgil has been accused of being a victim of his own "fondness for mixing up pieces of heterogeneous learning,"[15] but in representing time as it can be structured and understood differently *Eclogue* 4 also offers a historical perspective approximating reality. Like Virgil's gold and iron ages, the borders between historical eras tend to be indefinite and negotiable. To cite one obvious and very relevant example, the "end of the republic" can be assigned to various dates, whether Sulla's march on Rome, or Caesar's perpetual dictatorship, or the Battle of Actium, or even the assassination of Tiberius Gracchus. The "empire" or "age of Augustus" was not a new reality that arrived all at once, but a process developing over years and even decades.[16] Texts likewise rarely cooperate with attempts to confine them within borders defined by the beginnings and endings of historical institutions or by the milestones of a calendar. But that does not make periodization an unrewarding topic for discussion. Divisions between eras have to be sorted out in literature all the time as a consequence of intertextual relationships and of external factors. In the case of *Eclogue* 4, for example, it can be debated whether the poem belongs in the same time period as Catullus 64, or Lucretius *De rerum natura*, texts with which it shares the concern for historical and cultural transitions and much more. Alternatively, Virgil's poem might be said to look back on republican texts from a changed world due to the gravitational pull of political changes underway, or looming.[17] To resolve such a question by simply drawing a line between literary periods risks being seen as arbitrary or worse,[18] and instead of trying to finally categorize *Eclogue* 4 as a "republican" or an "Augustan" text or as something else, we might better focus on where and by whom these distinctions could be experienced in the light of the failure of periods of time to act like physical containers with discrete boundaries. To that end, Caroline Levine has recently made a case for thinking about temporal periods not through the spatial metaphor of a container but as changing "rhythms" and patterns of organizing experience that need not be mutually exclusive but often overlap and interact.[19]

---

[15] Conington and Nettleship 1898 ad *Ecl.* 4.5; cf. Nisbet 1995: 51: "Virgil's syncretism sometimes produces inconsistencies."
[16] The negotiation of this murky transition in literary texts of the empire is discussed well by Farrell and Nelis in their introduction (2013: 2–7), and by the contributors to their volume.
[17] Trimble 2013.   [18] The discussion by Perkins 1992: 61–84 has been rightly influential.
[19] Levine 2015: 49–81.

Such a view is consistent with the temporal complexity we encounter in *Eclogue* 4. In the poem, as we have seen, there is no line that defines where the golden age begins and the iron age ends. Rather, the difference between ages is marked by different experiences of time and of social life. The spontaneously abundant life in the golden age involves patterns of experience that are fundamentally different from life in the iron age, with its agricultural cycles, sailing seasons, and annual consular elections, all of which are examples of what Levine calls rhythms. In some ways, dividing time up and organizing life accordingly is itself a defining feature of the iron age, and a return to the golden age would mean removing not only the institutions of war, agriculture, politics, etc., that result from societal sin, but also the familiar patterns of life that accompany those institutions.[20]

Where the movement of time is conceived in terms of developing patterns, getting from one period of time to another and recognizing the change requires negotiating elements of continuity and disjunction. So in *Eclogue* 4, the Parcae voice an eagerness for time to pass quickly to reach the harmonious future (46–47):

> 'Talia saecla' suis dixerunt 'currite' fusis
> concordes stabili fatorum
> numine Parcae.

"Run across such ages," the Parcae said to their spindles, in unanimity by the unchanging authority of fate.

The running of the Fates' thread across the ages, backed by unanimous, unchanging authority, gives us a strong image of passing time seen as unbroken connection. This is consistent with the emphasis that the poem elsewhere puts on change through incrementalism. For example, the fields turn gold "gradually" *paulatim flavescet campus* (28). The child matures from cradle to adulthood without reference to the ceremonial milestones of a Roman boy's life, such as removing the bulla and donning the toga virilis, though the role of literary education in his maturation (26–27) does speak to realities of elite Roman life.[21] Pollio's consulship, the poem's historical touchstone, which might be seen as the culmination of a historical sequence in the form of the list of consuls, is represented first of all as the beginning of something that will advance as a process (11–12):

---

[20] So Feeney 2007: 116–17: "The ordering of time is a foundational element of what it takes to live in the Iron Age. It is not just an appurtenance, but a basic enabling constraint of civilization, and its absence is therefore a defining characteristic of the previous age."

[21] Nisbet 1995: 66 n. 98 cites the apt parallel of Cato's choices for his son's education (Plut. *Cat. Mai.* 20.5).

2. Eclogue 4 and the Futures of Rome

> teque adeo decus hoc aevi, te consule, inibit,
> Pollio, et incipient magni procedere menses;

> Under you Pollio, in your consulship, this glorious age will begin, and the great months will start to advance.

This orientation toward passing time represents the future not as a different reality segregated in another world somewhere off in time, but as what we might think of as a developing pattern.[22] The completion of such developments will, nevertheless, represent a fundamental break from the world of the present. And the poem conceives of that change in terms appropriate to the particular historical setting. Rome is facing the consequences of civil war, of society divided against itself, but the poem foresees a time without division, the golden age, a world in which the terrible disruptions and suffering of civil war are not possible because of the absence of vices that threaten social unity.[23] So division, we might say, is both Rome's problem and, in the form of time divided into separate eras, part of the solution. And yet, a basic question lingers, namely whether a golden-age Rome, a Rome without divisions, represents a better and purer Rome, or a society no longer recognizable as Rome. It is a habit of the Romans to perceive threats to their existence and identity in times of crisis. And this tendency is fed in *Eclogue* 4 both by the problems of the present, namely civil war, and by the uncertainty of how Rome's future is going to balance continuity – Rome remaining Rome – and the apparent necessity of a definitive end followed by a new beginning.

2.2 Rome, Civil War, and the Experience of Changing Eras

Two comparisons can provide some context for how the division of times operates in *Eclogue* 4. Like *Eclogue* 4, Horace's *Epode* 16 imagines a golden age as a change from and response to Rome's current troubles. But where Virgil's gold and iron ages blend into one another, Horace makes separation between them a reality through physical space and geography. Attaining the golden age means leaving Rome behind. Physical separation from Rome and from its ways of organizing time is also a factor in *Eclogue* 1 in the form of the divergent futures of Tityrus, who can stay on his little

---

[22] For history as process in *Ecl.* 4, see Jenkyns 1998: 199–208 and Hardie 2006 for the inversion of Lucretian ideas about permanence and change.
[23] For the undivided golden age, cf., e.g., *G.* 1.125–27, Tib. 1.3.35–44: no boundary stones dividing fields, a remedy for the particular trouble of Italy in the late 40s BC, where the need to divide land among owners was a source of civil strife, and an important theme of the *Eclogues*.

farm in the Roman *dintorni*, and Meliboeus, who must leave for parts unknown. The different patterns of life that they will follow also suggest that gold and iron ages are not merely segregated in separate worlds, but reflect differences of experience due to the asymmetrical impact of political and social change.

Horace's *Epode* 16 was written it seems nearly contemporaneously with the *Eclogues* and reveals close connections with Virgil's poems, especially *Eclogue* 4.[24] Horace, like Virgil, looks to a future golden age, but for him it is as much a distinct place as a different time. In the face of Rome's seemingly inexhaustible propensity for civil war, *Epode* 16 makes the outrageous proposal to abandon the city never to return in order to make for "blessed fields" *arva beata* (41) across the sea on islands in the streams of Ocean where the golden age, with its spontaneous agricultural abundance, lives on (41–62). Meanwhile, the progress and decline of the ages has advanced elsewhere, as is emphasized in the poem's last lines (63–66):

> Iuppiter illa piae secrevit litora genti,
> ut inquinavit aere tempus aureum.
> aerea dehinc ferro duravit saecula; quorum
> piis secunda vate me datur fuga.

> Jupiter set these shores apart for a pious race when he spoiled the golden age with bronze. And then he hardened bronze ages with iron. For those among them who are pious successful escape is now possible with me as prophet and guide.

A journey across the ocean is thus a journey to a former time, and Horace envisages not so much the restoration of the golden age as relocation to a place where it has always existed.

In comparison with *Eclogue* 4, Horace's post-urban and fugitive Roman future, which is also an expedition into the past, highlights a silence in Virgil's text. *Eclogue* 4 leaves the relationship between the new golden age and the city of Rome in need of being worked out. Virgil makes no mention of Rome as a geographical site. Pollio and his consulship represent the city as a political system and historical entity, and the reference to "our sin" *sceleris nostri* makes a gesture to the Roman people in their collective identity, but the *urbs* itself, the one that is, for instance, visited by Tityrus in *Eclogue* 1.19–25, is unseen. The absence of Rome the physical place may

---

[24] On the question of the relative dating of *Epode* 16 and *Eclogue* 4, Watson 2003: 486–8 and Clausen 1994: 145–50 uphold the different alternatives. The case for Horace as the imitator of Virgil would seem to be the stronger.

2. Eclogue 4 and the Futures of Rome

be a requirement of the idea of the return of the golden age as Virgil develops it, just as much as Horace's geographically isolated golden age requires leaving Rome behind to access it. At the most basic level, cities surrounded by walls are a reality of the iron age that, like sailing and plowing, is necessitated by sin (*cingere muris / oppida*, 32–33), and so a feature of culture whose disappearance must be contemplated in the process of imagining a return to a different way of organizing society. Another way of putting this is to say that for Rome the "return" of the golden age cannot be a return at all, since there never was a Rome in a past golden age.

The contemplation, furthermore, of a future without Rome in *Eclogue* 4 extends beyond just the tradition of the Hesiodic metallic ages. It is in fact common to many of the time schemes in play. It is explicit, for example, in the third sibylline oracle. That text, which originates among Hellenized Jews in Alexandria in the second century BC or first part of the first century BC,[25] shares with *Eclogue* 4 some of the idealized imagery of the golden age, and there is a strong case to be made that Jewish traditions have also influenced the idea of a miraculous child sent from heaven whose birth renews the world.[26] At the same time, the third sibylline oracle also foretells not only Rome's rise to power but also its eventual fall, which is described with relish.[27] Rome's destruction secures the redemption of people who suffer under the Romans as (the last in a series of) foreign conquerors (928–47, 954–88). A text whose prophecy of a blessed future is predicated on the destruction of Rome raises important questions about Virgil's access to sources and his purposes.[28] But if nothing else, the sybilline contribution to *Eclogue* 4's complicated vision of Rome's future is not anomalous. Thus, for example, Virgil's prophecy of a replay of the Trojan war as a step toward the golden age (35–36) evokes the repeated sacks that both end that city and produce a new beginning in the form of the rise of Rome. But the return expedition to Troy opens complicated possibilities. If hoped for eastern conquests, over Parthia for instance, are construed as another Trojan war, the Romans are in danger of being seen as destroying a version of themselves.[29] And rumors that Julius Caesar intended

---

[25] On the date and place of origin, see the up-to-date summary of evidence in Lightfoot 2007: 95–7.
[26] Nisbet 1995 reviews the possibilities, with a tendency to credit the likelihood of eastern influences on Virgil's poem.
[27] Rome's place in the cyclical history of civilizations: 188–235; curses on Rome and wishes for destruction: 399–412, 434–56. Cf. Chapter 10 by Gruen in this volume.
[28] One commonly cited vector of transmission is Pollio's Herodian connections: Feldman 1953, and some would assign Virgil the capacity simply to reverse the anti-Roman intent of the source material: Du Quesnay 1977: 77–8, Nisbet 1995: 49.
[29] As in Prop. 2.30.19–22 *Phrygias nunc ire per undas . . . spargere et alterna communes caede Penates.*

to move his capital to Ilium or Alexandria (Suet. *DJ* 79.3) represent another way in which a return to Troy could be seen as a threat to the future of Rome.[30] Furthermore, as already mentioned, the measurement of time itself in *Eclogue* 4 variously incorporates ideas of destruction followed by new birth. The concept of a "great year" would potentially see Rome destroyed in flame before society can begin again. The arrival of the *ultima aetas* would mean Rome is in its tenth age and so approaching the end of the lifespan of a nation.[31]

To be clear, in *Eclogue* 4 Virgil is not secretly wishing for the destruction of Rome. He is not even imagining a post-Roman world like Horace menacingly describes in *Epode* 16, in which the city falls to conquerors (11–14) and "the soil will again be occupied by wild beasts" (10), despite the congeniality of an un-urban Roman future with the imagery of pastoral in *Eclogue* 4: goats with full udders and other signs of rural bounty (21–30), sheep that dye their own fleeces (42–45). It is more the case that he is simply turning away from Rome to look outward to a different world. At the same time, as much as the golden age and the other futures of *Eclogue* 4 might represent a post-Roman world, it might also be construed as a fulfillment of the equation *urbs / orbis* in which the city is no longer distinguishable because it has come to occupy the whole globe. Thus in the *Aeneid* Jupiter will promise the Romans *imperium sine fine* (1.278–79) and a future in which, to quote Denis Feeney, "the people and the god will together occupy all available space, assimilating everything."[32] That idea is consistent with the desire in *Eclogue* 4 for the golden age to be universal and for the world to be undivided in it (*toto surget gens aurea mundo*, 9; *pacatumque reget orbem*, 17; *omnis feret omnia tellus*, 39; *venturo laetantur ut omnia saeclo*, 52). The Roman future in *Eclogue* 4 is, however, not only a convergence toward unification. The Virgilian golden age both extends and limits Roman power.[33] That is to say, the golden age might be found as far as the Romans extend their sway in the world (*Aen.* 6.791–95), but it can also be characteristic of places that stand apart from the ways and authority of the city (e.g., *G.* 2.458–540). In *Eclogue* 4 the golden age encompasses these radically opposed possibilities. It points to both a fulfillment of universal harmony under imperial Rome and a return to a world in

---

[30] See Kraus 1994: esp. 280–2 on these dynamics as they emerge from Livy's account of Camillus and the sack of Rome by the Gauls.
[31] Censorinus *DN* 17.6; Orac.Sib. 4.47, 8.199.   [32] Feeney 1991: 141.
[33] Perkell 2002 finds the point of Virgil's depictions of the golden age in their contradictions, for instance in the longing both for peace and for conquest and glory, as a challenge to the values of Virgil's Roman readers; cf. Thomas 2001: 1–7.

2. Eclogue 4 and the Futures of Rome

which there never was a Rome. The very contradiction suggests that there is something about the golden age that keeps it from being one thing for all Romans. This is a point on which Horace is again explicit where Virgil operates more by implication. In *Epode* 16 the achievement of the golden age has exactly the effect of perpetuating divisions in Roman society. It is a *melior pars* (15, 37) that makes the trip to the West, while the rest are left to their fate. In *Eclogue* 4 the golden age may be an expression of desire for an undivided world, but the poem's very multiplication of time schemes in conceiving the future represents the inevitability of the persistence of differences, at least as far as the experience of time goes.

On this point I turn to *Eclogue* 1, which is the poem in the book of the *Eclogues* that, after *Eclogue* 4, has the most to say about the future and how it will be experienced. The character Meliboeus voices extended descriptions of the future as he sees it for himself (64–78) and for his interlocutor, Tityrus (46–58). The differences are many, and Tityrus and Meliboeus are looking at futures lived, not just physically apart, but even, I suggest, in different eras of time. For Tityrus, Meliboeus sees a future defined by continuity and sameness. He says "the land will remain yours" (*tua rura manebunt*, 46), things will go on "as always" (*quae semper*, 53) in "familiar" surroundings (*flumina nota*, 51) amidst pleasantries that "will not cease" (*nec cessabit*, 58). By contrast, for himself the future is about uncertainty and dislocation. It stretches out in far, unknown distances (64–66), and the time before he might return home is long and indefinite (*umquam . . . longo post tempore*, 67). In contemplating this future he thinks in terms of harvests and planting seasons (*post aliquot . . . aristas*, 69; *haec tam culta novalia . . . has segetes*, 70–71; *his nos consevimus agros*, 72; *insere nunc, Meliboee, piros, pone ordine vites*, 73). He measures time, in other words, according to patterns of the iron age that would no longer be required in a spontaneously abundant golden age.[34] Meliboeus' iron age mentality is revealed also in the way he sees himself as part of a divided, warring society: *nos . . . alii*, "the rest of us" (64); *impius . . . miles* (70) and *barbarus* (71) vs. *cives* (71); *his nos* (72), dividing "them" from "us." Meliboeus is in this way also reminiscent of Horace's Romans in *Epode* 16, who are divided between a "better part," the valorous (*quibus est virtus*, 39), the pious (*piae . . . genti*, 63, and *quorum / piis*, 65–66) and the rest, and some at least are, like Meliboeus, looking at long exile (*Phocaeorum / velut profugit exsecrata*

---

[34] The recapitulation of this language at *Ecl.* 9.46–50, in association with the observation of the *Caesaris astrum*, evokes the speculation about the end of an age around Caesar's assassination and apotheosis; cf DServ ad 9.46 *sed Vulcanius aruspex in contione dixit cometen esse, qui significaret exitium noni saeculi et ingressum decimi*.

civitas, 17–18, cf. *Ecl.* 1.4 *patriam fugimus*).[35] But unlike those who will follow Horace to the distant West and their reward, Meliboeus' far journeys offer no hope of arriving at a better time; for him there are no *arva beata* somewhere else. Instead, Meliboeus sees a golden age that is right in front of him, but physically isolated (11–12) and exceptional (*fortunate senex*, 46).

Tityrus' idiosyncratic golden age is a protected space, but it is also a certain pattern of life conferred on him by his urban benefactor: "a god made these times of leisure for me" (*deus nobis haec otia fecit*, 6). For Tityrus the *otium* of watching cattle and making music (9–10) represents a change from the rhythms of life he was previously following: routines of market days and travel to and from the city, romantic entanglements, accumulating signs of aging (27–35). In response, his gratitude takes the form of a new pattern of observances, monthly offerings on a smoking altar to honor his patron (42–43). At the same time, the change Tityrus embraces means that some, apparently, can go back to doing things as they used to (44–45):

> hic mihi responsum primus dedit ille petenti:
> 'pascite ut ante boves, pueri; summittite tauros.'
>
> Here, he was the first to respond to my petition: "boys, go back to pasturing your cattle as before; raise your bulls."

Meliboeus at least is not among those able to return to the way things used to be. The conclusion is hard to miss, that Tityrus' generous god is also the author of Meliboeus' displacement, and what is spoken at Rome (*hic*, 44) produces different futures. The contrast between Tityrus' easy transitions among patterns of life and the uncertain relationship to time that will dominate Meliboeus' future reflects an unequal distribution of Roman authority in its impact on people.[36] In the different ways of relating to time experienced by Meliboeus and Tityrus, the selectivity and contingency of an attempt to impose periodization, a division of times, is exposed, despite the fondness of Roman authority for saying things like "conflict is over; go back to doing things as before" (*ut ante*, *Ecl.* 1.45) or "a new age has begun."[37]

---

[35] For further resonances of a Meliboeus-like perspective in *Epod.* 16 cf. also *barbarus* (*Epod.* 16.11); contemplating return (25–34); a group as "us" vs. them (35–41; *nos*, 41); amazement (*mirabimur*, 53; cf. *mirabor*, *Ecl.* 1.69).

[36] Cf. Thomas 2001: 7: "in political life one man's golden age will be another's age of iron."

[37] A gesture most fully associated with Augustus in the setting of the *ludi saeculares* of 17, but the intent may have been there from the first stages of the *princeps*' public life. The anecdote that a tenth age began with the appearance of Caesar's comet, upon the announcement of which the prophet

2.3 Conclusion

To return in conclusion to *Eclogue* 4, the model of divergent futures in the face of an intervention from Rome in *Eclogue* 1 and the dividing up of the Romans in *Epode* 16 confirm what we have already seen, namely, that the return of golden age need not be the same, will not be the same, for all people. In *Eclogue* 4 the multiplication of different ways of dividing and organizing time represents the possibility of living according to the rhythms of a golden age, while simultaneously, or alternatively, the ways of the iron age also persist. In that sense, the Rome of *Eclogue* 4 is like any other complex society. Dividing time, organizing it, transitioning between divisions is a fact of life lived in a society made up of many institutions and traditions, and it always happens in the presence of other divisions and systems.[38]

In important ways *Eclogue* 4 was right about the future: monarchy did come to Rome, and its arrival was accompanied and justified by peace. In the short term the poem was also very wrong. Events moved quickly. Hoped for children went unborn, or were born as girls rather than boys.[39] A peace celebrated as the dawning of a new era did not hold. The poem's mixed success as prophecy might have relegated it to the status of a curiosity, an artifact of the context of its creation that soon lost meaning. Instead, *Eclogue* 4's vigorously misappropriated afterlives testify to the poem's capacity for manifold relevance, which it achieves at least in part through its location of realities of the day within a view of history that is broad and flexible based on the multiplication of periods of time. The association of the golden age with the rule of one man suggests that in or around 40 BC it was possible to imagine a future in which a fundamental change in the political culture at Rome could represent the basis for a claim that one period of time has ended and a new one has begun. But it equally offers the possibility of recognizing that lives will be differently impacted by any such change. For all that some will embrace change and adapt accordingly and others struggle to cope with the consequences, there will also be a choice to go on living in total or occasional disregard of the claims

---

Vulcanius keeled over dead (cf. above n. 34), is attributed by DServ to Augustus himself *in libro secundo de memoria vitae suae*.

[38] So Levine 2015: 65: "a society organized by multiple institutions will be shaped not only by multiple points of origin but also by plural and conflicting rhythms." Feeney's account of such realities of Roman life as the different ways of measuring time in the city and the country, in the capital and in the provinces, in the republic and the empire (2007: 167–210) illustrates these "plural and conflicting rhythms."

[39] Both Antony and Octavian saw daughters born in 39 BC.

of a political authority to have altered the rhythms of life equally for all. So Virgil in the end is right about another thing. A change of eras will be as much a matter of interpretation, of recognizing patterns and balancing alternatives, in the political and social life of the Romans as it is in a literary text like *Eclogue* 4.[40]

---

[40] It is my pleasure to thank the editors for the invitation to contribute to the volume and for their and the press readers' suggestions for improvements. An earlier version was presented at Emory University, and I thank Christine Perkell, Niall Slater, Garth Tissol, and Susan Tamasi for their hospitality and input. Final thanks to Fiachra MacGóráin for reading and providing helpful comments on a draft.

CHAPTER 3

Imperium sine fine: *Rome's Future in Augustan Epic*

Ayelet Haimson Lushkov

> *Wouldn't Aeneas have asked: "What next?*
> *After this triumph, what portends?"* W. H. Auden, *A Secondary Epic*

After witnessing her son's shipwreck in *Aeneid* 1, the goddess Venus begs Jupiter to explain the apparent discrepancy between the Trojans' current plight and Jupiter's previous promises of their eventual, Roman dominion. Her most important words lie at the exact center of her speech, twelve lines from its beginning and end: *quem das finem, rex magne, laborum?* ("What end do you give to their toils, great king?" 1.241). Besides the meta-poetic reversal of epic convention – *beginning* in the middle – the centrality of ending is more than a matter of formalism and aesthetics: *finis* is the trigger that activates both Jupiter's response and the future to be realized by Aeneas and Rome.[1] Before he can reply, however, Venus points to yet another discrepancy, that between Aeneas' travails and Antenor's smooth escape from Troy as well as his foundation of a peaceful Padua (1.249 "now he is settled in serene peace" *nunc placida compostus pace quiescit*). The toil of the Trojans – encapsulated in the programmatic line, *tantae molis erat Romanam condere gentem* (1.33 "such a great effort it was to establish the Roman people") – is thus juxtaposed with the relatively effortless fate of Antenor and Padua: two parallel stories of foundation, two contrasting futures, two defining characteristics.[2] As the close of Jupiter's reply will emphasize, one day it will be Rome's fate to enjoy the peace here associated with Padua, but only following generations of war in stark contrast to

---

[1] Venus' language also echoes her son's earlier speech to his men, in which he attempts to put a brave face on their plight: 1.199 *dabit deus his quoque finem*. As if to further enhance the programmatic weight of *finis*, the word marks the beginning of the passage – yet another reversal – in which Venus and Jupiter's dialogue takes place: 1.223 *et iam finis erat*. On Vergil's clustering of *finis* in the first half of the *Aeneid*, see Mitchell-Boyask 1996: 293.

[2] Another important comparandum in the *Aeneid* is, of course, Carthage (1.437 *O fortunati, quorum iam moenia surgunt!*), in whose foundation Aeneas is participating when Mercury appears to him in Book 4 (4.265–7 *tu nunc Karthaginis altae / fundamenta locas pulchramque uxorius urbem/exstruis?*). For the parallel constructions of Rome and Padua, cf. Livy 1.1.2, with Ogilvie 1970: 35–7.

Venus' description of Padua and Aeneas' own hope for *sedes quietas* (1.205) in Latium. Venus' rhetorical question – *quem finem?* – appears unendingly complex as one temporal point folds into another: an end for Aeneas, for the Trojans, for the Romans.

Faced with this question, Jupiter reassures Venus of his constancy: his promise of foundation and glory remain unaltered. After recounting the future of Aeneas in Latium, he turns to the fate of his descendants:

> At puer Ascanius, cui nunc cognomen Iulo
> additur,—Ilus erat, dum res stetit Ilia regno,—
> triginta magnos volvendis mensibus orbis
> imperio explebit, regnumque ab sede Lavini   270
> transferet, et longam multa vi muniet Albam.
> Hic iam ter centum totos regnabitur annos
> gente sub Hectorea, donec regina sacerdos,
> Marte gravis, geminam partu dabit Ilia prolem.
> Inde lupae fulvo nutricis tegmine laetus   275
> Romulus excipiet gentem, et Mavortia condet
> moenia, Romanosque suo de nomine dicet.
> His ego nec metas rerum nec tempora pono;
> imperium sine fine dedi. Quin aspera Iuno,
> quae mare nunc terrasque metu caelumque fatigat,   280
> consilia in melius referet, mecumque fovebit
> Romanos rerum dominos gentemque togatam:
> sic placitum. Veniet lustris labentibus aetas,
> cum domus Assaraci Phthiam clarasque Mycenas
> servitio premet, ac victis dominabitur Argis.   285
> Nascetur pulchra Troianus origine Caesar,
> imperium oceano, famam qui terminet astris,—
> Iulius, a magno demissum nomen Iulo.   (Verg. *Aen*. 1.267–88)

But the boy Ascanius, to whom now the name Iulus is added – he was Ilus, while the kingdom of Ilium still stood – will fill thirty years with empire, and will transfer rule from the seat of Lavinium, and fortify Alba Longa with great force. Here they will rule, under the House of Hector, for three hundred years, until a royal priestess, Ilia, pregnant by Mars, will give birth to a double progeny. From there Romulus will rise, happy in the tawny cover of the nursing she-wolf, and will found Mars' walls, and will call them Romans after himself. On them I place neither boundaries nor endpoints, but give empire without end. Even harsh Juno, who now wearies the sea and earth and sky with fear, will change her mind to the better, and with me will favor the Romans, masters of all things, a people garbed in the toga; it has been decided. There will come a time with the passing ages, when the house of Assarcus will press Phthia and bright Mycenae in servitude, and will lord it over the defeated Argives. A Trojan Caesar will be born from lovely origin, who will bound his empire with the ocean, his fame with the stars – Iulius, a name descended from great Iulus.

The passage has a number of striking features, but for present purposes, the most prominent one is the lavish generosity with which Jupiter promises Venus that her descendants will enjoy empire without end, unfettered by space or time (278–9 *his ego nec metas rerum nec tempora pono; / imperium sine fine dedi*).[3] So unfettered will be their success, in fact, that even Jupiter's diction participates in it: *sine fine* immediately negates the very idea of ending, while *metas*, the boundary that the god does not impose, connotes not the very end, but rather the half-way point in a circular race-course, the marker at which the competing chariots turned back.[4] The verse, therefore, does more than just promise Roman greatness. It embodies also the formal rejection of a narrative doubling back on itself, and celebrates instead the linear teleology of Augustan triumphalism: the Romans will never have run half the race, since theirs is a never-ending march to glory. To Venus' question – *quem finem?* – Jupiter's answer is a resounding "none."

There are some obvious objections to such a reading, not least the simplicity it imposes on the complex narrative structure of the *Aeneid*, and of the political ideologies these narratives articulate.[5] And indeed, *imperium sine fine* is itself a complex phrase, both politically and ideologically. *Imperium*, however familiar a word, is a technical term of republican political theory, and one which Augustus was careful to navigate around, adopting for himself the more pliable *potestas* of the tribunes of the plebs. And in republican political terms, of course, *imperium sine fine* is anathema. By law and definition, the *imperium* that the Roman people bestowed on its magistrates, and which the senate bestowed on pro-magistrates, was

---

[3] The Latin word *finis* has a number of overlapping senses, the most relevant of which are temporal (a future or past point in time), spatial (a border or limit), and purposive or teleological (the goal towards which the poem is directed). Other senses exist as well, as, for instance, the ending of a speech. Note Mitchell-Boyask 1996: 263: "these usages are inseparable and Vergil ties them together." For *sine fine* as programmatic in the *Aeneid*, see O'Hara 1990 and Mitchell-Boyask 1996; for closure as a problematic feature of epic, see Quint 1993 and Hardie 1997; on the Homeric precedent, see Kelly 2007. On closure more generally, see Fowler 1989 and the essays in Roberts, Dunn and Fowler 1997.

[4] Mitchell-Boyask 1996: 262–3 points out that *meta* and *finis* are both available in the hexameter; the word cluster reminds us of the poet's other options. As it happens, *imperium sine fine* falls near, but not exactly at, the halfway point in Jupiter's speech, while Venus, who thinks they're more than halfway there, has her *quem finem* smack in the middle of hers.

[5] For surveys of critical approaches to the ideologies of the *Aeneid*, including the dominance of the Harvard School, see Harrison 1990 and Pandey 2017.

bounded not only by collegiality – with the exception of the dictator, magistrates were always elected in groups of two or more – but also by space and time, precisely what Jupiter specifies Roman *imperium* will not have. Magistrates served for a defined period, and were limited by clearly defined spheres of influence.[6] For all that Vergil qualifies that this *imperium* is given to all the Romans (*his*), in republican Rome *imperium sine fine* was simply *regnum*, a fitting idea for the king of heaven, but not for his worshippers below. In Augustan Rome, however, *imperium sine fine* was another matter altogether, a shared Roman project of expansion, and a practical if not legal definition of the scope of the *princeps'* power. If Venus' question – *quem finem?* – expects a republican answer, Jupiter's implicit answer of "none" heralds instead the new Augustan era.

What, therefore, does it mean to make an end in Augustan epic? More specifically, how can Augustan epic make an end for Rome? This question, which sits at the intersection of political ideology and literary genre, will preoccupy the rest of this essay, contrasting Jupiter's prophecy with Pythagoras' speech at the end of Ovid's *Metamorphoses*. I will argue, through a close formalist reading of the texts, that these two epic visions provide a fairly ambivalent terminus or boundary for Rome or its empire, and even more so in the case of Roman collapse or future non-existence. This is in keeping with a general resistance to closure in the epic tradition, whether as an inheritance of the cyclical epics of the Trojan War, or through the more extensive intertextual kinships of Latin epic.[7] This closural anxiety makes intuitive sense in a genre where literary filiation and continuation are so dominant a paradigm, but as a consequence the exchange between Venus and Jupiter can be read along two separate but related lines. The urgent question of "what end" has a qualitative as well as quantitative aspect – Venus wants to know not only whether there will be an end to Aeneas' labors, but also what kind of end it will be: peaceful, grisly, successful, or otherwise. As an answer to this kind of question, *imperium sine fine* is exactly what Venus wants to hear – there will be no real ending, therefore there is no need to fret over the fate of Aeneas and his men – and at the same time ducks the bigger question of what kind of ending is suitable from a generic or poetic point of view, not to mention the local question of Aeneas' specific experience. The *Aeneid*, after all, ends unsatisfactorily, not least for Vergil himself, who was allegedly

---

[6] For *imperium*, see, e.g., Brennan 2000: 12–20 and Beck 2011. Richardson 2008 offers the most recent survey of the uses of *imperium* in Latin and traces its semantic field, especially in relation to notions of empire.

[7] For the kinship networks wrought by literary intertext, Hardie 1992 and Hinds 1998 remain seminal.

displeased with his efforts and wanted the poem burned after his death. But if *imperium sine fine* exceeds the bounds of the poem, as it surely must, it also relates to the political realities of Rome. In other words, resisting a fixed end point is also a convenient way to avoid an explicit answer to some awkward, and potentially dangerous, questions about the identity of the thing – Rome – about whose end we are all curious: if Rome were to be identified with the republic, for instance, its end might already have occurred for the Augustan reader. More importantly, Jupiter's answer decouples the poem from its future. The god's promise of *imperium sine fine* assures the Roman reader that however much toil and trouble Aeneas must undergo, the continued success of his descendants is guaranteed. Turnus' death might make for a better or worse ending to the epic, but the end of the poem and the end of the Roman empire need not – indeed cannot – be one and the same.

The Venus-Jupiter exchange also reflects a more pervasive concern in Roman literature, whose authors and characters regularly think about what end there might be to their own individual and collective labors, what Rome's future might look like, and what choices such a future might entail for its people. Horace in *Epode* 16 describes an abandoned Rome, bereft of its citizens, and brought to wrack and ruin by civil war; Livy's Camillus imagines a similar outcome, but due to the Romans swapping their home for the more comfortable Veii. Later in Livy, the young Scipio Africanus threatens a group of young nobles who wish to escape over sea after the disaster of Cannae. Not even an enemy camp is more hostile than one in which such plans are hatched, he tells them, brandishing his naked sword, all while seemingly unaware that such an escape was – even as Livy was writing – being encoded in his countrymen's DNA by Vergil.[8] Aeneas fled in the wake of defeat; why should not his descendants? Such dreams of departure are inherently pessimistic, making an end of a Rome which was never meant to have such an ending, even as they also re-enact the persistent Roman anxiety about repeating, typologically and characteristically, the fate of Troy.[9]

In truth, Rome rarely faced a genuine existential threat, at least not in documented historical time. Narratives of potential flight from the city are instead primarily concerned with the potential impact on Roman

---

[8] Livy 22.53.8 *nulla uerius quam ubi ea cogitentur hostium castra esse*.
[9] On Rome and Troy as mutually exclusive entities, see Kraus 1994. On *Epode* 16, where Horace advises the "better citizens" to flee Rome for the Isles of the Blest, see Mankin 1995: 245 "the nature of their alternatives, to stay and perish or to flee to a place that cannot exist, still makes this a profoundly pessimistic poem." See also Brian Breed's Chapter 2 in this volume.

identity, illustrated, as in the case of Camillus, as a departure from Rome's republican character and geographical location, both prevailing anxieties of the triumviral and early Augustan period.[10] The future imagined for Rome is one where not only the place itself but also its values have been abandoned, and that negative image functions protreptically to defend the city and ensure its proper and more glorious future. But choice of ends is also a choice of futures, and the contest between parallel futures is especially characteristic of the epic genre, emblematized in the choice of Achilles between a long but inglorious life in Phthia and an early death at Troy that will bring him *kleos aphthiton* (*Il.* 9.410–6). As so often, Roman literature places a greater premium on the social and historical consequences of an individual's decision: Aeneas, in the clearest instance, rejects a life with Dido in Carthage for the sake of his son and his descendants. The immortality that is the epic hero's and epic poet's common goal thus becomes a feature of the nation itself, destined to live on through the collective and constantly renewed heroism of its leaders and citizens.

Imagining the future of Rome is thus prompted by and conducive to thinking about the end of Rome, and the corresponding tension between ending and continuity – just like the tension between parallel futures – is characteristic of the epic genre. Indeed, they are effectively the same tension, since the choice of Achilles, and subsequently of Aeneas, is one between foreclosing the epic and fulfilling its telos. That dynamic between closure and continuation has received ample attention in David Quint's classic study of the genre, *Epic and Empire*.[11] However, whereas Quint identified a cross-temporal tradition of winners' and losers' epics, characterized respectively by optimism and pessimism, this essay is necessarily more limited in scope and less invested in the affective attitudes structuring the works. Rather, the essay shows how moments in which the author reflects on the end of Rome or its future become more general meditations on endings and continuities – moments where formal and generic concerns overlap with historical and political ones.

3.1 *Quem Finem?*

The main argument of this essay is that epic poems, especially gestures like *imperium sine fine*, showcase a productive tension between a closural

---

[10] Miles 1995: 75–109.
[11] Quint 1993. This essay further builds on Mitchell-Boyask 1996, which systematically analyzes the poetics of *sine fine* in the *Aeneid* as a resistance to ending characteristic of epic.

imperative and an inherent desire to avoid any kind of closure.[12] This tension, as I have begun sketching out above, has both literary and cultural manifestations. In the following section, I want to focus on the mechanics of the text itself as well as on the formal features with which Vergil, and later Ovid, produce this tension. The two passages I analyze here engage the programmatic question of "what end?" but approach it in rather different ways. Vergil, I suggest, relies on structural figures and verbal play to undercut Jupiter's prophecy of endless Roman power, while Ovid, as appropriate to a poem of metamorphosis, evades the question of strict form in favor of offering an alternative view of continuous flux, with no strictly defined temporal caesurae. Both Vergil and Ovid peer into their own present from behind the looming shadow of Caesar's assassination, the following civil war, and ultimate deification, a point of congruence that fixes not only a historical boundary, but also the ontological boundary between man and god.

The tension between mortal and immortal is crucial to my reading of Jupiter's prophecy. This was a particularly live question for the Augustan age, when for the first time the Romans had in their midst a *deus praesens*, Augustus, who was both man and the son of a god, a ruler on earth yet one coming increasingly close to deification himself. Augustus thus posed a problem for the poets already in his own lifetime, and they in turn experimented extensively with defining both his status and their own relationship to this new prospective divinity.[13] In the *Aeneid*, the issue engages some of the epic's profound assumptions. Aeneas' project of bringing his people to Italy entails also a transfer of the Palladium and Roman penates, a divine migration important enough to appear in the epic's prologue: 1.6 *inferretque deos Latio* ("brought the gods to Latium"). But since the *Aeneid*'s project is genealogical as well as teleological, designed to establish the myth of Troy as the particular mythology of the Julian family, these new gods Aeneas brings with him extend to include Caesar and, in the future, Augustus as well. This is another moment where the transgression of endings is clearly visible: over the course of the *Aeneid*, Aeneas brings his gods to Latium only in so much as he physically unloads them from the ships onto the shore, but we never hear of them again.[14] Vergil can weave the

---

[12] The finest exemplar of this tension in Roman epic is perhaps Lucan, who falls outside the bounds of this paper; on his programmatic idea of endlessness and delay, see Masters 1992. On closure in Latin epic, see Hardie 1997, together with Fowler 1997 on closure between author and reader.

[13] Feeney 1998: 56 and Freudenburg 2014. Cf. e.g., Verg. *Ec.* 1.6–8, Hor. *O.* 1.12.

[14] The idea that the Trojan *penates* have arrived in Italy is confirmed by Turnus in 8.11–2 *victosque penatis / inferre*, but their appearance in the text decreases after Aeneas arrives in Carthage in Book 4. I am grateful to T. J. Bolt for drawing my attention to this point.

Julians into the fabric of the poem through mythical genealogies and prophecies, but Aeneas himself falls quite short of establishing his gods and his people as a natural and legitimate presence in Latium. The divine reconciliation in Book 12 promises an end, but the killing of Turnus shows that there is a distance to go before the two people can truly live side by side.

The tension between mortal and immortal organizes some ways of thinking about endings, since immortality in effect confers a bodily endlessness denied to mortals. This essential difference means that Jupiter has a fundamentally different idea of what limits entail.[15] This is perhaps nowhere better exemplified than in his echo of Venus at the end of the *Aeneid*, where he addresses Juno with the same question Venus once directed at him: 12.793 *quae iam finis erit, coniunx?* ("what will be the end, wife?"). The question emphatically rolls back the books, since it picks up not only Venus' *quem ... finem* in 1.241, but also the more declarative narratorial pause in 1.223, *et iam finis erat*. After twelve books and much fighting, even the once confident Jupiter has been reduced to wondering at the extent of Juno's hatred of the Trojans, a hatred that can (and will) quite literally go on forever.[16] The formal effect, likewise, produces a contradiction. On the one hand, here is a neat ring composition, with the epic bounded on either end by the word *finis*. On the other hand, each *finis* militates against the other, and the very echo undermines any closural work at either end: Venus asks about ends at the beginning and is promised endlessness; Jupiter asks about ends at the end, and promises an end of a very particular sort: a profound change in name, language, and culture for the people of Aeneas, underscoring and securing the end of Troy.[17] The promise that Juno extracts from Jupiter (12.826–8 *sit Latium ... / occidit, occideritque sinas cum nomine Troia*: "Let Latium live ... Troy has fallen, and let her remain fallen together with her name") allows the plot of the *Aeneid* to end as a sequel to the Trojan War and for the story of Rome finally to begin. This Roman story, meanwhile, has severe repercussions for the local inhabitants of Italy, for whom the *Aeneid* spells an end to the pre-Trojan era. The death of Turnus, perhaps the most definitive closural gesture of an epic whose ending is contested at best, exemplifies one aspect

---

[15] *Imperium* makes for a good example: any divine *imperium* is necessarily *sine fine*, since the gods will notionally always be around to enforce it. Roman *imperium*, however, was *sine fine* only in a theoretical sense, while in practice it was bound by time and collegiality (cf. n. 6).

[16] And indeed does; cf. Feeney 1984: 184: "What the scene in [*Aeneid*] 12 resolves is the question of Aeneas' settlement in Latium, and the final passing away of Troy; it does not resolve any more of Juno's grudges. The divine reconciliation is qualified to the extent that it reflects only so much of the Roman endeavour as has been accomplished so far: it leaves open what historically remains open."

[17] I will come back to the question of change as ending in the following section.

of that ending. Turnus's immortal sister Juturna wishes in lament that she could put an end to the endless grief (12.880–1 *finire dolores*) to which her immortality dooms her. Even as the Olympian gods look towards Roman expansion in step with their own immortality, Juturna is in the curious position of an immortal wishing she were not so – the very opposite of epic *telos* at the end of an epic.[18]

The divine resolutions at either end of the *Aeneid* offer an important element of prophetic vindication, or, looked at from the other direction, proleptic closure. Jupiter's vision, for all its views of endlessness, extends to a time when Juno might be persuaded to bend far enough (1.281–2 *consilia in melius referet, mecumque fovebit / Romanos* – "she will turn her counsels for the better, and with me favor the Romans") to allow the conquering Romans to lord over Juno's old favorites: Phthia, bright Mycenae, and Argos, the very places that produced the Greek vanquishers of Troy.[19] The *imperium sine fine* Jupiter imagines for the Romans therefore depends on making an end, on institutionalizing and affirming the end of Troy. *Imperium sine fine*, in this sense, is not a direct answer to Venus' question, but rather an answer that re-contextualizes her question and elevates the reader to a new perspective: Venus' *quem finem* is resolved by the end of the poem, while Jupiter's *sine fine* defines the horizons of everything outside and beyond the poem, a gleaming future which the *Aeneid* can only partially contain through scenes of prophecy.[20] But it is the last three lines of the prophecy that most capture the divine/mortal divide, for it is here that we meet Julius Caesar and the bounds of his *imperium*: *Caesar, / imperium oceano, famam qui terminet astris,—/ Iulius, a magno demissum nomen Iulo* (286–7 "Caesar, who will bound his empire with the ocean, his fame with the stars – Iulius, a name derived from great Iulus").[21] Within a prophecy that proclaims an endless empire, the very appearance of the verb *terminet* is curious and striking, even if the ocean and the stars make for rather grand, if somewhat fungible, boundaries. Still, the Latin itself highlights the interest in boundary formation: the name Caesar Iulius, placed in stark hyperbaton, brackets the line, with both parts of the name enjambed to the immediately preceding and following lines.[22] The verb

---

[18] Cf. Ovid's Sibyl ruing her immortal status in Ov. *Met.* 14.136–51. [19] Feeney 1984.
[20] On prophecy in the *Aeneid*, see O'Hara 1990.
[21] I follow Dobbin 1995 (with extensive further references in his n. 1) in taking *Caesar* as Julius Caesar rather than Augustus, not least because *Caesar Iulius* remains, as Dobbins points out, "an unexampled way to mention the Emperor" (7). For the passage as a grim vision of Roman prospects, see Hejduk 2009, with 290–1 on these lines in particular.
[22] On the spatial dynamics in these lines, see Gladhill 2012: 8.

terminet itself, meanwhile, is bound by a relative clause containing its object *famam*, yet simultaneously reaches beyond that clause to form a zeugma with the object *imperium*; and *imperium* is here literally *sine fine*, its *–um* ending elided with, indeed drowned by, the 'o' of *oceano*.

This conjunction of form and function – where the language both proclaims endlessness while enacting the tension between ending and continuity – can be found more broadly throughout the *imperium sine fine* prophecy. In particular, the passage is organized around two ring compositions, which focus attention on the twin issues of political power and its limitations. As such, the ring composition is a uniquely apposite device. It imitates the ring structure of the *Aeneid*, which starts and ends with the *quem finem* question, thus blending the prophecy and the poem in both form and content. It also engages the end/continuity tension at the level of form, using a structural figure to organize the chaotic flow of time, just as the potent image of *furor impius* (which arguably itself allegorizes the end of the *Aeneid*) is shackled at the end of the prophecy, an allegory of the peace and order imposed on the empire by the victorious Augustus and finally bringing Rome into the condition of Padua so envied by Venus.[23]

The first of the two ring compositions brackets the passage with the name *Iulus* (1.267–88), while another much smaller structure brackets the first half of the passage with the feminine cognate *Ilia* (1.268–74).[24] Strikingly, while the *Ilia* frame is clearly meant to separate the Julian story from the Romulean story which immediately follows, the two ring compositions nevertheless cohere structurally. The outer ring, built on the name *Iulus*, is symmetrical and chiastic: the name itself repeats twice (267, 288) in the same metrical *sedes*, and each time it is used to highlight a change in nomenclature, once from Iulus to Ascanius, and another from Iulus to Iulius. The *Ilia* frame, meanwhile, is a change of not only names, but also referents: in 268 *res Ilia*, it is adjectival, referring to the kingdom of Troy, while in 274 it refers to Ilia the mother of Romulus. As such, both frames begin in exactly the same spot – the myth of Troy – but they end in drastically different places: the outer *Iulus* frame ends with the deified Caesar, while the *Ilia* frame comes to a halting stop at Romulus.

This change, too, has political color. The *Ilia* frame contains a remarkable cluster of regnal words, appearing in three out of its five

---

[23] *Aen.* 1.294–6 *Furor impius intus, / saeva sedens super arma, et centum vinctus aenis /post tergum nodis, fremet horridus ore cruento*; on the ring compositional effect of ending with *furor*, see Galinsky 1988: 340–7.
[24] On ring composition, see Douglas 2007. On the etymologizing play on Iulus, see O'Hara 1996: 121–3; on metrical and teleological play, see Cowan 2009.

lines: 268 *regno*, 270 *imperio, regnum*, 272 *regnabitur*, 273 *regina*. Leaving aside the loaded word *imperium* for a moment, the transition from *regnum* to *regina* rewards closer inspection, since it traces a single process temporally, and, in a sense, causally. The *regnum* of 270 is a fairly abstract "sovereignty," and refers to Iulus' founding of Alba Longa. *Regnabitur* in turn describes the rule of the Alban Kings, here specified as a Trojan dynasty (273 *gente sub Hectorea*), while *regina* is the ultimate result of this reigning by generations of Aeneas' descendants: Ilia, the mother of Romulus. In contrast to the sovereignty of 268 *dum res stetit Ilia regno*, Romulus is distinguished by having neither *imperium* nor *regnum* of his own. He establishes the Roman "race" (276 *excipiet gentem*), founds the city walls (276–7 *et Mavortia condet moenia*), and names the Roman people after himself (277 *Romanosque suo de nomine dicet*). But it is to the nascent Roman people (278 *his* in prominent and accented first position) and not to Romulus that Jupiter gives *imperium sine fine* – to the Romans, and to Iulus, the only other entity in the passage to whom *imperium* is granted (270 *imperio explebit*), though his is admittedly not without end.[25] Finally, it's worth recognizing again the etymological connection between Iulus and Ilia, which, whether it is true or false, carries a political connotation with it: *regnum* will return to Rome through the descendants of a Julia, the Julians.

Iulus' *imperium* ends in two quite significant ways. The first is the rather prosaic fact of his death after thirty years of rule. The second, of course, is the demise of Alba Longa, from where hail Romulus and Remus (the *geminam . . . prolem* of 264), and which the Romans themselves eventually put to the sword, thus completing, finally and conclusively, the process of *translatio imperii* from Troy to Rome. In either case, however, the end of Iulus' *imperium* exceeds the scope of the *Aeneid*, which in turns falls short even of the completion of Aeneas' own mission of resettlement for his people. This temporal convergence is characteristic of epic prophecy, which was always anyway limited by the biographical facts of the poet, but in this case it provides another aspect of endlessness, or more precisely, of the sense that Rome is still not yet quite at its zenith, and therefore cannot yet – nor will ever – look towards any potential end. The recursive quality of prophecy here exists on a meta-poetic level as well. Iulus' *regnumque ab sede Lavini transferet* (270) picks up and directly continues Aeneas' own task, as spelled out programmatically at the opening of the

---

[25] The bibliography on Augustus and Romulus is considerable and collected in, e.g., Hinds 1992 and Starr 2009. Compare 6.781–97 on walls for another view on the idea of bounded imperium.

poem: 1.6–7 *inferretque deos Latio, genus unde Latinum, / Albanique patres, atque altae moenia Romae* ("and brought his gods to Latium, whence the Latin race, the Alban fathers, and the walls of lofty Rome"). Iulus, like many an epic descendant before him, builds on and expands his father's epic project, and Jupiter's prophecy therefore contains not just the *Aeneid* itself, but also its continuation: a *labor* quite literally without end.[26]

3.2 Sine Fine

Despite the structural and verbal play Vergil writes into Jupiter's prophecy, the essential message of the passage remains clear: however problematic, however arduous, Rome's trajectory is one of growth and imperial expansion. It will rise from modest beginnings, and will go on growing, and its empire shall be without end. In the epigraph for this chapter, however, W. H. Auden puts in the mouth of Aeneas a reasonable question: "what next?" Vergil's answer is written all over the *Aeneid*, in the Parade of Heroes and in the Shield of Aeneas, but it can only see as far as the death of Marcellus in 23 B.C. This limitation is partly imposed by Vergil's own mortality, his rootedness in a particular time and place; in that sense, at least, the *Aeneid* is not predictive. This answer, however, fails to address, or indeed verify, the issue of *imperium sine fine* and its ultimate scope. What can *imperium sine fine* mean after and outside of the *Aeneid*?

In this section, I want to offer not a definitive answer to that question, but rather to look at one alternative model, Pythagoras' speech in Ovid's *Metamorphoses* 15, which reworks the *Aeneid*'s linear teleology into a more flexible model of ebb and flow, with the attendant move away from *imperium sine fine* and towards an assumed endpoint.[27]

> Desinet ante dies et in alto Phoebus anhelos
> aequore tinguet equos, quam consequar omnia verbis

---

[26] *labor* in the *Aeneid* is programmatic: cf. e.g. 1.10 *tot adire labores*, where *labor* refers to the content of the *Aeneid* (the wandering and the fighting) and presumably also to the work Aeneas will have to undertake between the death of Turnus and the foundation of Rome. For the semantics of *labor* in the *Aeneid*, see Goins 1993; for the endlessness of the poem, see Hardie 1997: 142: "the question of an ending is thus complicated by the presence within the poem of more than one ending. One answer to the notorious problem of the killing of Turnus as the final scene of the epic would be to say that it is not an ending in any important sense; the real ending to the story of Rome is found instead in the survey of Roman history on the Shield of Aeneas . . ."

[27] The relationship between the *Metamorphoses* and the *Aeneid* is complex and extensive, not least in the ending of the *Metamorphoses*, which harks back to the opening phrases of *Aeneid* 1: Gladhill 2012 and Feldherr 2010.

3. Rome's Future in Augustan Epic

> in species translata novas: sic tempora verti 420
> cernimus atque illas adsumere robora gentes,
> concidere has; sic magna fuit censuque virisque
> perque decem potuit tantum dare sanguinis annos,
> nunc humilis veteres tantummodo Troia ruinas
> et pro divitiis tumulos ostendit avorum. 425
> clara fuit Sparte, magnae viguere Mycenae,
> nec non et Cecropis, nec non Amphionis arces.
> vile solum Sparte est, altae cecidere Mycenae,
> Oedipodioniae quid sunt, nisi nomina, Thebae?
> quid Pandioniae restant, nisi nomen, Athenae? 430
> nunc quoque Dardaniam fama est consurgere Romam,
> Appenninigenae quae proxima Thybridis undis
> mole sub ingenti rerum fundamina ponit:
> haec igitur formam crescendo mutat et olim
> inmensi caput orbis erit! sic dicere vates 435
> faticinasque ferunt sortes, quantumque recordor,
> dixerat Aeneae, cum res Troiana labaret. 437
> Priamides Helenus flenti dubioque salutis. 438
> (Ovid, *Met.* 15.418–37)[28]

The day will run short and Phoebus will plunge his panting horses in the sea before I can speak of all the transformations. So we see times change, and nations growing in strength with them, and others decline. Thus Troy, which was great in resources and men, and could bear through ten years' worth of blood, now is humbled, and has only old ruins to show, and tombs rather than ancestral wealth. Sparta was great once, Mycenae flourished, and what now is Oedipodian Thebes, but a mere name? What remains of Pandion's Athens, but a name? Now too the rumor is that Dardanian Rome is on the rise, which near the Tiber that flows from the Apennines puts down foundations under a great work: she will change her form in growing, and one day will be the head of the great world! Thus did the prophets say, and the fate-revealing lots, and to the extent I remember, Helenus the son of Priam thus said to Aeneas, when Troy was falling, and Aeneas was weeping and doubtful of survival . . .

There follow eleven lines of Helenus' prophecy, which manages both to summarize the *Aeneid* and expand upon it. Aeneas shall escape Troy, will resettle his people in a new land, and one of his, or more specifically, Iulus' descendants (*natus Iuli*) will make the city greater than any before or after it. In consequence, divine honors will be his: *caelumque erit exitus illi* (449). This prophecy is worth dwelling on for a moment longer, because, whether

---

[28] I use the text of Tarrant's 2004 OCT.

or not *illi* puns on *Iuli* two lines above it in the same *sedes*, Ovid's specification that this fabled Roman shall be born from Iulus is strikingly redundant as any descendant of Iulus is also, by definition, a descendant of Aeneas. The point must be, therefore, to establish him, etymologically at least, as Julius Caesar, rather than as Augustus, and thereby replicate the playful emphasis of the ring composition of *Aeneid* 1, discussed above. It matters, too, that this is Caesar, because *exitus* is a meta-poetic word, meaning both a biological end and the end of the book, as it does, for instance, in Horace's *Epodes*.[29] As it happens, the end of Book 15 of the *Metamorphoses*, which is also the end of the whole poem, describes the deification of Caesar, which thus makes real the prophecy of Helenus. But of course, the precise end of the *Metamorphoses* is not quite the death of Caesar: a *sphragis* follows (15.871–79), in which Ovid avers his literary success as coterminous with the Roman empire he has just prophesized.

The historiographical allusions that precede this prophecy are themselves prophetic in nature, and gnomically so; unlike the *Aeneid*, this passage *is* predictive, because it infers from globalized examples to the topical case of Rome. The allusions are drawn from Greek historiography, and more specifically from the two giants of Greek historiography, Herodotus and Thucydides, in that order. Lines 420–22, especially the contrast between rise and fall in *adsumere* in 421 and *concidere* in the immediately following line, clearly recall Herodotus' programmatic statements that cities that were once great are now small, and vice versa (Hdt.1. 5.4 τὰ γὰρ τὸ πάλαι μεγάλα ἦν, τὰ πολλὰ σμικρὰ αὐτῶν γέγονε· τὰ δὲ ἐπ' ἐμεῦ ἦν μεγάλα, πρότερον ἦν σμικρά). Ovid's references to Sparta and Athens as once great cities that are now but names (*uile solum Sparte est . . . nisi nomen, Athenae*) likewise participate in the Herodotean theme, but they add a further reference to Thucydides' famous statement that were both Athens and Sparta to be ruined, Athens' grand ruins would be more impressive than Sparta's meager ruins, and this despite the fact that Sparta was in fact a great power (Thuc. 1.10.2 . . . Ἀθηναίων δὲ τὸ αὐτὸ τοῦτο παθόντων διπλασίαν ἂν τὴν δύναμιν εἰκάζεσθαι ἀπὸ τῆς φανερᾶς ὄψεως τῆς πόλεως ἢ ἔστιν). Coming as they do just before a diptych of prophecies on Rome itself (Pythagoras's 'executive summary': 15.431–5; Helenus' prophecy: 15.439–49), these allusions condition the reader to take the prophecies as embedded within the same historical principles of ebb and flow that Herodotus and Thucydides describe. Just as Rome grows and

---

[29] Mankin 1995: 293 *ad* Hor. *Epod*. 17.81 *plorem artis in te nil agentis exitus?*: "an appropriate 'exit' for the book."

3. Rome's Future in Augustan Epic 61

changes (15.434 *formam crescendo mutat*), so too it is doomed to the same fate Pythagoras spells out for Athens, Sparta, Mycenae, or Thebes.

And what was that end? Part of the answer, I think, is punctuational, the idea that time is structured in recognizably discrete phases, even if the point of transition itself is not always easy to identify. All the allusions in this passage, both epic and historiographical, have in common an interest in moments of change and transition. Herodotus and Thucydides express their respective views precisely at a moment when they recall also the Trojan myth in order to make a programmatic point about their own work, and they both do so while talking about a metamorphosis of sorts. Herodotus makes his statement as he concludes his account of the reciprocal kidnapping of women that culminates in the Trojan War (and is the ultimate reason for the Persian wars), a passage of *dissoi logoi* which turns a Greek story into a Persian story and vice versa, and further changes myth into history as well. Thucydides, meanwhile, uses Athens and Sparta's hypothetical ruins to argue that *opsis* alone is insufficient without also taking account of historical change over time. This, in turn, allows him to assert, by comparison with Homer, that the Peloponnesian War was in fact the greatest *kinesis*: Athens and Sparta morph into their own dismal future, while the Peloponnesian War, a conflict whose precise shape still exercises scholars, morphs into its own written account (and, in a remoter future still, into a historiographical trope).[30] Thus both authors use the change from past to present to introduce their theme, establish their main preoccupations, and instruct the reader on an important methodological point, while poised exactly at the same myth/history boundary that Ovid has his Pythagoras construct.

Ovid further uses the moment programmatically. *In species translata novas* (420 "transformed into new shapes"), which introduces the sequence of historiographical allusions, recalls the opening lines of the *Metamorphoses*: *in nova . . . mutatas dicere formas / corpora* (*Met.* 1.1–2 "to speak of bodies changed into new forms"). And indeed the message of change, decline, and regrowth is appropriate in a poem whose main preoccupation is flux and change. Further, the *Metamorphoses* brings its narrative into the present tense in a way that the *Aeneid* remarkably fails to do, a poetic *translatio imperii* of its own. And indeed, the end of the *Metamorphoses* involves also a transition from mythical time to historical time. This transition is often organized around the Trojan War as

---

[30] Cf. Livy, 21.1, in which Livy emulates and expands on Thuc. 1.1. On the shape of the narrative, and of the war, cf. e.g. Price 2001, and Dewald 2005.

a "floating horizon," after which events and people become increasingly historical, that is to say, can be assigned a date and time, and belong to the realm of the "real" rather than the imaginary.[31] As such, Aeneas and the Trojan War have a somewhat problematic status, depending on what perspective one takes on proceedings. On the one hand, Aeneas and Troy belong in historical time, and can even have concrete (albeit manufactured) connections to the grandees of Augustan Rome.[32] On the other hand, the Trojan settlement in Italy still falls into a fairly foggy period of time, when evidence is impossible, and *fama* remains the best and only source (note *fama est consurgere Romam* ("now too the rumor is that Dardanian Rome is on the rise") in 431 above).[33] This latter perspective is also historiographical by nature, and indeed Livy identified the Sack of Rome as the earliest period from which documents could be obtained, and even that early date stretches the credulity of modern historians.

The two genres of epic and history are not mutually exclusive. Polybius, a Hellenistic historian who himself subscribed to the doctrine of constitutional *metabolai*, tells us that Scipio Aemilianus wept over the ruins of Carthage, seeing his own city's future and quoting from Homer a lament on the fall of Troy.[34] Here is a blend of epic and historical sentimentality, with the epic tradition reduced to a specific case-study in Herodotean principle. Ovid casts his own Pythagoras as not entirely trusting in Rome's surge to greatness: *fama est* hardly inspires confidence, and the implication is that this is simply the time for Rome, another small thing, to grow awhile before eventually subsiding. Helenus' prophecy, however, with its Vergilian overtones, moves from the historical mode into the epic: *sed dominam rerum de sanguine natus Iuli / efficiet, quo cum tellus erit usa, fruentur / aetheriae sedes, caelumque erit exitus illi* (15.447–49 "but a descendant of Iulus will make her the mistress of the world, and, once the earth has finished making use of him, the heavenly seats will rejoice in him, and the sky shall be his endpoint"). The arrival of Caesar marks the

---

[31] On Troy as the boundary between myth and history, see Feeney 2007: 82: " . . . in the historiographical and chronological traditions as well there is a tendency to locate a strong marker here [at the fall of Troy], fixing the Trojan War as pivotal or transitional, with myth lying on the other side of it."

[32] For the multiple versions of Rome's foundation, Bickerman 1952 remains important; on Trojan genealogies in Rome, see Wiseman 1974 and Feldherr 1995.

[33] Cf. Livy, 1.6 on the Trojan arrival in Italy: *duplex inde fama est*, and his ambivalence in 3.1 on Ascanius/Iulus: *Haud ambigam—quis enim rem tam veterem pro certo adfirmet?* On *fama* as source, see Miles 1995: 8–74; Hardie 2012: 226–72.

[34] Polyb. *Hist.* 38.22. On Scipio's tears, see Astin 1967: 282–7; Scullard 1960: 61; on the motif, see Rossi 2000 and the article by Price in this volume.

transition out of historical time and back into the mythic: gods now inhabit the earth again, as they did in the Golden Age.[35]

This approach to time, where events not only punctuate history, but can also reset it, is characteristic of some strands of Augustan thought, which held simultaneously that the *Saturnia regna* had returned and that the republic continued as it ever did.[36] Within that context, Ovid's fuzzy idea of the end of Rome as merely marking a change of key within a continuous movement speaks to live concerns: if Rome has risen it can also fall, while the nature of Rome can likewise mutate, from republic to autocracy to something not quite either. Are these changes an end, and if so, of what? Such views, however, also invite the Vergilian question *quem finem?*, because they move away from understanding *finis* as temporal or spatial, and therefore away also from teleological and purposive definitions of *finis*. If Venus' question might be recast as "what is the point?", the answer of Vergil's Jupiter might remain the same ideological commitment to striving eternally after supreme empire as its own reward, an ideology of control of self and other taken to its logical – and endless – extreme. Ovid's Pythagoras' answer, however, might be rather different, seeing the rise and fall of nations as a coincidence of nature, part of the cosmic *flux*, but without any assumptions regarding the eternity, or manifest destiny, of Rome. Ovid's *sphragis*, indeed, tacitly implies a time beyond Rome's empire, when he might no longer be in the mouth of the people. In the *Metamorphoses*, a poem which ends literally and figuratively with a decisive break in Rome's constitutional and religious growth, Rome's empire is *sine fine* in the sense that it is without a *telos*, which is not to say that it is without end. *Quem finem*, indeed.

Acknowledgments

I am grateful to Jonathan Price for inviting me to contribute to this volume, all the more so because it was with him that I first read Vergil in the original Latin. I am also grateful to Pramit Chaudhuri and T. J. Bolt for reading and commenting on drafts of the typescript.

---

[35] The presence of semi-divine figures was an important cognitive shift in the movement from republic to empire. Broadly speaking, 'good' emperors were decorous enough to avoid actual explicit divinization on earth, except in those cases that bordered on crazed tyranny, as in the case of Caligula. The bibliography is considerable, but useful points of reference include Weinstock 1971; Gradel 2002; Feldherr 2010; Koortbojian 2013; Cole 2013.

[36] On this productive tension, see now Luke 2014 and Hay 2017.

CHAPTER 4

Posterity in the Arval Acta
Greg Woolf

4.1 Rituals and Posterity

Romans, like ourselves, had many ways of imagining the future. They had premonitions and dreams, and sought foreknowledge from prophets, oracles and astrologers, and they tried to constrain the future with plans, precautions and restrictions. And like us too, they expressed many of their ideas about the future implicitly in habits and routines. In this chapter I aim to explore some ways in which ritual practice reveals Roman attitudes to the future, taking as its starting point the epigraphic records set up by the priestly college of the Arval Brothers during the first centuries CE.

No Roman rituals are as well documented as those performed by the Arval Brothers.[1] The detailed records of their cultic activities – among them sacrifices, vows, debates and many feasts – were inscribed on the marble furniture of the sacred grove of Dea Dia outside Rome. They were inscribed with such care and at such length that it has been suggested that the very process of recording was itself ritualized.[2] Exceptional as this documentation (both the process and the product) may be, the rituals described have been taken as a model of Roman cult. This paper argues that in the same way the Arval *Acta* offer insights into some ways in which the most elevated sector of early imperial society dealt with posterity.

Posterity is not the usual focus of discussions about ritual and time. Claude Lévi-Strauss once described ritual as a machine for the suppression of time.[3] He argued that a sequence of ritual acts gained their full significance only if experienced as if happening in a single moment. More recently Pascal Boyer has suggested that when actions are ritualized, one

---

[1] All modern studies of the Arval *Acta* begin from the researches of John Scheid (esp. Scheid 1990, 1998). My debt to this work is apparent in the pages that follow. I am also very grateful to members of audiences at the Tel Aviv meeting and also at the CAARE conference organized by Esther Eidinow and Tom Harrison at the Institute of Classical Studies in London in December 2016 for their responses to earlier versions of this paper.
[2] Beard 1985.   [3] Levi-Strauss 1972.

effect is to engage a set of cognitive procedures that include focusing attention on the here-and-now to the exclusion of our usual awareness of the surrounding contexts, including events that have preceded and will follow the performance.[4] Being 'lost in the moment' is both the basis of our experience of transcendence (one of the rewards that ritual performance delivers to participants) and also explains the obsessive attention to detail that characterizes ritual and has led to it being compared to the clinical symptoms of Obsessive Compulsive Disorder. Ritual, in short, disrupts our everyday experience of time.

Ancient historians might wonder how the experience of cyclical time generated by regular repetitions of rituals (or better iterations, since no two performances are ever identical) was related to the sequential time of lived experience. We ourselves often imagine the past as ordered in this way – how many birthdays, how many Christmases, how many wedding anniversaries and so on. Romans too celebrated their birthdays, and as families performed annual commemorations of the dead at *Parentalia* held every February, and at the *Lemuria* held in March. At a larger scale the civic ritual calendar provided the most authoritative means of dating.[5] During the Principate, imperial birthdays, and some other anniversaries, were celebrated across the empire. In all these cases, time is a social rather than an individual phenomenon.

Cyclical time is in fact an illusion: the passage of time is in reality one-directional. But it seems characteristically human to recruit astronomically recurrent phenomena such as the rotation of the earth, the phases of the moon, or the earth's annual orbit of the sun, to create a sense of cycles, and even to invent artificial cycles such as the seven day week. Only a little of this can be plausibly rationalized as a response to seasonality in high latitudes and its implications for food supply and reproduction. Why humans find cyclical time so reassuring is a rather bigger question than can be dealt with here, but perhaps it also operates to suppress a sense of entropy, a consciousness of the progressive loss of the past and diminishing of our personal futures.

Classicists have also been interested in how cyclical time was recruited by some ancient writers as a scaffold on which to construct various kinds of narrative.[6] Greek cities of the classical era dated by eponymous magistrates or priests, so if lists of them could be assembled they might provide a chronological framework. The periodic celebrations of the Olympic

---

[4] Liénard and Boyer 2006. See also Boyer 2001.   [5] Rüpke 1995.
[6] Clarke 2008 explores the connections between civic time and narrative time in historical writing.

Games provided something similar at a panhellenic scale. Larger schemas were developed along with large-scale historical writing, hence Herodotean synchronisms, Thucydides' correlation of civic dating systems and the emergence of Common (Universal) Histories. Rome followed a similar pattern, with eponymous consular years assembled at a later date to make a framework for projects of civic history. Much attention has been focused on the politicization of time and dating during the shift from political pluralism to autocracy.[7] The monumental consular and triumphal *Fasti* set up under Augustus provided both an authoritative organization of the past and a firm punctuation mark at the end of the Republic. Around the empire a variety of new systems emerged based on local versions of regnal years, another means of generating narrative out of cyclical time although in this case cycles of uneven length.

Yet in principle the annual ritual cycle of Rome remained independent of linear historical time. I shall argue that this is a key feature of Arval time. Ritual cycles were also as much about the future as about the past. The stability of the ritual year might be opposed to the sense of change evoked by sequential lists of past kings, magistrates or triumphs. When Horace wanted to assert the continuation of his reputation into remote posterity, he claimed he would be remembered for as long as the pontiff and the silent vestal made their annual climb up the path to the Capitol (*Odes* 3.30–6-9). Horace's Ode evokes not just posterity but also eternity, the extension of the present conceived of endless iterations of the ritual cycle. The expectation of a future that was essentially an extension of the present may have offered a palliative to the fear of oblivion, a fear often expressed in Roman writing. The establishment of regular commemorations, and monuments that might evoke them, responded to an expectation that the memory of most people and their deeds would perish.[8] Conversely, memory sanctions such as the tearing down of statues or the obliteration of names from public inscriptions, sought actively to impose oblivion on the dead.[9]

Romans were not unusual in these respects. The anthropology of ritual has made it clear that every ritual performance is unique. Actual performances, especially the larger collective rituals of communities, are often preceded by long discussions about exactly how the performance should unfold, who should occupy particular roles in it and so on. Those discussions provide space for interested parties to assert their claims, for

---

[7] Wallace-Hadrill 1987, Laurence and Smith 1995-6: 142–8, Feeney 2007, Hannah 2013.
[8] Woolf 1996.   [9] Flower 2006: 1–5.

competition for religious authority, even for social reproduction. But they also provide part of the build up, the mundane and human background noise against which transcendent experience and divine epiphany will shine out. Although no two ritual performances are identical, it is very common that a given performance takes part of its significance from its place in relation to others, some in the past, others imagined as yet to come. Participants are alive to subtle differences as well as to repetitions and references. That sense of iteration or re-enactment conjures up a particular view of the future, one that is imagined in quite specific terms, but also understood to be fraught with risk. The argument of this paper is that the early imperial use of monumental writing in ritual is particularly revealing of this double sense of the future as both predictable and risky. If modern societies have less confidence in continuity and more certainty of change, that is because we are the odd ones out historically speaking.

4.2 The Arvals and Their *Acta*

The Fratres Arvales – commonly the Arval Brethren or Brothers in English, or simply the Arvals – were one of the main priestly colleges through which the cults of the City of Rome were managed. There were twelve members and, once elected an Arval, a member served for life. The Arvals are best known today in the form into which their college was re-organized early in the reign of Augustus (probably in the 20s BCE). They are documented epigraphically during the first centuries CE. Very little testimony about the priesthood survives from the Republican period: the first certain witness is Varro (*de lingua latina* 5.15) and the most detailed testimony is that of Pliny the Elder.[10] There was, however, a consensus that the priesthood was among the oldest in the city.

Roman writers from at least the late Republic tended to operate with a tacit distinction between two categories of public cults. One group were believed to be very ancient – such as the *Lupercalia*, the rituals performed by the Vestals, the hymn of the Salian Priests and the restrictions placed on the *flamen Dialis* – all of which were said to have been founded before civilization, or during the reigns of the first kings of Rome.[11] Most myths are specific to particular cults, but there was also a tradition that the second king Numa created the cults of the community on the instructions of his

---

[10] Scheid 1990 collects and discusses all the testimonia.
[11] E.g. Cicero *Pro Caelio* 26 on the Lupercalia, Gellius *Noctes Atticae* 7.7.8 on the Arvals, Dionysius *Roman Antiquities* 2.71 on the Salians.

lover the nymph Egeria, just as other early kings were treated as founders of the political and military systems of Rome. A second group of cults had definite historical origins: these included the *Ludi Magni*, associated in some accounts with the expulsion of the Kings, or the cults of various deities brought to Rome such as the cult of Juno Regina from the Etruscan city of Veii reputedly installed in Rome in 392 BCE, that of Asclepius brought from Epidaurus in Greece in 291 BCE and that of Magna Mater Deorum brought from Pessinus in Asia Minor in 204 BCE. These latter introductions were typically presented as prompted by divine instructions (that is, the new gods were invited in by the divine establishment) even if to moderns they often look like responses to crises or the religious correlates of imperial expansion.

These two categories of cult were treated differently. In the case of the second category traces of their foreign origin were sometimes ostentatiously retained,[12] and they were overseen by a college of priests named the *quindecimviri sacris faciundis*. Some of these cults were conducted according to what Romans knew (but Greeks would not have recognized) as the 'Greek rite'.[13] There is some sign that Romans were less worried about change over time when it affected cults with historical origins, so for example the *Ludi Magni* underwent many changes of content, length and organization. In this sense Roman public religion was in effect recognized as a work in progress, an open system that expanded through the addition of new elements.[14] But the first category of public rituals was different. When emperors introduced changes to these foundational rites, as when Augustus and later emperors held Saecular Games, these changes tended to be represented as restorations.[15] Cults of this kind were easily recruited to establishing the eternity of Rome and the rituals performed by the Arvals were firmly among them. Augustus transformed the rituals of the college out of recognition, not least in centring their ritual activity around the imperial house. From a Roman perspective, however, this act could be presented as profoundly conservative or traditional.

The inscribed documents which are our main source for the rituals conducted during the early empire by the Arval Brothers were originally set up in the grove of the goddess Dea Dia, five miles from the centre of ancient Rome in the direction of the mouth of the river Tiber. This grove was not a remote wild place, as the term 'sacred grove' might seem to evoke, but rather an extensive sanctuary which by the end of the first century CE housed the temple of the goddess, a bath house for purification before

---

[12] Beard 1994.   [13] Scheid 1995.   [14] Bendlin 1997.   [15] Gros 1976, Wallace-Hadrill 1982.

rituals and before meals, an elaborate dining room (the *tetrapylon*), a temple of the emperors, the *Caesareum* (presumably added during the first century CE) and even a hippodrome for chariot races. How many worshippers it might accommodate, or even who attended apart from the Arvals themselves, is unclear. The *Acta* focus on the conduct of the priests but it is difficult to imagine chariot races taking place before just a dozen grandees, and we might suspect that crowds flocked out from Rome to the grove once a year for the festival of Dea Dia in May.

Formally the inscriptions we have are *acta*, official records of ritual proceedings. Not all the rituals or activity described in them took place at the grove of Dea Dia. Some were conducted in the central temples of the City of Rome, and on occasion the Arvals feasted and even sacrificed in the urban residence of the *magister*, their annual president. Most sacrifices were public, but some rituals took place in areas in the grove to which we believe access was restricted. There were also discussions and meals at which only the Arvals were present sometimes accompanied by young men of high birth. (Presumably their slaves were also silent participants in the background.) Fragments of these inscriptions have been known since the nineteenth century, but over the last thirty years our knowledge has increased enormously as a result of excavations at the site of the grove of Dea Dia, now located in the suburban sprawl around Rome at La Magliana. That work and the new editions and discussions of these documents has been masterminded by John Scheid. His study of the priesthood and epigraphic edition has set a benchmark for studies of Roman cults.[16]

The Arval Brothers were drawn from the most distinguished sector of Roman society. There were other priesthoods at Rome which were restricted to individuals of patrician status, and during the late Republic and early empire the major priestly colleges were filled entirely by senators.[17] Membership of the Arval Brothers was especially distinguished, however, at least to begin with, and this means that we know a great deal about their membership and how it changed over time.[18] Several versions of a foundation myth for the priesthood have been preserved, some at least originating in antiquarian speculations of the late Republic. According to one version the original Brothers were step-brothers of Romulus and he himself was a member.[19] The priesthood of the imperial period included

---

[16] Scheid 1990, 1998.
[17] Beard 1990 for an account of the structure. For the definitive prosopography see now Rüpke 2005.
[18] Scheid 1975, Syme 1980; now with Scheid 1990.
[19] On the myth and its creation, see Beard 1989.

some emperors and members of the imperial house, and to begin with the other members were typically very distinguished senators.

What did the Arvals do? It is a modern convention to distinguish three kinds of priestly activity at Rome, and to say that all priests performed in at least one capacity. Most common was *ritual action*, that is presiding at sacrifices, saying prayers and so on. A second role was as *ritual experts*, meeting formally to decide on exactly what ritual actions were called for in particular circumstance, for example when a temple had been struck by lightning or when a particular religious offence had been committed. Religious knowledge at Rome, as Clifford Ando has lucidly argued, was most of all knowledge about how to perform rituals.[20] The third function, the rarest, was *to manifest specific ritual prohibitions*, such as the rule that the priestesses of Vesta should be chaste, or that the priest of Jupiter should not leave the city for extended periods.

The Arvals did not, as far as we know, manifest specific prohibitions in their regular lives, although there were certain prohibitions on what might be done in the grove without expiation, such as bringing in iron. But there is ample evidence in the *Acta* for both ritual action, and some for their exercise of ritual expertise. From their *Acta* we see them perfuming and adorning statues in the temple, making vows, consecrating animal victims, performing sacrifices of grain and various domesticated animals, engaging in ritual feasts that followed animal sacrifice, holding annual elections of their officers, the *magister* and the *flamen*, and presiding over games. Details are provided of the costumes they wore for certain rituals, and the lists of the specific victims designated for particular deities assert the complexity of the rituals they performed and their mastery of that complexity. On 7 November in 224 CE extraordinary sacrifices were offered in expiation for having dug up some trees in the grove which had been struck by lightning, and for having cut them up with iron tools and burned them.[21] The explanation implies considerable prior discussion, both about how to deal with the damage to the trees, and also about how to restore the sacred *status quo* after the works were complete. This was the kind of issue on which religious expertise was most likely to be deployed.

Annual vows were taken by the priests together every January for the safety of the emperor in the coming year. These vows were modelled on traditional vows for the safety of the Republic. Each year too an assessment was made of whether or not the emperor had been kept safe in the preceding twelve months, and so whether or not the promised sacrifice

---

[20] Ando 2008, 2010.   [21] CIL VI.2107, ILS 5048.

4. Posterity in the Arval Acta 71

was due. Imperial birthdays were also celebrated, and on some occasions the Arvals thanked the gods for the discovery of plots directed against the emperor of the day. Statues of at least some emperors were present in the grove, perhaps in the Caesareum.[22] But the cult was not only about the emperors. Varro and Pliny were clear that the Brothers originally performed rituals in connection with the coming harvest, and this seems supported by the sacrifices of cereals during the three day festival held every May. In other words, the 'reform' of their rituals reflects some familiar Augustan transformations, in which the safety of the state was wrapped up with the safety of the emperor, and its agrarian prosperity assimilated (as on the Ara Pacis) with political security.

Nor was cult only paid to Dea Dia. During the extraordinary sacrifices of November 224 CE victims were also sacrificed to Janus Pater, to Jupiter, to Mars Pater Ultor, to deity male or female, to the Virgin Deities, to the attendant deities, to the Lares, to the mother of the Lares, to Fons, to Flora, to Summanus Pater, to Vesta Mater, to Adolenda and Coinquenda, to the genius of the living emperor and to the divi, the deified emperors. It is very difficult now (and was perhaps already difficult then) to explain why some deities were included and other excluded from this list, beyond noticing the absence of deities treated as of foreign origin. But why were Juno, Minerva and Venus not included, or Mercury, Hercules, Saturn or Vulcan and what is the significance of some of the minor deities that are little more than names to us? Perhaps the best we can do is notice that the cult of the Arvals was not only complex, but *advertised itself as complex*, declaring at the same time the punctiliousness and expertise with which these extraordinary rituals had been designed and performed. The inscribed record of deities, together with the care with which they are ordered and appropriate victims assigned to each, also makes clear that the genius of the living emperor and the cult of the divi were inserted into a larger cosmological schema.[23]

Quite likely other priestly colleges made records of their debates and rituals. What makes the Arvals unusual is that their records were inscribed on stone furniture in the grove, rather than kept on papyrus roles in some ancillary building. Who decided what would be inscribed? Presumably the Arvals themselves or the annual officers acting on behalf of the college. It is interesting that the opportunities for formulaic repetition and

---

[22] Fejfer 2008: 86–8.
[23] On the significance of this ordering, see Scheid 2003. On the emperor, the Arvals and Italy, see Gradel 2002.

standardization were avoided. When we have fragments that describe multiple iterations of the same rituals, such as the three day sacrifice that took place every year in May, we find different words used, different details recorded and a tendency over time to record in more and more detail.[24] For what audience were these records intended: priests or other worshippers? humans or gods? And, if inscription was itself a ritual activity, to what ends was it designed? Answering these questions involves considering the use of epigraphy in early imperial ritual in more general terms, and returns us to the question of Roman futures.

4.3 Epigraphy and Ritual

Latin epigraphy was transformed at the beginning of the principate into something of a mass medium. Explosion is for once not an overstatement. Less than 5,000 Latin inscriptions are known from the Republican period, while the latest estimate for the empire is around 300,000.[25] Many studies have tracked the process through which the number of inscriptions produced increased first in Italy, and then in the provinces, especially in the vicinity of Roman colonies, military camps and major urban settlements. The chronology is disputed. Growth was rapid during the first century CE and perhaps tailed off in some regions during the second century. But in some areas mass epigraphy persisted well into the early third century CE. Late antique epigraphies – if different and less intense – persisted in some areas. The phenomenon is sometimes termed the epigraphic habit or epigraphic culture, and the reasons for it have been much discussed. How it relates to similar but different trends in imperial Greek epigraphy is less well explored.[26] Once the habit of setting up of monumental writing had become established, we can infer a range of subsidiary motivations for participation. These might include competition for status within a peer group, emulation of social superiors, conformity within a community, assertions of adherence to a set of admired values or behaviours exemplified by former owners, aristocrats, Roman colonists or soldiers and so on. At the most general level, the use of writing to assert the importance of social relationships was perhaps a response to a more and more volatile social world.[27]

---

[24] Beard 1985. [25] Beltrán Lloris 2014.
[26] On the epigraphic habit (MacMullen 1982, Meyer 1990, Woolf 1996, Cooley 2002, Mouritsen 2005, Beltrán Lloris 2014). On epigraphic culture more widely (Corbier 2006, Cooley 2012, Sears, Keegan, and Laurence 2013, Keegan 2014).
[27] For this argument at greater length (Woolf 1996).

4. Posterity in the Arval Acta

What is not always emphasized is that the vast majority of Latin inscriptions of the early empire were the products of private ritual activity. A few dozen municipal decrees and imperial letters exist from the west, and other semi-public bodies such as collegia also generated some epigraphy. These documents included building inscriptions, honorific notices on statue bases, laws, regulations and the occasional epigraphic transformation of a standard civic document such as a land register or an *album* (register) of decuriones. But the vast majority of monumental inscriptions on stone were either epitaphs or votive dedications, texts placed on offerings dedicated to a god in fulfilment of a vow.[28] The spread of Latin epigraphy through Italy and the western provinces in effect tracks the spread of a set of ritual practices, some funerary, some about communication with the gods. It was also largely a private phenomenon, an expression of individual religious impulses rather than traces of the performance of *officia publica*. The only sense in which these documents were public is that they were displayed for others to read, records of the pious performance of duties to the dead and to the gods by named individuals.

Why incorporate writing into these private rituals? Neither formal burial of the dead nor the making of vows to the gods was new, and writing was essential to neither. Many graves were unmarked or had no epitaph, and many votives were uninscribed.[29] The habit of using writing in these rituals seems to have become common over time. Funerary epigraphy was very old in Rome: unsurprisingly the earliest extant examples relate to the most powerful individuals and families. The same is true of those few vows attested from the Republican period, recorded mostly in literary testimony. Generals might make battlefield vows to offer a share of the *manubiae* (the proceeds of the sale of booty) to a specific deity in the event of victory. Yet neither the making of the vow nor the formal declaration that the god had kept his or her side of the bargain required writing. The dedication of terracotta anatomical votives in central Italy from the fourth century BCE *might* represent something similar to the *solutio* (paying off) of a vow made to a god in return for a hoped-for benefit, in this case presumably a cure, good health or reproductive success. By the early empire, formulae such as VSLM (*votum solvit libens merito*), particularly associated with votive altars, shows the spread of the custom of making a vow and paying it later if the god provided the desired benefit.

---

[28] Carroll 2006.
[29] On the poorest graves, see Graham 2006. For an account of an important set of largely uninscribed votives, see Hughes 2017.

One possibility is that writing helped differentiate offerings made in fulfilment of a vow, from other kinds of gifts to the gods. The agricultural rituals recommended by Cato the Elder in *On Agriculture* 139–141 involved saying prayers and making offerings *before* coppicing and tilling. In the case of the ritual for purifying the land, initial prayers and an offering were to be followed by the taking of omens. Only if the omens were not favourable would further offerings be made. Similar offerings and divination were performed before troops went into battle. Explanatory texts allowed dedicators to make clear the reasons for their gifts. In so doing worshippers advertised the success of their appeal, and the receptiveness of the gods to prayer. Putting one's name on an offering was a means of claiming public recognition of one's piety.

One other thing that writing contributed to funerary rituals and to vows alike was to extend a transient performance into the future. Most rituals do not take long to perform. Even the grandest games of the City of Rome lasted only a few days. The Saecular Games celebrated by Augustus in 17 BCE took over the city for about two weeks: the three days and nights of sacrifices were preceded by elaborate invitations and purifications and followed by *ludi scaenici* and *ludi circenses* (dramatic performances and chariot racing). The dedication of the Flavian Amphitheatre by Titus in 80 CE supposedly lasted for a hundred days.[30] Most public rituals took place within a single day, most private ones just a few hours or minutes. Elaborate planning and preparation might extend the period of involvement at least for a core group. From the perspective of participation, of course, sustained engagement of the kind that Boyer describes, was impossible. The intense concentration involved in ritual action cannot be maintained for long, except perhaps by adepts, and/or with the aid of psychotropic substances. Often such short intense rituals are sufficient. Most of the ethnography has been carried out on small-scale societies which typically make little use of writing. It has been argued that one way societies of this kind pass on important knowledge from one generation to another is by collective participation in rituals that are short-lived but reiterated at intervals. On each iteration the circle of participants will be different but there will be enough continuity to ensure the transmission of social memory to posterity.[31] Roman society was much larger than these small-scale communities, and the need to involve the dispersed body of citizens and subjects was more pressing.[32] Augustus not only organized his

---

[30] For slightly sceptical discussion of what this might mean (Hopkins and Beard 2005: 42–50).
[31] Connerton 1989.
[32] On the effects on rituals of the need to widen participation see Burkert 1987.

4. Posterity in the Arval Acta

Saecular Games in great detail, but had a monumental record of their performance set up, and Horace's *Carmen Saeculare* was widely disseminated.[33] These strategies of memorialization helped extend the range of participation, in space and in time.

Incorporating writing into these rituals did more than simply record them. As Mary Beard writes:

> the vast majority of the many thousands of inscriptions detailing vows and the performance of sacrifices can hardly have been widely consulted – or intended to be so; instead they instantiated and made permanent the ritual act itself. Writing, in other words, could be as much an integral part of religious symbolism as an external record of it.[34]

Writing might extend the experience of ritual in time but it also compromised the closure of the performance. Funerary rituals are quintessential rites of passage in which the identities of the main participants are transformed. The funerals of Roman grandees illustrate this perfectly. The living became socially dead, perhaps ancestors; the power and property of a *paterfamilias* was dispersed among his children, creating new *familiae* in the process; wives became widows; some slaves became free and so on. And at the end of a rite of passage, in van Gennep's sense, liminal time closed and the social landscape – slightly reconfigured – returned to normal. Set up a stele, of course, and that social closure is not only advertised, it is also undermined. Annual rituals like the *Parentalia* temporarily reconstituted *familiae* that had passed away, and reasserted the primacy of individuals whose roles had since been assumed by others. Ancestor masks had the power to rebuke as well as inspire their descendants.

The ritual of the vow was in principle even more temporary in span. There were many variants but they all revolved around two moments, the first when a human made a conditional promise to a deity, and a second moment at which the dedicators would publicly affirm that the god had delivered, and would pay what had been offered (the *solutio*). These moments might be close in time – during and after a battle in the example discussed above, or at intervals of a year in the case of the Arval vow for the safety of the emperor – but in principle once the *solutio* had been performed, the bargain was completed and the debt discharged. Memorializing it in stone prolonged the relationship between deity and

---

[33] Schnegg-Köhler 2002 for the latest version of the text with commentary and discussion.
[34] Beard 2007: 133.

worshipper. The medium of a votive altar achieves a similar effect. Sacrifice consumes the victim. At the end the animal or food offering is no more. But an altar – even one never used for an actual sacrifice – propels the gesture of sacrifice into the future, makes the ephemeral permanent, and expresses the desire of the dedicator for an enduring relationship with the deity in question.

Funerary altars and inscribed epitaphs also involved new participants in ritual. If *writing down* the details of a ritual is potentially part of religious action rather than 'just' a commentary on it, so too is *reading* those records. It is usually impossible for us to reconstruct the ancient experience of reading texts created in this way. The exception is when ancient acts of reading are themselves transformed into new texts. Pliny's much discussed account of writings he observed at the source of the Clitumnus is perhaps the closest we can get to over-looking as an ancient observer was inspired to theological reflection by written traces of the experiences of others.[35]

Reading and writing can inspire each other. Sites where writing generated around ritual was displayed, often seem to have provided an incitement to further acts of writing. The gradual filling up of the grove of Dea Dia with texts that eventually covered much of the stone furniture is a case in point. We might also think in this way about the factors that promoted the accumulation of votive altars in particular sanctuaries, and also the growth of cemeteries. Each new inscribed stele added to a cemetery was both a commentary on those already there, and provided a potential incentive to imitation. These clusters of inscriptions can be thought of as indices of what Alfred Gell called an object distributed in space and time.[36] What we are observing is the way writing enables discrete ritual actions to snowball, preventing closure, drawing in new worshippers and inciting new ritual actions. In a sense, of course, sanctuaries had always operated in this way, as centres of accumulation that inspired iterations and elaboration of ritual action. But writing provided new mechanisms through which the acts of individual worshippers were coordinated.

A similar set of arguments has been advanced by John Barrett who argued that Latin inscriptions characteristically evoke two different notions of time. In *commemorative* mode they referred (back) to particular moments or events in the past, like a military victory or sacrifice, but without inserting these events into a narrative sequence or using them to delimit blocks of time. In *dedicatory* mode they were orientated towards

---

[35] Pliny *Epistles* 8.8 with commentary by Veyne 1983, Beard 1991, Scheid 1996, Dubourdieu 1997.
[36] Gell 1998: 242–58. See also Gell 1992.

long-term projects or ideas extended forwards into the future, and evoke a sense of time as a passage of ongoing obligations. The same inscription might operate in both modes, commemorating a particular funeral for example or the specific achievement of a deceased general, while also looking forward to the intergenerational obligations of *pietas* that bound together the generations of a family. Neither mode depended on or produced the narrativized history for which epigraphy is generally recruited today. For Barrett monumental inscriptions:

> enabled those who raised and who could read them to understand two different forms of chronological order, both of which differ from the sequential narratives which the stones are now used to illustrate[37]

As Barrett points out, modern uses of epigraphy embrace their commemorative function, often using them to provide data that the historian can order in different ways including chronologically. For ancient Romans, the forward looking power of epigraphy to keep a ritual act open, and to prolong good relations with the divine, may have been just as important.

4.4 Arval Futures I: Continuity and Security

New Arval Brothers were recruited only when a space fell vacant through death. The *magister* proposed a name and the others voted, although presumably in this and in the regular annual elections, no proposal was made until a name had already been agreed. As far as we can see most Arvals were recruited in their late twenties, not long after they had begun their senatorial careers.

The new Arval was immediately involved in a series of temporalities, experiences of time inculcated by the actions he was henceforth committed to perform. The priesthood was for life, so adlection marked a punctuation point before and after his elevation. At the most banal level he would have known he had arrived and his future career was secure. But he had also entered a much more intimate world than the Roman senate. He had eleven fellow priests – some very eminent, a few of them members of the imperial family – and would get to know most of them very well, some for decades. We know little about the Arval Brothers of the Republic, and perhaps their imperial successors were almost as ignorant. But there must have been some sense of entering into a very ancient tradition. Becoming an Arval must have been like stepping into one of the deeper channels of

---

[37] Barrett 1993: 236.

Roman history, and knowing that one would spend the rest of one's life there. The sacred grove and its buildings would accumulate personal memories as well as inscriptions, and some ritual activities, such as the three day ceremony each year, would become very familiar. Priests, more than any other Romans, were brought close to that sense of eternity evoked by annual reiterations of rituals that were believed central to the perpetuation of the state. The newly recruited Arval was taking on a lifetime of service.

Alongside the annual rhythm there were other cycles. Each year the Arvals elected a president (a *magister*) and a priest named a *flamen*. The *magister* in particular seems to have had significant duties and prominence, during his year in office. We hear of *magistri* convening the Brothers, presiding at the dedication and sacrifice of victims, acting as president of the Games and entertaining the other Brothers to eat in his house. Some of these duties might be discharged through deputies, but the responsibility was clearly taken seriously. Any given Arval would be *magister* every ten years or so, so maybe three or four times in his life. The years of one's first, second, third presidency and so on would be significant personal milestones, even given that the same men could also expect to hold all the great magistracies of the Roman state as well if they so wished.

The *Acta* themselves were scrupulously dated in traditional fashion. Consider the entry in *ILS* 5037 for the May ceremonies in what we would call 87 CE. The sacrifice is dated by consular year (the consulship of Natalis and Proculus) and by the Roman calendar, fourteen days before the Kalends of June. For a hypothetical Roman reader in the grove trying to work out how these *Acta* related to those from other years, the task was not made easy. The fragments we have were apparently not arranged in sequence – although the *Fasti* shows Romans were quite capable of doing so in other contexts. Few individuals can have known the names of the *consules ordinarii* for each year well enough to be able to convert consular dates into a linear series. Should we be surprised that even in a priesthood which devoted so much attention to the emperors, and which on occasion had emperors and or imperial princes among its members, there is no regnal year, not even in the form of the number of Domitian's grants *tribunicia potestas*? The *Acta* do mention these grants, but they do not use them to mark time. In other words the *Acta* conform to Barratt's notion of commemorative time, the recording of key events but in isolation, not as points on a sequence or moments in a narrative. Perhaps we might even see these dating conventions working actively to suppress any sense of history unrolling. At each moment of inscription those responsible will have been

4. Posterity in the Arval Acta

aware of the accumulation of *acta* in the grove: finding new spaces for ever longer texts must eventually have proved difficult. But these *acta* were piled up at random like items in a treasury. Together they conveyed a sense of how often annual sacrifices had been performed for the goddess. But the order in which the rituals took place seems to have been irrelevant.

The dating formulae provide one other surprise, since it is apparently a redundancy: they are dated not only by the names of the consuls of the year but also by the name of the year's *magister*. The two systems of dating were not completely synchronized: the *magistri* and the *flamines* served from one Saturnalia to another while *consules ordinarii* (whose names dated the year) took up their office at the new year on 1 January, a few weeks later. Does this represent an assertion that inside the grove it is Arval time that matters? Or is it simply an assertion of the pre-eminence of the Brothers? After all, being an Arval Brother was a more exclusive honour than being a consul, given how few Arvals there were, and how long each served. But perhaps it is better to read these notices more as a monument of a given mastership masquerading as a date, rather than as a dating formula. Indeed perhaps *all* the dating formulae do more to evoke a consciousness of the (supposedly) unchanging rituals of the city than to correlate particular performances with external measures of time. Perhaps the *Acta* were not 'published' to provide a history of the Arvals and their rituals but to proclaim them as lying outside history. The rituals so carefully documented are not closed, but bleed into each other. What I am suggesting is that the *Acta* construct a kind of continuous present in place of a sense of time flowing unidirectionally from past to future via the present. The implications for the future are clear. If change is always inconsequential and non-directional – Brownian motion more than entropy – then the future is envisaged as essentially a prolongation of the present.

It is more complicated yet. Because alongside this emphasis on an absence of change, was coupled an intense sensitivity to the most minor variations between one performance to another. There seems a connection here with Boyer's thesis that ritual engages cognitive routines in which the participant becomes temporarily less aware of the wider context, and more intensely focused on the minutiae of the immediate moment.

This is most easy to illustrate in relation to the May sacrifice to Dea Dia since it took place every year and the fragments of the *Acta* preserve several quite full accounts of their performance.[38] The general pattern seems to have been for the sacrifice to take place over three days, the first being

---

[38] Scheid 1985; and see more generally Scheid 2005.

a bloodless sacrifice in Rome at the house of the *magister*; the second (two days later) being a full day at the grove with animal sacrifice, a banquet and the election of the officers for the next year, followed by chariot racing; and a final day back in Rome for a closing banquet and additional sacrifices of cereals. Wherever we have records they punctiliously record the date and location of each event and those present at it. More detail appears on the later *Acta*, providing information on banqueting around the sacrifices, on the costumes worn, on who else was present and so on. It is very tempting to use detail from late records to fill out the rather sketchy accounts from the first century CE and construct a normative and rather stable ritual. That said, the basic pattern seems secure.

Yet the individual records are not at all formulaic. I have said already that an opportunity for standardization was missed in the composition of the Arval *Acta*. By that I meant that notwithstanding the fact that the rituals were mostly the same, from year to year, and that detailed records of them increasingly filled the grove, there is no sign that standard formulae of words came to be adopted, or that past inscriptions were used as model or templates for the composition of new ones. Scheid examined precisely this question and found that although naturally some words and phrases recurred, strict formulae did not develop.[39] Take for example the words that record the participation of boys of high status in the May sacrifice. I reproduce Scheid's examples, omitting reconstructions and expansions (which tend to homogenize):

81 CE	pueris ingenuis senatorum filis patrimis matrimis ministrantibus, ture et vino, referentibus ad aram in pataris
84, 90 CE	pueri senatorum fili patrimi [vacat] aram rettulerunt
105–155 CE	pueri patrimi matrimi praetextati cum publicis ad aram retullerunt
183, 186 CE	ministrantibus pueris patrimis et matrimis senatorum filis illis cum publicis ad aram retullerunt
218 CE	et per pueros praetext [vacat]orum filios et public ad aram pertul
239, 240 CE	ministrantibus pueris praetextatis et cum public ad ar pertulerunt
241 CE	ministr puer praetextatis et c[vacat]

There is no sign here that the roles assigned to a group of boys of senatorial status whose parents were both still alive and were on the verge of

[39] Scheid 1990: 484–505.

4. Posterity in the Arval Acta

adulthood changed over the century and a half for which we have records. But it is also clear that there was no attempt to make each set of *Acta* conform precisely to earlier accounts of the same rituals. In fact there is no real sign that the *Acta* were ever consulted – although conceivably they may have been, whether in their monumental form or on papyrus – in the course of the careful discussions that must have preceded many performances. Institutional memory, in the form of the recollections of more senior Arvales, might well have provided most of the guidance the priests had for deciding tricky questions such as what to do if one of the trees in the grove fell down, or how to handle an annual *solutio* if the emperor for whom the vow had been made was no longer alive a year later. A consensus has emerged that Roman religious texts did not describe paradigmatic rituals, nor did they provide liturgical recipes for future performances.[40] In this respect the *Acta* are quite conventional.

Alongside variations in the way similar elements of the ritual were described, there were actual variations from one year to another and these too were faithfully recorded. For instance in 87 CE the central day in the grove began with the immolation of two additional sows in expiation for gardening work carried out in the grove. These works were clearly much less of an intrusion than those that would occasion the very elaborate extraordinary sacrifice recorded in *ILS* 5048 after trees had been brought down in the autumn storms. Naturally another key area of change was personnel. Care was taken in the records of every ritual performance or banquet to record not only who presided (as *magister* or his deputy), but also which of the Brothers were present. Often it seems no more than half the number attended, for the start of year ceremony termed the *indictio* and sometimes no more than three. There is no sense that this was intended to establish a quorum had been present (if indeed sacrifices and other rituals had a quorum in the way a deliberative body had) nor are the individuals listed as witnesses as in some Roman documents, both records of financial transactions and occasional imperial grants of citizenship. Simply one way each year's ritual was unique was in who attended.

Finally there is variation in what was thought worth recording: here the expansion of the *Acta* over time is significant. The record from 240 CE is very detailed, specifying the costume and actions of those presiding in great detail. At one point the vice-magister conducts a sacrifice, returns to the dining room (the *tetrastylon*) and orders it to be noted down in the *codex* that he had been present, had conducted the sacrifice and had offered up

---

[40] Rüpke 2004. See also the conclusions of the chapters on religious themes gathered in Moatti 1998.

the entrails. Among all those whose participation is recorded at every stage, the identity of the person with the codex is not revealed. Presumably the Arvals' recording angels were slaves, as were presumably the gardeners and cooks and other *ministri* at the grove. But even in the first century CE, from which we have more records, there is a lack of consistency in what precisely was written down, as if each act of recording too were a unique performance.

We are presented then with the spectacle of formal minutes being taken of the ritual performances, minutes that presumably contributed in some form to the composition of the *Acta* that would themselves eventually be inscribed in what some have supposed was a ritual process. But the texts refer explicitly to actions (including speech acts), and they implicitly reject any notion of intertextual play with documents already in the grove. Every stone record directs us back to an individual performance.

Over time the grove became filled up with more and more epigraphic documents until they cover the stone furniture as well as more conventional places of display. That general dynamic of accumulation is a familiar one. The sanctuaries of Italy, like those of Asia Minor, had by the early third century accumulated a vast mass of statuary, votives and epigraphic documents in stone and metal. Equally the cemeteries around major Roman cities were becoming filled with inscribed tombstones. The Arvals were not the only cult to make their own idiosyncratic appropriation from this trend. An accumulation of votives, of cure testimonies or of *acta* might seem to offer reassurance about the efficacy of repeated rituals, the stability of the present and the security of the future.

4.5 Arval Futures II: Uncertainty and Risk

So far, the *Acta* create (at least for us, and perhaps for the Arvals too) a vision of a future very like the present, a set of familiar events and actions that in its grand lines repeats itself each year, with minute if carefully documented variations. The grove and the iterations of ritual and recording seem outside historical time, even if historical individuals repeatedly stepped in and out of it. Yet the rituals performed also evoked the possibility of change, even of cataclysmic change. To the extent that ritual was a way of managing risk and uncertainty, it operated with a notion of the future as something very far from secure.

Consider two sets of risk, interconnected in the thought of the Arvals.

The first is the risk that the carefully managed relation between the Roman community and the gods – here mediated most importantly by the transactions between the Arvals and Dea Dia – might break down. The rituals of November 224 CE when an expensive and elaborate expiation was performed for bringing iron tools into the sanctuary is a case in point. Lightning strikes were often taken as prodigies, events believed to signal disruption in relations with the gods and requiring ritual remedies. Lightning striking trees in a sacred grove of a cult devoted to the safety and prosperity of the state must have been particularly disturbing. The works needed to repair the damage clearly went well beyond the regular pruning attested elsewhere in the *Acta*. The examples highlight the precarious nature of relations between gods and men, and therefore the precariousness of Rome's future. The Brothers devoted such time to debating and performing rituals precisely because if they did not then Rome would be exposed to significant risk.

The second kind of risk is the (to us more realistic) belief that the emperors' lives were constantly in danger. Most emperors did in fact face a serious threat of assassination. The storms of the autumn of 224 CE came early in the reign of Severus Alexander who had succeeded to the throne on the murder of his cousin Elagabalus, a murder allegedly engineered from within the imperial family. As Fik Meyer put it, 'emperors don't die in bed'.[41] The Arval Brothers were recruited from those senators who were closest to the imperial court, and so were more aware than most Romans of the perils surrounding the princeps: many will have been involved in actual conspiracies and/or their suppression.

There is of course a question of perspective here. To us the Roman Principate seems unbelievably stable, a political entity that lasted for centuries with surprisingly few major changes, and so we are attracted to the idea that Romans might have had confidence in a future that simply extended the present situation onwards indefinitely. Rituals like those performed by the Arvals might seem to reflect that confidence, or even to have helped create it, both in terms of experience, by rejecting sequential time and accentuating cyclical reiterations and perhaps ideologically too by helping fashion a connection between the imperial order and the cosmos. Yet get up closer, and watch the Arvals at work, a small group of the most powerful individuals in the empire, devoting time and emotional energy to devising, performing and recording rituals on which the safety of their world depended, and we get some sense of their anxiety about the immediate future, a future haunted by the risk of plots, murders, violence, military

---

[41] Meijer 2004. See also Woolf 2006: chapter 3.

defeats and also spectacular collapses in that bit of the Roman state's relationship with the gods that was their responsibility and no-one else's.

These various Arval futures, I suggest, remained in unresolved tension with each other. While to us the grove looks like a memory theatre, accumulating a greater and greater documentation of the past, there is no sign it was ever used as such: in contemporary experience it seems to have been focused wholly on posterity, the short-term future of the emperor, and the long-term future of Rome that the Brothers hoped to ensure through punctilious attention to the cult of Dea Dia.

CHAPTER 5

The Future of Rome in Three Greek Historians of Rome

Jonathan J. Price

A historical theory of uncertain origin is directly relevant to how Roman historians, particularly those who wrote in Greek, understood the future of Rome: four empires have dominated the world, Rome is the fifth, signifying either the continuation of a natural process or the end of the historical cycle. This 4+1 model of world empires occurs also in Jewish and Christian apocalyptic, deriving ultimately from the Book of Daniel, where it may be a reworking of a Zoroastrian tradition.[1] So compelling was the idea for the Jews and Christians living in the Roman Empire, nursing messianic dreams, that its *absence* in a major Jewish thinker of the first century requires explanation.[2] Among historians of Rome the model first appears as a tool of explanation and prediction in Polybius' Greek history of Rome, then in Latin Aemilius Sura[3] and Pompeius Trogus – in each of these first cases, indirectly, or in quoted fragments – then certainly in Dionysius of Halicarnassus and later Greek writers. Thus, the 4+1 scheme appears in Greek prose literature from as early as the second century BCE, around the time that the Book of Daniel was being redacted.

Philologists and historians have naturally been drawn to the compelling questions of origin, dating, and influence, i.e., the direction and circumstances of travel of an idea and literary trope. This problem, even if it could be conclusively solved, is unimportant to understanding the three Greek historians under investigation here, whose cosmos of literary reference was Greek and Roman historiography and other literature. A foreign germ entering the Greek stream was beyond their ken.

---

[1] In this volume, see the chapters by Noam (Chapter 9), Gruen (Chapter 10), Berthelot (Chapter 6), and Inglebert (Chapter 13); and on Josephus' use of the model, Davies (Chapter 8) and Rocca (Chapter 7). The connection to the Avesta was made by Flusser 1972: 148–75. The main studies on the four-empires scheme, esp. its Greek manifestations, are: Swain 1940: 1–21; Momigliano 1982: 533–60, esp. 542–6; 1980: 157–62; Hasel 1979: 17–30; Alonso-Núñez 1983: 411–26; Mendels 1981: 330–7; Wiesehöfer 2013: 59–69.

[2] Cf. Chapter 6 by Berthelot in this volume.   [3] Probably second century BCE, see Swain 1940.

In fact Polybius and the other historians found the idea of the succession of empires in rudimentary form in Herodotus, who defined the chronological periods of empires in the East, and had thus already put into place the first three empires in earlier versions of the model. As a prelude to the narrative of the rise of Cyrus and beginning of Persian rule, Herodotus notes that the Assyrian and Median Empires had preceded Cyrus, and he gives precise calculations of the duration of each (1.95, 130). The Persian Empire, replacing the previous two, was of course still strong in his day. It is true that Herodotus' purpose was not to describe or circumscribe all world history according to those empires, but the sequence was soon adopted for that purpose. Ctesias was apparently the first to do that, constructing the first six books of his *Persica* according to the sequence of Assyrians-Medes-Persians – as summarized in Diod. Sic. 2.1–34.[4] After Alexander's conquests, the Macedonians became the fourth empire.

Rome, which suppressed and broke apart other empires in establishing its domination, was obviously the next in line of world powers. After Pydna, this was indisputable. Greek historians, struggling to understand Rome's achievement and the proper attitude towards it, as well as the Romans themselves, saw Rome as the fifth in the sequence of world empires (and not as the fourth, with retrospective adjustment of the sequence). In Roman literature, the quotation of Aemilius Sura by Velleius Paterculus seems to be the earliest surviving trace: he asserts that after the Assyrians, Medes, Persians and Macedonians, "the world power passed to the Roman people."[5] Pompeius Trogus organized his history around the succession of empires,[6] and there are traces elsewhere in Latin historians (cf. Tac., *Hist.* 5.8.1), but the very poor state of preservation of Latin historiography has certainly obscured the real extent to which the model was used. Rome's exceptionalism was elaborated by Romans in various compartments of literature.[7] Apocalyptic authors adjusted the

---

[4] See Muntz 2017: 36–7, whose thesis is that Diodorus, exceptionally, rejected the succession of empires as a way of organizing history.

[5] Vell. Pat. 1.6.6: *Aemilius Sura de annis populi Romani : Assyrii principes omnium gentium rerum potiti sunt, deinde Medi, postea Persae, deinde Macedones ; exinde duobus regibus Philippo et Antiocho, qui a Macedonibus oriundi erant, haud multo post Carthaginem subactam devictis summa imperii ad populum Romanum pervenit. Inter hoc tempus et initium regis Nini Assyriorum, qui princeps rerum potitus est, intersunt anni mdccccxcv.* The genuineness of this passage is disputed, but see Swain 1940.

[6] Muntz 2017: 40–1; it seems Trogus envisioned a sixth empire to replace Rome, namely Parthia.

[7] E.g., Liv. 5.7.10; Verg., *Aen.* 1.279 (*imperium sine fine*: without geographical or chronological limit?), see Chapter 3 by Lushkov in this volume; on Cicero's ideas of Rome, see Chapter 1 by Carlos Lévy in this volume; Woolf 2001: 311–22.

sequence of empires to make Rome the fourth, and God's empire the fifth and last.

The greater traceability of the 4+1 model in Greek historians may be just an accident of survival. All historians of Rome had to face the question, in one way or another, whether Rome was the next in a possibly endless succession of empires, or possessed exceptional qualities that would allow it to end the pattern. This is the question that informs the present investigation of the model in the writings of Polybius, Dionysius, and Appian.

5.1 Polybius

Polybius' *History* contains the earliest instance of the full 4+1 model in surviving Greek literature. It is the earliest, but also the most difficult case, not only because the crucial passage is contained in a contested, second-hand text, but also because it does not seem to be consistent with Polybius' initial judgment of Rome, as he set out to write his expansive *History*, with an apparently different, more startling view of the future of the city and of the world.[8]

The typological succession of 4+1 empires appears near the end of the work. In 146 BCE, gazing on Carthage in flames, Scipio turns to Polybius and declares, "A glorious moment, Polybius; but I have a dread foreboding that some day the same doom will be pronounced upon my own country" – an utterance that Polybius judges could not have been "more statesmanlike and profound."[9] The sequel to this dramatic scene (38.22) is missing from the manuscripts but preserved by Appian (Punica 628–30, [132]):

> Scipio, beholding this city, which had flourished 700 years from its foundation and had ruled over so many lands, islands, and seas, rich with arms and fleets, elephants and money, equal to the mightiest monarchies but far surpassing them in bravery and high spirit (since without ships or arms, and in the face of famine, it had sustained continuous war for three years), now come to its end in total destruction – Scipio, beholding this spectacle, is said to have shed tears and publicly lamented the fortune of the enemy. After meditating by himself a long time and reflecting on the rise and fall of cities, nations, and empires, as well as of individuals, upon the fate of Troy, that once proud city, upon that of the Assyrians, the Medes, and the Persians,

---

[8] This will bring us unfortunately but inevitably into the thicket of the question of the *History*'s composition; I shall try to avoid getting entangled by relating only to those parts relevant to the question of "the future of Rome" in Polybius' thought. Recent speculation on Polybius' "teleological" thinking is contained in J. Grethlein 2013: 224–67.

[9] πραγματικωτέραν καὶ νουνεχεστέραν, 38.21, trans. W. R. Paton in Loeb edition.

greatest of all, and later the splendid Macedonian empire, either voluntarily or otherwise the words of the poet escaped his lips: – "The day shall come in which our sacred Troy | And Priam, and the people over whom | Spear-bearing Priam rules, shall perish all." (Iliad, vi, 448–449) Being asked by Polybius in familiar conversation (for Polybius had been his tutor) what he meant by using these words, he said that he did not hesitate frankly to name his own country, for whose fate he feared when he considered the mutability of human affairs. And Polybius wrote this down just as he heard it. (trans. H. White in Loeb edition of Appian)

There has been great uncertainty as to whether Appian's quotation of Polybius represents a genuine fragment or a later elaboration on the preserved passage in Polybius. Doubt ensues not only from the fragmentary Pol. 38.21 (of which crucially the beginning is missing), in which Scipio tells Polybius that he sees in Carthage's destruction a sign or message (παράγγελμα) of Rome's own future destruction, but also from the briefer report in Diodorus Siculus 32.24 (itself plagued by textual problems), which reports Scipio's weeping, his quotation of Homer, and interaction with Polybius but not the historical sequence of empires. Appian's is the only version that attributes the reflection on the four empires preceding Rome to Scipio; Polybius' greater distance from Appian than Diodorus has exacerbated doubt. Opinions are many, and sharply divided.[10] I hestitate to disagree with great Polybian scholar Frank Walbank, who saw "no reason to include this passage ... as a fragment of P.,"[11] but arguments offered since then have made the Polybian authorship of the passage rather more acceptable. Appian was able to read the complete text of Polybius and claims to be quoting Polybius directly (καὶ τάδε μὲν Πολύβιος αὐτὸς ἀκούσας συγγράφει), which should be taken seriously; the absence of the model in Diodorus' abbreviated account is not the same as a contradiction of Appian. It is true that in Appian's account, Scipio's reported *words* are only the quotation of Homer and foreboding about Rome, whereas his reflection of the succession of empires is confined to his silent thought; but the ancient historians routinely entered the minds of their actors, and there is nothing foreign in the passage to Polybius' way of writing history. In fact, a meta-historical pattern to which all actors, human and state, are subject, is typical of Polybius' thinking and historical

---

[10] A good up-to-date survey of the debate is in Baronowski 2011: 153, 209 nn. 2–3; he defends the authenticity of the passage, as does Momigliano (see n. 1) and Muntz 2017: 38–9; against authenticity are Astin 1967: 282–3 and Mendels (see n. 1).

[11] Walbank 1957–1979: vol. III, 725.

5. The Future of Rome in Three Greek Historians 89

presentation.[12] Thus it is believable that Appian reflects Polybius' full account of Scipio's thoughts and words as he viewed Carthage in flames.

We shall not know for certain what Polybius wrote without the miraculous recovery of a lost manuscript. It is undeniable, however, that *some* scene of Scipio lamenting the future of Rome was written by Polybius towards the end of his *History*, because the text at 38.21 is genuine. It was bold of Polybius not only to write the dramatic scene – certainly including a quotation from Homer, probably also the 4+1 model of empires – when Rome seemed to be at an unprecedented and indisputable pinnacle of power, but also to put the words in the mouth of its great general and statesman. Polybius explicitly interpreted the sentiment as a sign of Scipio's greatness of character, but still it was a brave choice, as well as an effective literary maneuver, to focalize his own ponderings about Rome's imperialist actions and (philosophically) uncertain future through its most successful general of the time, the dominant figure in the later books who stood out as uncorrupted by greed and the other faults that attended Rome's management of its empire so rapidly achieved.[13] It was put near the end of the entire work in its expanded form, as a kind of climax to the last year covered in the *History*.[14]

That scene takes the reader back to the very beginning of the work, which Polybius was writing, decades earlier, as a different man with a different historical vision and purpose. Famously, when he began writing history, Polybius was deeply impressed by Rome's unique achievement, and by the consequent need for a unique form of historical writing, which he claims to have invented. He opens with a bold claim about the unprecedented extent and importance of the subject of his investigations and narrative – the Roman Empire – which he phrases for dramatic and didactic effect in the form of a question (1.1.5), in one of the most-quoted passages in his entire surviving work:[15]

> For the extraordinary nature of the events I decided to write about is in itself enough to interest everyone, young or old, in my work, and make them want to read it. After all, is there anyone on earth who is so narrow-minded

---

[12] This is now a wide topic, see the recent dissertation, Herchenroeder 2010.
[13] Eckstein 1995: 139–40 and *passim*, and on Scipio see 268–9; Champion 2004: 179–80 suggests that Scipio cultivated the image of old-time Roman morality; Baronowski 2011: 156–8.
[14] This is not to disregard the similar musings by Demetrius of Phalerum on the eventual end of Macedonian rule at Pol. 29.21, i.e. at the end of the work as originally conceived by Polybius. If that was intended to contain a hint of Rome's eventual fall – which may be doubted – then the hint was made explicit in Scipio's lament on Rome; see Eckstein 1995: 268–9; Baronowski 2011: 154.
[15] See Alonso-Núñez 1983: 411–13 and *passim*. For a detailed narratological analysis of this *prokatasekue*, Miltsios 2013: 8–13; cf. Walbank 1957–1979: vol. I, 40.

or uninquisitive that he could fail to want to know how and thanks to what kind of political system almost the entire known world was conquered and brought under a single empire, the empire of the Romans, in less than fifty-three years – an unprecedented event?[16]

The opening statement of theme and purpose is unqualified, and although the claim of the unprecedented nature and extent of the Roman Empire will become typical in prefaces of historians of Rome, Polybius writes as if he is saying something entirely new and unexpected (*paradoxon*); and the thematic program will be repeated.[17] It is a clear statement of premise and purpose as he started his great project.

As Polybius had learned from Thucydides' widely imitated claim that his subject was the *megiste kinesis* in all human history,[18] a grand opening assertion of the unprecedented nature of a historical subject required proof in the form of a brief, curated historical survey of all possible comparative examples. This is just what Polybius provides (1.2.1–7):

> The extraordinary and spectacular nature of the subject I propose to consider would become particularly evident if we were to compare and contrast the most famous empires of the past—the ones that have earned the most attention from writers—with the supremacy of the Romans. The empires that deserve to be compared and contrasted in this way are the following. The Persians once held sway over a huge realm, but whenever they endeavoured to go beyond the boundaries of Asia, they endangered not just their rule, but their very existence. The Spartans strove for leadership of the Greeks for a long time and achieved it, but maintained a secure grip on it for barely twelve years. Although in Europe Macedonian dominion extended only from the Adriatic region to the Danube—nothing but a tiny fraction, you might think, of this continent—they later gained control of Asia too, by overthrowing the Persian empire; but despite the view that never had more places, nor greater power, been in the hands of a single state, they still left most of the known world in others' hands. They made not the slightest attempt, for example, to take over Sicily, Sardinia, and Libya, and they were, to put it bluntly, completely unaware of the existence of the extremely warlike peoples of western Europe. The Romans, however, have made themselves masters of almost the entire known world, not just some bits of it, and have left such a colossal empire that no one alive today can resist it and no one in the future will be able to overcome it.

---

[16] τίς γὰρ οὕτως ὑπάρχει φαῦλος ἢ ῥᾴθυμος ἀνθρώπων ὃς οὐκ ἂν βούλοιτο γνῶναι πῶς καὶ τίνι γένει πολιτείας ἐπικρατηθέντα σχεδὸν ἅπαντα τὰ κατὰ τὴν οἰκουμένην οὐχ ὅλοις πεντήκοντα καὶ τρισὶν ἔτεσιν ὑπὸ μίαν ἀρχὴν ἔπεσε τὴν Ῥωμαίων, ὃ πρότερον οὐχ εὑρίσκεται γεγονός. Translations by Waterfield 2010. On the question of *pragmatike historia*, see Walbank 1972: 66–96.
[17] As Walbank points out, e.g.: 1.4.1; 3.4.1, 1.9, 2.6, 3.9 and 118.9; 8.2.3.
[18] Marincola 1997: 34–43; Price 2001: 207–10.

5. The Future of Rome in Three Greek Historians

This is Polybius' first proof. There is nothing typological in the series of empires. It does not reflect the sequence of 4+1 empires that became standard afterwards, or any other established sequence of empires, but rather Polybius' wide knowledge of history and analytic mind. Polybius' chronological series of Persia-Sparta-Alexander-Hellenistic empires is a direct appeal to the Greeks' experience and historical memory, i.e. all the empires that were relevant to Greek history – except perhaps Egypt, which is absent from the 4+1 model as well.[19] Comparison with Rome impressed: the Persians, despite their fabled might, never succeeded outside of Asia; the Spartans' hegemony was little more than a blip in history; and the Macedonian success neglected Europe. The proof is obvious: Rome's empire exceeds the extent of all others worth comparison, and "need not fear rivalry in the future,"[20] which is an important comment not only on Rome's stability but on its foreseeable longevity.

It is to be noted that Polybius' first proof is focused through one of his most complex, inconsistent, and debated media for historical explanation, the workings of *Tyche*. The first statements on this are unambiguous, positive, and even positivistic: *Tyche* "has guided almost all the affairs of the world in one direction and has forced them to incline towards one and the same end" (1.4.1, trans. Paton in Loeb), and Rome's empire was "the finest and most beneficent of the performances of Fortune. For though she is ever producing something new and ever playing a part in the lives of men, she has not in a single instance ever accomplished such a work, ever achieved such a triumph, as in our own times" (1.4.4, ibid.). Without Polybius' subsequent contradictory and complicating statements on *Tyche*, the reader understands, on first meeting Polybius' historical thought, that *Tyche* is a benign, active force with a good purpose.[21] This is, at least, what Polybius conveyed, and evidently thought, and felt, as he set down those first sentences.

Comparison of empires is only Polybius' first proof of Rome's unique achievement. His full proof is multi-faceted, emerging in all its pieces as the

---

[19] Philo, who did not employ the topos, does refer to Egypt in his historical comparisons, see Chapter 6 by Katell Berthelot in this volume.
[20] See Walbank's note on the reconstruction of this defective passage, 1957–1979: vol. I, 41–2, which seems right; the words τοῖς ἐπιγινομένοις seem correct, and that is what is important here.
[21] See Walbank 1972: 68: "Tyche and Polybius are shown as being in a sense complementary to each other: each is a creative artist in the relevant field, the one producing the unified oecumene, the other its counterpart in the unified work of history–σωματοειδῆ. In this way Polybius gives a new meaning to universal history, in so far as he identifies it with the history of his own time and no other." On the problem of *Tyche* in Polybius' *History*, Walbank 1972: 58–65; for recent discussions with up-to-date bibliographies, Deininger 2013, 71–111; Baronowski 2011: 151–2 with his long note at 208 n. 17.

History proceeds. Thirty books were originally planned, with a logical structure. One half, i.e. fifteen books, would cover the Second Punic War (220–201 BCE), and the second half the conquest of the East down to the Roman victory at Pydna (168 BCE), with the first two books devoted to the prelude to the Second Punic War, long and important digressions on the uniqueness of the Roman army and the Roman constitution and institutions in Book 6, and Book 12 consisting of a polemic on historiography.[22]

The digressions on the army and the constitution were especially important tools of explanation. The innovative structure and functioning of the army explained how Rome conquered all rivals more efficiently and thoroughly than any army previously seen in history (6.19–42). Aside from the peculiarly Roman inventions and innovations, the Romans were quick to adopt improvements from other armies (6.25.11), the Roman army demonstrated καλὰ καὶ σπουδαῖα in the field (6.26.12), the discipline and system of rewards and punishments lead to brilliant success (6.39.11), the virtues of the Roman army camp were highly effective and the exact opposite to the Greek method (6.42.1). The world had never before seen such a tool of social discipline and military conquest.

Rome's mixed constitution was, in Polybius' first innovative construction, so perfectly balanced as to be able to stop or significantly slow down the cycle of constitutions (*anacyclosis*), to which all other states in history have been subject. Although this long and discursive passage contains contradictions posing serious interpretive problems, it is at the outset (6.2.3) explicitly presented as a fulfillment of the pledge offered at the beginning of the *History* (1.1.5) to explain Rome's unprecedented fifty-three-year conquest of most of the world: the constitution was one of the main reasons. Polybius seems to have believed at first that the Roman political system could, unprecedentedly, self-correct when needed, and thus attain stability for an extraordinarily long time, if not forever. The original scope and structure of the *History*, and Polybius' plan to explain the Roman achievement by means of demonstration and comparative analysis, reflect the optimisim, one might say euphoria, in Rome after Pydna.[23]

Yet both the opening thesis laid out in the Preface and the proofs by the army and constitution, are compromised by what appear to be contradictory statements. This is one of the most obvious, long-noticed, and

---

[22] Roughly, each two books covered one Olympiad. Cf. Walbank 1972: 97–129; Marincola 2001: 116–24.

[23] Cf. 1.63.9 (where *Tyche* is used in a different way, but Polybius reinforces his original assertions). Discussion in Alonso-Núñez 1983.

5. The Future of Rome in Three Greek Historians

much-discussed problems in the *History*. Here is the problem, briefly.[24] In his "second preface" in at 3.4, he announces his intention to expand his composition in order:

> ... to see clearly whether the Roman rule is acceptable or the reverse, and future generations whether their government should be considered to have been worthy of praise and admiration or rather of blame. And indeed it is just in this that the chief usefulness (ὠφέλιμον) of our history for the present and the future will lie. (3.4.7–8, trans. Paton in Loeb edition)

This statement contradicts the program enthusiastically announced at the beginning, where the purpose was to describe and explain an astounding achievement unprecedented in history, which was sufficient in itself and did not require further moral assessment. The "usefulness" was reflected as well in Polybius' allegedly original method and conception of a "synoptic" history. The purpose has now explicitly changed:

> The final end achieved by this work will be, to gain knowledge of what was the condition of each people after all had been crushed and had come under the dominion of Rome, until the disturbed and trouble time that afterwards ensued (ἐπιγενομένης ταραχῆς καὶ κινήσεως.). About this latter, owing to the importance of the actions and the unexpected character of the events, and chiefly because I not only witnessed most but took part and even directed some, I was induced to write as if starting a fresh work. (3.4.12–13, trans. Paton in Loeb edition)

I am fully aware of the strong current in Polybian scholarship to fuse these disparate statements into a single, coherent program. But the large volume of scholarship devoted to this task attests in itself to the failure by a notoriously finicky and self-aware writer to do the same. It is curious and significant that Polybius did not go back and try to harmonize his two statements of purpose and program for research and writing. There is no hint in Polybius' first introduction that the results of his grand project would need to be reevaluated, or that the overall assessment of Rome's achievement would be less than splendid praise. As he laid out his plan for a History in thirty books, Polybius was not concerned with the "opinions and appreciations" of the ruled, nor with whether the Roman rule was

---

[24] Walbank, 1957–1979: vol. I, 292–7 and 1972: 19–31, with bibliography of previous treatments; most important is Petzold 1969: 53–64; a different approach now in Grethlein 2013: 234–40. Recent discussion with more up-to-date bibliography in Baronowski 2011: 160–2. Baronowski and Ferrary 1988: 276–91, both try to harmonize the two introductions into a unified plan. The compositional problem is complex and open to multiple nuanced interpretations; the treatment in the scope of this chapter is naturally condensed and allusive instead of thorough.

"acceptable" to their subjects, nor with a close assessment, with strong ethical overtones, of Rome's management of its empire. In fact, through verbal echoes, Polybius practically undermines his original statement of purpose. Note the contrasts in the following two passages:

> 1.1.4–6. αὐτὸ γὰρ **τὸ παράδοξον τῶν πράξεων**, ὑπὲρ ὧν προῃρήμεθα γράφειν, ἱκανόν ἐστι προκαλέσασθαι καὶ παρορμῆσαι πάντα καὶ νέον καὶ πρεσβύτερον πρὸς τὴν ἔντευξιν **τῆς πραγματείας**. [5] τίς γὰρ οὕτως ὑπάρχει φαῦλος ἢ ῥᾴθυμος ἀνθρώπων ὃς οὐκ ἂν βούλοιτο **γνῶναι πῶς καὶ τίνι γένει πολιτείας** ἐπικρατηθέντα σχεδὸν ἅπαντα τὰ κατὰ **τὴν οἰκουμένην** οὐχ ὅλοις πεντήκοντα καὶ τρισὶν ἔτεσιν ὑπὸ μίαν ἀρχὴν ἔπεσε τὴν Ῥωμαίων, ὃ πρότερον οὐχ εὑρίσκεται γεγονός, [6] τίς δὲ πάλιν οὕτως ἐκπαθὴς πρός τι τῶν ἄλλων θεαμάτων ἢ μαθημάτων ὃς προυργιαίτερον ἄν τι ποιήσαιτο τῆσδε τῆς ἐμπειρίας;

> For the extraordinary nature of the events (τὸ παράδοξον τῶν πράξεων) I decided to write about is in itself enough to interest everyone, young or old, in my work (τῆς πραγματείας), and make them want to read it. After all, is there anyone on earth who is so narrow-minded or uninquisitive that he could fail to want to know how and thanks to what kind of political system (γνῶναι πῶς καὶ τίνι γένει πολιτείας) almost the entire known world (σχεδὸν ἅπαντα τὰ κατὰ τὴν οἰκουμένην) was conquered and brought under a single empire, the empire of the Romans, in less than fifty-three years – an unprecedented event? Or again, is there anyone who is so passionately attached to some other marvel or matter that he could consider it more important than knowing about this? (trans. R. Waterfield, *Polybius, The Histories*)

> 3.4.12–13. διὸ καὶ **τῆς πραγματείας ταύτης** τοῦτ' ἔσται τελεσιούργημα, **τὸ γνῶναι τὴν κατάστασιν** παρ' ἑκάστοις, ποία τις ἦν μετὰ τὸ καταγωνισθῆναι τὰ ὅλα καὶ πεσεῖν εἰς τὴν τῶν Ῥωμαίων ἐξουσίαν ἕως τῆς μετὰ ταῦτα πάλιν ἐπιγενομένης **ταραχῆς καὶ κινήσεως**. [13] ὑπὲρ ἧς διὰ **τὸ μέγεθος τῶν ἐν αὐτῇ πράξεων καὶ τὸ παράδοξον τῶν συμβαινόντων**, τὸ δὲ μέγιστον, διὰ τὸ τῶν πλείστων μὴ μόνον αὐτόπτης, ἀλλ' ὧν μὲν συνεργὸς ὧν δὲ καὶ χειριστὴς γεγονέναι, προήχθην οἷον **ἀρχὴν ποιησάμενος ἄλλην γράφειν**.

> So my work (τῆς πραγματείας ταύτῃ) will be complete when it has clarified how all the various peoples felt from the time when the Romans' victories had brought them worldwide dominion, up to the disturbed and troubled period that came afterwards (ἐπιγενομένης ταραχῆς καὶ κινήσεω). As far as this period is concerned, the scale and the extraordinariness of the events (τὸ μέγεθος τῶν ἐν αὐτῇ πράξεων καὶ τὸ παράδοξον τῶν συμβαινόντων) that took place then, and most importantly the fact that I myself witnessed very

5. The Future of Rome in Three Greek Historians

many of them, mean that I had no choice but to write about it as if I were making a fresh start (ἀρχὴν ποιησάμενος ἄλλην γράφειν).

What is clear from the comparison of just these two passages is that the knowledge that the historian hopes to gain and transmit to his readers through the study of history, the purpose to which that knowledge is put to use, and the definition of τὸ παράδοξον and other elements in his two programmatic schemes, changed from his first to his second introduction. The παράδοξον in the first introduction relates solely to the Romans' astonishingly vast and rapid conquest of nearly all the known world, whereas in the second the "extraordinariness of the events" has to do with the turn that the events took, into the "disturbed and troubled period", of which there is not a hint in the Preface. The first introduction asks almost hubristically whether anyone would not want to know (γνῶναι) how the Romans conquered the world, using what sort of constitution, without any sign of trouble or disturbance, whereas the second introduction promises knowledge (τὸ γνῶναι) of how each conquered people felt after being crushed (μετὰ τὸ καταγωνισθῆναι), a purpose which is peripheral, if not contradictory, to the first stated one. The second introduction quotes the first, with a dissonant ring.

I shall not enter here into – ultimately – unfruitful speculation about when exactly Polybius modified and expanded his plan, wrote the second introduction, possibly changed parts in the first thirty books and composed the final ten books in accordance with his changing view. It will be enough to agree with a widely held view that Polybius grew more uncomfortable with his original optimism as he observed the Romans as imperialists more closely and over time, and that this change of heart took a sharp downturn in or after 146 BCE, the year Rome wantonly destroyed both Carthage, which Polybius witnessed, and Corinth.[25] What is pertinent here is that Polybius finished his work before the end of his long life, and decided to leave in place both introductions, with their explicit and implicit contradictions. Much against his tendency to hyper-explain, he let the reader puzzle out the meaning of the contradictions. This is, I think, the best way to understand the presence of the two incompatible introductions, preferable to efforts to flatten them into a unified view. Deliberately enigmatic writing, rather than incompletion, or lack of opportunity because of untimely death,[26] signals that Polybius revised his original blithe

---

[25] Walbank 1972: 16–31. After 146 BCE, the conviction spread in the Greek world that "Roman hegemony had changed into open despotism," Gabba 1991: 196.
[26] Pseudo-Lucian, *Macrob.* 22.

and sympathetic view of Rome's achievement – pointing to a belief in Rome's everlastingness – to a more complex and subtle one; and that complexity and subtlety are conveyed by a textual puzzle. By posing the question in the second introduction, whether Rome's achievement was worthy of praise or blame, Polybius provides sufficient material and authorial direction to guide the reader towards the more complex view. The reader will understand the implicit critique of a certain view of Rome, and of Rome itself.

What is plain, so plain as almost to need no elaboration, is that the later Polybius, with a more pessimistic and darker view of the Romans' imperial accomplishment, took over the earlier Polybius, who was deeply impressed by the Romans' rapid and complete conquest of the *oikoumene* as a unique historical achievement worthy in itself of study and contemplation. This is clear from the parts of Books 31–40 which do survive, as well as comments scattered throughout (possibly inserted into) the original thirty books. As Walbank has pointed out,[27] after Pydna, Polybius witnessed inexplicable instances of brutality, cruelty, growing greed, and the shattering of unity as Rome was inundated with wealth and irresistable opportunities for gain. Polybius' "growing pessimism," in Eckstein's phrase, is discernible throughout the *History*.[28]

A similar interpretive and much-studied compositional problem is present in the discussion of Rome's constitution.[29] An exposition of its unique qualities was intended from the beginning, and Polybius duly signals to the reader that, as he opens Book 6, his intention is to fulfill his promise, and he will explain the peculiar features of the Roman state that allowed it to persevere and prevail in the most trying of circumstances (6.2.3–7). Aside from explanation of Rome's unprecedented achievement, his purpose is explicitly to predict the future of the Roman state (6.3.3). The theory of *anacyclosis* is then offered in interesting and colorful detail, in what appears to be written as a set-piece (6.5–9). It is familiar to all students of Polybius:

---

[27] Walbank 1972: 170–83.
[28] Eckstein 1995: 254–71. It should be stressed that, however one interprets Polybius' change in attitude, it should not be conceived as a linear development: despite his original optimism, his mind was critical and alert from the beginning, not blind to problems in the Roman character; see e.g., 18.35.1, 31.25.5, and discussion of *anacyclosis* below; Gruen 1984: 346–51, although I am not so sure that "it was not Polybius' purpose to moralize"; Petzold 1969: 60–3.
[29] Given that Polybius VI is the main source for the theory of the mixed constitution in antiquity, an enormous bibliography has grown up around it. See Baronowski's recent discussion, 2011: 154–6 (denying a contradiction between the two political theories); especially important is Petzold 1969: 64–90; Walbank 1972: 130–56 (rejecting Petzold's approach and arguing for unification of the two theories), and 1998: 45–59; and now the articles by Erskine 2013: 231–45 and Seager 2013: 247–54, in Gibson and Harrison 2013.

5. The Future of Rome in Three Greek Historians

as a law of nature (6.5.1, 9.10), all states pass through six stages in a never-ending cycle, i.e., good and corrupt forms of single rule, the rule of the few and the rule of the many. By identifying the particular form of a state's constitution, an observer will know with fair precision the state's immediate and long-term future: thus a scientific concern for knowing a state's future. At the end of this first set-piece, Polybius remarks that by applying keen observation from the *anayclosis* to Rome, we can also know about the stage in its natural growth and its eventual end:

> And especially in the case of the Roman state will this method enable us to arrive at a knowledge of its formation, growth, and greatest perfection, and likewise of the change for the worse which is sure to come some day. For, as I said, this state, more than any other, has been formed and has grown naturally, and will undergo a natural decline and change to its contrary. (6.9.12–13, trans. Paton)

Yet the expectation to find the place of Rome in the *anacyclosis* is belied by the second set-piece on the constitution in Book 6, namely the famous exposition of Rome's mixed constitution (6.11.11 – 18.8). Here in fact is the actual realization of Polybius' initial promise of explaining Rome's unprecedented achievement, for the main point is that Rome, by a perfect balance of all three constitutional elements, has defeated the cycle, perhaps even stopped it. The cooperation and the balance between the monarchical, aristocratic, and democratic elements in the Roman state "is adequate to all emergencies, so that it is impossible to find a better political system (πολιτεία) than this," which is sufficiently strong and well-designed to withstand all external *and internal* threats (6.18.1–7). "All in fact remains as it has been" (πάντα γὰρ ἐμμένει τοῖς ὑποκειμένοις, 6.18.8). The idea, at least when this section was written, seems to have been that Rome had conquered history itself. The exposition of the other constitutions in Book 6, pointing out the weaknesses of each, shows just how they differ from Rome's stronger and well-balanced system; it is like the comparison of previous empires at the beginning of the *History*.

Yet this presentation of Rome's constitution, not only without any indication of internal flaws or weaknesses but asserting that all threats and dangers from without and within will be checked, contradicts the assertion that Rome will live a natural life of birth, growth, peak, decline, and death, following a law of nature applying to all states, without exception. That law of nature is repeated towards the end of the book, following the long digression on the Roman army and the discourses on other states, all with the implied or explicit purpose of comparison to Rome.

> That all existing things are subject to decay and change is a truth that scarcely needs proof; for the course of nature is sufficient to force this conviction on us. There being two agencies by which every kind of state is liable to decay, the one external and the other a growth of the state itself, we can lay down no fixed rule about the former, but the latter is a regular process. (6.57.1–2, cf. 51.4, trans. Paton)

Polybius' explicit previous statement about Rome's mixed constitution overcoming both kinds of danger, external and internal, is not so far away in the text here as to be forgotten by the attentive reader. Thus in Book 6 Polybius says both that Rome has defeated the inevitability of the *anacyclosis* and is subject to it. Polybius applies to Rome two theories of political change which lead to opposite conclusions about Rome's future.

Walbank believed that the problem was intellectual and textual: "The consequent contradictions between 57 and the account of the mixed constitution are all to be explained as arising out of P.'s rather tortuous attempt to reconcile theories not ultimately consistent and his treatment of the *anacyclosis* as the form in which the general biological law finds expression in a political context."[30] Another possibility, an old suggestion consonant with our interpretation of the two inconsistent introductions, is that Polybius could not reconcile early theory with later reality, so that he offered a second theory which better explains the developing situation without disavowing or canceling the first theory; the seams draw the reader's attention. That is, when Polybius first set out to explain "how and with what system of government" (πῶς καὶ τίνι γένει πολιτείας) Rome conquered nearly the entire world in an incredibly short span of time, he was certain that Rome's constitution was as unprecedented as its achievement, and had even stopped the cycle of growth and decay because of a perfect internal balance; the open-ended future was as unprecedented as the present. Yet as he changed his mind and saw that Rome was as inherently flawed as other states – flaws are more easily seen in states after they fail – he believed that Rome would eventually fail as a result of its success. In 6.57.5–9, Polybius gives a generalizing analysis, reflecting the Roman moralists' own opinions, about the corrupting effects of prosperity and luxury as the root cause; he was particularly worried about an overconfident and empowered populace. But for a historian interested deeply in cause and causation, those superficial sentences are few and inconclusive.

---

[30] Walbank 1957–1979: vol. I, 743; 1972: 133–4.

As with the two introductions, so with the two life-cycles of states, the contradiction, which cannot be facilely dismissed as incomplete editing, draws the reader to ponder the historian's true intention. There have been many attempts to demonstrate a unified conception,[31] but these strenuous efforts in themselves are the kind of mental exertion which Polybius' ambiguity was meant to elicit from his readers. And again, like the case of the two introductions, the more pessimistic view, predicting Rome's inevitable decline and death, seems to prevail over, and be illuminated by, the more optimistic model of perpetuity. Modern exegeses of Book 6 tend to conclude that Rome, according to Polybius, is subject to the same natural laws of decline and death as all other states, and the mixed constitution was *not* seen by Polybius as a formula for perpetual existence, but as the basis for a *longer* period of prosperity and stability than other states in history. This may be, but Polybius, the hyper-explainer of his intention and his material, never clearly resolves a glaring problem. The contradictions can be read, rather, as an indictment of innocence.

Let us now return to the matter of Rome's place in the succession of Rome's empires, and its implied future. A reader who persevered through Polybius' thick text, including the appended decade, and remembered the beginning of the first scroll, would notice the contradiction in Polybius' use of previous empires to judge Rome's achievement: in Book 1, previous empires are used, in no typological way, to demonstrate Rome's surpassing them and overcoming the problems which brought their failure. Near the end of the expanded work, in Book 38, a received model of four successive world empires followed by a fifth was exploited by Polybius to predict Rome's eventual fall, for it was afflicted by the same inherent flaws as the other empires, the seeds of its own destruction. Thus Polybius showed two possibilities in one work: using historical precedent to confirm Rome's uniqueness and unique stability, with the implicit or explicit conclusion that it can last forever; and the subjugation of Rome to universal historical laws, becoming the next but not the last in a string of empires which arose, flourished, and perished, each for its particular reason but all according to the universal law. The final word is given to the universal law.

5.2 Dionysius and Appian

Dionysius of Halicarnassus and Appian of Alexandria, Greek historians living in Rome's empire during very different periods from Polybius and

---
[31] See the works cited in n. 29.

from each other, invoked the 4+1 model of past empires when contemplating Rome's future. Each may have been reacting mimetically to Polybius (whom at least Dionysius definitely read) and others who had used the model before them. Yet whereas Polybius, through Scipio, viewed Rome's inevitable demise configured in the succession of past empires, Dionysius and Appian, each in his own way, saw it differently.

Dionysius uses the 4+1 model at the outset of his *Roman Antiquities* in a way that is both typical and innovative.[32] *Typical*, since he makes the same routine claim as so many Greek historians did after Thucydides, viz. that his subject was the greatest and most important in history. After Polybius – really, after the Second Punic War, and certainly after Rome's conquests in the Greek world – that greatest subject for the historian was perforce the Roman Empire.[33] Such a claim required proof, even if the subject was the vastly powerful empire under which all potential Greek readers of Dionysius and Appian lived, with varying levels of satisfaction or resentment. The historian was compelled not only to explain the worthiness of Rome as a historical subject, but also his unique insight into Roman history which made his history worthier to read than previous ones, as well as his original and effective method of narrating and explicating that greatness. Thus in the manner of prefatorial proofs in the Thucydidean manner, Dionysius compares Rome's imperial achievement with previous empires and finds them wanting. Ultimately, of course, Dionysius' real topic will be revealed not as the unprecedented achievement of the empire but Rome's allegedly Greek origins; that was his *innovation*. But his claim for innovative method and research will not occupy us here.

The empires Dionysius marshals are the four in the model. His decision to use the ready-to-hand model means that he, too, excluded other comparable empires, like Egypt. He states his conclusion first (1.2.1):

> For if anyone turns his attention to the successive supremacies both of cities and of nations, as accounts of them have been handed down from times past, and then, surveying them severally and comparing them together, wishes to determine which of them obtained the widest dominion and both in peace and war performed the most brilliant achievements, he will find that the supremacy of

---

[32] On Dionysius' introduction, see Alonso-Núñez 1983: 413–17 and *passim* for discussion; Gabba (n. 25), 192–4.

[33] The place of Rome in Timaeus' *History* is contested. A. Momigliano believed that Timaeus realized the importance of Rome, cf. 1977a: 37–66; Pearson expressed doubts, see 1987: 84–5. Most recently, Champion (2010) in his commentary on Timaeus in Brill's New Jacoby maintains, reasonably, that "Timaios may well have been the first writer to see clearly the importance to the western Greeks of the victor of the great Sicilian war, whether it be Rome or Carthage, which he could not have divined."

the Romans has far surpassed all those that are recorded from earlier times, not only in the extent of its dominion and in the splendor of its achievements – which no account has as yet worthily celebrated – but also in the length of time during which it has endured down to our day.[34]

This is followed by an efficient survey: the Assyrian Empire is judged to have been territorially limited, the Median short-lived, the Persian short-lived and also exclusive of Europe, and the Macedonian power (δυναστεία) broken apart by internal dissension after Alexander's death and, even before that, not encompassing the whole known world (1.2.2–3). Briefly dismissing the inferior Greek powers as unworthy of comparison – for the benefit of his Greek readers, who would ask the question[35] – he offers the unsurprising but still dramatic conclusion that

> Rome rules every country that is not inaccessible or uninhabited, and she is mistress of every sea, not only of that which lies inside the Pillars of Hercules but also of the Ocean, except that part of it which is not navigable; she is the first and the only State recorded in all time that ever made the risings and the settings of the sun the boundaries of her dominion. Nor has her supremacy been of short duration, but more lasting than that of any other commonwealth or kingdom.[36]

The totality of Rome's rule is an improvement on Polybius' σχεδὸν δὲ πᾶσαν τὴν οἰκουμένην – Rome had made objective imperial gains since Polybius, but Dionysius was one-upping his predecessor.[37] Moreover while Polybius (presumably) used a *different*, non-formulaic series of empires at the beginning of his *History* to *prove* Rome's unprecedented achievement, and then the 4+1 model to *question* Rome's enduring strength and lament its eventual fall, Dionysius uses the latter model to *affirm* Rome's achievement and bright future. Dionysius also differs pointedly from Polybius in

---

[34] Translations by E. Cary in the Loeb edition.
[35] Mentioning the peak of glory of Old Greece as even more limited than the Asian and Macedonian powers not only puts the Greeks' imperial accomplishment in sobering perspective, but also provides Dionysius with a platform for comparing Roman virtues with Greek, and in fact to claim that Rome's highest virtues were Greek, since Rome was founded by Greeks. As Irene Peirano put it, in her article (2010: 42): "What starts as a narrative of Roman superiority thus becomes a demonstration of how Rome is in effect carrying on the Greek cultural project."
[36] He continues: "From the time that she mastered the whole of Italy she was emboldened to aspire to govern all mankind (ἐπὶ τὴν ἁπάντων), and after driving from off the sea the Carthaginians, whose maritime strength was superior to that of all others, and subduing Macedonia, which until then was reputed to be the most powerful nation on land, she no longer had as rival any nation either barbarian or Greek; and it is now in my day already the seventh generation that she has continued to hold sway over every region of the world, and there is no nation, as I may say, that disputes her universal dominion or protests against being ruled by her."
[37] On Dionysius' relation to Polybius – with typically penetrating insights into Dionysius' view of Rome's future – see Pelling 2016: 155–73.

the reason he identifies for Rome's success. Polybius stressed systemic and political factors such as Rome's constitution and army, with relatively little emphasis on collective Roman virtue *per se*; while there is a strongly felt moralistic strain in his work and clear admiration for aristocratic virtue in a Greek mode found in individuals, there is conspicuously no systematic meta-historical digression on inherent Roman virtue to match the digressions on the Roman constitution and army, which Polybius felt were unique inventions.[38] By contrast, Dionyius lavishly praises "the infinite examples of virtue in men whose superiors, whether for piety or for justice or for life-long self-control or for martial virtue, no city, either Greek or barbarian, has ever produced" (1.5.3), and this becomes a repeated theme throughout the twenty books of his history. More importantly, the subject and scope of Dionysius' history exceed Polybius' since, instead of writing on an extraordinarily *brief* fifty-three-year period of conquest and then another twenty years of maintenance, Dionysius' Rome has proven its worthiness and mettle, its brilliance and its unprecedented achievement, in its surviving and thriving for more than 700 years. This is not only one-upmanship, but also *perhaps* an implicit answer to Polybius' doubts about the durability and eventual collapse. Perhaps; we shall see that there may be small cracks in Dionysius' confidence.

Dionysius comes rather close to affirming his belief in Rome's immortality, or at least his inability to predict not only that Rome would some day fall. At 1.6.4 he declares that "both the present and future descendants of those godlike men (τῶν ἰσοθέων ἀνδρῶν) will choose, not the pleasantest and easiest of lives, but rather the noblest and most ambitious (τὸν εὐγενέστατον καὶ φιλοτιμότατον)," the Romans' near-divinity implying everlasting life bringing earthly glory. Rome's future was the destiny of the world (τὸ πεπρωμένον). Dionysius says romantically about the village of the first founding (1.31.3):

> Yet this village was ordained by fate to excel in the course of time all other cities, whether Greek or barbarian, not only in its size, but also in the majesty of its empire and in every other form of prosperity, and to be celebrated above them *all as long as mortality shall endure*.[39]

---

[38] The Romans' moral decline is a theme guiding the later narrative, but with no separate philosophical discussion of Roman virtue *per se*, see (n. 13) Eckstein; Champion: 193–203, and succinctly 237–8; Candou Morón extracts the Polybius' idea of "Roman ethos" from the passages we have been discussing: 2005: 307–28.

[39] ἣν ἔμελλε τὸ πεπρωμένον σὺν χρόνῳ θήσειν ὅσην οὔθ' Ἑλλάδα πόλιν οὔτε βάρβαρον κατά τε οἰκήσεως μέγεθος καὶ κατὰ δυναστείας ἀξίωσιν καὶ τὴν ἄλλην ἅπασαν εὐτυχίαν, χρόνον τε ὁπόσον ἂν ὁ θνητὸς αἰὼν ἀντέχῃ πόλεων μάλιστα πασῶν μνημονευθησομένην.

This is the final and most important programmatic statement in which Dionysius offers a historical vision exceeding and superseding Polybius': his lack of pessimism, and his apparent belief in Rome's future rule so long as mortal humans rule the earth.[40]

From Dionysius' thematic introduction, then, there is nothing obvious in Rome's origins or present state of power to raise doubts about the stability and future of its rule, or its worthiness to rule. At least, I can find no traces of figured speech, subversive rhetoric, or any subtle trick to undermine his positive interpretation in this preface or in any other of the programmatic statements guiding his long narrative. At the outset, he uses the topos of 4+1 world empires plainly to reveal that Rome had broken the pattern of the rise and fall, as demonstrated by the very extent and long duration of its conquests, and its avoidances of the vices to which other empires succumbed.

As a *coup de grâce* to Polybius, Dionysius asserts in his Preface and elsewhere in his *Roman Antiquities* that Fortune had *no role* in Rome's history, rather, Rome's success was and is a product of the Romans' innate virtue. This is connected with his innovative theory that Rome was in fact a Greek foundation. In this he contradicted the Romans' own foundation legends, but he created a solid footing for his polemic against bitter Greek critics of Rome who contended that the Romans were barbarians who blundered into Empire with the help of blind Chance.[41] On the contrary, Dionysius writes, in a passage already quoted, that it was the Romans' virtue, piety, justice, discipline, and skill that accounts for their constant success (1.5.3). This is a theme restated throughout his work.[42]

---

[40] The idea of *Roma Aeterna* first appears in Cicero, and is attested through the Principate, but only occasionally and sporadically, as Benjamin Isaac 2017 points out in his study: 33–44; and see Chapter 1 by Lévy in this volume.

[41] 1.4.2: "For to this day almost all the Greeks are ignorant of the early history of Rome and the great majority of them have been imposed upon by sundry false opinions grounded upon stories which chance has brought to their ears and led to believe that, having come upon various vagabonds without house or home and barbarians, and even those not free men, as her founders, she in the course of time arrived at world domination, and this not through reverence for the gods and justice and every other virtue (εὐσέβειαν δὲ καὶ δικαιοσύνην καὶ τὴν ἄλλην ἀρετήν), but through some chance and the injustice of Fortune, which inconsiderately showers her greatest favours upon the most undeserving. And indeed the more malicious are wont to rail openly at Fortune for freely bestowing on the basest of barbarians the blessings of the Greeks."

[42] E.g., 14.6.5: "For I considered that Greeks are distinguished from barbarians, not by their name nor on the basis of their language, but by their intelligence and their predilection for good behaviour, and particularly by their refraining from any inhuman behaviour towards one another. All in whose nature these qualities prevail I believe ought to be called Greeks, but those of whom the opposite is true, barbarians."

Fortune is presented as a source of adversity that the Romans overcame. Witness Fabricius' impressive answer to Pyyrhus (19.14.1), showing that Rome does not rail against *Tyche* or blame *Tyche* for poverty, to which Pyrrhus responds with praise of the Romans' εὐγένεια τῆς ψύχης, a natural, innate nobility (seen through the whole exchange between Fabricius and Pyrrhus at AR 19.14–18)[43]. Throughout his narrative, Dionysius emphasizes the Romans' "reverence for the gods and justice and every other virtue" (εὐσέβειαν δὲ καὶ δικαιοσύνην καὶ τὴν ἄλλην ἀρετὴν, 1.4.2) – resonating, perhaps, with the Augustan program in his period, but also specifically contrasting them with Greek city-states which failed in the same virtues. True to their alleged Greek roots, the Romans excelled in virtues which were quintessentially Greek, in a far more consistent and demonstrative way than any Greek state was able to do. In his final encounter with the Romans, Pyrrhus is made to remark that they were "the most pious and most just among the Greeks" (πρὸς ἀνθρώπους ὁσιωτάτους Ἑλλήνων καὶ δικαιοτάτους, 20.6.1).

Is Dionysius' view of Rome really so positive, optimistic, and unnuanced? Most long and complex works evoke the urge in readers to seek subtlety and sophistication even where none is immediately apparent. Recently, in an elaborately argued article, Irene Peirano[44] has claimed that Dionysius' praise of the virtue of Rome's first heroic generations as "godlike men" contains an implied contrast with the present generation. She highlights passing comments by Dionysius, particularly on tyranny, as "scathing criticism" of the present generation of Romans, and even anti-Augustan. The problem with Peirano's clever observations is that none of them arises from an ambiguity or disturbance in the text itself, but requires importing information and opinion which Dinoysius' readers may or may not have agreed with. The same may be said for her strongest case for ambivalence in Dionysius, arguing for a "re-barbarization" of the Romans at the end of the *Roman Antiquities*. Yet aside from the fact that the actual end of the work is lost, the execution by public humiliation, scourging, and beheading – a sign of the alleged Roman barbarity – was not new or recent behavior resulting from empire, but a standard Roman method; the victims were the status of slaves; and it was a punishment not unprecedented in the Greek world. Moreover, the supposedly subtle linguistic clues criticizing contemporary Romans would have provided little comfort

---

[43] This seems to have been followed by account of Rome's empire stretching to limits of earth, thus suggesting a causative connection between the Romans' virtue and their domination. See n. 41 above.

[44] See n. 35.

to Dionysius' Greek readers, and I doubt a Roman leader, even and especially a corrupt one, would have taken him very seriously. Even if (which to me seems far-fetched) Dionysius employed his panoramic and ambitious twenty books of Roman antiquities to send a subtle admonition to the decadent elements of the Roman ruling class in his time, this does not impinge on his optimism, expressed in various ways throughout the work, beginning with the first pages, that future of Rome's empire was contiguous with the future of humanity.

The supreme Greek vice which the early Romans were able to overcome was *stasis*, which Dionysius says had brought down the Diadochi.[45] In *Roman Antiquities* 7.66, he says that it was important to record all the speeches given in his account of the first secession of the plebs – a true *stasis* – since by rhetoric the Romans were able to avoid violence in their internal conflict; that is, reason and persuasion won out over violence and preserved the Republic. Dionysius criticizes other historians for leaving out speeches from accounts of *stasis*, not recognizing their importance in the historical developments. Before that, in 7.54–6, in Valerius Maximus' famous speech, Rome's constitution had been presented as a most perfect system, so that by its very nature it prevents the outbreak of *stasis* among the different elements of Rome's society. Gabba has called this "probably the single most complete theoretical programme for the mixed constitution as applied to the Roman republic."[46] It is important to note that in attributing the defeat of *stasis* to the Roman constitution, Dionysius is referencing Polybius while removing all the ambiguity Polybius showed in applying the theory to Rome.

The biggest problem with Dionysius' apparently optimistic treatment of Roman *stasis* in its early formative period is the brutal civil wars that many of the first readers of the *Roman Antiquities* had experienced. Here, the absence of clear information on Dionysius' view of Augustus is felt: Did the historian see the Princeps as a benevolent monarch who imposed order and restored Rome to itself, thus overcoming *stasis*? Or as one who really, as Augustus presented himself, restored the Republic? The only mention of Augustus in the surviving portions of the *Roman Antiquities* is at 1.7.2, where he discloses that he arrived in Italy "at the very time that Augustus Caesar put an end to the civil war," which could reflect Augustus' boast of the same, but does not unequivocally present it as an accomplishment, just a chronological reference point.[47] The mere mention of the solution of

---

[45] On what follows, see Schultze 1986: 121–41 at 131–3.   [46] Gabba 1991: 205.
[47] τῷ καταλυθῆναι τὸν ἐμφύλιον πόλεμον ὑπὸ τοῦ Σεβαστοῦ Καίσαρος, cf. Res Gestae 34.1: *bella civilia exstinxeram.*

civil conflict by a stable government is consistent with the presentation of *staseis* in the Republic which ended with "a positive development"[48]; the Roman constitution, on its face, was saved, and the Empire, without equivocation, was preserved. Thus the bland reference to Augustus can be construed as a continuation of the pattern of Romans preserving their state and their power after *stasis*, in direct contrast to the conclusion of almost all Greek *staseis* and to the prediction of the *stasis* model in Thucydides, which Dionysius quotes with a certain level of understanding and perception.[49]

Still, the precautionary tone in Dionysius' text is felt when the topic of civil war emerges. Now it is true that references to the civil wars after G. Gracchus (to whose tribunate Dionysius dates the beginning of the brutal civil wars ending the Republic) are scattered throughout the work, but as Gabba has remarked, they are "marginal and are never developed in Dionysius' historiography."[50] Yet they are there nonetheless, and Dionysius knew that at least his first readers, who had experienced or witnessed the last brutal episodes of those wars, would feel a jolt at every mention, as well as the strongly implied – but never explicitly stated – contrast with the *concordia* that Dionysius consistently attributes to the earlier, successful generations of Roman imperialists, as one of their most important qualities. Moreover, resonance with recent events, and attendant worries about the Roman character, would have been felt in Dionysius' preference for a particularly troubling version of the story of Romulus' murder of his brother as the foundational act of the city of Rome. He describes that first *stasis* in terms which would strongly recall the recent civil wars of the extinct Republic,[51] leading Wiseman to observe: "Conspicuously in Dionysius, less prominently in Plutarch, the theme of discord, rivalry and selfish ambition presents the twins as an aition for the origins of political strife in Rome."[52] Dionysius reflects, if faintly, what some authors at the end of the Republic felt to be "a congenital defect of Rome."[53] This is a topic that requires more detailed discussion than is possible here; I raise it only as a *possible* hedge to Dionysius' otherwise very clear statements.

---

[48] Schultze 1986: 132.   [49] See Pelling 2010: 105–18 at 112–15.   [50] Gabba 1991: 153.
[51] 1.85.4–5: ... αἴτιον δὲ τοῦ μεγίστου κακοῦ, στάσεως, ἐγένετο. οἵ τε γὰρ προσνεμηθέντες αὐτοῖς τὸν ἑαυτῶν ἡγεμόνα ἕκαστοι κυδαίνοντες ὡς ἐπιτήδειον ἁπάντων ἄρχειν ἐπῆρον, αὐτοί τε οὐκέτι μίαν γνώμην ἔχοντες οὐδὲ ἀδελφὰ διανοεῖσθαι ἀξιοῦντες, ὡς αὐτὸς ἄρξων ἑκάτερος θατέρου, παρωσαντες τὸ ἴσον τοῦ πλείονος ὠρέγοντο.
[52] Wiseman 1995: 143.   [53] Breed, Damon and Rossi 2010: 9.

Yet all this does not amount to a systematic warning or admonishment to the present generation, or a pessimistic conclusion that Rome had degenerated irrevocably from its heroic days. Such views or messages cannot – so far as I can tell – be found in the *Roman Antiquities* or any text Dionysius has left us. As Gabba wrote, Dionysius "reproached Rome for her most recent history, while offering an example for the future."[54]

In a later epoch of Rome's history, during the third dynasty of Roman emperors, Appian of Alexandria decided to write a sort of universal history of the Roman Empire in an unusual – but not completely unprecedented – way, by ethnic division. The result was a Roman History in twenty-four books. I have written about Appian's plan and vision before, and shall add only a few key points to that previous study.[55] Appian opens not with a programmatic statement but a geographical survey of the entire Empire, after which he reaches the standard and necessary conclusions that Rome has reached an unprecedented pinnacle of achievement. Yet this standard assertion evokes the standard proof used by the Greek historians before him, viz. the model of four previous empires, with Rome's as the fifth having surpassed them all: "No government down to the present time ever attained to such size and duration"[56] (Praef. 29–42). In his case, his use of the model to the exclusion of his native Egypt is particularly poignant.

Appian, too, claims to have a unique perspective and method. He justifies the ethnographic, non-linear arrangement of his history as a way "to compare the Roman virtue in all its aspects with that of every other nation," in order to grasp "the weakness of these nations or their power of endurance, as well as the virtue or good fortune of their conquerors or any other circumstance contributing to the result" (Praef. 46, 48–9). This unusual way of demonstrating the range and versatility of the Romans' virtues as conquerors sets up a deliberate contrast with the Greeks in particular and other previous imperialists in general. Thus, addressing his Greek readers first (with their lingering resentment even in the second century CE!), he dismisses, in the manner of Polybius and Dionysius, the very comparability of Greek empires, which are not part of the standard model because they largely consisted of hegemony over other Greeks, they failed in foreign ventures, and were neither extensive nor durable; the Greek mastery of parts of Asia is hardly worth mentioning, because of its ease and simplicity.

---

[54] Cf. Gabba 1991: 204–12.
[55] See my article, Price 2015: 45–63. On the future in Appian see now Pitcher 2016: 281–92.
[56] Translations of Appian based on the translation by H. White in the Loeb edition of Appian's works.

The first three empires in the standard model are then efficiently lumped together: the longevity of the Assyrians, Medes, and Persians, taken together, do not total the duration of Rome's long life and rise to world domination, nor did they collectively cover as much territory – the Roman Empire essentially encompassing all the known world worth conquering: "They possess the best part of the earth and sea," and their "boundary is the ocean both where the sun-god rises and where he sinks, while they control the entire Mediterranean, and all its islands as well as Britain in the ocean" (Praef, 26, 35–6). Finally, the last empire worth comparing to Rome was as usual Alexander's, which is subject to the usual critique: "The empire of Alexander was splendid in its magnitude, in its armies, in the success and rapidity of his conquests, and it wanted little of being boundless and unexampled, yet in its shortness of duration it was like a brilliant flash of lightning" (Praef. 38), for it quickly broke apart into smaller empires, which in turn were constantly plagued by empire-destroying *stasis*, as Appian notes in a significant gnomic statement (Praef. 42): "Yet all these resources were wasted under their successors by warring with each other. By means of such civil dissensions alone are great states destroyed."[57]

Appian's purpose, both in ethnographic arrangement and in historical comparison of previous empires, is to highlight the reason for the Romans' success. Their virtues are revealed as stated in their fullness only by comparison with each of the conquered peoples and nations, in which the Romans demonstrated different aspects of their virtue. The overall Roman achievement demonstrates their general character: "Through prudence and good fortune has the empire of the Romans attained to greatness and duration in gaining which they have excelled all others in bravery, patience, and hard labor. They were never elated by success until they had firmly secured their power."[58] As we know from Appian's predecessors, the Greeks were keenly aware of the Romans' capacity for hard work, unflinching bravery, and unbreakable persistence, and this perception of the Roman character became part of the standard explanation of Rome's empire – even if the Greeks did not always see these Roman virtues as completely civilized.

---

[57] ἀλλὰ πάντα ἐς τοὺς ἐπιγόνους αὐτῶν συνετρίφθη, φθαρέντας ἐς ἀλλήλους, ᾧ μόνως ἀρχαὶ μεγάλαι καταλύονται, στασιάσασαι.

[58] τὰ δὲ Ῥωμαίων μεγέθει τε καὶ χρόνῳ διήνεγκε δι' εὐβουλίαν καὶ εὐτυχίαν ἔς τε τὴν περίκτησιν αὐτῶν ἀρετῇ καὶ φερεπονίᾳ καὶ ταλαιπωρίᾳ πάντας ὑπερῆραν, οὔτε ταῖς εὐπραγίαις ἐπαιρόμενοι, μέχρι βεβαίως ἐκράτησαν, Praef. 43, cf. also 44: τὴν ἀρχὴν ἐς τόδε προήγαγον καὶ τῆς εὐτυχίας ὤναντο διὰ τὴν εὐβουλίαν.

5. The Future of Rome in Three Greek Historians

Like Dionysius, Appian refers to *stasis* as the main cause of the Greeks' failure and as the cause of the failure of all great empires. It may be asked whether his gnomic statement about empire-destroying *stasis* contains a veiled warning to Appian's Roman patrons. It can be read to mean either that all great states are inevitably destroyed by *stasis*, or more likely, that great states, when they fall, are always destroyed by *stasis*. Rome was the great state still standing, with the greatest extent and longest history, in Appian's time. The question was whether it, too, would be destroyed by *stasis*.

On that question, we must settle with an even more equivocal answer than that offered for Dionysius. For whereas Dinoysius all but ignored the Roman civil wars at the end of the Republic, Appian broke from his ethnographic scheme of his universal history to write five books about them. He could very well have mentioned the civil wars of 68–69 CE in the lost books, but their contents are obscure.[59] As I have previously suggested, Appian appended such an extended treatment of the Roman *stasis* to his panoramic history in order to explain how, contrary to the prevailing Thucydidean theory of *stasis*, the Roman conflict did not entirely destroy or transform the entity in which it took place, namely the Roman Empire, but in fact preserved and even strengthened it. That is, the Roman Republic was surely and thoroughly ruined, but, contrary to all ability to predict by historical theory and precedent, the Roman Empire was not only not destroyed by the Roman civil war, but emerged stronger and was even expanded by the stable monarchy that followed. In this unique way – in addition to the extent and duration of the Roman Empire – Rome appeared to break precedent and even defy Thucydides' *stasis* model and previous patterns of history.

Thus, in regard to the main question here: if the Roman Empire has survived *stasis*, "by which alone great empires are destroyed," and emerged from internal conflict with a stable system to maintain the Empire, then Rome, according to Appian, may have solved the problem "by which great states are destroyed."[60]

Appian writes with little nuance and no subterfuge. He openly expresses confidence in Rome's continuing strength and domination; it had survived *stasis* by becoming stronger than before. Rome's endurance was a theme in his century. Aelius Aristides in fact invoked the 4+1 model to convey his

---

[59] See Osgood 2015: 23–44.
[60] Weissenberger 2002: 262–81, from very different arguments, also concluded that Appian believed that the Roman Empire was "das Ende der Geschichte."

hope that Rome would be the last empire in history: "History records five empires, and may their numbers not increase."[61] Plutarch suggested that Rome, unlike all previous political entities, may have defeated Fortune herself.[62] Yet doubt lingers: Were *five books*, more than a fifth of the entire composition, really necessary to make the point of Rome's endurance – especially when those books are filled with ever more hideous examples of "the measureless ambition of men, their dreadful lust of power . . . "? The Romans had overcome internal division – but through military means; the second-century reader may have wondered whether the Romans had overcome innate human tendencies as well. The historian does not say.

5.3 Conclusion

All three historians discussed here were impressed by Rome's empire, claimed historiographical innovation, offered an explanation for Rome's achievement, and used the 4+1 model in their explanation. Polybius, while beginning his panoramic *History* with the belief that Rome had broken historical precedents to enable it to last forever, seems to have changed that view and come to believe that Rome in fact was as subject to the laws of nature and history as any other state, its end was foreseeable, its eventual fall inevitable. That is all Polybius' understanding of history required: it was not possible or necessary to predict what would come after Rome. The 4+1 model was not for him the end of history; there would be a sixth dominant empire, then a seventh, and so forth.

By contrast, Dionysius and Appian used the 4+1 topos not as vehicle for critique of Rome's power, but as a formalized tool of explanation, judgment, and justification (to a still-resentful Greek audience, apparently), reaching the apparent conclusion that Rome had no foreseeable end; its future *seemed* open-ended, its accomplishment lasting. Neither was responding, in all likelihood, to the Roman idea of *Roma Aeterna*, which was rather weakly purveyed in the Late Republic and Principate. Neither made a definitive statement to that effect, however; there are faint but real reasons in each text for nuance or doubt that Rome had overcome the problem most fatal to states: *stasis*.

It would be facile to offer here any causative or determinisitic explanation for the differences between Polybius, who lived in a dynamic and contentious time in Rome's history, and the later Greek historians who

---

[61] Aelius Aristides, *Panathenaic Oration* 234 (183–4).
[62] *On the Fortune of the Romans* 1, 2; see Chapter 6 by Berthelot in this volume.

enjoyed the fruits of peace under stable monarchy.[63] A full explanation would have to take into consideration not only the different periods in which the historians lived, but also their different personalities and temperaments, as well as their reactions to the historiographical literature preceding them. It should be observed nonetheless that Polybius lived in a period, at least towards the end of his life, of creeping corruption and cruelty in Rome's rule, of expanding luxury and changing morality, incipient worry about the good old Rome and Romans, and increasingly prominent internal division. Pessimism was a prominent feature of Roman literature in the late Republic. Dionysius witnessed the end of the Republic, the recovery from the civil wars and the inauguration of a new Golden Age; Octavian chose to become not Romulus but Augustus. There is nothing in Dionysius really to contradict this central message, nor should anything like this be expected to be found. By the time Appian wrote history, the Roman monarchy was a long-established fact. It had emerged strong and stable after a brief episode of *stasis* between the first and second dynasties. The Roman Empire appeared to be as strong and enduring as ever before. Appian did perhaps leave subtle hints about the possibility of Rome's collapse from within, but he was not explicit about it, and no external power in his time threatened Rome's dominance in the Mediterranean. Appian's use of the 4+1 model in the Preface to his universal history seems uncompromised and unconditioned, confidently resting on the proof of history, more so than his predecessors. Rome's empire superseded and exceeded the four previous ones, and no end was in sight.

In contrast to the apocalyptic visionaries of the time, neither Dionysius nor Appian seem to think that the end of Rome, if it ever came, would be good for the world. Only one Greek historian of the first century CE clearly believed in Rome's eventual, inevitable demise. That was Josephus, who was in the grip of Biblical prophecy whose truth he could not doubt.

---

[63] Weissenberger 2002: "Das allgemeine historischpolitische Umfeld bestimmt am stärksten alle drei Gestaltungen des Themas: bei Polybios Roms rapide, unwiderstehliche Expansion, bei Dionysios die sowohl reale als auch propagandistisch überhöhte *pax Augusta*, bei Appian die Politik der Defensive und Stabilität, an der seit Hadrian im wesentlichen festgehalten wurde."

CHAPTER 6

Philo on the Impermanence of Empires

Katell Berthelot

Reflections on empires among ancient writers can take different directions. Some focus on the succession of specific empires and speculate about the number of empires destined to rule the world, as does the author of the Book of Daniel, for example.[1] Such writers are in various ways concerned with history and how it continues from the past, through the present, and into the future. In some cases, this leads them to speculate about the end of time.[2] Other authors are interested in comparing the empires of the past to the one(s) of their own day. In the Roman period, for example, many orators praise the Romans for establishing an empire that has surpassed all others. This type of comparison is not restricted to orations and can be found in various literary genres. Finally, there are writers who are prone to more philosophical reflections on empires and what causes their rise or decline, their intrinsic instability, or the political factors that help certain ones endure.

All these questions may be asked by a single author, though one generally expects a particular problem to dominate the work of any individual. Here, I shall examine whether and how these three lines of thought are present in Philo's work, starting in each case with a brief survey of discourses by ancient Greek writers such as Demetrius of Phalerum, Polybius, Dionysius of Harlicarnassus, Plutarch, Appian, and Aelius Aristides, albeit the last three were active only after Philo's death and, in the case of Appian and Aelius, extend into the second half of the second century CE. I shall then compare their discourses with that of Philo, in

---

[1] See Dn 2:31–35, 39–43. The ambiguity of this text allows for at least two interpretations: four or five empires could be alluded to. In a dream, the king sees a statue made of gold, silver, brass, iron, and a mixture of iron and clay, and Daniel interprets these materials as different kingdoms. The mixture of iron and clay could be interpreted as being a sub-part of the iron part, or as a distinct part and thus as a distinct kingdom.

[2] See Chapter 9 by Vered Noam in this volume.

6. Philo on the Impermanence of Empires

order to better appreciate the specificity of Philo's thought on empires and its implications for his understanding of the future of Rome.

6.1 Philo and the Greek Scheme of the Succession of Four or Five Empires

6.1.1 From Herodotus to Appian

By the fifth century, Greek historians such as Herodotus had developed a particular historical model that spoke of the succession of three different empires: that of the Assyrians, the Medes, and the Persians. In the wake of Alexander's conquests, the Macedonian Empire was added as the fourth great entity to the model. Later, when Rome overcame the Hellenistic kingdoms, it began appearing as the fifth great empire on the list.[3]

However, when referring to past empires and the way in which they succeeded one another, Greek writers did not necessarily follow the above order in every detail. Thus, at the beginning of his *Histories*, when discussing the ancient empires that bear comparison to Rome, Polybius refers to the Persians, the Macedonians, and the Lacedemonians (despite the fact that their dominion was limited to Greece), but not to the Assyrians or the Medes (*Histories* 1.2.1–6). By contrast, when Dionysius of Halicarnassus similarly justifies his choice of topic – Roman history – by comparing Rome to previous empires, he follows the classical model of the four empires (*Roman Antiquities* 1.2.1–4), while commenting on the hegemony of Athens, Sparta, and Thebes separately so as to emphasize that the comparison is not really relevant in their case (1.3.1–2).[4] At the beginning of his *Roman History*, Appian likewise compares Rome to the ancient empires. First, he examines those of the ancient Greek states (Athens, Sparta, etc.), then those of the Assyrians, the Medes, the Persians, and the Macedonians (§8). Lastly, when Aelius Aristides compares Rome to its predecessors, he basically follows the traditional model by stating:

---

[3] See Chapter 5 by Jonathan Price in this volume. Whether Greek and Roman authors considered Rome a fifth and everlasting empire in as early as the second century BCE, as a fragment of Aemilius Sura may attest, is debated. See Swain 1940, Mendels 1981 (according to whom, the *topos* of Rome as the fifth empire became commonplace in Rome only in the second half of the first century BCE), and Alonso-Núñez 1989, who maintains that Aemilius Sura saw Rome as the fifth empire: "From the fragment of Sura we can deduce that one aim, maybe the most important, of his work *De annis populi Romani* was to glorify Rome's achievement in its expansive policy in the Mediterranean area *and perhaps to predict for her an everlasting rule*, though we have no elements in the fragment that allow us to state this plainly" (emphasis mine).

[4] For a different interpretation of this particular passage, see Jonathan Price's chapter in this volume.

"Macedonians had a period of enslavement to Persians, Persians to Medes, Medes to Assyrians" (§91). Thus, even if not adhered to in a systematic manner, in every detail, or referred to in only a cursory way, the model of the four empires (preceding Rome) is a recurring pattern among Greek authors reflecting on the Roman Empire.[5]

6.1.2 Philo's Personal Use of the Greek Model

The first thing one needs to recall is that Philo never refers to the Book of Daniel, a point that strongly distinguishes him from Josephus.[6] The scheme of the four or five empires found in Daniel 2 (in which the Assyrians are replaced by the Babylonians) therefore plays no role in his work.[7] On the contrary, Philo refers to the great empires that preceded Rome in a way that recalls what can be found in Greek works.

Nonetheless, Philo does not merely repeat Greek *topoi*. He has his own perspective and selects only certain examples, while also adding new ones that are not usually found in the writings of Greek authors. In *De Iosepho* 134–136, for instance, he starts with the example of Egypt's past glory, and probably has Pharaonic Egypt in mind as he speaks separately of the Macedonian kingdoms. Moreover, when tackling the case of the Macedonians, he singles out the Ptolemies as those who ruled over Egypt.[8] This kind of "Egypt-centered" perspective appears again in *Deus* 175, another text that deals with the succession of empires, and one that shows that Philo was influenced by the place in which he lived. None of the Greek writers mentioned ever refer to Egypt as one of the important empires of the past, but instead remain faithful to the more "Eastern" perspective initiated by Herodotus. In *Deus* 174, we find another example of Philo's independence vis-à-vis the conventional Greek list of empires; here he evokes the past glory of Carthage (alluding to the Phoenician

---

[5] It is also found in the works of Roman historians, possibly in Aemilius Sura's *De annis populi Romani* in the second century BCE (see n. 3), and as early as the first century BCE in the work of Pompeius Trogus, if the *Epitoma* of Justin can be trusted.

[6] See Biblia Patristica 1982. Although Philo's works consist merely of commentaries of the Pentateuch, they do quote from the prophetical books of the Hebrew Bible, but only in passing. On Josephus' understanding of Daniel's vision of the statue representing different empires, see Chapter 8 by Jonathan Davies in this volume.

[7] The model of the four empires is considered of Oriental origin (see Gruen 1984: 315–16 and 328–29), though Arnaldo Momigliano claimed that the author of Daniel derived the idea from the Greeks. See Momigliano 1984.

[8] *Ios.* 136: "Where is the house of the Ptolemies, and the fame of the several successors (of Alexander) whose light once shone to the utmost boundaries of land and sea? ... " (transl. Colson, Loeb Classical Library (LCL), 205).

control of the Mediterranean), thereby pointing to the contemporary domination of Rome, which caused Carthage's power to vanish. His reference to Carthage obviously has to do with his Roman context. However, he does not really single out Carthage despite its having been the great enemy of Rome, but rather mentions it together with Ethiopia, Libya, and the kingdom of Pontus, etc. Philo's combined references to Egypt, Carthage, Libya, and Ethiopia may have to do with his "African" context.

It must be emphasized that Philo never mentions the Assyrians or the Medes, and thus never resorts to the Greek model of the four empires as such. Going one step further, one may state that Philo is concerned neither with the way(s) in which empires succeed each other from a historical point of view nor with the details of their political history. As we shall see, he is interested in past empires (be they Egypt, Persia, or the Macedonian kingdoms) merely as examples of a past glory that has gradually faded, sometimes in brutal fashion. Even more fundamentally, he turns to them for examples of the fact that human and terrestrial realities have no intrinsic permanence. The fact that the Persians historically preceded the Greeks is of no significance to him. Similarly, Philo does not reflect on the role that Persia or the Macedonian kingdoms played in the history of Israel.

Finally, insofar as Rome is concerned, Philo refers to the fall of the Hellenistic kingdoms several times without mentioning the Roman Empire by name, but merely alluding to its existence.[9] Nowhere does Philo speculate about Rome being the fourth or the fifth empire, or affirm or suggest that it is supposed to be the last one in human history.

6.2 Philo and the Comparisons of Different Empires

6.2.1 From Polybius to Aelius Aristides

From Polybius onward, the chief reason for Greek writers' references to the great empires of the past seems to have lain in their need to compare these to Rome, to indulge in a kind of comparative "imperiology" dominated by the claim that this latest empire was of a superior kind, hitherto unseen in world history. An important recurrent element in all their comparisons of it to earlier empires is the emphasis they lay on the exceptional extent of the

---

[9] See *Quaest. Gen.* 4.43; *Deus* 173; *Ios.* 134–136, and the analysis in §6.3, as well as Berthelot 2011, in which I show that Philo did not agree with the discourse that celebrated the eternity of Roman rule and saw in Rome the final, everlasting empire.

Roman Empire, from both a geographical and chronological point of view. The physical breadth of the empire seems the more striking of the two, but Greek writers generally drew a close association between its longevity and geographical scale, at least from the first century CE onward (in Polybius's time, it was obviously too early to celebrate the duration of Rome's control over the world).

Let us first look at the beginning of Polybius's *Histories*:

> How striking and grand is the spectacle presented by the period with which I intend to deal, will be most clearly apparent if we set beside and compare with the Roman dominion the most famous empires of the past, those which have formed the chief theme of historians. Those worthy of being thus set beside it and compared are these. The Persians for a certain period possessed a great rule and dominion, but so often as they ventured to overstep the boundaries of Asia they imperiled not only the security of this empire, but their own existence. The Lacedaemonians, after having for many years disputed the hegemony of Greece, at length attained it but to hold it uncontested for scarce twelve years. The Macedonian rule in Europe extended but from the Adriatic region to the Danube, which would appear a quite insignificant portion of the continent. Subsequently, by overthrowing the Persian Empire they became supreme in Asia also. But though their empire was now regarded as the greatest geographically and politically that had ever existed, they left the larger part of the inhabited world as yet outside it. For they never even made a single attempt to dispute possession of Sicily, Sardinia, or Libya, and the most warlike nations of Western Europe were, to speak the simple truth, unknown to them. But the Romans have subjected to their rule not portions, but nearly the whole of the world and possess an empire which is not only immeasurably greater than any which preceded it, but need not fear rivalry in the future.[10]

Although this passage clearly focuses on the exceptional geographical size of the Roman Empire, Polybius ends with a remark that suggests that its rule will be equally exceptional in terms of length for reasons that he explains throughout the *Histories*.

Writing during Augustus's principate, Dionysius of Halicarnassus is able to emphasize the stability of Roman rule in a new way, thus stating:

> If anyone turns his attention to the successive supremacies both of cities and of nations, as accounts of them have been handed down from times past, and then, surveying them severally and comparing them together, wishes to determine which of them obtained the widest dominion and both in peace and war performed the most brilliant achievements, he will find that the

---

[10] *Histories* 1.2.1–7 (transl. by W. R. Paton, rev. by F. W. Walbank and Christian Habicht, LCL, 5–7).

supremacy of the Romans has far surpassed all those that are recorded from earlier times, not only in the extent of its dominion (τὸ μέγεθος τῆς ἀρχῆς) and in the splendour of its achievements – which no account has as yet worthily celebrated – but also in the length of time (τὸ μῆκος τοῦ χρόνου) during which it has endured down to our day.[11]

Dionysius goes on to prove his point by examining the length and geographical extent of the empires of the Assyrians, the Medes, the Persians, and the Macedonians. He repeats his conclusion in 1.3.3–5:

But Rome rules every country that is not inaccessible or uninhabited, and she is mistress of every sea, not only of that which lies inside the Pillars of Hercules but also of the Ocean, except that part of it which is not navigable; she is the first and the only State recorded in all time that ever made the risings and the settings of the sun the boundaries of her dominion. Nor has her supremacy been of short duration, but more lasting than that of any other commonwealth or kingdom ... there is no nation, as I may say, that disputes her universal dominion or protests against being ruled by her.[12]

Later, and with even sounder reasons, Appian similarly states in his preface that "No government down to the present time ever attained to such size and duration," and that its "boundary is the ocean both where the sun-god rises and where he sinks" (§8). He thus falls back on the literary *topos* already used by Dionysius.[13]

Aelius Aristides, too, celebrates the extraordinary geographical breadth of the Roman Empire (*Roman Oration*, §28), but also introduces a qualitative element linked to the very nature of Roman rule, which he considers even more significant for a proper appreciation of its exceptional character: "Vast and comprehensive as is the size of it, your empire is much greater for its perfection than for the area which its boundaries encircle" (§29).[14] By this he means that the power of Rome is not that of a despot, that Roman rule is wholeheartedly supported by all peoples who fall under it (a point already made by Dionysius), that its subjects are free men (§36), and that the Romans rule according to nature (§91). Logically enough, in §29 Aelius goes on to state that "for the eternal duration of this empire, the whole civilized world prays all together." In §108 he adds that "to compose the oration which would equal the majesty of your empire" would "require just about as much time as time allotted to the empire, and that would be all

---

[11] *Roman Antiquities* 1.2.1, transl. by Earnest Cary, LCL, 7. On this passage see Alonso-Núñez 1983.
[12] Transl. by Earnest Cary, LCL, 11.
[13] For a more detailed analysis of the similarities and the differences between Dionysius and Appian, see Weißenberger 2002.
[14] The translation used for Aelius's *Roman Oration* is that in Oliver 1953.

eternity." Aelius therefore contemplates the possibility, at least rhetorically, that Roman rule will last forever.

Finally, one should emphasize that in §106, Aelius suggests that Hesiod was wrong to locate the golden race of men in the distant past. He points out that, in any case, the iron race ended when the Romans began ruling the *oikoumenē*, implying therefore that their empire amounts to a new Golden Age. Aelius's discourse thus recalls motifs found in the writings of Latin poets before and during Augustus's principate, which considered Augustus's rule the beginning of a new Golden Age.[15]

6.2.2 Philo's Praise of the Roman Imperial Order in the Legatio ad Gaium

In general, Philo does not refer to great former empires in order to compare them and analyze their respective achievements and failures. Although he does sometimes juxtapose the customs and norms of the Persians, Greeks, and other peoples, he does not compare empires as such, probably because in his eyes, they were all fundamentally similar in their arbitrariness and volatility.[16]

In the *Legatio ad Gaium*, however, one finds a passage with a description of the empire's geographical expanse that seemingly recalls those of the Greek authors whose works we have examined so far. In it, Philo describes the situation of the Roman Empire at the onset of Caligula's reign and celebrates the achievements of Augustus and Tiberius, with particular emphasis on the *pax Romana*. First, he notes that Caligula received "the sovereignty of the whole earth and sea" (τὴν ἡγεμονίαν πάσης γῆς καὶ θαλάσσης, §8), and then describes the empire as:

> A dominion not confined to the really vital parts which make up most of the inhabited world, and indeed may properly bear that name, a world (οἰκουμένην), that is, which is bounded by the two rivers, the Euphrates and the Rhine, the one dissevering (us) from the Germans and all the more brutish nations, the Euphrates from the Parthians and from the Sarmatians and Scythians, races which are no less savage than the Germans, but a dominion extending, as some have already said (ὡς εἶπον ἤδη), from the rising to the setting sun both within the ocean and beyond it.[17]

---

[15] The idea of an imminent Golden Age already appears in Virgil's *Fourth Eclogue*, as well as in later writings. See Chapter 2 by Brian Breed in this volume.

[16] See §6.3.

[17] *Legat.* 10, transl. F. H. Colson, LCL, 7–9, slightly modified. See also *Legat.* 143–147 and 309 for an encomium of the reign of Augustus and of the universal peace it brought about; these passages, however, entail no comparison with previous empires.

6. Philo on the Impermanence of Empires

Philo seems to fully agree with the view that the world that deserves to be called *oikoumenē* – the civilized world – stops at the Rhine and the Euphrates, beyond which only savage barbarians live. He thus equates the civilized world with the Roman Empire.[18] By mentioning the Euphrates and the Rhine, the Germans and the Parthians, Philo refers to the boundaries of the Empire, which somehow undermines his later claim that the empire extends "from the rising to the setting sun both within the ocean and beyond it." As we have seen with the writings of Dionysius, this statement is actually a *topos*, as Philo himself admits with the words ὡς εἶπον ἤδη ("as some have already said").[19]

In the paragraphs that follow, Philo describes the first seven months of Caligula's reign and the universal joy that prevailed during this period and then compares them to the age of Saturn:

> In these days the rich had no precedence over the poor, nor the distinguished over the obscure, creditors were not above debtors, nor masters above slaves, the times giving equality before the law. Indeed, the life under Saturn, pictured by the poets, no longer appeared to be a fabled story, so great was the prosperity and well-being, the freedom from grief and fear, the joy which pervaded households and people. (*Legatio ad Gaium* 13)

By comparing the beginning of Caligula's reign to the age of Saturn, i.e., to the Golden Age, Philo repeats ideas that had been in the air during Augustus's principate, and that would still be echoed in Aelius Aristides's *Roman Oration*.[20]

In short, this passage shows Philo reproducing a conventional discourse. Nonetheless, his reference to both the Germans and the Parthians, the chief threats to the Roman Empire, may be interpreted in at least two ways; not only is he emphasizing that the Empire encompasses the entire civilized world (the obvious meaning of his text), but he is also astutely pointing out the real limits of Roman rule despite claiming that these coincide with the entire world. We shall see that other references to the Parthians in Philo's work seem to entail a similar underlying message on the limits of Roman

---

[18] Hadas-Lebel 2012 : 63 concludes thus: "Philon, Juif de la Diaspora, n'a pas d'aspirations nationalistes ; dans sa cité d'Alexandrie, il se sent partie intégrante du grand Empire romain étendu aux dimensions de l'univers." For a different view, see Berthelot 2011.
[19] On this passage, see Niehoff 2001: 113–18, who notes that "Philo's assumption of literally universal and unchallenged Roman dominion reflects imperial ideology" and that in his *Res Gestae*, Augustus had "elegantly passed over the fact that the Germans and Parthians had not been truly conquered" (*Philo*, 114; see *Res Gestae* 3:1, 6:1, 8:5, 26:3–4, 32:2, 34:1). On the idea of the *Urbs* as *orbis terrarum*, see Ovid, *Fasti* 2:684.
[20] See n. 14.

hegemony, not only in terms of geographical extent, but also in terms of duration.[21]

6.3 Philo's Philosophical Reflections on Empires and Their Implications for the Future of Rome

6.3.1 The Debate on the Instability of Empires and the Role of Fortune

Written at the beginning of the Hellenistic period, Demetrius of Phalerum's philosophical work *On Fortune* includes a passage on the instability of empires, which is quoted with approval by several later authors, such as Polybius and Diodorus. In a passage in Polybius (*Histories* 29.21), Demetrius argues that Fortune (*Tychē*) is a free agent, who has "show[n] all people, by establishing the Macedonians in the prosperity that used to be the Persians', that it has lent these blessings to them as well until it arrives at a different decision concerning them."[22] Demetrius thus states that both Persian and Macedonian rule were gifts of Fortune, and that both had therefore been intrinsically unstable insofar as Fortune's decisions are always changing. Reflecting on Demetrius's statement, Polybius claims that it was, in fact, a prophetic utterance proven true by the Roman defeat of Perseus, king of Macedonia, at Pydna in 168 BCE.

Polybius thus seems to share Demetrius's perspective on the role played by Fortune in the growth and decline of empires. As far as Rome is concerned, however, Polybius's discourse is complex and ambiguous. In some passages of the *Histories* he seems to attribute the successes of Rome at least in part to Fortune, whereas in other passages he clearly emphasizes other factors, such as Rome's political institutions and the extraordinary discipline of its military.[23] Towards the end of his life, he did in fact predict

---

[21] The *Legatio* itself contains only one more reference to the Parthians, who Caligula himself describes as ruling the peoples of the East. See *Legat.* 256 (in Caius's letter to Petronius): "You concern yourself with the institutions of the Jews, the nation which is my worst enemy; you disregard the imperial commands of your sovereign. You feared their great numbers. Then had you not with you the military forces which are feared by the nations of the east and their rulers the Parthians (καὶ ἡγεμόνες αὐτῶν Παρθυαῖοι)?" (transl. F. H. Colson, LCL, 131–133).

[22] See Fortenbaugh and Schütrumpf 2000: 149 (n°82A). See also Diodorus Siculus, *Historical Library* 31.10.

[23] On this issue in Polybius, see in particular Ferrary 1988 : 265–76, esp. 271: "A ceux qui attribuaient à la Fortune l'extraordinaire succès des Romains, Polybe n'opposait pas l'idée d'un empire éternel voulu par le Destin : il montrait que les Romains avaient méthodiquement réalisé un projet raisonnable bien que sans précédent, car fondé sur une juste estimation de leurs possibilités." On Polybius and the rise of Rome, see also Walbank 1957–79: vol. 1, 16–26; Walbank 1972: 157–83; Walbank 1974: 1–38; Walbank 2002: 243–92; Pédech 1964: 331–54; Eckstein 1995: 194–236; and Guelfucci 2010. Walbank, Pédech, and Eckstein maintain that for Polybius, *Tychē*, along with other

6. Philo on the Impermanence of Empires

the decline of Rome, but connected it to social, political, and moral factors rather than to the changing will of Fortune.

If an author admits that Fortune played a role in the rise of the Roman Empire, does this mean that he also believes that it will pass away just as its predecessors did? Some Greek authors who were critical of Roman imperialism clearly express this view and are censured by Dionysius of Halicarnassus for doing so.[24] According to Dionysius, Roman successes have been due not to mere Fortune, but rather to divine providence (*pronoia*). This view makes it possible for him to claim outstanding longevity for Rome in contrast to the decline and decay experienced by earlier empires.

Plutarch is another interesting Greek voice in this debate. In his treatise *On the Fortune of the Romans*, he wonders whether it is Virtue (*Aretē*) or Fortune (*Tychē*) who is the main cause of Rome's achievements. On the ethical level, *Tychē* symbolizes the elements or circumstances faced by the moral agent, which he or she cannot influence, whereas *Aretē* represents the inner disposition of the individual that depends on him or herself.[25] In Plutarch's work, both *Tychē* and *Aretē*, in fact, enhance Rome's superiority. In §1, Plutarch already asks:

> Who, then, will not declare, when Rome shall have been added to the achievements of one of the contestants, either that Virtue is a most profitable thing if she has done such good to good men, or that Good Fortune is a thing most steadfast if she has already preserved for so long a time that which she has bestowed?[26]

In other words, due to Rome's lasting dominion over the *oikoumenē*, the argument that Roman successes are a gift of Fortune necessarily entails that she is not as unstable and uncertain as generally argued. It thus means that Fortune can be recognized as playing a role in the ascent of Rome without being loaded with the usual pejorative connotations associated with *Tychē*. Moreover, Plutarch actually affirms that in the case of Rome, Fortune and Virtue have joined forces:

---

factors, played a major role in the ascension and supremacy of Rome – not as mere chance but as a teleologically oriented force. Polybius's references to *Tychē*'s role are not entirely consistent with his rational explanation of Rome's rise. See also Jonathan Price's Chapter 5 in the present volume, where he argues that *Tychē* changes from a guiding to an irrational force in Polybius as the Greek historian changes his mind about Rome.

[24] See *Rom. Hist.* 1.4.2.   [25] See Frazier 2010: III–XXIII, esp. XIV.
[26] Transl. by Frank Cole Babbitt, LCL, 323.

> Even as Plato asserts that the entire universe arose from fire and earth as the first and necessary elements, that it might become visible and tangible, earth contributing to it weight and stability, and fire contributing colour, form, and movement; but the medial elements, water and air, by softening and quenching the dissimilarity of both extremes, united them and brought about the composite nature of Matter through them; in this way, then, in my opinion, did time lay the foundation for the Roman State and, with the help of God (μετὰ θεοῦ), so combine and join together Fortune and Virtue that, by taking the peculiar qualities of each, he might construct for all mankind a Hearth, in truth both holy and beneficent (τὸ οἰκεῖον ἀπεργάσηται πᾶσιν ἀνθρώποις ἑστίαν ἱερὰν ὡς ἀληθῶς καὶ ἀνησιδώραν), a steadfast cable, a principle abiding for ever, 'an anchorage from the swell and drift,' as Democritus says, amid the shifting conditions of human affairs.[27]

Thus, in Plutarch's opinion, the foundation of Rome and the extent of its domination do not lack a providential dimension (μετὰ θεοῦ). It is true that in §1, Plutarch wonders whether the city of Rome owes its existence to the work of *Tychē* or *Pronoia*, which reminds us of the debate in which Dionysius of Halicarnassus was involved. However, the first paragraph makes it unclear whether Plutarch's question reflects his concern for the stability of the Roman Empire, or is simply one of terminology.[28] In any case, §2 shows that Plutarch viewed Rome's fate as being at least in part the result of a divine scheme, and the Roman state as something particularly stable.[29]

Later, in §4, Plutarch describes Fortune's actions and her particular relationship with Rome as follows:

> Fortune, when she had deserted the Persians and Assyrians, had flitted lightly over Macedonia, and had quickly shaken off Alexander, made her way through Egypt and Syria, conveying kingships here and there; and turning about, she would often exalt the Carthaginians. But when she was approaching the Palatine and crossing the Tiber, it appears that she took off her wings, stepped out of her sandals, and abandoned her untrustworthy

---

[27] *On the Fortune of the Romans* 2, transl. by Frank Cole Babbitt, LCL, 326.

[28] In a different yet similar way, when Livy writes about the difficult beginnings of Roman history, he mentions Fate as a determining factor in the development of the empire, with no negative connotation: "But Fate (*fatum*) was resolved, I suppose, upon the founding of this great city, and the beginning of the mightiest of empires, next after that of the gods" (*Rom. Hist.* 1.4.1; transl. B. O. Foster, LCL, 17). Here, Fate is more or less equivalent to divine providence.

[29] Swain 1989 argues that Plutarch sees divine providence as being involved in Roman history: "Plutarch did not simply muddle what happened with what was destined to happen. The present order and good government of the world was pleasing to the divine in his eyes, and indeed divine interest was obvious in the natural world around him also" (276). Babut 1969 is more cautious in his assessment of the role that Plutarch assigns to providence in history.

6. Philo on the Impermanence of Empires

and unstable globe. Thus did she enter Rome, as with intent to abide, and in such guise is she present to-day, as though ready to meet her trial.[30]

Plutarch builds on the scheme of the succession of empires to create a personal version that does not merely mention the Macedonians, but refers specifically to the Ptolemies and the Seleucids as well as the Carthaginians, the former enemies of Rome,[31] in order to show that Fortune has established a different relationship with Rome, a city in which she seems willing to abide permanently.

All in all, by discussing the respective roles of *Aretē* and *Tychē* in the rise of Rome, Plutarch does not mean to undermine Roman successes or suggest that the Roman Empire will disappear as its predecessors did. On the contrary, Rome enjoys a very special relationship with *Tychē* that thus leaves open the possibility of long-lasting stability. At least, this is the point of view reflected in Plutarch's *On the Fortune of the Romans*, which may have been a scholarly exercise meant to facilitate his integration into Roman society.[32] As Françoise Frazier rightly notes, this work is probably insufficient to credit Plutarch with a real "philosophy of history."[33]

6.3.2 Philo's Position in the Debate

Unlike Plutarch, Philo sees Fortune as something consistently negative; contrary to *pronoia*, it cannot be considered an expression of God's will,[34] God's blessing or God's punishment,[35] even if it does not represent an independent power at work in the universe, insofar as God controls everything. Nowhere does Philo say that God's providence (*pronoia*) is at work in the Roman Empire, or that the Empire enjoys divine support. Yet, he also never explicitly affirms that the Romans rule the world thanks to a fickle and unfair Fortune. However, at the very beginning of the *Legatio* – a work in which he deals with the threats against the Jews and the Temple of Jerusalem under Caligula, as well as with providential salvation – he shares some general thoughts on *Tychē*, and elsewhere (*Legat.* 284), has Agrippa speak about Caligula's destiny and power in terms of *Tychē*.

---

[30] *On the Fortune of the Romans* 4, transl. by Frank Cole Babbitt, LCL, 332.
[31] In their reflections on fallen empires of the past, Philo and Plutarch both mention the Ptolemies, the Seleucids, and the Carthaginians, but nowhere does Philo speak about Fortune in positive terms or state that Fortune or Providence shall remain on Rome's side. See §6.3.2.
[32] See Frank Cole Babbitt, LCL, 320. [33] See Frazier 2010: XIX. [34] See *Spec.* 2.231.
[35] It seems that in this respect Philo differs from Josephus, for whom Fortune can sometimes be an expression of God's will. There is one apparent exception in Philo's writings (*Deus* 176); see further discussion in this chapter.

Furthermore, Philo's work offers us at least three quite telling instances of his reflections on the instability of empires. The first example is found in the final section of the treatise on the subject "That God is immutable," *Quod deus sit immutabilis* (from §140 onward), where Philo comments on Genesis 6:12, which states that "all flesh had corrupted his way upon the earth." Philo understands "his way" as referring to God's way, which lies in wisdom. This is the way taken by Israel, who leaves behind all the worldly goods that correspond to the kingdom of Edom and are unreal. To the earthly and worthless man, symbolized by Edom, Israel (or Philo) says:

> 171 For in very truth "the matter" which has so engaged your zeal is absolutely "nothing." 172 Or do you think that aught of mortal matters has real being or subsistence, and that they do not rather swing suspended as it were on fallacious and unstable opinion, treading the void and differing not a whit from false dreams? 173 If you care not to test the fortunes of individual men, scan the vicissitudes, for better and worse, of whole regions and nations. Greece was once at its zenith, but the Macedonians took away its power. Macedonia flourished in its turn, but when it was divided into portions it weakened till it was utterly extinguished. 174 Before the Macedonians fortune smiled on the Persians, but a single day destroyed their vast and mighty empire, and now Parthians rule over Persians, the former subjects over their masters of yesterday. The breath that blew from Egypt of old was clear and strong for many a long year, yet like a cloud its great prosperity passed away. What of the Ethiopians, what of Carthage, and the parts towards Libya? What of the kings of Pontus? 175 What of Europe and Asia, and in a word the whole civilized world? Is it not tossed up and down and kept in turmoil like ships at sea, subject now to prosperous, now to adverse winds? 176 For circlewise moves [or: dances] the divine design [or: plan] which most [people] call Fortune (χορεύει γὰρ ἐν κύκλῳ λόγος ὁ θεῖος, ὃν οἱ πολλοὶ τῶν ἀνθρώπων ὀνομάζουσι τύχην). Presently in its ceaseless flux it makes distribution city by city, nation by nation, country by country. (*Deus* 171–176)[36]

In short, "mortal matters," which include glory, power, prosperity, and the like, have no intrinsic stability and are even devoid of reality; they are comparable to dreams. The fortune of nations is as unstable and fugitive as that of individuals. Prosperity will give way to adversity. For Philo, however, a divine plan lies beyond what most people call Fortune. This is an important claim, which seems to indicate that he did develop a certain theology of history. Moreover, the end of the passage may be interpreted as meaning that Rome's present rule owes its existence to the movement of

---

[36] Transl. Colson, LCL, 95–97, slightly modified.

the divine *logos*. Philo seems to think that Roman rule is not the result of mere chance, insofar as God controls everything on earth; at the same time, however, it cannot be described as a divine gift as that would imply that divine providence works on behalf of the Romans. In Philo's work, providence seems to be covenantal: it sustains the cosmos or benefits Israel, and thus corresponds to the covenant with Noah after the flood, on the one hand, and to the covenant with Israel, on the other.[37] This may explain why in this case, when referring to God's plan, Philo uses the term *logos* rather than *pronoia*.

The fact that this discourse on the instability of fortune (according to the common sense of the term, with reference to prosperity, glory etc.) is addressed to the wretched Edom raises an important question: Did "Edom," the terrestrial kingdom, symbolize Rome in Philo's eyes? The identification of Rome with Edom or Esau is only attested in Jewish sources from the late first century CE on. It appears allusively in apocalyptic writings, and later in rabbinic literature, but mostly from the fourth century CE on (despite a few occurrences in Tannaitic works).[38] It is unclear whether this identification was already common in the early first century, or present in Philo's work. There is no real way of answering this question conclusively. Still, the fact that Philo addresses his speech on the instability of empires to Edom is quite interesting, as is the fact that in accordance with the biblical narrative, he explicitly states in §180 that the divine *logos* shall stop Edom and those who follow him. According to §176, it is this divine *logos* that distributes good fortune to cities and nations.

Another passage by Philo that deals with the instability or impermanence of empires appears in *De Iosepho* 134–136, within a more general discussion on the theme of "life is a dream," to which Philo adds the idea – based on the story of Joseph – that the political man is the interpreter of dreams. Turning at one point to empires, Philo writes:

> 134 For nothing at all anywhere has remained in the same condition; everywhere all has been subject to change and vicissitudes (τροπαῖς δὲ καὶ μεταβολαῖς). 135 Egypt once held the sovereignty over many nations, but now is in slavery. The Macedonians in their day of success flourished so greatly that they held dominion over all the habitable world, but now they pay to the tax-collectors the yearly tributes imposed by their masters. 136 Where is the house of the Ptolemies, and the fame of the several successors [i.e., of Alexander] whose light once shone to the utmost

---

[37] See Berthelot 2011: 177–79.
[38] The bibliography on Rome as Esau or Edom is vast; see the seminal article Cohen 1967; and Berthelot 2016 for a recent review of the bibliography.

boundaries of land and sea? Where are the liberties of the independent nations and cities, where again the servitude of the vassals? Did not the Persians once rule the Parthians, and now the Parthians rule the Persians? So much do human affairs twist and change, go backward and forward as on the draught-board. (*De Iosepho* 134–136)[39]

In this case, Philo is not concerned about the *translatio imperii* as such, or about any kind of chronological succession of historical events. What he wants to emphasize is the impermanence of wordly realities, which, like scales, go up and down,[40] appearing and disappearing. Wisdom, he claims, lies in being aware of this intrinsic impermanence of both wordly powers and individual fortunes.[41]

Zealous to demonstrate his point, Philo lacks rigor and exaggerates the geographical extent of the Macedonian kingdoms, which never conquered Europe or North Africa (beyond Egypt) and thus could not be described as "all the habitable world" (§135). This hyperbole may have to do with the unnamed successor of these kingdoms, namely, the Roman Empire, which by contrast, was viewed as holding dominion over "all the habitable world," the *oikoumenē*, in quite an exaggerated manner even in Philo's time.[42] The rule according to which all things are subject to change and vicissitude also applies beyond the realm of Rome, to the Parthian kingdom; it is truly universal. It is also firm and stable. Thus the rule of continuous change and vicissitude is eternal. Logically enough, those, namely the Romans, who now treat Egypt as a slave (δούλη, §135) and are the present masters of the Macedonians, shall one day live under the dominion of other masters. In other words, Rome's power and glory too shall pass as did those of its predecessors.

Still, one could argue that in *De Iosepho* 134, Philo speaks about the way in which the world used to run (in the past tense) until the Romans achieved world domination, and that things are different now. In order to strengthen the interpretation proposed above, let us look at a passage in the *Quaestiones in Genesim*, which, in André-Jean Festugière's view, closely resembles Demetrius of Phalerum's *On Fortune*:[43]

---

[39] Transl. Colson, LCL, 205.
[40] Compare *Ios.* 136 with *Deus* 177–178. Munnich 2011: 176 argues that "le *Quod deus* souligne la relativité des empires, alors que le *De Josepho* insiste sur leur disparition." However, it seems to me that both emphasize the transient nature of all things, point to the disappearance of past empires, and use the image of ups and downs (ἄνω καὶ κάτω in *Ios.* 136, the image of a balance in *Ios.* 140; the image of the tide in *Deus* 177–178) to suggest that while certain things fade, others make their appearance, and that when some people go down, others go up.
[41] See *Ios.* 140 and 144 for the use of *tychē*, in the plural in this case.
[42] See Philo's *Legatio* 8–10 and §6.2.   [43] See Festugière 1949: 523–25.

> When the Persians ruled land and sea, who expected that they would fall? And again, when the Macedonians (ruled)? But if anyone had dared to say so, he would most certainly have been laughed at as a fool and a simpleton. And no less necessary a change awaits those nations that opposed them, though they have become illustrious and conspicuous in the meantime; so that those at whom (others) laughed are beginning to laugh (at them), while those who laughed are becoming (an object of) laughter for thinking that things which are by nature mobile and changeable are immobile and unalterable. (*Quaestiones in Genesim* 4.43)[44]

The Greek original of this passage is only partly preserved. The Greek word for "change" is probably *metabolē*, as similar passages confirm. That wordly goods and situations are not permanent, but subject to multiple changes, is a recurring theme in Philo's work, as we have seen.[45]

The most striking aspect of this passage lies in the fact that Philo unambiguously foretells the fall of Rome. The sentence "no less necessary a change awaits those nations that opposed them, though they have become illustrious and conspicuous in the meantime," which refers to those who overcame the Macedonians, that is, the Romans, leaves no doubt as to the latter's fate. Like the empires that preceded them, the Roman one will ultimately fall and be replaced by another power.

6.3.3 *Philo's Theological Perspective on History and the Future of Rome*

Of the three texts on the impermanence of empires, the passage in *Deus* 176 quoted above is the only one in which Philo refers to the action of the divine *logos* in history. That he had a certain "theology of history" is apparent from other passages in his work, however, and from his so-called historical treatises, *In Flaccum* and *Legatio ad Gaium*.

Let me first quote a passage from Book 3 of *De Specialibus Legibus*, in the section dealing with the prohibition of murder. After dealing with the murder of free men, Philo tackles the issue of the murder of slaves (or servants):

> 137 Servants rank lower in fortune, but in nature can claim equality with their masters, and in the law of God the standard of justice is adjusted to nature and not to fortune (τῷ δὲ θείῳ νόμῳ κανὼν τῶν δικαίων ἐστὶν οὐ τὸ τῆς τύχης ἀλλὰ τὸ τῆς φύσεως ἐναρμόνιον). And therefore the masters should not make excessive use of their authority over slaves by showing arrogance and contempt and savage cruelty. For these are signs of no

---

[44] Transl. Marcus, LCL, 318. [45] See Munnich 2011.

> peaceful spirit, but of one so intemperate as to seek to throw off all responsibility and take the tyrant's despotism for its model. 138. He who has used his private house as a sort of stronghold of defiance and allows no freedom of speech to any of the inmates but treats all with the brutality created by native or perhaps acquired hatred for his fellow-men, is a tyrant (τύραννός) with smaller resources. 139. By his use of them he gives proof that he will not stay where he is, if he gets more wealth into his hands, for he will pass on at once to attack cities and countries and nations, after first reducing his own fatherland to slavery, a sign that he will not deal gently with any of his other subjects (ὑπήκοοι). 140. Such a one must clearly understand that his misconduct cannot be prolonged or widely extended with immunity, for he will have for his adversary justice, the hater of evil, the defender and champion of the ill-used, who will call upon him to give an account for the unhappy condition of the sufferers. (*De Specialibus Legibus* 3.137–140)[46]

Philo's starting point lies in the biblical laws pertaining to the murder of a slave (Exod 21:20–21). However, he switches from the abuse of individuals to the oppression of countries and nations (ἔθνη). The figure of the tyrant, known from Greek political writings, is merged here with that of the Hellenistic king or, more probably, with that of the Roman *imperator*, who conquers and subdues many nations. Although nowhere does Philo advocate the suppression of slavery as such,[47] he condemns the arrogance and the cruelty that may characterize a slave master and warns that punishment shall fall on those who abuse and mistreat others, be it in the private sphere or at the level of an entire empire. In other words, he is implicitly warning the Roman governors or emperors who are currently ruling over the Jews to be careful, lest they be punished by God, who is the only true source of justice (*Dikē*).

This is actually the point that Philo makes in *In Flaccum* – Flaccus perishes miserably due to his responsibility for the riots against the Jews in Alexandria – as well as in *Legatio*, where Caligula's murder is the punishment he suffers for attempting to erect a statue of himself in the Temple of Jerusalem. Significantly, as we saw above, the *Legatio* opens with some general thoughts on the opposition between *Tychē* and Nature that recall those in *De Specialibus Legibus* 3.137. How can we be so blind, Philo asks, as to hold "fortune, the most unstable of things, to be the most unchangeable, [and] nature, the most constant, to be the most insecure? . . . The reason is that, having no forethought for the future, we are ruled by the present, following erratic sense-perception

---

[46] Transl. F. H. Colson, LCL, 563–565.
[47] In line with other Greek, Roman and Jewish sources of the period; see Urbach 1964.

rather than unerring intelligence."[48] Some people are thus led to believe that there is no divine providence for Israel (§§3–4). Philo uses the story of Caligula precisely to show that such assumptions are wrong: whereas Caligula's amazing prosperity (described at length at the beginning of the *Legatio*) was put to an end – implying that all things are ruled by Fortune[49] – Israel was saved, thanks to God's providential care for His people.[50]

In short, from Philo's perspective, the only human community that shall endure all the vicissitudes of life is Israel. The Roman Empire shall fade away, as does every worldly power. Roman rule may last longer if emperors truly attempt to govern in a just manner and respect the right of Israel to live according to its ancestral laws. However, it may end sooner than most people think if the Romans behave unjustly and challenge God's providential care for Israel. In the end, God is the one who will put an end to the Empire.

All in all, Philo's allusive reflections on the future of the Roman Empire do not differ substantially from those of Josephus or the rabbis. They may all be said to share the following vision: divine providence has not abandoned Israel; Rome rules today but shall one day collapse. Ultimately, the spiritual rule of Israel shall prevail.[51]

Acknowledgment

This research has been funded by the European Research Council (ERC) under the European Union's Seventh Framework Program (FP/2007–2013)/ERC Grant Agreement no. 614 424. It has been conducted within the framework of the ERC project Judaism and Rome, under the auspices of the Centre National de la Recherche Scientifique (CNRS) and Aix-Marseille University, UMR 7297 TDMAM (Aix-en-Provence, France).

---

[48] *Legat.* 1–2, transl. F. H. Colson, LCL, 3.   [49] Cf. *Legat.* 284.
[50] Philo's treatment of the episode is comparable to Josephus' in *Antiquities* 18, insofar as both consider that all historical events are ultimately controlled by God. On this aspect of Josephus' work, see Chapter 8 by Jonathan Davies' in this volume. Both Philo and Josephus also suggest that what is good for Israel is also good for Rome, as Caligula was likewise a disaster for the Romans.
[51] On this idea in Philo's work, see Berthelot 2011: 184–86, and the bibliography therein.

CHAPTER 7

From Human Freedom to Divine Intervention
Agrippa II's Address on the Eve of the Jewish War

Samuele Rocca

7.1 Introduction

King Agrippa II's address to the people of Jerusalem (Josephus, *BJ* II.342–404) is one of the most impressive and outstanding rhetorical statements from classical antiquity to have survived. Scholars have been dealing with this well-known passage, so central to our understanding of Josephus's *Jewish War*, since early in the last century. Until quite recently, most studies focused on the central part of the address – the description of the Roman Empire – extracting information on the political, economic, and, above all, the military situation of the Roman Empire between the final years of Nero's reign and the early years of Vespasian's rule.[1] A notable exception is M. Rostovzeff. By the early twentieth century, this Russian-American scholar already understood the importance of Josephus' use of rhetoric and quoted the aforementioned address in an article on the history of political speeches in the Roman Empire. Most scholars who have written on the passage in recent years have followed in Rostovzeff's footsteps, emphasizing the importance of rhetoric and its influence on the depiction of the Roman Empire.[2]

Agrippa's speech occupies an important place in the *Jewish War* as it marks the turning point at which peace transitions into war. The use of rhetoric, therefore, is very important. Like most of Josephus' speeches in the text, Agrippa II's address imitates those found in Thucydides and serves the purpose of communicating or drawing attention to the author's interpretation of events. But such obvious use of a Thucydidean model does not

---

[1] Good examples of this are Domaszewski 1892: 207–18; Kubitschek and Ritterling 1924. See also Picard 1956: 163–73.
[2] Rostovtzeff 1904. Notable subsequent studies include Gruen 2011; Rajak 1991; Roduit 2003; Price 2005; Kaden 2011; and Berthelot 2011. See also Berthelot 2019.

7. Agrippa II's Address on the Eve of the Jewish War

mean that Agrippa II never delivered such a speech.[3] There is no reason to believe that as King of Judaea and as "friend and ally of the Roman people" Agrippa II did not do the utmost in his power to prevent a limited rebellion, one restricted to Jerusalem, from escalating into a full-fledged war against Roman might.[4]

The war had the character of both a *polemos*, or war between Jewish provincials and Roman power, and a *stasis*, or civil war between the ruling class of Judaea, which accommodated itself to Roman rule, and the Zealots, who wished not only to overthrow the Roman overlords, but also to put an end to the Empire's aristocratic supporters. Agrippa II stood as the *de facto* and *de jure* head of what Martin Goodman rightly defines as the ruling class of Judaea – as the king and ruler who had the power to appoint and dismiss high priests. Therefore, it is important to argue that one of the primary tasks of the speech is to exonerate not only King Agrippa, but also Josephus – both members of Judaea's ruling class – from any responsibility for the outbreak of the Jewish War. Hence, though the main protagonist of the speech is, of course, the orator, King Agrippa II, behind his speech, we can recognize Josephus' voice. A. Roduit argues even more unambiguously that the speech reflects the point of view of the narrator, Josephus, and not that of the orator, King Agrippa II. T. Rajak, in turn, argues that Agrippa II needed an *a posteriori* exculpation far more desperately than Josephus did, and from both the Jewish and Roman side. He had to be defended by Josephus in light of the highly dubious role he played at the outbreak of the revolt. Thus, though the voice is that of Josephus, the arguments serve primarily to justify the Jewish king's behavior during the event. By the same token, Agrippa II's speech is meant to exculpate Josephus as well. The reason is obvious; both are members of the ruling class of Judaea and are going to play a key role in the war. Much, therefore, is at stake. Indeed, Rajak argues that it was Agrippa II's incompetence that led the Jewish provincials to wage war against Rome. On the other hand, the king's incompetence was mirrored by the inability of Judaea's ruling class – which included Joseph Ben Mattatihu, the priest – to restrain the mob. The ruling class, therefore, was no less responsible for

---

[3] See Thucydides, *History of the Peloponnesian War* I. 22.2. Rajak points out that Josephus chose the words that Agrippa uttered: for there is no doubt, in view of their recurrent themes and patterns, that Josephus in common with Thucydides invented his speeches for the most part and used them to communicate or set off his own interpretation of what happened. See Rajak 1991: 122.

[4] See Rajak 1991: 122. On the background, see also Roduit 2003: 367–8. It is possible that parts of this speech reflect what King Agrippa said during a real encounter between the Jewish king and select members of the ruling class of Judaea, including Josephus, who was probably a witness, in order to avoid an escalation from a circumscribed rebellion to a doomed war against Rome.

the incumbent tragedy. Just as Agrippa II was unable to convince, so too Josephus was incapable of hearing and understanding the obvious. Indeed both Agrippa II and Judaea's ruling class failed miserably at controlling and restraining his subjects and keeping them faithful to Rome.[5]

Donna Runnals has argued that in terms of the canons of rhetoric, the king's address contains the standard four features: *Exordium* (*BJ* II.345–347), *Statement* (*BJ* II.348–357), *Proofs* (*BJ* II.358–387), and *Epilogue* (*BJ* II.388–401).[6] Yet, the best approach to the speech probably lies in Roduit's article.[7] According to the French scholar, the speech begins with the *Exordium* (*BJ* II.345–347). The first part of the speech consists of an analysis of the motivations made to justify the war (*BJ* II.348–361). The preamble (*BJ* II.348–350), is followed first by the list of the grievances against the procurators (*BJ* II. 350–354), and afterwards by the statement that the real cause of rebellion lay in the zeal for liberty burning in the heart of the Jews (*BJ* II.355–361). Here – following a Thucydidean model – Agrippa II differentiates between the immediate causes or pretexts and deeper motivations. If the immediate pretext is the rough behavior of the Roman *procuratores*, the real cause of rebellion is, of course, the deep love of freedom burning in the heart of each Jew. Indeed this part, which addresses the past – a past of freedom – shall be discussed in greater detail below. The second part of the speech is a careful and detailed discussion of Roman invincibility vis-à-vis the meagerness of the resources available to the Jews (*BJ* II.361–395). While the preamble consists of a summary of the Jews' weakness (*BJ* II.361–362), the main feature of this section is a detailed list of Roman conquests (*BJ* II.363–387). And whereas afterwards the king discusses in brief the question of the allies (*BJ* II.388–389), arguing that no one shall follow the Jews in their path to rebellion, he concludes the second part of his speech with the theme of the Alliance of God (*BJ* II.390–395). Most important in the eyes of the Jewish king, therefore, is the forceful argument – the most forceful of all – that the Jews cannot rely on their Alliance with God. Unlike the first part, the second part addresses the present; the present is dominated by the might of Rome that has enslaved all the peoples of the *oikoumenè*. The situation is justified on a theological level by the fact that it was by God's wish that Rome came to dominate the *oikoumenè*; to rebel against Rome, therefore, is tantamount to rebelling against God and breaking the Alliance. The third and final part of the

---

[5] See Roduit 2003: 366. Rajak 1991: 126–9 depicts Agrippa II's rule as a failure from the start.
[6] Runnalls 1997: 737–54. Mason 1994 follows the same approach and accepts the four part division, yet, the *confirmatio* (proof) extends to *BJ* II.399. See Mason 1994: 161–91. See also Kaden 2011: 490.
[7] See Roduit 2003: 368–74.

speech focuses on the possible consequences of the conflict and thus on the future. Agrippa II clearly states that to begin a war with Rome shall endanger not only the Jews living in Judaea, the Mother Country, but all the Jews living in the *oikoumenè* (*BJ* II.396–400). Indeed, the Romans shall spare no one as they shall make an example of the Jews (*BJ* II.397), and the war shall place the Jews living in foreign cities (*BJ* II.398) in mortal danger and lead to the total destruction of Judaea and the Temple (*BJ* II.400). The speech ends in a final peroration (*BJ* II.401–404), in which the king once again condemns the rebellion. This final section is devoted to a discussion of the future, or to be more exact, of various futures, as the choice lies in the Jews' hands. Although the Jewish king recognizes *prima facie* the possibility that the Jews, once they break their Alliance with God, shall be severely punished, it is quite clear between the lines that Agrippa II is also contemplating the possibility that Roman rule may not last forever and therefore the prospect that God shall one day transfer his favor back to the Jews.

7.2 A Past of Freedom

The Jewish king addresses the theme of the past in the *Exordium* (*BJ* II. 345–347), at the very beginning of the speech. The main feature of this past is that all the peoples of the *oikoumenè*, including the Jews, lived in a state of collective independence before the Roman conquest, enjoying freedom and liberty. Indeed, a closer look at the text shows that the state of freedom that preceded the Roman conquest corresponds to the Greek ideal of *eleutheria*, or political independence, and of *autonomia*, or internal autonomy. In addition, it is important to argue that in the mind of Josephus this state of independence and freedom was achieved through Divine Intervention, but that man, being free, shared in the strife preceding the conquest of freedom equally with the divinity.

However, the idea of freedom and its close connection with a distant past, first mentioned in the *Exordium*, is discussed mainly in the first part of the speech, the *Statement*. Here, the king offers an acute analysis of the Jews' reasons for justifying the war (*BJ* II.348–361).[8] Agrippa II (or Josephus) is careful to differentiate, in accordance with the Thucydidean model, between immediate causes or pretexts (rough behavior of the Roman *procuratores*) and deeper motives (deep love of freedom of each Jew). Therefore the king "shall first separate those pretenses that are by some connected together." Yet the behavior of the *procuratores* is merely

---

[8] See Roduit 2003: 369–70.

a pretext, not the real cause. In the main argument (*BJ* II.355–361), the king discusses the Jewish passion for liberty, an argument that the orator sees as already belonging to a distant past rather than the present, as the Jews have already lost their chance. The king is clear on this point: "However, as to the desire of recovering your liberty, it is unseasonable to indulge it so late; whereas you ought to have labored earnestly in old time that you might never have lost it; for the first experience of slavery was hard to be endured, and the struggle that you might never have been subject to it would have been just (*BJ* II.355)." The Jews ought to have fought for freedom and liberty when they were free men, under Hasmonean rule, rather than afterwards, when Judaea was already annexed to the Empire and had become a province, and the Jews mere slaves. Agrippa II argues that it would be natural and right for a people to revolt at the moment of provincialization. Therefore the Jews, by now slaves, have already missed their chance to wage war against the Romans, which they ought to have done in the days of Pompey. Agrippa states his argument quite clearly: once Judaea became a province, Jews became nothing more than slaves. And slaves do not rebel against their master. Only free men can successfully and rightfully wage war for freedom and liberty. Rajak compares King Agrippa's first attack on the idea of freedom to Calgacus' speech in Tacitus' *Agricola*. Like Calgacus, Agrippa II too is a realist. He clearly states that Jews are enslaved to the Romans.[9]

According to Josephus, this ideal, faraway period, when freedom and liberty ruled supreme, is symbolized by Hasmonean rule. It is interesting that in contrast to the First Book of the Maccabees, Josephus does not refer to the rule of the early Hasmoneans, such as Simon, but rather to that of the last Hasmoneans, who assumed the Greek title of king, or *basileus*, along with that of high priests. Thus, a close look at the first book of *War* and the thirteenth book of *Antiquities* shows that Josephus looked back with nostalgia at the final years of the rule of Alexander Jannaeus and, of course, to the reign of Salome Alexandra. That Josephus is referring to the final Hasmonean rulers is clear from the text of the speech, in which the Jewish king argues that "our ancestors and their kings, who were in much better circumstances than we are, both as to money, and strong bodies, and [valiant] souls" (*BJ* II.358). The text therefore refers to "our ancestors," that is, to the ruled, together with the kings, the rulers. Furthermore, in the speech, Agrippa II speaks of the Hasmoneans not as high priests, but only as kings. This reference to the Hasmoneans as kings frames the period from

---

[9] See Rajak 1991: 128. See Tacitus, *Agricola* 29–38. See Josephus, *BJ* II.256–357.

the reign of Judah Aristobulus I to that of Queen Salome Alexandra (104–66 BCE).[10] According to Josephus, this period was ideal as the Jews were rich and possessed both strong bodies and valiant souls. The body-soul binomial used in the speech greatly strengthens Josephus' argument. In his mind, the perfect state of independence is that of a kingdom, a strong local power that can keep its enemies at bay, while the ideal state of autonomy is that of a monarchy presided by an absolute ruler, albeit one surrounded by well-meaning counselors.

It is interesting that Agrippa II depicts the Hasmonean rule as the Golden Age. We must remember, however, that the Hasmonean family was the common denominator of Agrippa II, the orator, and Josephus, the narrator. Both Agrippa II, a Herodian king, and Josephus had Hasmonean blood running in their veins – Josephus on his maternal side and the Jewish king through his father, Agrippa I, the son of Aristobulus, one of the two sons of King Herod the Great by his second wife, Mariamne. This connection with the Hasmonean family is very important for both figures as it defines them as leading members of the ruling class of Judaea. Indeed as members of such, the king and the priest complement each other. Agrippa II, the Herodian, was a lay ruler, King of Judaea, and friend of the Romans. Josephus, a priest, possessed a pedigree no less impressive than the king's.[11] Even the fact that at the very beginning of the revolt Josephus took the side of the rebels, and Agrippa II, that of the Roman overlords, does not erase the similarity between these two leading members of Judaea's ruling class. Afterwards, both Agrippa II and Josephus were to be intimately connected again from 69 CE on, after Vespasian's rise to the throne. In fact, despite the fact that they made opposite choices at the beginning of the war, they still enjoyed common ground. Both miserably failed their Jewish subjects and Roman overlords. Yet their Hasmonean ancestry forged a positive tie between the Jewish king and priest to the primary idea of pristine freedom. In other words, a harkening to the physical descendants of the Hasmoneans and not rebelling against Rome shall restore freedom, albeit as salvation through the grace of God.

However, the Jews were not the only people to have enjoyed a state of freedom and liberty that came to an abrupt end with the Roman conquest. Indeed, they are not the only *ethnos* that enjoyed liberty before this brutal event. For this reason, at the very beginning of the speech, Josephus

---

[10] On the last Hasmonean rulers in Josephus, see on Judah Aristobulus I, *AJ* XIII.301–319, *BJ* I.70–84. On Alexander Jannaeus, see *AJ* XIII.320–404, *BJ* I.85–106. On Queen Salome Alexandra, see *AJ* XIII.405–432, *BJ* I.107–119.

[11] See Josephus, *Vita* 1.

compares the Jews' glorious free past to the *poleis* of Athens (*BJ* II.358), Sparta (*BJ* II.359), and the Kingdom of Macedonia (*BJ* II.360). While the final years of the quite autocratic Hasmonean kingdom were considered the Golden Age of freedom and liberty for the Jews, every *polis* and *ethnè* had enjoyed its own golden age of freedom and liberty in different circumstances, under completely different forms of rulership. Thus while independence had had more or less the same meaning for each political entity, the meaning of freedom as autonomy had differed from city to city. The examples of Athens, Sparta, and Macedonia are striking for the difference in their definitions of the very concept of freedom and liberty. Athens is depicted as the perfect democracy.[12] Josephus chooses a well-defined time frame to outline the perfect state of freedom and liberty that graced Athens at the dawn of the classical era. It is interesting that Sparta's Golden Age of freedom and liberty fits within the same chronological framework, from the end of the Archaic to the very beginning of the classical period. Yet, the form of government chosen by Sparta was, in fact, that of an aristocracy.[13] Contrary to Athens and Sparta, Macedonia's Golden Age coincided with the reign of the Argead rulers, Philip II and Alexander. The form of government that characterized Macedonia in that period and complied perfectly – at least according to Josephus – to the ideals of freedom and liberty was that of an absolute monarchy. As in the political writings of Plato (e.g. the *Republic*), of Aristotle in the *Politics*, of Polybius in the *Histories*, and slightly later in Plutarch, so here, we have a comparison of the three ideal forms of government: democracy, which fits the Athenians; aristocracy, which suits the Spartans; and monarchy, which is, of course, appropriate to the Macedonians. All three forms of government fit each of these peoples perfectly. A close look at the text shows that the reference to the Aristotelian and Polybian cycle or *anakyklosis* is chronological, though Josephus opts for a contrary order.[14] Hence, the earliest constitution presented by Josephus is that of democratic Athens, which is defeated by aristocratic Sparta, which, in turn, is

---

[12] On Cleisthenes, see Herodotus, *Hist.* VI.131. See also Aristotle, *Ath.Pol.* 20–21.

[13] Although in theory a monarchy, classical writers referred to Sparta as an oligarchy. See Aristotle, *Pol.* III.I285a. The best reference to Sparta as an oligarchy, and not a monarchy is by Isocrates, *Panath.* III.24. On the Spartan constitution, see Plutarch, *Lyc.* 5–7, 28–29. See also Xenophon, *Lac.* 30.

[14] Plato, *Rep.* VIII already divided governments into five basic types: democracy, or government by the many; oligarchy, or government by the few; timocracy, or government by the honored or valued; tyranny, or government by one for himself; and aristocracy, which for Plato is the ideal form of government. On the cycle of subsequent rules, see Aristotle, *Politics* II–VII. According to Polybius, it was the constitution of Republican Rome that realized the ideal mixed constitution. See Polybius, *Hist.* VI.1–18. See also Plutarch, *Mor. (On Monarchy, Democracy and Oligarchy)*.

conquered by monarchic Macedonia. Josephus' order is not random. As we have discussed above, the ideal form of government for the Jewish priest is the monarchy, the Hasmonean dynasty of kings-high priests. Indeed, in *Against Apion*, Josephus coins the term "theocracy" to define the perfect form of government for the Jews.[15] Here, too, is another reference to Polybius, although this time it requires reading closely between the lines. A perfect democracy, Athens, a perfect aristocracy, Sparta, and a perfect monarchy, Macedonia, is opposed Rome, which has successfully conquered all three countries for the very simple reason that its government includes elements of monarchy, aristocracy, and democracy, all mixed together, thus leading to a perfect constitution.[16] It is therefore possible to say that the ideals of freedom and liberty described by Josephus are relative as each people chose a different form of government that best fit it, regardless if that was democracy, oligarchy, or monarchy.

In the second and middle part of the address, the Jewish king comes back to the former liberty enjoyed by the various peoples subjected by the might of Rome as he enumerates all the peoples conquered by Rome and now subservient to it. This time, however, Josephus refers not only to Greece, the center of the *oikoumenè*, but also to other *ethnè* and *poleis* that once enjoyed freedom and liberty no less than Jews had. Thus, early in the middle part, Josephus returns to the Greeks, "who were esteemed the noblest of all people under the sun." Now, however, the noblest of all people under the sun are kept in an abject state of subjection by the Romans with "six bundles of Roman rods" (*BJ* II.365). The contrast between the Greeks, the noblest of all peoples, and the *fasces lictorii*, the brutal symbol of the Roman magistrate's authority, could not be more striking. Josephus once again refers to the Macedonians, who "have juster reason to claim their liberty than you have" (*BJ* II.366).

Now, however, the idea of former liberty encompasses all the peoples of the *oikoumenè* subservient to Rome. Hence, the reference to a former state of liberty in correlation to more or less all those that Josephus mentions. The Henlochi, the Colchi, the Tauri, the Bosphoraeans, the nations around Pontus, and Meotis, which once "knew not so much as a lord of their own," are now subject to Rome (*BJ* II.367–368). What is interesting here is that Josephus, who is obviously dealing with Barbarian *ethnè*,

---

[15] See Josephus, *C. Ap.* II.165–166. Josephus writes that "A Theocracy, by ascribing the authority and the power to God, and by persuading all the people to have a regard to him, as the author of all the good things that were enjoyed either in common by all mankind, or by each one in particular, and of all that they themselves obtained by praying to him in their greatest difficulties."

[16] See Polybius, *Hist.* VI.1–18.

suggests that the state of pristine freedom and liberty consisted of a more or less perfect state of anarchy, very near the primitive state of Nature. The *ethne* of Bithynia, Cappadocia, Pamphylia, Lycia, and Cilicia, too, have a claim to liberty (*BJ* II.369). The ideal pristine liberty, until now claimed by peoples living in the Hellenized east, is extended by Josephus to those living in the west. The best example of a western people who once lived in a state of freedom and liberty are, of course, the Gauls (*BJ* II.372–374). Although they fought an eighty-year-long war to preserve their liberty, they are now enslaved by Rome. Josephus characterizes the Gauls as a valiant and noble people. Here again, as in the case of the Jews under Hasmonean rule, he associates liberty with virility and nobility. The Spaniards (*BJ* II.375–376), Germans (*BJ* II.378), and Britons (*BJ* II.379), once enjoyed a pristine state of liberty, albeit it was more akin to anarchy than to any organized form of government. Although in this list of *gentes devictae*, Josephus deals with various other peoples, the best example of one that formerly enjoyed liberty in his final section of the oration's second part, is, of course, the Carthaginians (*BJ* II.381). He defines the Golden Age of freedom and liberty in Carthage chronologically. Once again, Josephus winks at Polybius by defining this Golden Age as the period in which Carthage was dominated by the figure of Hannibal. The life-and-death struggle between Hannibal's Carthage and Rome is, in fact, one of the main topics of Polybius' *Histories*. Philo too refers to Carthage, without, however, emphasizing his imperial past. But then, Philo's writing is not influenced by the historical Polybius in the way that Josephus' is.[17] Indeed, Josephus and the Greek historian-politician have the same attitude to the Roman Empire. Moreover, as we shall discuss in detail later on, the idea that *Tychè* lay behind the Empire's growth and gave the rule of the *oikoumenè* to the Romans – one of the leitmotifs not only of the king's speech but also of Josephus's *War* – is shared by Polybius.

7.3 A Present of Slavery

The present, on the contrary, is characterized by a dire state of slavery in Rome. Man, once a slave, cannot change this state of affairs as he had lost all pride, dignity, and self-respect. The here and now is dominated by Rome. It is in this part of the speech, in the description of a present dominated by Rome, that God's role in history is introduced. As previously stated, it is the rule of the *procuratores* that serves the rhetoric of the speech,

---

[17] See Philo, *Deus* 174. See also Berthelot 2019: 3.

which is to bring the observer from the distant past of freedom to the present state of slavery. The first and main pretext, therefore, relates to the behavior of the *procuratores*. Here the king, using philosophical arguments rooted in Stoic philosophy, shows how it is possible to attenuate the sufferings provoked by a greedy and cruel government (*BJ* II.351). Roduit argues that much in the speech mirrors Seneca's attitude to the Empire. Indeed, Josephus, like the Roman stoic philosopher, considers the Empire an unquestionable reality. Moreover, like Seneca, he condemns all those who exploit the *proviniciae* for their own personal ends.[18] Yet, as A. D. Kaden argues, we have to be aware that the similarity stops here. Josephus the narrator and Agrippa II the orator are provincials and subjects, while Seneca is a Roman citizen, living and acting for the emperor at the center of power. The Jews are urged to be patient because not all Romans have a hostile attitude. Surely the next *procurator* shall be better than the previous one, or at least friendlier. Therefore it is simply absurd to wage war against all Romans on account of a specific individual (*BJ* II.353). The behavior of the *procuratores* arises once more at the end of the speech (*BJ* II.402). Rajak argues that Agrippa II was accountable to Rome, more so than high priests and other members of the ruling class of Judaea. The Jewish king thus orders the Jewish magistrates to pay tribute. He well knows that the failure to pay tribute is clearly an act of defiance and revolt against Rome. For Roman authorities, the first duty of a *rex-cliens* and the native ruling members of the province is that of maintaining order. Failure to do so results in merciless penalties for native authorities.[19] Thus, as we know from *Antiquities* even more so than from the *War*, Josephus regards the rule of the *procuratores* as a rising crescendo in misrule, bad government, corruption, and greed. However, while in the earlier period we can always discern the hand of the emperor, who, even at the last moment, dismisses the wicked governor, now, in the present, the emperor no longer intervenes. On the contrary, as in the case of the dissensions in Caesarea, Nero takes the "other" side. Therefore, in as much as the rule of the *procuratores* is tempered by imperial intervention, we can argue for a past tense. Yet now that the emperor no longer takes a stand favorable to the Jews, we can point to the present situation.[20] Unlike Josephus, who focuses

---

[18] See Roduit 2003: 393–4.
[19] See Rajak 1991: 127–8. See also Josephus, *BJ* II.308 on Florus' merciless execution of Jewish members of the equestrian order.
[20] On the rule of the *procurators*, see Josephus, *BJ* II.117–308. See also Josephus, *AJ* XVIII–XX. On the disturbances that occurred at Caesarea Maritima under the procuratorship of Felix, see *BJ* II.266–270 and 284–292. See also *AJ* XX.173–178 and 182–184.

on the present, Philo may be making a negative reference to Roman emperors and governors, who rule the Jews as tyrants in atemporal terms, and be equating them with past Hellenistic kings and Greek tyrants, whom he equates with cruel masters who mistreat their slaves. Philo uses strong terms to criticize the arrogance and cruelty of masters over slaves, warning his reader that regardless of whether the case is one of a master versus slave in a private framework, or a tyrant versus his subjects in the public realm, all shall meet their deserved punishment at the hands of divine justice, or *Dikē*. More specifically, while *In Flaccum*, the Roman governor dies as a wretch due to his responsibilities vis-à-vis the Jews of Alexandria, in *Legatio*, Gaius Caesar is stricken down because he wishes to erect a statue of himself inside the precinct of the Temple in Jerusalem. Yet, a careful reading shows that though Flaccus, the subordinate governor, is evil, the emperor is merely mentally unstable and thus not really responsible for his action. Thus, in the end, Philo's attitude is not that different from that of Josephus-Agrippa II.[21]

Nonetheless, according to Roduit's careful analysis, it is the second part of the speech – the *Proofs* – that is dedicated to demonstrating the weakness of the resources available to the Jews and the Romans' invincibility (*BJ* II.361–395).[22] The second part of the speech thus has a double objective: to show that *Tychè* is by now in the Roman *castra*, and that Jews have no real men to confront or even fight the Romans. No doubt the main theme of this central part is the universal rule of Rome, which at present dominates the *oikoumenè*. According to Kaden, the *gentes devictae* are listed here as a comparative measure.[23] The preamble of the second part is dedicated to exposing Jewish weakness in the face of the Romans (*BJ* II.361–362). Agrippa thus argues that in order to wage a successful war against the Romans, the Jews ought to prepare a fleet and army, and, of course, need financial means (*BJ* II.361). However, they lack all of this! Then, in order to show how ridiculous are the claims of the Jews, he discusses the Roman conquests in amazing detail (*BJ* II.361–387) as well as the huge expanse of the Roman Empire and the resources with which it can quell the revolt. This is the most important part of the speech. The king also addresses the question of potential allies (*BJ* II.388–389). Indeed, Agrippa argues that the Jews can rely on no one as all the peoples of the *oikoumenè* are under

---

[21] See Philo, *Spec*.3.137–140 on the slave master as tyrant. See *Flacc*.114–115; 162–191. Philo emphasizes that Flacco was arrested at the same time as Jews were celebrating Sukkoth, the Feast of Tabernacles, thus emphasizing God's providential intervention. See also *Legat.* 346 on Gaius Caesar's attempt to set a statue in the Temple of Jerusalem. See also Berthelot 2019: 16–17.
[22] See Roduit 2003: 370–1. [23] See Kaden 2011: 491.

7. Agrippa II's Address on the Eve of the Jewish War 141

Roman rule. Even the Parthians are in no mood to wage a war against Rome. Last but not least, to demolish all claims to wage war against the Romans, Agrippa II brings up a traditional *topos*, the Alliance between God and the Jews (*BJ* II. 390–395). It is the discussion of this *topos* that brings us to the future. Indeed, most important in the eyes of the Jewish King is the forceful argument – the most forceful of all – that the Jews cannot rely on their Alliance with God. First, the Romans, who at present dominate the *oikoumenè*, acquired their power with Divine Assistance; hence God now stands with them (*BJ* II.390). Furthermore, a war shall render impossible the Temple's cult, which ought to be the Jews' primary purpose. Should the Jews, therefore, wage war against the Romans, they would forfeit Divine Assistance (*BJ* II.391–393). Hence the conclusion that "all men that go to war do it either as depending on divine or on human assistance; but since your going to war will cut off both those assistances, those that are for going to war choose evident destruction" (*BJ* II.394).

Thus, the central part of Agrippa II's speech consists of a highly detailed portrayal of the Roman Empire (*BJ* II.363–387). The question remains whether this description is a genuine description of the Empire in the last years of Nero, or simply a piece of Flavian propaganda in which Josephus tries to convey the majesty of the Roman Empire to his Jewish and Gentile readers and to warn them never to disturb the *Pax Romana*.

Nicolet and Roduit argue, quite successfully, that a possible primary-source available to Josephus was the *Breviarium Totius Imperii*, which has not survived.[24] Another source that he may have used alongside the *Breveriarum* is the *Res Gestae Divi Augusti*. Nicolet thus argues for the similarity between the speech of Agrippa, filled with geographic detail, and the *Res Gestae*. Besides, even more importantly, the *Res Gestae* – which, unlike the *Breviarium*, was probably just a detailed list – had a clear propagandistic purpose as one of its main topics was to celebrate the fact that Augustus had extended the rule of the Roman Republic to the entire *oikoumenè*.[25] All these sources, however, date to the Augustan period. New provinces, notably Britannia, which is in fact mentioned in King Agrippa's speech, had been added to the Empire. It is therefore clear that the source available to Josephus did not reflect the situation in 14 CE, but rather the Roman Empire in a more recent period. The question, of course, is precisely when. Some scholars, such as Saulnier, have argued that the

---

[24] This document, dated shortly before the death of Augustus and deposited in the care of the *Vestales*, included a summary of the condition of the entire Empire. See Suetonius, *Aug.* 101.6–7. See Tacitus, *Annales* I.11.7. See also Dio Cassius, *Hist. Rom.* LXVI.33.2.

[25] See Nicolet 1988: 97. See also Kaden 2011: 496–7. See *Res Gestae Divi Augusti* 26–33.

Empire as depicted by Agrippa II in his powerful address mirrors the situation in 74/75 CE, when Josephus published the *Jewish War*. In such case, the description of the Roman Empire would, in fact, be an example of Flavian propaganda.[26]

Yet there are two principal reasons for dismissing Saulnier's claim. The first is that a detailed review of the various provinces, peoples, cities, and the military situation points to the final years of Nero's rule.[27] In addition, as Rajak argues, one of the main characteristics of Agrippa II's address is that it goes backward, not forward. The Jews who oppose the war against Rome have some practical justification for doing so, even if the moral balance sheet is something different. Thus, the view that with this speech Josephus wished to dissuade Jews from rebelling after the destruction of the Temple is incorrect. The justification adopted by Josephus and put in the mouth of Agrippa II is *a priori*, not *a posteriori*. In other words, the king's intention in this speech is not to deter Jews from rebellion. His address conveys another message, namely, that even if the Jews have every right to complain, Realpolitik suggests submission. Hence, the speech cannot have served Flavian propaganda. It would have been useless for Josephus to have used data pertaining to the Flavian period, as it would not have conveyed his ideological message.[28] In conclusion, Roduit, like Nicolet before him, argues that Josephus relied on the Augustan *Breviarium* along with other, unidentified "intermediate" sources, which as a group, offered an up-to-date image of the Roman Empire of around 66 CE.

Nevertheless the idealized vision of the Roman Empire, at whose very center stands the Hellenistic East, does correspond to a highly realistic depiction of the Roman Empire, whose legions keep at bay the various *ethne*. Indeed Kaden argues that Josephus chose to depict the Roman *oikoumenè* in a trifold manner. Hence, at the center of imperial space stands the civilized world, the Greek islands and Egypt, around which lie the Romanized peripheries, mainly the northern and western *ethne*, which, in turn, come to an end at the frontier where the Dacians and Arabs dwell.[29] The decision to begin the list of *gentes devictae* in the Greek world may reflect Josephus or Agrippa II's perception of the Empire. As Agrippa II was an eastern, Hellenized ruler, the Greek east rather than the Latin east stood at the center of the civilized *oikoumenè*. Kaden forcefully argues that the idea to include *gentes devictae* in the list is also present in the poetical writings of Augustan poets, such as Virgil, as well as in visual

---

[26] See Saulnier 1991: 199–221.   [27] See Roduit 2003: 374–80.   [28] See Rajak 1991: 131–2.
[29] See detailed list quoted by Kaden 2011: 494–5. See Josephus, *BJ* II.358–387.

depictions of the Empire.³⁰ Last but not least, Kaden claims that the list is a perfect example of colonial mimicry – as defined by Homi Bhabha – because the list of *gentes devictae* originated in the periphery, in a conquered province, and not in the center, in Rome.³¹ Therefore, it makes no difference whether this section originated with Josephus or indeed with Agrippa II; while the primary source from which the document originated was Roman, the secondary source that transmitted the document was provincial.

As Rajak notes, possibly the main characteristic of this section, which deals with the present, is the realistic argument for Roman rule adopted by Agrippa II, which also carries Josephus's voice. Polybius, one of Josephus' most important models, already does not praise Roman rule as such. Indeed, not blind to the shortcomings of Roman rule, he presents Roman power as brutal and cruel. Its power, its invincibility, not its present benevolence, is the recurring motif in the writings of the Greek historian. Indeed, a closer look at Polybius shows a notable number of criticisms of Rome.³² Neither Polybius nor Josephus praises the benefits that Rome has brought to the world. Therefore, like Polybius before him, Josephus does not welcome the rule of Rome, the peace, prosperity, and security of living in the embrace of the Empire. Therefore, as in the writings of Polybius, so too in the king's speech, the power of Rome and its invincibility rather than its generosity are the recurring motif. As Rajak observes, Agrippa II depicts the *Pax Roma* as brutal and the Roman governors of Judaea as vicious, cruel, and greedy. Moreover, in his description of the Empire, he argues quite clearly and more than once that Rome uses brutal force to keep at bay its provincial subjects and shamelessly exploits its provinces.³³ In his article on the attitude of Josephus to the present state of the Roman Empire, P. Stern forcefully argues that the king's oration contains no *Laus Imperii* and is totally different from the oration of Aelius Aristides, who praises the *Pax Romana*. The king

---

³⁰ See Virgil, *Georg.* III.25–33. On Aeneas's prophetic shield see Virgil, *Aen.* VIII. 722–728. For examples of the visual depictions of the Empire, see Augustus' funeral procession in Dio Cassius, *Hist. Rom.* 56.34.1–3. See also the Sebasteion of Aphrodisia in Smith 1988, 50–77. Last but not least, see the Theatre of Pompey, which listed fourteen conquered nations in Suetonius, *Nero* 46.1. On the *Porticus ad Nationes*, which contained images of conquered nations, see Servius, *Commentary on the Aeneid* VIII.721. See also Pliny, *Nat. Hist.* XXXVI.39. Spain and other nations were listed among the conquered in the Forum of Augustus. See Velleius Patercolus, *Hist. Rom.* II.39.2.
³¹ See Kaden 2011: 488–9.
³² See Gruen 2011: 152–5. The most important studies on Polybius and the rise of Rome are Walbank 1957–1979; Walbank 1972: 157–83; Walbank 1974; Walbank 2002: 243–92.
³³ See Gruen 2011: 152–8.

describes the contemporary *Pax Romana* in an ambivalent light and not as a benefit to subjects.[34] Thus, in his speech, the invincibility of Rome rather than its benevolence are reflected in his use of terms of quiescence in the roster of peoples who have yielded to Rome, as well as in his depiction of the Roman Empire's natural resources, deterrent power, and the sheer scale of its exploitative transactions.[35] As Rajak rightfully argues, the voice of Agrippa II is also the voice of Josephus the realist, who knew what it was like to live under an empire and was aware that usually it was necessary to wait. Hence, both the orator and the narrator are realists who well understand why their fellow countrymen hate Rome even if they deplore their actions. Understanding Philo's real attitude to the Roman Empire and the *Pax Romana* is a bit more difficult. At the beginning of the *Legatio*, he describes the geographic extent of the Roman Empire at the accession of Gaius Caesar, albeit briefly. Rome rules over the *oikoumenè*, "the most numerous, valuable and important portions of the whole world, which can be indeed fairly called the whole world." Later on, Philo focuses on Augustus' achievements, such as the end of the civil wars, his conquests, and the benefits these brought to Greeks and Jews, such as freedom for their cities. Moreover, within this framework, Philo emphasizes that Augustus respected the peculiar needs of the Jews and gave them special privileges. Indeed, he ends this part by extolling the enviable situation of the Jews living in Rome. Later on, in a different context, Philo lauds Augustus as a man of "virtue and good fortune," who spread peace everywhere. All the same, he perceives Fortune, one of Augustus' attributes, as consistently negative. Furthermore, nowhere within the framework referring to the Augustan Empire does Philo mention Divine Providence. Yet, it is clear that his perception of the Augustan empire is on the whole positive – as long as it protects Jewish rights. The French scholar M. Hadas-Lebel rightly argues that "Philo, Jew of the Diaspora has no nationalistic aspirations; in his city of Alexandria, he feels part of the great Roman Empire extended to the dimensions of the universe."[36]

---

[34] See Rajak 1991: 129–34. See also Josephus, *BJ* II.371.
[35] In terms of quiescence, see the section on Athenians in Josephus, *BJ* II.358. On the depiction of the natural resources of the Empire compare Josephus, *BJ* II.372 to Aelius Aristides, *Orat. 26 (To Rome)* 11. On Rome's power as deterrent, see, for example, Josephus, *BJ* II.373, where he points out that the Gauls are kept in order with the help of only 1200 soldiers. On the sheer size of the exploitative transaction, see Josephus, *BJ* II.382–383, where Josephus describes the resources of Africa used to nourish Rome. See Rajak 1991: 129–34.
[36] See *Legat.* 10 on the extension of the Roman Empire; 143–147 on the achievements of Augustus, 148–151, on the honorary tribute to Augustus in the Greek world and more specifically in Alexandria,

7. Agrippa II's Address on the Eve of the Jewish War 145

Josephus/Agrippa II's attitudes towards Rome have not passed unnoticed in post-colonial studies. Kaden, for example, argues that Agrippa II's speech reveals Josephus' hybrid position as a simultaneously conquered Judaean and Roman citizen. This position is no less true of Agrippa II, hence his ambiguous stance as revealed by careful analysis of the speech. Moreover, Agrippa II's attitude as a provincial to the Empire is revealed by the fact that he attributes its expansion not to the deities of Rome, but to his own God, who had His Temple in Jerusalem. This view of Rome obviously resembles that of the Greek intellectuals as it reflects one from the distant periphery rather than from the center.[37]

However, the main argument of the middle part of Agrippa II' speech, which discusses the current situation – the *oikoumenè* under the aegis of Rome – is that Rome acquired its Empire with divine support. Hence, God now stands behind the Romans (*BJ* II.390). It is interesting that as in Polybius, so here, the concepts of God and *Tychè* appear together. In fact, God or *Tychè* has been behind the growth of the Empire in the past and continues to support it in the present. God has moved to Rome's side, granting it rule over the entire *oikoumenè*. Indeed, according to Polybius, the Roman acquisition of world supremacy has been guided by an invisible hand that has led to a predetermined outcome that he calls *Tychè*. Hence *Tychè* is a form of divine fate that guarantees Rome's success in bringing the entire world under a single rule and dominion, something never accomplished before. According to P. Pédech, A. M. Eckstein, and W. F. Walbank, Polybius presents the plan of *Tychè* not as something depending merely on chance, but as something teleologically directed,

---

and 152–160 on Augustus and Tiberius' favorable attitude to the Jews and the privileges they bestowed on them. See *Legat.* 309 on Augustus and the Pax Romana. See Hadas-Lebel 2012: 63. See also Berthelot 2019: 7–8. Berthelot argues that Philo's mention of the Germans and the Parthians – the main threats to the Roman Empire – could be interpreted as the underlying message emphasizing the limits of Roman hegemony not only in terms of geographical extent, but also in terms of duration. However, neither the Germans, nor the Parthians could have been perceived as a threat to Rome at the accession of Gaius Caesar. See, for example the reference to the Germans and Parthians in Strabo, *Geog.* VI.4.1. In this passage, the Greek geographer discusses the causes of Rome's preeminence, conquests, and hegemony while focusing, as does Philo, on Augustus. Thus, according to Strabo, Augustus brought an end to the civil wars, extended Roman conquests, was successful in handling Parthia, and brought peace and prosperity to Italy and the Roman Empire. The teleological character of the last part of the passage is emphasized by the statement that the only possible solution to the civil wars was to give dominion over the *oikoumenè* to one man, Augustus, who not only brought peace and prosperity, but also chose Tiberius, along with Germanicus and Drusus (the son of Tiberius), as his heirs. Tiberius, since he made Augustus "the model of his administration and decrees," was successful in continuing his predecessor's policy of peace and prosperity. See Dueck 2000: 96–106.

[37] On hybridity, see Kaden 2011: 481–5.

even if his rational explanation to clarify the rise of Rome is not always coherent with his use of the idea of *Tychè*.³⁸ The similarity between the teleology of Polybius and that reflected in Agrippa II's speech is striking. In the speech, Josephus also employs the term *Tychè* in the context of transferring world domination to Rome. Here, however, God and *Tychè* seem almost interchangeable. Agrippa asserts that God has moved on the side of Rome, a role that he assigns to *Tychè* a few lines earlier. This overlap between the two concepts makes for a conspicuous conjunction. Indeed, the Polybian concept of *Tychè* also appears in other passages in the *Jewish War*. *Tychè* has thus advanced the aims of Vespasian, a deed that the Roman ascribes to *Pronoia*, or *Providentia*. When Josephus tries to justify his surrender, he quotes a prayer to God affirming that divine will accords with the passage of *Tychè* to the Romans. Last but not least, in his speech outside the walls of the city at the instigation of Titus, Josephus urges Jews to yield to Rome, arguing that there is no use in defying the masters of the universe as *Tychè* has passed to the Romans, and God, who has transferred imperial power from nation to nation, has now set it in Italy.³⁹ Both Polybius and Agrippa II warn that any challenge to Rome will end in disaster.⁴⁰ Polybius thus repeatedly brands the enemies of Rome as irrational, irresponsible, and even mad.⁴¹ Indeed, the main characteristic of this madness is the failure to understand that it was *Tychè* who gave the Romans control over the *oikoumenè*. This concept is also clearly expressed by Josephus, albeit in a different way. According to him, because God has made the Romans the masters of the *oikoumenè*, the Jews, wishing to rebel against the divinely appointed Romans, cannot rely on their Alliance with God. Therefore, if the Jews wage war against the Romans, who were chosen by God to dominate the *oikoumenè*, they shall forfeit Divine Assistance (*BJ* II.391–393) and the war shall end in disaster. The Jewish king therefore argues that it is not up to the Jews to change this state of affairs. In other words, it is clear that he is preaching acquiescence to

---

³⁸ In Polybius, Tychè carries various connotations, such as chance or randomness, even happenstance. However her meaning is closer to fate or providence. See Polybius, *Hist.* I.2.2–4; XVIII.28.5; XXIX.21.3–5 (as capricious fortune); XXXVI.17.2 (as chance or the unexpected); XV.20.4–6; XXXVIII.7.11; XXXVIII, 8.8; XXXIX.8.1–2 (in the sense of watchful spirit with the power of punishment). On Tychè as the divinity that guaranteed the success of Rome, see Polybius, *Hist.* I.4.1–5; VIII.2.3–6; 21; XVI.8. See also Gruen 2011: 150–1. See Pédech 1964: 331–54. See also Eckstein 1995: 194–236.

³⁹ See Josephus, *BJ* II.360, 373, 390. On Tychè advancing the aims of Vespasian, see Josephus, *BJ* IV. 622; On Josephus' justification for his surrender, see Josephus, *BJ* III.351–354; On Josephus' speech outside the walls of the city, see Josephus, *BJ* V.367–368; 412. See also Gruen 2011: 151–2.

⁴⁰ See Polybius, *Hist.* I.2.7–8; I.3.7–10; III.14.

⁴¹ See Polybius, *Hist.* II.21.2; V.102; VII.2–7; VIII.24.10.

Roman rule for the time being. Unlike Polybius and Josephus, Philo depicts *Tychè* in negative terms and in opposition to *Pronoia*, as something not beyond the bounds of God's power, but also not as an expression of his will. Besides, as already stated, *Pronoia* is nowhere associated with the rise or rule of Rome.[42]

In concluding this section, one must emphasize that the theme of Divine Providence governing history is not one taken up by Polybius or Josephus. Kaden rightly claims that the theme of Divine Providence governing a history that culminates in the Empire also appears in Roman poetry as well as in the plastic arts that decorate the monuments celebrating Augustus' achievements in Rome. Good literary examples appear in Horace's *Carmen Seculare* and Ovid's *Fasti*. In Roman visual art, the best example is the teleology behind the reliefs depicted on the Ara Pacis.[43]

7.4 A Future of Redemption?

The third part of the speech, the *Epilogue* (*BJ* II.396–400), is dedicated to the possible consequences of the conflict.[44] Quite dramatically, Agrippa invites the Jews to be his witnesses of the fact that he has done everything in his power to avoid the imminent conflict. Agrippa II warns that the consequences of this war shall be catastrophic not only for the Jews living in Judaea, but for all the Jews in the Roman Empire (*BJ* II.396–400). In order to set an example, the Romans shall not spare anyone, as moderation at this stage is useless (*BJ* II.397). The Jews living in foreign cities shall be exposed to retaliation (*BJ* II.398–399); what is more, the very existence of the Mother Country and the Temple is under direct threat (*BJ* II.400). In a short, final peroration (4 *BJ* II.01–404), the king condemns the rebellion.

Here, a close reading of Josephus' text outlines two possible choices for the future. Josephus is quite clear that like the Pharisees – whose beliefs he has already introduced at the beginning of the second book of *War*, though he discusses it in depth only in *Antiquities* – he believes that God had given free choice to all of mankind. Hence the Jews still have time to choose and determine their destiny.[45] The first choice is clear. If the Jews shall rebel against Rome, they shall bring on themselves a catastrophe. The reason is obvious. As God supports the Roman Empire and stands behind it, Jews who rebel again Rome are, in fact, revolting against God and therefore shall

---
[42] See for example, Philo, *Spec.* 2.231. See also Berthelot 2019: 12.
[43] See Kaden 2011: 503. See also Ovid, *Fasti.* V.550–564; Horace, *Saec*; Galinsky 1996: 91–3, 148.
[44] See Roduit 2003: 371–374.
[45] On the Pharisees, see Josephus, *BJ* II.162–166; *AJ* XIII.288–298 and XVIII.12–15.

be punished. Hence, *prima facie*, the only possible future for them is one of wanton destruction. And yet, if Jews do not rebel against Rome and instead patiently wait for God's salvation, another, brighter future lies in store for them. Divine Providence shall reward Jews with a future of freedom, complete independence, and autonomy – in other words, a future without Rome. Nevertheless, it is also clear from Agrippa II's speech that this course of events depends only on God, and that Jews, by now no more than slaves, are merely mute, passive witnesses of a present and future history.

Indeed, in view of the negative present as well as a negative depiction of the Roman Empire as brutal, Josephus, like Polybius before him, foretells the end of Roman rule, which may not last forever. Both historians suggest a future without Rome, a not unwelcome future. Thus, in the final part of his book, which deals with the siege and conquest of Carthage, Polybius warns the reader through a speech delivered by Scipio Aemilianus, the conqueror of Carthage, that *Tychè* can turn. For the Greek historian, in fact, the capriciousness of Fortune shall result in the end of the Roman Empire in a not so distant future. The Roman Empire is therefore not really different from the mighty empires – most notably the Persian and the Macedonian Empires – that dominated the world in the past. Just as these empires once rose to prominence, dominated the world, then fell down, so too the Roman Empire shall come to an end. Thus, Polybius's cyclical concept of history is mirrored in the prediction of a not distant end of the Roman Empire.[46]

The end of the Roman Empire also appears between the lines of Josephus' writings. A good example of this already appears in his own speech to the Jews in the fourth book of the *War*, where, inviting the rebels to surrender to Roman might, he argues that *Tychè* has passed over to the Romans and that God, having granted supreme rule to various nations, one by one, "now" rests in Italy. E. Gruen argues that this "now" is pregnant with meaning as it points to the end of Rome in a not distant future.[47]

---

[46] On the capriciousness of Fortune, see Polybius, *Hist.* XXXVIII.21–22. On the cyclical theory of empires, see Polybius, *Hist.* I.2.4–7. On the cyclical theory of empires, see also Dionysius of Halicarnassus, *Ant. Rom.* I.2–6. Dionysius mentions the Assyrian, Median, Persian, and Macedonian Empires. The text of the Greek historian living in Augustan Rome is quite ambiguous, and again, reading between the lines, one has the impression that Rome, like previous empires, shall too one day fall. Appian likewise discusses the theory of empires; Rome was preceded by the empires of the Assyrians, Medes, Persians, and Macedonians. The Alexandrine historian is no less ambiguous than Polybius and Dionysius on the future of Rome. See Appian, *Hist. Rom.* I.32–37.

[47] See Josephus, *BJ* V.367.

7. Agrippa II's Address on the Eve of the Jewish War   149

There are, of course, other examples. Most notable lies in the tenth book of *Antiquities*, where Josephus paraphrases Nebuchadnezzar's dream in the Book of Daniel. The gold, silver, brass, and iron statue that appears in the dream to the king symbolizes the four different "kingdoms" that shall in turn rise and come to an end. While according to the traditional interpretation, these "kingdoms" are Babylonia, Media, Persia, and Macedonia, and thus mirror the political conditions of the Near East in the second century BCE, according to Josephus, they are Babylonia, Media, Persia, Macedonia, and Rome. Gruen therefore rightly argues that by the second half of the first century CE, the part of Daniel's prophecy that refers to the great stone that shall eventually be pulverized by the Kingdom of God was seen as depicting the Roman Empire just as it had once been viewed as signifying the Hellenistic kingdoms. Therefore, within the ideological framework that characterizes the interpretation of Daniel's apocalyptic vision in the first century, it is clear that Daniel's prediction refers to the end of the Roman Empire. The eschatological future is plain enough as the demise of Rome has already been foreordained by Daniel, and Josephus is simply making a point of calling attention to this, without stating it explicitly. Gruen's interpretation is shared by P. Spilsbury, who argues that the Jewish historian, albeit very carefully, is addressing the future fall of Rome. Hence, as all kingdoms shall meet their end, even the last one, Rome, shall not be an exception.[48]

Unlike Josephus, Philo nowhere mentions the Book of Daniel. Thus, the Jewish philosopher from Alexandria never refers to the succession of empires, the "four kingdoms" present in the Dream of Nebuchadnezzar.[49]

On the other hand, the passage in *Antiquities* where Josephus paraphrases Bala'am's prophecy is less known. According to Spilsbury, it is already possible to perceive an implicit admonition addressed to the Romans in this prophecy. Josephus warns that *Pronoia*, divine providence, shall always protect the Jews from total destruction, stating that "no entire destruction can seize upon the nation of the Hebrews ... for the Providence of God is concerned to preserve them from such a misfortune" (*AJ* IV.127–128). Even when momentarily defeated they shall once more "flourish and bring fear upon those who caused injury to them." Thus, the Roman Empire, which in the present is dominating the Jews, shall one day too come to an end. Spilsbury argues that this passage

---

[48] See Daniel 2.31–35. See also Josephus, *AJ* X.203–210. See also Mason 1994: 172–3.

[49] According to Berthelot, Philo's attitude to the succession of empires mirrors that of Greek historians. See *Quaest. Gen.* 4.43; *Deus* 173; *Ios.* 134–136. See also Berthelot 2011: 166–87; and Berthelot 2019: 3–4.

can be regarded as evidence that Josephus hopefully wished for the resurrection of a Jewish state, even in a distant future.[50]

The view that the Roman Empire shall, one quite distant day, meet its end is consistently found in all of Josephus' literary output. As Gruen points out, it is possible to read the future demise of the Roman Empire even between the lines of *Contra Apionem*. Here Josephus remarks that only a few nations have had an opportunity to be an empire or *egemonia*, and even they have suffered changes in fortune that have reduced them to servitude. Thus shall come a day when Rome too shall be reduced to servitude.[51]

But is this negative attitude to the future of Rome also present in Agrippa II's speech, which dates to the very beginning of Josephus's literary output? It is clear that Agrippa II cannot explicitly discuss or welcome the end of the Roman Empire as in the eyes of the people he is, in fact, the representative of Rome. Yet, Josephus's teleology, which envisions the end of Rome in the future, also emerges in the king's address. Towards the end of the speech he states clearly that "Divine Assistance ... is already on the side of the Romans; for it is impossible that so vast an empire should be settled without God's Providence" (*BJ* II.390). Therefore if the Jews do wage war against Rome, the dire consequence shall be that they shall completely forfeit God's support as they shall voluntarily transgress Divine Law. Indeed, while waging war, the Jews shall not be able to observe their religious customs zealously. Thus, if they rebel against Rome, they shall incur the wrath of God, who elevated Rome, thus allowing it to dominate the entire *oikoumenè*. Yet, by reading between the lines, one may give a different and broader interpretation to this passage. If the Jews do follow Agrippa II's advice and do not wage war against Rome, they shall be able to fully meet their obligation towards God and will thus be rewarded with Divine Assistance. And what is this "Divine Assistance?" Josephus does not state it clearly, but in light of other passages in the *War*, *Antiquities*, and *Against Apion*, the idea of Divine Assistance hints at the possibility that one day, probably in the distant future, God shall transfer his favor back to the Jews. Thus if the Jews carefully observe His Law, they shall be able to win back divine favor. God shall put an end to the Roman Empire, and the Jews shall be free of the shackles of Roman domination. Jonathan Price claims that Josephus argues for the centrality of the

---

[50] On Bala'am's Prophecy, see Numbers 22–24. See also Josephus, *AJ* IV.112–128. See Spilsbury 2002: 306–27, esp. 317. See also Spilsbury 2003: 1–24. For a similar conclusion, see Goodman 2007: 195–6.

[51] See Josephus, *C. Ap.* 2.127. See Gruen 2011: 159–60.

7. Agrippa II's Address on the Eve of the Jewish War

relationship between God and the Jewish people, who are defined as *theophileis* or the Beloved of God in his teleological view of history. Hence, it is clear that in the same way that God has alternatively favored the various ruling powers and the Jews, rewarding each for their righteous behavior, so in the future He shall grant success once more to the Jews, the "Beloved of God."[52] Yet, it is also clear from Agrippa II's speech that this course of events depends solely on God, and that the Jews, because by now they are no more than slaves, shall be merely mute and passive witnesses in the present and future.[53] Thus, Jews have to be patient and wait for God's salvation.

The Italian historian E. Gabba has already pointed out that in Agrippa II's speech – very much as in Polybius – there is a concept of a cycle of sin, punishment, and salvation, with an eventual new beginning that lies beneath the transference of God's favor.[54] Like Gabba and Gruen, Rajak too has noted a certain similarity to Polybius' argument that *Tychè* is unstable and that God, though now siding with the Romans, will one day change sides. As Rajak states, "the implication of the Josephan doctrine that God is siding with the Romans must surely be that the day will come when the tables will be turned, when He will change sides once more."[55]

We can compare Josephus' view of the future of Rome to Philo's. According to Berthelot, it is possible to infer from the final section of Philo's *That God is Unchangeable*, which reflects on a passage in *Genesis*, that mortal matters are not inherently consistent and can even be compared to a dream. Thus, the fortunes of individuals as well as those of nations are unpredictable. Good fortune can be followed by misfortune. Nothing is stable. History is ruled by *Logos*, the divine Word, which is responsible for the rise and fall of empires, such as those of the Persians and the Macedonians. *Pronoia*, or Divine Providence, is nowhere mentioned in connection with the rise and fall of empires, but plays a definite role only in association with Israel. *Pronoia*, which provides the Jews with blessings throughout history, is not responsible for the rise of the Roman Empire. *Tychè* is the real force behind the creation of the Roman Empire. But *Tychè*, which works in opposition to Nature, cannot be considered an expression of God's will and is thus presented in a negative way. In other words, while the Law of Moses is firmly grounded in Nature, and, as an expression of God's will, is eternal, the Rome an Empire, like any other

---

[52] See Josephus, *BJ* V.381 on *theophileis* or the Beloved of God. See Price 2005: 101–18.
[53] See Josephus, *BJ* II.391–395.   [54] See Gabba 1976–1977: 189–94.   [55] See Rajak 1991: 122–34.

empire, is only temporary as it is rooted in *Tychè*. However, it is in a passage in *Quaestiones in Genesim* that Philo specifically presages the ultimate fall of Rome, after stating that "no less necessary a change awaits those nations that opposed them (the Macedonians), though they have become illustrious and conspicuous in the meantime." Those nations may refer to Rome, but the use of the plural – "those nations" – leaves a question mark. Contrary to Josephus and Agrippa II, Philo rejects *in nuce* the idea that the Roman Empire is the outcome of Divine Providence. However, like Josephus and Agrippa II, he expects Roman rule to fade and hopes for a new bright future for Israel.[56]

Rajak too points to a certain similarity between the teleological conception of the future of Rome in Josephus and the one mirrored in rabbinic literature. The words of the dying Rabbi Yose ben Kisma, who urged Jews who wished to defy the might of Rome to be patient, presents a striking similarity to the final part of Agrippa II's speech. The Jewish sage warns that it is God who has ordained that Rome shall rule, even if the Romans have burned down the Temple. Yet it is also clear that one day God shall punish the Romans for their sins, and that He shall restore the Jews to divine favor.[57] The best example, of course, is a well-known *midrash* dedicated to the Dream of Jacob. Its subject is the future of the four "kingdoms," namely, Babylonia, Persia, Greece, and Rome, all of which have oppressed the Jewish people, who are symbolized by Jacob-Israel. Yet, God's prophecies to Jacob foretell that in the end, Israel shall triumph.[58] There is a clear similarity between the cyclical concept of the empires shared by Polybius and other Greek historians, on the one hand, and Josephus and the Rabbis, on the other. Accordingly, Rome is just one of the "kingdoms," albeit the ruling one. A day will come, as prophesized by Daniel, that Rome too shall fall. However, for the time being the Jews ought to be patient and carefully observe Divine Law.

---

[56] See Philo, *Deus* 140–182, esp. 173–176. See also Philo, *Quaest. Gen.* 4.43. Berthelot 2011: 177–9. See also Berthelot 2019: 12–15. Berthelot tends to identify Edom with Rome, arguing that Edom is seen as the paradigm of Rome in Rabbinic literature. Yet, in the period in question the Idumaeans were still existing as a separate entity within Judaism, as a nation or *ethnos*, and lived on its land, Idumaea, but had totally embraced Jewish religion. The Idumaeans took part as a semi-independent entity in the Jewish War. See for example, Josephus, *BJ* IV.224–353 on the Idumaeans' intervention in Jerusalem during the war.

[57] See b. *Avodah Zarah* 18a. See also Rajak 1991: 132–3.

[58] See Genesis 28:12–13. See also *Pirqe Rabbi Eliezer* 35; *Genesis Rabbah* 68, 14; *Leviticus Rabbah* 29, 2. According to the *midrash*, since Jacob refuses God's invitation to ascend, he condemns his progeny to serve the four empires until the final redemption.

Last but not least, Divine Providence is a conditional concept even in Augustan Rome; it is not absolute. Galinsky argues for an Augustan ethos tied to continuous effort and pursuit. Even if Augustus has brought back the Golden Age of Saturn, only continuous endeavor and exertion shall permit Rome to rule the Empire, as Virgil writes, *parcere subjectis et debellare superbos*.[59]

7.5 Conclusion

In his address to the people of Jerusalem, King Agrippa deals with the issue of liberty, which he presents as independence and autonomy in the past, present, and future. The speech, though specifically addressed to the Jews, is characterized by a particularistic view as the main topic addresses the freedom of the Jews. Nonetheless it is discussed against the background of the freedom of all the cities and peoples of the *oikoumenè*, now enslaved to Rome. Thus here, as in many other passages in Josephus, there is a universal aspect, in this case dealing with the topic of freedom.

The issue of liberty is addressed though a temporal analysis of the past, when the Jews and every other people were free from Roman domination, and the present, in which Rome rules the *oikoumenè* as well as an uncertain future. Yet behind the choice between liberty and slavery stands God, the Master of the Universe. If in the past it was God who allowed each people in the universe to enjoy independence and autonomy, in the present, it is He who stands behind the growth of the Roman Empire. Hence, the present *Pax Romana* mirrors the wish of God. Thus, rebelling against Rome is equivalent to defying God. Yet Agrippa II also suggests the possibility that if the Jews abide with God's laws and wishes, then, in the future, God's grace shall bring an end to the wicked Roman Empire. Although Agrippa II and Josephus are silent on the topic, it is clear that the end of the Roman Empire shall also bring back freedom to all the peoples of the *oikoumenè*, not only the Jews. It is therefore necessary for the Jews to wait patiently for divine salvation. This shall come, perhaps in the near future, perhaps at the end of time. And then the Jews, the nation chosen by God to bring His Word to mankind, shall once again worship God without the hindrance of a brutal war and bring salvation to all of

---

[59] See Kaden 2011: 503. This Augustan ethos is highly evident in the visual arts, as, for example, in the *Ara Pacis*, where the bucolic image shows a snake ready to bite, as well as in the poetry of Horace. See Galinsky 1996: 91–3, 148. Galinsky underscores that though Virgil's *Fourth Eclogue* evokes the return to the Golden Age of Saturn, effort and pursuance, so typical of the Augustan ethos, is absent from it.

mankind. The message of Agrippa II's speech is thus once again universal, as an Israel that worships God shall bring freedom to all nations, through the grace of God.

Acknowledgments

This research has been funded by the European Research Council (ERC) under the European Union's Seventh Framework Program (FP/2007–2013)/ERC Grant Agreement no. 614 424. It has been conducted within the framework of the ERC project Judaism and Rome, under the auspices of the Centre National de la Recherche Scientifique (CNRS) and Aix-Marseille University, UMR 7297 TDMAM (Aix-en-Provence, France).

CHAPTER 8

Josephus, Caligula and the Future of Rome

Jonathan Davies

8.1 Introduction

A Jewish priest, Roman citizen and Greek historian, Flavius Josephus (born Yosef ben Matityahu) is an author whose works are strongly marked by the confluence of traditions. Both the Jewish tradition in which he had been raised and the Graeco-Roman tradition in which he chose to write had long and varied histories of thinking about the future and Josephus, a "prophet" learned in both cultures, could draw on a variety of literary models when forecasting what was to come. Polybius, for instance, one of Josephus' most important sources, articulates a belief in the Greek idea of cyclical history, but is able to accommodate this schema to the realities of his times by arguing that the Roman constitution had found a way to arrest the inevitable degeneration of *anakyklosis*. The composite Roman state had been able to postpone its decline and win extraordinary success, but nevertheless its decline would surely come some day.[1] The Jewish tradition too had things to say about futurity, and specifically about the futures of gentile kingdoms that would occupy Judaea. At the more elaborate end of the spectrum, some streams of Jewish thought predicted eschatological events in meticulous detail; more broadly speaking, all Jews believed in a covenant, a special relationship between God and his people, which could be temporarily interrupted but would always be reinstated. However severe the temporary setbacks faced by the Jewish people, God would always restore his favour eventually, meaning that Roman hegemony could never be anything more than a temporary state.

Situating Josephus' view of the Roman future within the complementary matrices of these two traditions, themselves diverse and multifaceted, is no easy task. Previous scholarship on Josephus' Roman future has focused almost exclusively on three passages, two re-workings of biblical prophecies

[1] Polyb. 6.5–7.

in the *Antiquities* and a piece of rhetoric in the *War* with both Jewish and Graeco-Roman intertexts. Broadly speaking, the lesson of these three passages (which will be sketched out in this chapter) is that the Jewish God has total control over the future of Rome, a view which may have been rather more striking to Roman readers than is usually emphasized in the scholarship, and that the Jewish God will, when the time is right, transfer the sceptre of hegemony elsewhere. Josephus' predictions of a divinely-engineered end to Roman dominion are valorised by a vision of history to which God is central; indeed, not only does Josephus not shrink from documenting God's control over world affairs in the Roman period, he markedly strengthens his emphasis on divine rule over gentiles in the Roman portions of the *Antiquities*.[2] Divine control over the Roman superpower is the theme which connects the predicted failure of the Roman state with the present and the recent past, anchoring the biblical prophecies to the solid bedrock of history. And nowhere is divine control over Roman affairs clearer than in the account of the reign of the emperor Gaius Caligula in Books 18 and 19 of the *Antiquities*.

However, the Caligula material is rarely read in this way or used to illustrate this theme. As I shall argue below, existing scholarship on Josephus' Caligula narratives tends to regard theological concerns as of secondary importance, with scholars more interested in mining the text for details about the emperor or reconstructing Josephus' lost Roman sources. This is a missed opportunity. In this chapter, after taking stock of existing scholarship on the Roman future in Josephus, I shall attempt to read the Caligula narrative as it stands, taking the theological dimension seriously, in the hope that we can learn from it something about the divine control of Roman affairs that underpins Josephus' vision of the prophesied end of empire.

8.2 Three Visions of the Future

The first of the three predictive passages mentioned above occurs at *BJ* 5.367, where Josephus (as a character in the narrative) is addressing the Jerusalem rebels. Resistance is futile, Josephus maintains, and he explains why: μεταβῆναι γὰρ πρὸς αὐτοὺς πάντοθεν τὴν τύχην, καὶ κατὰ ἔθνος τὸν θεὸν ἐμπεριάγοντα τὴν ἀρχὴν νῦν ἐπὶ τῆς Ἰταλίας εἶναι ('Fortune has passed over

---

[2] For some important observations on God's control over the wider political situation and the implications of this for his relationship with the Jewish people, see Klawans 2012: 188–98. A local or provincial god's arrogation of control over Roman affairs was not unique to Josephus in the Greek East: for parallels, see Edwards 1996: 38 (on 2 *Baruch* and 4 *Ezra*); 58 (on Aphrodite of Aphrodisias); 65–8 (on the Christian God) and 64–5 (further comments on divine control over Rome in Josephus).

entirely to them [i.e. the Romans], and God, having led pre-eminence around the nations, is now upon Italy'). This vision of the divine transfer of hegemony from one nation to another has both classical and Jewish precedents; what is really interesting is that there is no clear indication in the text that this constant transfer of pre-eminent power has come to a permanent stop in the present age.³ Indeed the text seems to imply quite the opposite; rarely in Greek prose has the word νῦν been so suggestively deployed. Thus hegemony rests over Italy, but it is there by divine grace and its sojourn is temporary.⁴

The other two passages are both retellings of Biblical prophecies in the *Antiquities*. At *AJ* 10.203–210, Josephus presents an intriguing adaptation of Daniel's interpretation of Nebuchadnezzar's dream of the sequence of four kingdoms that would rule over the Middle East, concretised in the form of a statue whose body parts are made of four distinct materials.⁵ In the original book of Daniel, the fourth kingdom (represented by the statue's feet of mixed iron and clay) signifies the Macedonian successors of Alexander. Josephus, by collapsing the Persians and the Medes into one, makes the final kingdom refer instead to Rome. On reaching the part of the narrative concerning the stone which smashes the feet of the statue (and therefore Rome, the fourth kingdom) before growing to fill the whole world, Josephus indulges in a bit of 'publicly-enacted self-censorship'.⁶ He writes:

> ἐδήλωσε δὲ καὶ περὶ τοῦ λίθου Δανίηλος τῷ βασιλεῖ, ἀλλ' ἐμοὶ μὲν οὐκ ἵστορ εῖν τὰ παρελθόντα καὶ τὰ γεγενημένα συγγράφειν οὐ τὰ μέλλοντα ὀφείλοντι.

> And Daniel also interpreted the stone for the king, but it does not seem right for me to explain this, bound as I am to write about things that are in the present or have passed and not what is to come.⁷

This is restraint indeed from a self-proclaimed prophet, but given that this particular prophecy concerns the coming destruction of Rome, numerous scholars have suspected that Josephus had diplomatic reasons for declining to interpret this part of the vision, and indeed that his very mentioning of it affirms a fundamentally non-Roman agenda: this passage is a coded

---

³ A commonly-cited classical precedent is the prediction of Demetrius of Phalerum of the decline of Macedonian power, quoted by Polybius at 29.21. Price 2011: 240–1 suggests that for Jewish readers this passage would suggest Daniel's Four Kingdoms schema.
⁴ This passage is discussed in Nikiprowetzky 1971: 484–5; de Jonge 1974: 211; Mason 1994: 181; Bilde 1998: 54.
⁵ C.f. *Dan.* 2:31–45. ⁶ For this phrase, see Dominik, Garthwaite and Roche 2009b: 3.
⁷ *AJ* 10.210. Josephus goes on (perhaps rather optimistically) to suggest that interested readers should consult the original *Daniel* for further information.

message to Jewish readers about the impermanence of Roman hegemony.[8] On this point we ought to pay heed to Mason's wise caveats: it would not take an especially sensitive reader to understand the import of Nebuchadnezzar's vision in Josephus' presentation (not least because soon after this Josephus explicitly tells his readers that Daniel predicted Roman rule over Judaea), and if Josephus is attempting to communicate secret messages here, he has done a poor job of concealing them.[9] Nonetheless, here is a second passage clearly drawing attention to the fact that in Josephus' historical imagination Roman rule was a passing phase.

More underhand is Josephus' account of the prophecies of Balaam.[10] Josephus gives us a substantially compressed account of the gentile prophet who, despite being ordered by King Balak to curse the Israelites, cannot do anything but break out in rapturous prophecies of Israel's future blessings. He recounts one substantial prophecy in direct speech, which omits from Balaam's oracles two biblical predictions (at least one of which was later taken as Messianic) of the overthrow and destruction of Israel's conquerors.[11] In a second prophecy, repeated briefly and in indirect speech, Josephus mentions that Balaam foretold the downfall of the nations from remote antiquity right down to Josephus' own day. Josephus concludes knowingly: not all of Balaam's prophecies have yet come true, we are told, but they will. It is hard to see how this could be interpreted as anything other than a coded prediction of the downfall of Rome, most easily comprehensible to readers who happened to know the book of Numbers, which in context has to mean Jews.[12]

It is important to be clear about precisely what can and cannot be said about these passages. It would be a stretch (or at least it would require further argument) to label any of them 'Messianic' or 'eschatological'. Josephus clearly foresees a post-Roman age, but he nowhere specifies precisely that he expects this post-Roman age to be the *eschaton*; indeed he nowhere gives us any information at all about what he thinks this post-Roman age will involve. Moreover, as Mason has pointed out, it may be unjustified to consider these passages 'subversive'. It was in no sense obligatory in the first century to believe that Roman hegemony was the

---

[8] Bruce 1965; de Jonge 1974: 207–11; Sterling 1992: 294; Spilsbury 2003: 1–14; Spilsbury 2005: 224–6; Bilde 1988: 188.
[9] Mason 1994: 171–2. Explicit statement about Daniel and Rome: *AJ* 10.276.
[10] *AJ* 4.112–125, cf. *Num.* 22–24. [11] *Num.* 23:24, 24:17–24.
[12] This passage is discussed in Sterling 1992: 292–3; Bilde 1998: 52–3; Spilsbury 2005: 226–7; Nikiprowetzky 1971: 488.

8. Josephus, Caligula and the Future of Rome

end of history or *imperium sine fine*, and several classical authors speculate on the fall of the empire.[13] What matters in these passages is that there is no indication that this foretold end of Roman power was in any way imminent, and the predictions could therefore be read merely as harmless speculation about an undefined future. However, although the bare fact of speculating about a post-Roman future cannot be said to be subversive or politically awkward, these passages do share a feature which may have seemed surprising, perhaps impertinent, to putative Roman readers. Underneath all three passages lies the rather shocking belief that the small god of the Jews – the national deity of a provincial backwater and its scattered, maligned people, a god comprehensively defeated in recent memory by the imperial pantheon of Rome – held nothing less than the Roman future in his power.

But it is not only in his brief and gnomic visions of the future that Josephus places God at the centre of world events. The arrogation of control over Roman power on behalf of the Jewish God is one of the most striking aspects of the later books of the *Jewish Antiquities*, and it serves to ground Josephus' predictions of a divinely-engineered post-Roman future in the observable reality of the present and the recent past. Now I will turn to consider the clearest and most complete example of divine control over Roman history in Josephus, the long account of the reign of Gaius Caligula in the eighteenth and nineteenth books of the *Jewish Antiquities*, and in particular that emperor's divinely-engineered assassination.

8.3 Caligula, Rome and Divine Authority

Josephus' status as an author whose study cuts across the disciplinary boundaries between Classics, Jewish Studies and the New Testament has had unfortunate consequences for scholarship on certain parts of his work, perhaps never more so than his account of the death of Caligula in the nineteenth book of the *Antiquities*. Largely ignored by Jewish Studies scholars, this section has been left to the Roman historians. Roman historians, in turn, have not fully appreciated all aspects of the account.[14] In particular, classicists seem persistently to underestimate the importance of Jewish theological concerns to this narrative, the sort of concerns that

---

[13] Mason 1994: 172–3.
[14] For example of Roman historians engaging in various ways with this part of Josephus, see Birley 2000; Pagán 2005: 93–108; Wilkinson 2005: 65–72.

Jewish Studies scholars might be interested in if only they would turn their attention to this part of Josephus' *oeuvre*.[15] I hope to argue that theological and political aspects of this divinely-engineered assassination are entirely enmeshed, and that a reading of this material which takes the theological dimension seriously can do much to clarify our understanding of both Josephus' view of God's role in historical causation and his political conception of a world ruled by Rome.

A brief survey of the relevant material in Books 18 and 19 clearly reveals the extent of divine supervision over Caligula's affairs. God's involvement in the reign of Gaius begins with his accession, when God signals his will concerning the succession by frustrating Tiberius' ploy to favour Tiberius Gemellus (*AJ* 18.211–214). Josephus begins to lay the foundations for Caligula's divine punishment as early as *AJ* 18.222, where the aged Tiberius warns Gaius that he may suffer divine punishment if he kills Gemellus, which he promptly does.[16] Later, at 259–260, he recounts Philo's encounter with the emperor when he led an embassy to Rome in 39 or 40 CE. Caligula, inflamed by the anti-Jewish allegations of Apion, scornfully dismisses Philo from his presence, but Philo takes great comfort from this meeting, since what he has seen convinces him that the emperor has already turned God against himself. Josephus proceeds to describe Caligula's attempt to install a statue of himself in the Jerusalem Temple.[17] The new Syrian legate Petronius is commanded to oversee the work but, after representations from the Jews and the Herodian family at Ptolemais and Tiberias, the governor realises that he will not be able to carry out his orders without provoking intolerable dissent. He calls together the local population, announces that he will write to Caligula and urge him to change his mind, and he includes in his oration what can only be read as a prayer to the Jewish God to favour his request. The prayer is immediately answered by a surprise rain shower – another indication that God has a hand in these events.[18] Meanwhile in Rome, Agrippa I manages to trick Caligula into agreeing to abandon his plan to install a statue in the Temple, but the *princeps* still decides to punish Petronius for failing to follow his earlier command. However, the emperor is struck dead, and news of the

---

[15] Deliberate neglect of the theological dimension is particularly noticeable in T. P. Wiseman's commentary (1991) which is unfortunate because the commentary is excellent in many other respects. This *desideratum* may be addressed to some extent by the publication of the relevant volume of the Brill *Josephus* commentary series, which is not yet in print at the time of writing.

[16] Tiberius' almost supernatural insight here into the ways of gods and men perhaps reflects popular Roman traditions of Tiberius as a pious sage, as discussed by Champlin 2008.

[17] *AJ* 18.261–309.   [18] Petronius' 'prayer' and the rain shower is at *AJ* 18.281–285.

assassination reaches Judaea before Petronius' death warrant, thus saving the legate's life – a clear sign, says Josephus, of the providence that has guided events.[19]

There follows a substantial break in the narrative in which Josephus deals with Parthian affairs, before he returns to pick up the thread of the God-cursed emperor at the beginning of Book 19.[20] He begins by providing a potted overview of the outrages and insanities of Gaius. He then states that he wishes to give a full account of Caligula's death specifically because it furnishes an undeniable demonstration of God's concern for justice, and πολλὴν ... πίστιν τοῦ θεοῦ τῆς δυνάμεως ('great assurance of the power of God').[21] He goes on to introduce the three leading conspirators, Cassius Chaerea, Annius Minucianus and Aemilius Regulus, and their reasons for conspiring.[22] The rest of the conspiracy narrative is focalised through Cassius Chaerea's perspective. Josephus tells us that Chaerea grew increasingly sick of the unpleasant jobs Caligula handed him and of being forced to be the instrument of innocent people's misery (though he also mentions Caligula's incessant teasing of Chaerea, which is cited as Chaerea's prime motivation in Suetonius).[23] Chaerea begins to recruit associates for his conspiracy, before finally working up the courage to attempt a communication with Minucianus. The day after he seals his treasonous compact with the senator, Chaerea, while entering the palace, hears a mysterious voice urging him to continue on his planned course and telling him that providence was on his side. Josephus suggests that this may have been the voice of God.[24] Over time the conspiracy attracts more participants, but the assassination is repeatedly delayed, until it is decided that Caligula should be killed during a series of spectacles held on the Palatine. Delays strike again; just prior to the final day of the spectacles, Chaerea gives a speech to galvanise his confederates. The next day, a sequence of ill omens presages what will come, further proof of divine oversight.[25] Caligula leaves the theatre, and his assassins crowd around him

---

[19] *AJ* 18.309.
[20] The following summary is based on *AJ* 19.1–161. I will only give specific references to details of particular interest to this chapter.
[21] *AJ* 19.15–16, Whiston's translation.
[22] Chaerea's role in the assassination is well known – see Suet. *Cal.* 56.2. Wiseman 1991: 47 suggests that 'Annius Minucianus' is a garbled version of the name of L. Annius Vinicianus, attested at Tac. *Ann.* 6.9 and Dio Cass. 60.15.1. In this analysis, I will follow Josephus in referring to him as 'Minucianus', since I am considering this account as a literary artefact and am not primarily interested in questions of its historical accuracy.
[23] *AJ* 19.37. The tipping point is the torture of the Roman citizen Quintilia. On Caligula's teasing, see *AJ* 19.29, cf. Suet. *Cal.* 56.2.
[24] *AJ* 19.60–61.   [25] Portents: *AJ* 19.87; 94–95.

in a narrow passageway and strike him down. One Aquila delivers the killing blow, although Josephus opines that it is Chaerea who truly deserves the credit for the deed. The conspirators escape the scene, and Caligula's narrative of the emperor's death is rounded off with a description of the chaos unleashed by Caligula's German guards in the city.

Even from the above summary, it should be clear that Josephus takes every opportunity to highlight God's responsibility for these momentous events. To summarise all the signs of divine involvement in order, we have Tiberius' thwarted plot to favour Gemellus in the succession, Tiberius' prediction of Caligula's divine punishment, Philo's conviction that God opposed the emperor, the rain shower sent to Petronius, Josephus' expressed conviction that the delay in the death warrant reaching Judaea demonstrates God's role in saving Petronius, Josephus' comments that the emperor's death demonstrates the power of God, the mysterious voice heard by Chaerea and the omens on the day of the assassination. Taking all this together, it certainly seems difficult to agree with Wiseman's assessment that the theological dimensions of this narrative are of only secondary importance.[26] This story clearly presented Josephus with an opportunity to demonstrate and validate his vision of God as the ultimate arbiter of human justice, and as a key causative influence in human history. However, as a first step in illuminating what this divine intervention can show us about God and Rome in Josephan historiography, an altogether more basic question must first be addressed: what is this material doing in the *Antiquities* in the first place?

It is not immediately clear why Josephus opts to devote such a large portion of his work to these Roman political events, which seem rather removed from his work's focus on the history of the Jewish people, even if these events impinge on the Jews because of the developing situation in Judaea. The usual explanation is that Josephus lacked adequate sources for events in Judaea in this period and so included this narrative as filler. This may be true (the account of Judaean history in the same period in the *Jewish War* is also rather sparse), but rather than dismiss this material as tangential padding, it is more productive to ask how Josephus attempts to make it coherent and relevant in the broader context of the *Antiquities*. The question is further complicated by the fact that the Caligula narrative is part of a longer stretch of the *Antiquities* where Josephus loses his focus on Judaea. We have already seen how the accounts of the attempt on the Temple and Caligula's assassination are separated by a Parthian excursus.

---

[26] Wiseman 1991: xiv.

After Caligula's death Josephus keeps the narrative in Rome, giving a similarly detailed account of the stand-off between the Senate and the Praetorians that developed prior to the accession of Claudius.[27] No sooner is Claudius on the throne than Josephus is eager to digress again: after a short section dealing with the reign of Agrippa I we are once more far from Judaea, this time in the Parthian sphere for an account of the tribulations of the royal house of Adiabene.[28] This is a large amount of apparently extraneous material. It is true that throughout the whole of the *Antiquities*, Josephus has shown that he is not a narrowly regional historian: he has followed the Jews into captivity in Egypt and Babylon, and reported other stories of them abroad (as in the case of his retelling of the Esther story, set at the Persian court). However, in the final sections of the *Antiquities*, beginning in Book 18, Josephus seems to be entering a new phase of the project, with a marked rise in his interest in foreign affairs, and also with a marked increase in his God's tendency to meddle in the political business of non-Jewish peoples. In quick succession we see the accessions of both Caligula and Claudius, the death of Caligula, the extraordinary political careers of the bandit–governors Anilaeus and Asinaeus and the successful anti-Parthian resistance of the royal family of Adiabene all directed by the hand of God.[29] This is not quite a case of Josephus turning to write universal history, since all of this material has a Jewish angle, Caligula because of his assault on the Temple, the Parthian and Adiabenean narratives because they feature Jewish protagonists, and Claudius' accession because of the important role played in the proceedings by Agrippa I.[30] Nevertheless Josephus' eagerness to show the highest political affairs of gentiles being directed by the will of God sets these sections of the work apart from most of what has gone before.

So what prompted this marked change of focus and emphasis? The answer to this problem may lie right back at the beginning of the *Antiquities*, in the programmatic preface at the start of Book 1. Here, Josephus tells us, very clearly, that the *principal lesson* of his book is that God is sovereign over all, and that those who obey his will will prosper and

---

[27] *AJ* 19.167–273. [28] *AJ* 20.17–96.
[29] Divine supervision of the accessions of both Caligula and Claudius is asserted at *AJ* 18.211–214 and *AJ* 19.69.
[30] Price 2011: 229 attempts to class the *Antiquities* as a universal history, on the grounds that it tells the complete history of the Jewish people and that it emphasizes the universal power of God. I am not quite convinced that this is enough to constitute a 'universal history' on the usual definition, and (unlike Polybius) Josephus nowhere claims to be writing a universal history.

succeed, whereas those who do not will suffer.[31] In other words, the principal express purpose of the *Antiquities* is to demonstrate the centrality of God's will and judgement over human history. Bearing this in mind, we see that all of these digressions in fact are far from digressive, and they all further the express aim of the *Antiquities*, to show the power of the Jewish God over human affairs. In choosing to recount stories from both the Roman and the Parthian spheres, Josephus demonstrates that God recognises no geopolitical limits to his authority; the Jewish God is no celestial client–king, running the affairs of an obscure Middle Eastern province, but rather (in the words of Isaiah) 'the whole earth is full of his glory'.[32] Moreover, in the Roman sections, Josephus is undertaking a daring rhetorical manoeuvre, and one which we have seen echoed in his predictions of a divinely-engineered post-Roman age. The greatest affairs of Roman history, it turns out, are decided by the God of the Jews. Josephus appropriates Roman history and subordinates it to Jewish theology: the voice of God ringing out for Cassius Chaerea in Caligula's palace is the most strikingly concretised expression of this act of intellectual reverse-imperialism, where a defeated God controls the high politics of the people who will go on to defeat him.[33] Caligula had tried (and failed) to intrude into the Jewish sacred space by erecting his statue in the Temple; the God of that Temple has no difficulty whatsoever in intruding into the heart of the Roman political sphere, successfully reversing Gaius' attempt to impose his power by violating spatial boundaries.[34] Gaius' power is temporal and contingent, dependent (as the Petronius episode shows) on the goodwill and loyalty of his subordinates; God's power is autonomous, and therefore complete. On this reading, divine intervention is not of secondary importance to Josephus' account of the principate and death of Caligula; in picking up on the lessons promised to us in the prologue, it is the central consideration behind its inclusion in the *Antiquities* in the first place.

A subordination of Roman power to the Jewish God is practically necessitated by this change of emphasis, but there are signs in the text that Josephus was conscious of the potential political difficulties that such

---

[31] *AJ* 1.14. Elsewhere in the preface Josephus insists on the power of God to punish those who are not virtuous, at 1.23.

[32] Is. 6:3.

[33] It may be added that this striking arrogation of control over Roman history on behalf of the Jewish God is paralleled by Josephus' insistence, in the *Jewish War*, that Vespasian's rise to the throne was the work of God (*BJ* 6.312–313). On this, see Thérond 1981: 243.

[34] For a sophisticated reading of the spatial politics of this episode, see Von Ehrenkrook 2008.

8. Josephus, Caligula and the Future of Rome

a move may involve, and he seems to take steps to render this stark emphasis on the overwhelming power of God more palatable to Roman readers. The question of precisely how the downfall of Caligula is orchestrated in the *Antiquities* is of some significance. It is striking, although Josephus makes it clear that Caligula's downfall is unquestionably the will of God and he links this through the sign sent to Petronius to the assault on the Jerusalem Temple, that the actual conspiracy itself proceeds with no reference whatsoever to Jewish affairs. Josephus is too astute to try to convince his readers that Chaerea and his associates did what they did out of concern for the religious sensitivities of the Jews. What we see in this story is an approach to the relationship between divine and human agency closely related to the causative over-determination commonly seen in classical historiography, the simultaneous attribution of entirely sufficient supernatural and natural explanations for the same phenomenon. Josephus gives us a story that would be perfectly comprehensible if all references to God were removed, while nevertheless continually insisting that the Jewish God lay behind everything. Thus the conspirators enact the will and the punishment of God without having any awareness that this is what they are doing. This has an interesting effect on the narrative: it serves to equate the interests of Rome with the will of God. Thus, when Josephus emphasizes the outrages Caligula perpetrated on Romans as well as Jews, and when he puts speeches in the mouth of Cassius Chaerea justifying the assassination in purely secular Roman terms, he makes it plain that Caligula, though emperor, does not represent the real Rome.[35] His death benefits Romans as much as it does Jews, and therefore a divinely-orchestrated assassination of a Roman emperor should not imply an inherent opposition between Rome as a system or an abstract concept and the Jewish God. No doubt this distinction was easy for Josephus to make because of the political fact that under the Flavians denigration of Caligula was permitted, and perhaps even encouraged.[36] So in Josephus, even when he is striking down an

---

[35] Caligula's perversions: *AJ* 19.1–15, c.f. 19.201–211; speeches of Chaerea: *AJ* 19.40–43, 78–83. Note particularly Chaerea's explicit opposition between the interests of Caligula and those of the 'Roman rule' (ἀρχῆς τῶν Ῥωμαίων) at 19.42.

[36] Scholarship on the Flavians and their use of imperial precedents has revealed a pointed aversion to attempting to connect the family to any part of Gaius' legacy. Levick 1999: 73–4, for instance, finds clear signs that Vespasian sought to appropriate elements of the images of Augustus, Tiberius and Claudius, but not Nero or Caligula. They are also the only two Julio-Claudians whose names and examples are not cited in the inscription known as the *lex de imperio Vespasiani* (*CIL* 6.930 = *CIL* 6.31207 = *ILS* 244), which delineates Vespasian's powers with reference to Julio-Claudian precedents. As for active denigration in contemporary literature, every single authorial comment on Gaius in Pliny the Elder is negative, and on a striking number of occasions he pairs Caligula with

emperor, the God of the Jews is working in harmony with the values and interests of Rome.

Similar diplomatic strategies can be detected in the Petronius material in Book 18 of the *Antiquities*. Considering the precise role of Petronius himself in this narrative is revealing, particularly in the context of depictions of Roman–Jewish tension elsewhere in Josephus' works. When dealing with incidences of conflict between Rome and the Jews of Judaea, Josephus often employs a particular narrative scheme which is discernible in both the *War* and the *Antiquities*. Trouble is provoked by the conduct of a poor Roman administrator, usually an equestrian governor of Judaea. Rebellious Jews react to this, or else such a reaction is threatened. Resolution usually comes from a more senior figure in the Roman administration, either the proconsular governor of Syria or the emperor.[37] This narrative scheme suits Josephus perfectly: it enables him to criticise Romans without criticising Rome. In this way he legitimises to some extent the grievances of rebellious Jews, while always demonstrating that, in the ordinary course of events, Roman justice is adequate to the task of punishing or preventing misgovernment.[38] Thus in some ways Petronius perfectly fits the Josephan mould of a responsible, moderate Syrian governor when he takes the decision to resist Caligula's orders in the interests of the Jews, and our positive assessment of the man is guaranteed when we see God preserving him from danger by killing Caligula before his death warrant can take effect. But beyond the conventional role of Petronius, we can see that the typical Josephan narrative is here completely inverted. Ordinarily, subordinates cause problems and, through a process of appeal to higher authority which Josephus consistently emphasizes, these problems are corrected by superiors. This is an essentially reassuring narrative structure, designed to emphasize that, when things are working properly, Rome can be trusted to correct its own abuses, because it presides over a fundamentally, albeit not infallibly, just system. However, in the Petronius narrative in the *Antiquities* we have a situation where the people

---

Nero, who was frequently denigrated in Flavian Rome (Pliny, *HN* 4.10, 7.45, 11.143, 13.83, 35.18, 36.74, 36.111).

[37] As examples of situations that were resolved by Syrian governors, I would cite the problems under Pontius Pilatus (*AJ* 18.55–88), and the failed attempts of Cestius Gallus and his envoy Neapolitanus to calm the unrest provoked by the outrageous Gessius Florus (*BJ* 2.333–341). For Judaean misgovernment corrected by the emperors, see the accounts of the governorship of Cumanus (*BJ* 223–245 = *AJ* 20.103–127), the recall of Felix (*AJ* 20.182) and the trouble between Fadus and his subjects over the High Priestly vestments (*AJ* 20.6–10).

[38] My characterisation of Josephus' portrayal of the role of governors in provoking dissent is indebted to the discussions of Rajak 1983: 65–77, Sanders 1992: 35, and Goodman 1987: 7–9.

of Judaea cannot appeal to a higher authority to address their grievances and, in a complete inversion of how the system usually works, they are reduced to appealing to a subordinate (Petronius) about the emperor's conduct. The inversion motif is strongly reinforced by Josephus' long account of the many perversions and idiosyncrasies of Gaius mentioned above: this is a man who turns everything upside down, and under whose authority the ordinary mechanisms of imperial justice simply cannot function. In this case, and unusually, Rome simply cannot address the complaints of its subjects, because Caligula's destabilising personality has subverted the fundamental justice underpinning the Roman *imperium*. Thus the standard channels of justice are clogged up, and resolution can only come from one quarter, the one entity in existence more powerful than Gaius Caligula.

Josephus thus creates a situation where nothing but a divine intervention can restore justice to the world. God therefore acts against a Roman emperor, but in the least subversive way possible. He acts against a man who has inverted the values of Rome, whose removal is in Rome's interests just as much as it is in the interests of the Jews, and whose vilification was positively encouraged by the ruling dynasty at the time of the *Antiquities*' composition. Here, Josephus can depict God intervening in human affairs against an unjust gentile tyrant just as he did in biblical times in defence of his people, but he can do so in such a way that his account does not emphasize hostility between Rome and the Jews, but rather the harmonious congruence of their interests. God may be in control of Roman affairs, but he is not countermanding or subverting Roman justice: he is complementing it, correcting it and thus ensuring a return to the fundamental justice of the Roman system after the brief but violent interruption brought about by Gaius Caligula.

8.4 Conclusions

The Caligula material in the *Antiquities* thus provides useful insights into the mechanics of divine oversight over the high politics of Rome. Josephus' focus on the confluence of the interests of Rome with those of God in the assassination of Caligula suggests that, as long as God approves and promotes Rome's global hegemony, he will intervene in political affairs to promote the genuine interests of Rome. However, there is little real comfort for Roman readers here. The prophetic passages make it clear that divine support for Rome is ultimately a temporary phenomenon; that the very same power which has guided Rome to global dominion will one day turn against it, as it did in the case of Babylon, and bring about its end and the liberation of the Jewish people. Beneath the diplomatic language and apologetic strategies, divine authority over the Roman superpower is a constant feature of Josephus' thought; the *Jewish War* brings this theme right up to the present, by illustrating how Rome's triumph over the Jews and the Flavians' rise to the purple were also sponsored by the divinity. The strange story of the wicked governor Catullus, punished by God for his outrages against the Jews of Cyrene and Rome, the story with which Josephus concludes the *Jewish War*, demonstrates that even after the defeat of his people and the destruction of his Temple God continues to drive Roman history.[39] Thus divine power over Rome runs like a thread through Josephus' works, from the Julio-Claudian past, through the post-70 present and into the indeterminate future as foreseen by Balaam and Daniel and even Polybius.[40] For all the Hellenistic colouring of his rhetoric and for all the attempts to render this schema less shocking to his putative Roman readers, this is a fundamentally Jewish, covenantal expectation of the future, looking ahead to the day when the words God spoke through Zechariah will be fulfilled: וְהָיָה בַּיּוֹם הַהוּא אֲבַקֵּשׁ לְהַשְׁמִיד אֶת־כָּל־הַגּוֹיִם הַבָּאִים עַל־יְרוּשָׁלָם ('and on that day I will seek to destroy all the nations which come against Jerusalem').[41]

Acknowledgement

I would like to thank Professor Martin Goodman, who supervised the MPhil thesis from which much of this chapter is derived, and who kindly read and commented on a draft. I also thank the participants in the classics work in progress and Jewish history and literature seminars at Oxford, who offered me valuable comments and suggestions.

---

[39] *BJ* 7.437–453.
[40] The speech of Agrippa II in *BJ* 2.345–401 seeks to extend the history of divine rule over Rome further back in time by arguing that Rome could not have acquired its empire without God's assistance.
[41] Zech. 12:9.

CHAPTER 9

"Will This One Never Be Brought Down?"
Jewish Hopes for the Downfall of the Roman Empire

Vered Noam

9.1 Introduction

R. Nachman opened [his homily, with the verse]: "therefore fear not, O Jacob my servant, says the Lord, neither be dismayed, O Israel; for I will save you from afar, and your seed from the land of their captivity. And Jacob shall again be quiet and at ease, and none shall make him afraid" (Jer. 30:10). This speaks of Jacob himself, [for it is written:] "And he dreamed, and behold a ladder set up on the earth, and the top of it reached to heaven; and behold the angels of God ascending and descending on it" (Gen. 28:12). R. Samuel b. Nachman said: do you think that these were angels? These were not angels, but rather the princes of the nations. He showed him the prince of Babylon ascend seventy rungs, and the prince of Medes ascend fifty-two rungs, and the prince of Greece ascend a hundred and eighty rungs, *and the prince of Edom ascend and ascend, and* [Jacob] *knew not how many rungs. He said before Him* [the Lord]*: Lord of all the worlds, will this one ever be brought down?* The Holy One, blessed be He, said: Jacob, even if you see him rise to the skies, I will bring him down. As it is said: "Though you make your nest as high as the eagle, and though you set it among the stars, I will bring you down from there, declares the Lord" (Ob. 1:4).[1]

The scene portrayed in this midrash from Leviticus Rabbah, whose components are attributed to two third-century sages, the Babylonian Rav Nachman and the Palestinian R. Samuel b. Nachman, is one of the rabbinic depictions of the paradigm of the four kingdoms in the Book of Daniel (Chapters 2 and 7, see also Chapter 8). According to this archetype, the entire history of the world, which is divinely predestined, is divided into four major periods in which each one of these kingdoms reigns in

---

[1] Leviticus Rabbah, 29:2, author's translation.

succession and is followed by a messianic era in which all collapse and Israel is released from any human yoke. This "future history" is revealed to the biblical Jacob. The rise and fall of the great empires is portrayed not as the outcome of complicated historical processes, but rather as the preordained dramatic setting of the relationship between God and His chosen people.[2] The verse of encouragement, quoted from the book of Jeremiah, "therefore fear not, O Jacob my servant," originally addressed to the entire nation, is here interpreted as a consolatory message and directed personally to the biblical Jacob as he is dreaming in Bethel. However, this individualization of the prophecy is merely a literary dramatic device, since Jacob is immediately transformed into a personification of the entire nation – or more accurately, the Jewish populace of late third-century Palestine – which desperately sought the Roman Empire's downfall. The comforting words on the future fall of Rome are based on Obadiah's eschatological prophecy regarding the fall of the Edomites. This probably means that the homilist expected the downfall of Rome to occur only at the End of Days, by the hand of God, with no involvement on Jacob's part.

This midrash demonstrates how actual political anxieties and messianic expectations were integrated into Scripture, and how a biblical scene may have served as a powerful vehicle for political-theological visions of the fall of Rome. Indeed, a key method for understanding Judean-Jewish political and cultural attitudes towards the Roman Empire is through the examination of exegetical expansions of biblical scenes that reflect the fears, hopes, and desires of their authors and addressees.

In order to follow transformations in the Jewish political ideas concerning the future of Rome, we begin our journey with Qumran texts of the first century BCE, namely, at the beginning of the Roman occupation of Judaea, and from there proceed to the apocryphal work known as the Second Baruch, to the Palestinian Amoraic midrash, and finally to the Babylonian Talmud, which is set in Late Antiquity. These texts, with their varied literary techniques, demonstrate the intriguing shift – sometimes manifested even in exegeses of a single biblical pericope – from divine assurance of the contemporary revolt's success, through rational, concrete hopes for the collapse of Roman rule thanks to military action by world powers, and, finally, to passive expectation of the fall of Rome through divine intervention in a messianic future. An examination of the wording of some of these eschatological visions has surprisingly shown that

---

[2] See Yerushalmi 1989: 22–3.

contemporary Jewish liturgy may echo ancient hopes for the demise of the Roman Empire.

9.2 Qumran

The Qumran library provides several references to Rome under the epithet "Kittim." The word is first mentioned in the biblical "Table of Nations" in Genesis, in which it is listed as the term for the descendants of Japheth and Javan (Genesis 10:4). Other biblical references construe it as a general label for western nations and the inhabitants of the Mediterranean islands. The reference most relevant to our needs is the concluding verse of Balaam's prophecy to the nations: "Ships shall come from the coast of Kittim, and they shall afflict Asshur, and shall afflict Eber, and he also shall come to destruction" (Num. 24:24). As Hanan Eshel observes, "Balaam's prophecy was understood as eschatological – that the Kittim would rule over Asshur and Israel as well but would eventually perish. Since this was understood as a description of the End of Days, the identification of the Kittim was of great significance to those who were waiting for the End of Days in the Second Temple period."[3]

In its post-biblical function, however, the term "Kittim" is ambiguous as in certain works dating to the Second Temple period, it can be used to designate nations other than Rome, such as Greeks and Macedonians,[4] or Mediterranean tribes in general.[5] On the other hand, it was used to designate the Romans as early as the Maccabean revolt (Daniel 11:29–30). Similarly, in the Qumran library we encounter occurrences of Kittim that clearly refer to the Romans, and others, to be discussed below, that are vague and therefore subject to scholarly debate.

The Kittim receive mention mainly in the War Scroll and related texts (1QM=1Q33; 4Q491; 4Q492; 4Q285),[6] and in four of the pesharim (1QpHab; 1QpPs^b=1Q16; 4QIsa^a=4Q161; 4QpNah=4Q169).[7] In Pesher Nahum and Pesher Habakkuk, the reference is clearly to the

---

[3] Eshel 2008: 163–4. [4] 1 Macc. 1:1, 8:5. [5] Jub. 24:28–29; 37:10. See Josephus, *Ant.* 1:128.
[6] The word "Kittim" should undoubtedly also be restored in 4Q496 3:6, which parallels 1QM 1:6.
[7] The Psalms Pesher (1Q16=1QpPs) frags. 9–10:3–4 is too fragmentary for its attitude towards the Kittim to be assessed. The Isiah Pesher^a will be discussed further in this chapter. For an additional fragmentary mention in 4Q247 and a suggested restoration in 4Q332, see the full review by Brooke 2015: 17–32. For general discussions of the Kittim in the DSS and the sectarian attitude towards Rome, see e.g. Amusin 1977: 123–52; Brooke 1991: 135–59; Lim 2000: 470; Eshel 2001: 29–44; Alexander 2003: 17–31. For a recent comprehensive review of the scholarship and a fresh discussion, see work of Sharon 2016: 357–88.

Romans,[8] who "trampled" Jerusalem (4QpNah 3–4 i:3). Described as swift, cruel, and mighty conquerors coming from distant sea coasts, fear of whom exists in all nations (1QpHab ii:10–17; iii; iv; vi:1–12; ix:4–7), they are also divine agents for the destruction of the wicked in Jerusalem (1QpHab 9:4–7; 4QpNah 3–4 ii:3–6; iv:1–4). Several scholars have suggested that these pesharim represent an earlier stance of the *Yahad*, whose initial approach to the Romans was either neutral or favorable, due to the sect's opposition to the Hasmonean state, which was terminated by the Roman conquest.[9] Others object to this view, pointing at expressions of deep hostility towards the Romans in the pesharim, in which the Romans are depicted as cruel and evil, act cunningly and deceitfully (1QpHab iii 5, 12–13; iv.10–13), are accused of idolatry (1QpHab v.14–15), and, most importantly for our purposes here, are anxiously expected to get their due. Thus, for example, the biblical verse: "You have ordained them for judgment, and You, O Rock, have established them for correction" (Hab. 1:12, JPS 1917) is interpreted in Pesher Habakkuk as heralding the judgment of the nations, including the above-mentioned rulers of Kittim (iv.16–v.1ff.), by God's chosen. "God will not destroy his people by the hand of the nations, but into the hand of his chosen God will give the judgment of all the nations" (1QpHab v.3–4).[10] The sea mentioned in Nahum's prophecy – "He rebukes the sea, and makes it dry" (Nah. 1:4) – is identified with "all the Ki[ttim . . .] so as to ren[der] a judgment against them and to wipe them out from upon the face of [the earth]" (4QpNah 1–2 ii:3–4).[11]

By contrast, the contexts in which the Kittim appear in other Dead Sea Scroll (DSS) texts are different and their precise identity is unclear. These works – the various manuscripts or versions of the War Scroll and a parallel section of one of them in Pesher[a] Isaiah – prophesize the Kittim's future defeat rather than their being the means through which God will destroy the wicked.

In these texts, this nation is often mentioned as the major enemy of the Sons of Light in the eschatological war. Thus, "the troops of the Kittim of Asshur" are enumerated among the enemies of the Sons of Light. The [king

---

[8] On the Romans in Pesher Nahum, see Berrin 2004: 87, 101–4 and Berrin 2005: 65–84. On the Romans in Pesher Habakkuk see Atkinson 1959: 243; Brownlee 1979: 81; Nitzan 1986: 125–8.
[9] Stegemann 1998: 131–2; Atkinson 1999: esp. 445; Vermès 2007: 139.
[10] Cited from Horgan's translation in Charlesworth et al. 2002: 169.
[11] Cited from Horgan's translation in Charlesworth et al. 2002: 147. See Brooke 1991: 155. On the ambivalence towards the Romans in these two pesharim, see Brooke 2015 and Sharon 2016: 379–85.

9. Jewish Hopes for the Downfall of the Roman Empire

of?] the Kittim will [enter, fight, or fight in] Egypt, and march against the kings of the north, but will also try to exterminate and cut off the horn of Israel (1QM 1:4–5). The scroll describes in detail the war waged by the Sons of Light and their encampment directed against the king of Kittim and the entire army of Belial gathered around him (15.2–3). The camps of the Kittim, their lines, their "mighty men," their slain soldiers, as well as "the multitude of Assyria," and "the forces of all the nations" are colorfully depicted (16.3, 6, 8, 9; 19.10, but also 4Q491 10 ii; 11 ii; 13; 4Q492 1.9, 12). Eventually, "the day of the Kittim's fall" will arrive, and "the Kittim's dominion shall come to an end," so that wickedness can be "subdued without a remnant" (1QM 1.9.6; 4Q496 3.6).[12]

Further events of this future war are described in the fragmentary War Scroll^b (4Q285). These have to do with a flight to sea and probably the king of the Kittim, and finally describe the joy of the Sons of Light after their victory.

All the fragments and versions of this rich eschatological vision share a prominent feature: that the defeat of the Kittim, though wrought by the God of Israel, is not miraculous. It will follow an active war waged by the Sons of Light.[13]

Another feature of these texts is the use of and allusions to biblical passages. Fragment 7 of War Scroll^b serves as a prominent example. It is, in fact, a pesher on Isaiah 11, which has a better preserved parallel in Pesher Isaiah (4QpIsa^a = 4Q161, iii 6–21, which relates to Isaiah 10–11):

6) [" ... and the th]ickets of [the forest will be hacked down] with an axe, and Lebanon by a mighty one
7) will fall" (Isaiah 10:34). They are the] Kittim, wh[o] will fa[ll] by the hand of Israel. And the Poor Ones of
8) ... all the nations, and the mighty ones will be filled with terror, and [their] cour[age] will dissolve
9) [... "And those who are lofty] in stature will be cut down" (10.33). They are the mighty ones of the Kitt[im]

---

[12] Citations and paraphrases follow Duhaime's translation in Charlesworth et al. 1995: 97–141.
[13] Flusser 2007b: 165 underscores the heavenly interference at the very end of the war as presented in the War Scroll, which describes a supernatural final victory and mentions "the sword of God" (1QM 19:9–13). However, the entire war is clearly a battle between human armies. The scroll describes priestly encouragement of the warriors before the war (xv, xvii) and their bravery in battle (xvi–xvii). Moreover, when the author declares that the battle is God's and that the enemy's defeat is due to "the power of your hand" (xi:1), it is clear that what he means is that God grants victory to the righteous party, rather than a miraculous deliverance. "For in the hands of the poor ones you will deliver the enemies" (xi:13).

10) [...] *d* "and the thickets of [the] forest will be hacked down with an axe." Th[ey are]
11) [...] *m* for the battle of the Kittim. "And Lebanon by a mi[ghty one]
12) [will fall." . . . .] Kittim, who will be giv[en] into the hand of his great ones [...]
13) [...] *ym* when he flees from befo[re Is]rael [...] *m* [...]
14) . . . .
15) [There will come forth a shoot from the stu]mp of Jesse, and a branch [will grow] out of [his] ro[ots. And] on him [will re]st the sp[irit of]
16) [God, a spirit of] wisdom and discernment, a spirit of coun[sel and might,] a spirit of knowle[dge]
17) [and fear of God, and his delight (will be) in fear of] God [...][14]
22) [...] David, who will take (his) stand in the lat[ter days ...]
23) [... .] his [ene]my. And God will sustain him with [a mi]ghty [spirit ...]
24) [... a th]rone of glory, a h[oly] crown, and garments of variegated stu[ff.]
25) [...] in his hand, and over all the n[ation]s he will rule, and Magog
26) [... al]l the peoples will his sword judge [...][15]

In this passage, the Kittim are identified with Lebanon, who will fall by "a mighty one," along with "the lofty," who will be cut off, and with "the thickets of the forest," which will be hacked down with an ax, all mentioned in Isaiah 10:33–34. These events will come to pass "in the latter days," when the messianic ruler, the son of David, will again assume the throne.

Most scholars understand the verses in Isaiah as a metaphor for the failure of some Assyrian raid on Judaea in the final quarter of the eighth century BCE.[16] "Lebanon"[17] is the Assyrian king or army, and the "mighty" is the Lord. This was probably how the prophecy was also interpreted in Second Temple times, but with two modifications: (a) the enemy was no longer biblical Assyria, but rather a current world power,[18]

---

[14] The Pesher cites Isaiah 11:1–5, but I skip the rest of the citation here.
[15] There is a continuation that is not included here. Cited from Horgan's translation in Charlesworth et al. 2002: 92–95, slightly revised. The biblical verses integrated into the Pesher are cited according to their translation therein.
[16] In accordance with the reasonable assumption that verses 33–34 relate to the previous verses addressed to Assyria rather than to the following verses (11:1 ff.) addressed to Judah. See Oswalt 1986: 273–4; Blenkinsopp 2000: 261–2.
[17] For a review of the meanings of "Lebanon" in the Bible and in postbiblical interpretations, see Vermès 1973: 32–9; Gordon 1992; Japhet 2003: 707–11.
[18] Teeter 2012: 197–8 observes that "eighth-century Assyria has been absorbed – already in Isaiah – into a larger, typological role in its capacity as the rod of divine wrath that is itself destined to destruction ... the historical particulars of Assyria's role and fate become features of an archetype."

which, in this pesher, is labeled "Kittim"; (b) its rule would end "by the hands of Israel" (l. 7) rather than by heavenly action.

The exact identity of the Kittim in both the War Scroll and Pesher Isaiah is still a matter of debate, with most scholars identifying them as the Romans, and a minority arguing that they were the Seleucids or the Ptolemies.[19] Nadav Sharon has recently reviewed this scholarly debate in detail, adding weighty reasons for favoring the Roman identity of every reference to the Kittim in the DSS. One is based on Flusser's discovery that column 1 of 1QM leans heavily on Daniel 11:40ff., where the epithet "Kittim" clearly designates the Romans, and the "King of the North" is undoubtedly a Seleucid monarch.[20] It is therefore unreasonable, according to Sharon, to suppose that the author of 1QM would have utterly inverted his source and applied the term "Kittim" to the Seleucids, and "King of the North" to their enemies. Another argument is that the Seleucid Empire was in decline around the time of the composition of the scroll and was therefore poorly suited to fill the role of the ultimate eschatological enemy. It should also be taken into account that historically, the Seleucids were defeated by the Hasmoneans, whom the sectarians heartily despised and opposed.[21] In addition, I note that elsewhere in Second Temple Jewish literature, both the cedar of Lebanon imagery and the vision of a wicked dominion that will come to an end are associated with the Romans, as shown further in this chapter.

Moreover, there is no doubt that from the second half of the first century BCE, that is, after the Roman conquest, Kittim was used solely as a reference to the Romans. This is evident from the above-mentioned peshers on Nahum and Habakkuk. Thus, even those scholars who opt for the Hellenistic identification of the Kittim in 1QM and in 4QpIsa^a admit that "in the second half of the first century BCE . . . this term is given also the 'Roman' meaning in texts being copied contemporaneously."[22] George Brooke convincingly argues that "as the text of 1QM was variously edited and reused, there was nothing in the second half of the first century BCE to prevent the later reader or hearer of 1QM 1 from understanding that the text referred to the Romans." The same applies, in his opinion, to Pesher Isaiah, extant only in a late first-century BCE copy.[23] It is also noteworthy

---

[19] For identification of these Kittim with the Romans, see e.g. Yadin 1962: 245–6; Alexander 2003: 30; Sharon 2016. For identification with the Seleucids, see e.g. Amusin 1977: 123–52; Flusser 2007a: 154–5; Eshel 2001. For a review of the data and the scholarly stances and a more nuanced opinion, see Brooke 2015.
[20] Flusser 2007a. [21] Sharon 2016. [22] Schultz 2009: 135. Cited by Brooke 2015: 26.
[23] Brooke 2015: 26–7.

that all the manuscripts of the War Scroll that mention the Kittim date to the Roman period. From the Roman occupation onwards, both the eschatological enemy of the War Scroll and the prophecy of Isaiah on the fall of the cedar of Lebanon must have been understood to represent a future victory over the Romans rather than the Greeks, who were no longer in power. According to both texts, the anticipated fall of the Roman enemy will be carried out by Israel and occur after an eschatological war. In both cases, the prophecies draw on biblical passages from Habakkuk, Nahum, and especially Isaiah 10–11, which originally referred to the defeat of Ashur.

9.3 Second Baruch

Several scholars have shown that the apocalyptic tradition found in the War works and the Isaiah Pesher from Qumran is also manifest in the apocryphal book, 2 Baruch.[24] This Jewish pseudepigraphical text, written shortly after the destruction of the Second Temple in 70 CE, is attributed to the biblical Baruch, Jeremiah's scribe, and thus formally associated with the sixth-century BCE destruction of the First Temple.[25] The first and larger section of the book, the *Syriac Apocalypse of Baruch* (chapters 1–77; the second section consists of the *Epistle of 2 Baruch* and comprises chapters 78–87), deals with the theological crisis engendered by the destruction, and its apocalyptic text includes, inter alia, revelatory scenes followed by heavenly interpretations. In a vision described in chapters 36 to 40 and followed by a divine interpretation, the author sees a forest, a vine, and a nearby fountain. Suddenly, the fountain floods the forest and uproots all its trees, leaving only one fallen cedar. Thereupon the vine says to the cedar:

> (7) Are you not that cedar which remained of the forest of wickedness, and because of whom wickedness persisted and flourished all those years, and goodness never? (8) And you kept conquering that which did not belong to you, and you did not show compassion to that which did belong to you. And you kept extending your power over those who were far from you, and you kept those who drew near to you in the toils of your wickedness, and you prided yourself always as one that could not be uprooted. (9) But now your time has passed and your hour has come. (10) Do you also, therefore,

---

[24] See William Horbury's comment in Vermès 1992: 89–90; see also Bauckham 1995 and Flusser 2007b. On connections between 2 Baruch and 4 Ezra, on the one hand, and wisdom texts, Pseudo-Ezekiel, and the Apocryphon of Jeremiah C from Qumran, on the other, see Dimant 2013: 31–61.

[25] On 2 Baruch, see Bogaert 1969; Gurtner 2009; Sayler 1984.

9. Jewish Hopes for the Downfall of the Roman Empire

depart, O cedar, after the forest which departed before you, and become dust with it, and let your ashes be mixed together? And now, recline in anguish and rest in torment until your last time comes, in which you will return and be tormented even more (Chapter 36).[26]

Eventually the author sees the cedar burning and the vine growing (Chapter 37). In this case, there is no doubt as to the identity of the wicked cedar, since God interprets the vision for the dreamer,[27] prophesizing the rise and fall of the four kingdoms, based on the paradigm in the Book of Daniel, and clarifying that the vision pertains to the fall of the fourth kingdom:

> (5) And after these things a fourth kingdom will arise, whose power will be more harsh and more evil than those which were before it, and it will rule many times like the forests on the plain, and it will hold fast for times, and will exalt itself more than the cedars of Lebanon.[28] (6) And truth will be hidden by it, and all those who are polluted by unrighteousness will flee to it, as evil beasts flee and creep into the forest.[29] (7) And it will be when the time of its completion is coming, that it should fall. Then the reign of my Messiah will be revealed, which is like the fountain of the vine, and when it is revealed it will uproot the multitude of its hosts (Chapter 39).[30]

As Richard Bauckham observes, "Baruch's vision is constructed from a detailed exegesis of Isa. 10:33–11:5, including the messianic interpretation of 10:34," an exegesis "very similar to that found in 4Q285 and 4QpIsa^a." Besides the shared image of the cedar of Lebanon that symbolizes Rome, which has also been pointed out by others, Bauckham mentions many other features here that resemble the Isaian prophecy and several other scriptural passages.[31] To these I would like to add some of its similarities not to Scripture, but rather to the peshers discussed above. Thus, the vine accuses the cedar that "you kept conquering that *which did not belong to you*" (על דלא דילך 36:8). The same accusation appears in Pesher Habakkuk: "they come to smite and to loot the cities of the land. For this is what it says (Hab. 1:6): To take possession of dwelling places *not their own* . . ." (לרשת משכנות לוא לו 4QpHab iii:1–2). The vine continues to censure the cedar: "And you did not show compassion (מן מתום רחמא 36:8) to that which did not belong to you". Pesher Habakkuk too describes the Romans as having no compassion (לוא ירחמו 4QpHab vi:12). In Baruch, the cedar is also condemned for keeping those near him "in the toils of [his]

---

[26] Gurtner 2009: 71. See the parallels in 4 Ezra 4:13–19; 5:23–24; 11:38–12:3.
[27] Cf. 4 Ezra 12:4–35.   [28] Cf. 4 Ezra 12:13.   [29] Cf. 4 Ezra 5:1, 14:18.   [30] Gurtner 2009: 73–75.
[31] Bauckham 1995. Citations from 209, 208, respectively.

wickedness" (במציצדתא דרושעך 36:8). This is a typically sectarian expression (cf. 1Qha 11:27 ויפרשו כול מצודות רשעה; CD 4:15 מצודות בליעל).

These similarities make the difference between the Qumran texts and 2 Baruch even more striking. Whereas the Qumran works, composed shortly after the Roman occupation, envision an eschatological war between the Sons of Light and the Romans, the Baruch apocalypse, authored after the failure of the First Jewish Revolt and the destruction of the temple, prophesies a miraculous heavenly victory over the Romans, with no human involvement.

9.4 Traces of Homiletic Traditions Current during the First Jewish Revolt

We now turn to a tradition preserved in rabbinic literature, in which we encounter a surprising shift in the exegetical role played by the same verses in Isaiah regarding the future of Rome. In the famous story of R. Yohanan b. Zakkai's escape from Jerusalem during the Roman siege, retold in four different rabbinic works,[32] the sage meets the Roman commander Vespasian, whom he addresses as "king."[33] In response to Vespasian's rejection of this title, R. Yohanan declares that according to the Lebanon verse in Isaiah, the temple will be delivered only into the hands of a king.

> When [R. Johanan b. Zakkai] reached [Vespasian] he said: "Peace to you, O king, peace to you, O king!" He [Vespasian] said: 'Your life is forfeit on two counts: one, because I am not a king and you call me king; and again, if I am a king, why did you not come to me before now?' [according to the parallel sources, Vespasian expressed anxiety that he himself would be executed for being called king]. He replied: "As for your saying that you are not a king, in truth you are a king [in the parallel sources: eventually you will be a king], since if you were not a king Jerusalem would not be delivered into your hand [in the parallel sources: since this house (the temple) will be destroyed only by a king]. For it is written, "And Lebanon by a mighty one will fall"[34] (Is. 10:34).[35]

---

[32] There is a huge amount of scholarship on this tradition, its date, historicity, aim, relationship to Josephus's testimony etc., which is beyond the scope of my chapter in this volume. See, e.g., Alon 1977; Doeve 1977, 50–65; Schalit 1975; Baer 1971; Schäfer 1979: 43–101; Moehring 1984: 864–944.

[33] From parallel sources it appears that the blessing was a Latin one: "*vive domine imperator*"or "*ave domine imperator*." See Rosenthal 1987: 4–5.

[34] The BT adds here: "'Mighty one' [is an epithet] applied only to a king, as it is written, 'And their mighty one shall be of themselves, his ruler shall come from his midst' (Jer. 30:21); and Lebanon refers to the Sanctuary, as it says, 'This goodly mountain and Lebanon' (Deut. 3:25)". This addition is missing in the parallel sources.

[35] BT *Gittin* 56a–b. For parallels, see *Avot de-Rabbi Natan* A, 4; *Avot de-Rabbi Natan* B, 6; *Lamentations Rabba* 1:5. Josephus reports a similar story regarding himself, *War* 3.391–408.

9. Jewish Hopes for the Downfall of the Roman Empire 179

This midrash on Isaiah 10:34 stands in absolute contrast to the messianic interpretation that is explicit in 4Q285 and Pesher Isaiah and implicit in 2 Baruch. R. Yohanan's homily understands the word "Lebanon" as representing the temple rather than the enemy, and the word "mighty" as referring to the enemy rather than to the messiah of Israel. In other words, the same biblical prophecy is now used – in contrast both to previous interpretations and its plain meaning – to herald Jewish *defeat* rather than the promise of redemption. Menahem Kister suggests that these two opposing interpretations of Isaiah 10:34 belong to an ideological-exegetical struggle that took place between the supporters and opponents of the First Jewish Revolt. The plain meaning of the prophecy refers to the defeat of the Assyrians, symbolized by the cedars of Lebanon, and this defeat serves as an archetype of a miraculous victory over a northern empire that has besieged Jerusalem. According to Kister, it is reasonable to suppose that the rebels used this prophecy – just as the sectarians had used it over a century earlier – to describe a marvelous victory over the Romans. However, the rebels did not expect this victory to take place in some remote messianic era, but rather in the here and now. This may explain what it was that motivated those opposed to the revolt to interpret the same verse in the opposite manner, as describing the destruction of Jews at the hands of the Romans.[36] The various meanings provided for the verse in apocryphal and Qumran literature, on the one hand, and in rabbinic tradition, on the other, have led several scholars to suggest that this prophecy is, in fact, the χρησμὸς ἀμφίβολος, the "ambiguous oracle," found, according to Josephus, in the sacred Scriptures. Its prophecy was "that ... one from their country would become ruler of the world." Josephus explains that the Jews believed this ruler would be one of their own, whereas the oracle actually signified the sovereignty of Vespasian.[37] Roman historians also claim that an ancient prophecy of a person coming from Judaea to rule the world hints at Vespasian and Titus.[38]

In sum, we can trace *four* distinct homilies on Isaiah 10:34, each of which represents different circumstances and diverse Jewish circles, and each of which reveals a different political and theological Jewish stance with regard to the Roman Empire. The sectarian exegesis, which immediately followed the Roman occupation, interprets the prophecy as a human victory over the Romans in a messianic future. During the First Jewish Revolt the rebels

---

[36] Kister 1998: 514.
[37] *War* 6.312–313. See Hahn 1962: 131–8; Kister 1998: 512–7; Ben Shahar 2017, 648–50.
[38] Tacitus, *Histories*, V.13.2 [Stern 1980: 23, 31]; Suetonius, *Divus Vespasianus*, 4.5 [Stern 1980: 119–20].

probably used it to justify their active mutiny, whereas moderate Jews, who objected to the uprising, employed the same verse in a polemic attempt to refute rebellious tendencies and foretell the forthcoming destruction. Finally, after the destruction, 2 Baruch returned to the optimistic interpretation in an attempt to console desperate souls with the glory of messianic salvation, but this time as an apocalyptic vision of *heavenly* rather than human punishment of Rome at the End of Days.

9.5 Jewish Liturgy

The post-destruction tendency – evident in 2 Baruch – to transpose the fall of Rome to a messianic future and leave it solely in divine hands, is also evident in Jewish liturgy. I suggest that remnants of Second Temple texts expressing fervent hopes for the fall of the Roman Empire can still be traced in present-day Jewish liturgy. The adaptation of Second Temple traditions and expressions in these later rabbinic texts sheds light on the evolving image of the messianic era in Jewish eyes. David Flusser has pointed to the similarity between 1QMyst (1Q27 5–7=4Q300 3)[39] and a passage in the prayer ובכן תן פחדך ("We pray, then, that you place Your reverence"), which is integrated into the third benediction of the High Holiday Amidah.[40] The relevant passage in the prayer reads as follows:

> All the creatures will bow down to You, and all of them will form a single throng, doing Your will whole heartedly. The righteous will see and rejoice, and the upright will be glad, and mouth of wickedness will be shut up, and all evil (רשעה) will disappear like smoke, for You will banish the rule of wickedness (ממשלת זדון) from the earth, and You alone will reign over all your creatures.[41]

Here is the comparison as formulated by Flusser:

Flusser observes here the only example of "discernible Essene influence on the religious creation of the sages."[42] Based on this similarity, he tries to define "the precise nature of the evil that will dissipate like smoke" in the prayer. He submits that the expression "rule of wickedness" (ממשלת זדון) is

---

[39] See Barthèlemy and Milik 1955; Schiffman 1997; Tigchelaar 2003; Elgvin 2006; and Kister 2009: 302–4.

[40] Flusser 2007c.   [41] I prefer the translation in Kister 2004: 36.

[42] Flusser 2007c: 138. However, I tend to conjecture that the presence of terms and concepts typical of the Qumran library (see further in this chapter) in the prayer does not attest to direct sectarian influence but rather to a shared Second Temple background. Scholars have also questioned the ascription of the Mysteries to the *Yahad* sect. See Weinfeld 1997: 357; Elgvin 2003: 55, 63; Kister 2004: 43.

9. Jewish Hopes for the Downfall of the Roman Empire

1QMysteries	Prayer
בהסגר מולדי עולה [. . .] When all that is born of sin is locked up	ועולתה תקפץ פיה and mouth of wickedness will be shut up
וכתום עשן ואיננו עוד כן יתם הרשע לעד As smoke vanishes, and no longer exists, so will evil vanish forever	והרשעה כולה כעשן תכלה And all evil will disappear like smoke
וכול תומכי רזי פשע אינמה עוד ודעה תמלא תבל And all those who support the mysteries of sin will no longer exist of evil	כי תעביר ממשלת זדון מן הארץ For You shall will banish the rule of wickedness from the earth

clearly an epithet for the "wicked kingdom" of Rome, and that this reading "certainly suits the general spirit of the 'Kingship verses'[43] and the meaning of the Rosh Ha-Shanah holiday itself." He also acknowledges that early liturgical traditions interpreted the prayer in this way. Nonetheless, he still argues that "the kingdom that is to be destroyed is understood in cosmic-ethical terms, rather than [as] a political entity . . . wickedness will disappear altogether."[44] This conclusion relies on the similarity of the passage to 1QMyst, which refers to a universalistic, cosmic exorcism of evil from the world.

Menahem Kister is skeptical of this comparison, claiming that though the similarity between this benediction and Qumranic terminology at large is indeed striking, its resemblance specifically to Mysteries is only in terms of subject, tone, and allusion. He thus points out that the term ממשלת זדון, which, in fact, is similar to some typical Qumranic expressions, does not appear at all in the Mysteries. Instead, Kister proposes a different comparison, to 4Q215a 1 ii. This passage does bear an impressive similarity to the opening line of the prayer[45] and also contains the term ממשל (rule) – albeit with reference to the good and just, rather than evil rule. In my opinion, however, it resembles the prayer only in terms of general content and ideas.[46]

I would like to suggest here another hitherto unrecognized parallel, namely the War Scroll, which bears on our theme of the evolving attitude

---

[43] In accordance with Ezra Fleischer's assumption that this prayer is probably a remnant of an alternative "Kingship Blessing." See Flusser 2007c: 138, n. 66.
[44] Flusser 2007c: 134–6.
[45] See the comparison in Kister 2004: 38, regarding the future unity of all creatures in the worship of and bowing down to the one and only God. For references to the editions of and publications on this text, see 37 n. 105.
[46] Kister 2004: 36–45. All the parallels between the prayer and 4Q215a enumerated on pages 39–40 are clearly in terms of content rather than style and wording.

War Scroll 1Q33 I 4–6	Prayer
[...] ולהכרית את קרן And cutting off the horn ...	[...] וצמיחת קרן לדוד עבדך And growth of the horn of David Your servant
וכלת עולמים לכול גורל בליעל Everlasting dissipation for all the lot of Belial	והרשעה כולה כעשן תכלה And all evil will dissipate like smoke
להכניע רשעה לאין שארית [...] Evil being subdued without a remnant	
וסרה ממשלת כתיים The Kittim's government shall pass away	כי תעביר ממשלת זדון מן הארץ For You shall pass the government of evil from the earth

of the Jews towards Rome. The table here compares the ancient prayer to the opening of the War Scroll discussed above. Identical expressions are marked by underlining.

The textual similarities: קרן, רשעה, כל"ה, כולה/לאין שארית and especially כי תעביר ממשלת זדון/וסרה ממשלת כתיים are impressive. It is also clear that the epithet "Kittim" in the War Scroll is equivalent to ממשלת זדון in the prayer. In other words, the appellation ממשלת זדון in the prayer – which Flusser admits is "a political formula par excellence" (135) – probably hints at a well-known and despised, political power – the Romans, who in the parallel Qumran passage are referred to as Kittim. Note that I am not arguing here for a direct dependence of the later benediction on the War Scroll, but rather for what Torleif Elgvin has defined as "common origins in eschatological traditions in the Land of Israel in the early second century BCE."[47] These pre-rabbinic roots were adopted and adapted within the later liturgy, and the adaptations exemplify both continuity and change in the Jewish approach to Roman rule.

Note the intriguing change between the Second Temple text and the later rabbinic prayer. Whereas the War Scroll designates a certain nation (ממשלת כתיים), albeit vaguely, the rabbinic prayer universalizes the designation to an appellation (ממשלת זדון) broad enough to be understood in abstract terms.[48] More importantly, whereas in the War Scroll the government of Kittim will

---

[47] Elgvin 2003: 63. In my mind, however, his comparisons of various ideas in multiple layers of the later liturgy of Rosh Hashanah to a wide array of texts and ideas in the Qumran literature is far too general.

[48] On other aspects of universalization in rabbinic liturgy, in contradistinction to pre-rabbinic prayers and blessings, see Kimelman 2005.

collapse after a lengthy war with Israel, the later prayer prophesies that "*You* [i.e., God] shall pass the government of evil from the earth." Whereas in the sectarian work, the Sons of Light will have to work hard in order to exterminate the wicked, in the rabbinic prayer, the "righteous," the "upright," and the "virtuous" need only "see and rejoice." Similar tendencies are apparent in the famous *Birkat HaMinim* (the benediction against heretics) in the daily *Amidah*, which pleads that "the wicked kingdom (מלכות זדון) be uprooted." There is wide scholarly consensus that these words express the hope for the fall of the Roman Empire.[49] The same appellation is being used here and the benediction describes the eschatological event in the passive ("be uprooted"),[50] as an act of salvation to be executed by God, rather than as the result of an envisioned victory by Israel. It is worthwhile noting that these prayers, in turn, further support the Roman identity of the War Scroll's Kittim.

9.6 Tannaitic Literature

After the failure of the Bar Kokhba revolt, the rabbis appear to have refrained even from passive expectations for redemption from the yoke of Rome.[51] The following Tannaitic maxim was undoubtedly aimed at suppressing messianic hopes altogether:

---

[49] The versions, development, and meaning of this benediction have drawn an immense amount of scholarly discussion, which is beyond the scope of the current article. See Flusser 2007d. For the identification of the "wicked kingdom" in the benediction with the Roman Empire, see 89, 115 (Flusser apparently believed that this epithet preceded the Roman occupation but was applied to the Romans when this part of the benediction was first authored); See the review of research in Langer 2012: 16–39. For a different opinion, ascribing the very formulation of the benediction to "a clear anti-Roman mark," see Schremer 2010: 57–9.

[50] Flusser 2007d: 91.

[51] The rabbinic attitude towards Rome has generated vast scholarship, of which I will mention only several representative works. Samuel Krauss collected rabbinic sources on Persia and Rome in his 1947 volume (Krauss 1947). Neusner 2008 authored a later, English compilation. Louis Feldman reviewed the rabbinic attitude towards Rome in the third century; see the useful summary of previous scholarship in Feldman 1992: 41–4. Schwartz 2001; Schremer 2010; and Lapin 2012 have written more recent surveys of various aspects of the rabbinic approach to the Roman Empire. A fresh look on the rabbinic perception of Roman culture from the perspective of the Mishnah's creation has recently been offered by Rosen-Zvi 2017. The article describes the novel scholarly interest in the Roman influence on the Jewish population in Judaea against the background of comparative studies on "Romanization" in the provinces at large. See also the collected essays in Kalmin and Schwartz 2003. While the pendulum of the rabbinic treatment of Rome in general may swing "from the most extreme praise … to the fiercest condemnation" (Feldman 1992: 46), my focus here falls specifically on the expectations of the fall of the empire, as expressed through biblical exegesis.

> There are seven things hidden from men, and they are these: The day of death; the day of comfort; the depths of judgment. No man knows by what he can make profit. No man knows what is in the heart of his fellow man. No one knows when the Kingdom of David will be restored to its former position, *nor when this wicked kingdom will be uprooted.*[52]

This beautiful proverb juxtaposes three examples of human ignorance in everyday life with four kinds of eschatological lack of knowledge. Just as a man does not know from what he will make a profit, what lies in his neighbor's heart, or the date of his own death, thus the end of the "wicked kingdom" and the rise of the messianic dynasty, as well as the "comfort" and judgment involved at the End of Days, are entirely beyond his understanding. Put differently, the fall of Rome will occur only at the End of Days, and no one can predict, nor – more importantly – accelerate, the processes that will bring down the Roman Empire. Note the verb used in this Tannaitic source: "uprooted" ([53]תעקור, תעקר), and its juxtaposition with the rise of the kingdom of David. Both these features bear clear traces of the Second Temple messianic exegetical tradition discussed earlier in this chapter, which the rabbis clearly wished to suppress.

9.7 Amoraic Literature

Moving on in time, from second-century CE Tannaitic Palestine to Talmudic Palestine and Babylonia, we encounter a further shift in cultural attitudes with respect to the Roman Empire. Politically concrete hopes for the decline of Rome reemerged at this point, albeit not in as active a fashion as during the First Jewish Revolt. The new perspective was rather that of passive onlookers, spectators of a war waged by others.

> R. Joshua b. Levi in the name of Rabbi said: Rome is designed to fall into the hand of Persia, as it was said: "Therefore hear ye the counsel of the LORD, that He hath taken against Edom; and His purposes, that He hath purposed against the inhabitants of Teman: surely the least of the flock shall drag them away, surely their habitation shall be appalled at them" (Jer. 49:20, BT Yoma 10a)[54]

R. Judah the Prince is probably reacting to the Roman wars against the last Parthian kings. Caracalla's planned invasion of Parthia was cancelled due

---

[52] Mechilta de Rabbi Yishmael, Vayassa 5 in Lauterbach 2004: I, 248. Also quoted in BT Pesahim 54b.
[53] In the BT version: תכלה, תפול ("will fall down, will come to an end").
[54] For a thorough analysis of the entire *sugya*, including the sections cited in this chapter, see Kalmin 2008: 88–99. For previous scholarship, see 90 n. 11; Naiweld 2016: 265–9.

to his murder in 217 CE, and Artabanus V's counterattack against the Romans had an early success. R. Judah seems to view Parthia as a "reincarnation" of biblical Persia that will prevail over the Roman Empire, which he identifies as biblical "Edom." Nevertheless, the continuation of the discussion proves that the Babylonian rabbis were not entirely sure whether the Persians were the party that should be victorious.[55]

> Rabbah b. 'Ullah demurred to this: what intimation is there that "the last of the flock" refers to Persia? [Presumably] because Scripture reads: "[As for] the ram which you saw having two horns, they are the kings of Media and Persia" (Dan. 8:20). But say [perhaps] it is Greece, for it is written, "and the rough he-goat is the king of Greece" (ib. 8:21)! When R. Habiba b. Surmaki came up [to the Land of Israel], he reported this interpretation before a certain scholar. The latter said: should he who does not understand the meaning of the verses respond to Rabbi's comment? Indeed, "the least of the flock" means the youngest of his brethren, for R. Joseph learnt that "Tiras" means Persia (BT *Yoma* 10a).

Although the Palestinian rabbis who bore the yoke of the Roman Empire expected Rome to be defeated by Persia, their Babylonian counterparts, who lived under the yoke of the Sassanid "Persians," were far more skeptical. Rabbah b. 'Ullah, a Babylonian, apparently suggested identifying the victorious "least of the flock" as Greeks rather than Persians, but this was rejected out of hand and rather sharply by another Palestinian rabbi, who set out to defend Rabbi Judah the Prince's homily. The latter argued that in Jeremiah, the term "least" refers to the youngest of the sons of Japheth enumerated in Genesis 10:2, as quoted earlier in the *sugya*: "the sons of Japheth: Gomer, Magog, Madai, Javan, Tubal, Meshech, and Tiras." Since Tiras is elsewhere identified with Persia, Persia is the power destined to defeat Rome.

Even though the debate is disguised as merely exegetical, its motivation was probably political. Ron Naiweld claims that while the Babylonian Rabbah b. 'Ullah's attitude may have been merely scholastic, the Palestinian Rabbi's sharp reaction is understandable in view of his Palestinian background, under Roman rule.[56] Indeed, the political undercurrents are swiftly revealed in the rest of the *sugya*:

---

[55] According to Naiweld 2016: 267, R. Judah the Patriarch ("Rabbi") already represents some retreat from R. Judah Bar Ilay's resolved belief in the defeat of Rome (see further in this chapter) as the latter did not need a biblical verse for support.

[56] Naiweld 2016: 268.

> Rabbah b. Bar Hana in the name of R. Johanan, on the authority of R. Judah b. Illai, said: Rome is designed to fall into the hands of Persia. That may be concluded by inference *a minore ad maius*: if in the case of the first Sanctuary, which the sons of Shem [i.e., King Solomon] built and the Chaldeans [i.e., the Babylonians] destroyed, the Chaldeans fell into the hands of the Persians [meaning Cyrus' victory over the Babylonian Empire], then all the more so should it be with the second Sanctuary, which the Persians built and the Romans destroyed, that the Romans should fall into the hands of the Persians (*Yoma* 10a).

The rabbis believed that world history was determined by the attitude of the various world powers towards the Jews. R. Judah b. Illai, a sage who lived in Palestine in the second half of the second century CE, witnessed a series of wars between the Romans and Parthians, which took place after Trajan's invasion of Parthia. According to the argument presented here, since the Persian Cyrus had built the Second Temple in Jerusalem, the Parthians, considered his heirs, had to triumph seven centuries later (!) over the Romans, who had destroyed that very temple.

In Babylonia, however, the Jewish community was further detached from the direct effects of Roman rule, but occasionally suffered from Sassanid persecutions. Therefore, it did not seem to harbor such a hostile view of the Romans as did their brethren in Palestine:

> Rav said: Persia will fall into the hands of Rome. Thereupon R. Kahana and R. Assi asked of Rab: [shall] the builders fall into the hands of the destroyers?— He said to them: yes, it is the decree of the King. Others say that he replied to them: they [the Persians] too are guilty, for they destroy synagogues.
>
> It has been taught in accordance with the above: Persia will fall into the hands of Rome, first because they destroy synagogues, and then because it is the King's decree that the builders fall into the hands of the destroyers. For R. Judah said in the name of Rav: the son of David will not come until the wicked kingdom of Rome will have spread [its sway] over the entire world for nine months, for it is said: "Therefore Israel will be abandoned, until the time when she who is in labor bears a son, and the rest of his brothers return to join the Israelites" (Mic. 5:2 [5:3 in the RSV]).

In contrast to the previous view, presented by R. Judah b. Illai, Rav – who migrated to Babylonia c. 220 – takes a far more hesitant view of the Persians. His reservations can be understood as a political statement that reflects a negative reaction to the shift from the favorable Parthian regime to the threatening Sassanian dynasty in the early third century CE.[57] However,

---

[57] See Gafni 1990: 39–40.

9. Jewish Hopes for the Downfall of the Roman Empire

according to the first version of his response – and in contrast to the views held by R. Kahana and R. Assi – Rav does not use any arguments to justify Rome's future triumph, but instead assumes that it will happen by divine decree, thereby implying his belief in an arbitrary aspect of history.

The reasoning in the second reply cited in Rav's name, according to which "they too are guilty, for they destroy synagogues," may either allude to events that occurred in Rav's own lifetime, during the reign of the first two Sassanid kings,[58] or be a later addition to the text, inserted during the persecutions of the Mazdaic priest Kerdir in the late third century, after Rav's death,[59] or even, as recently suggested, a post-redaction addition responding to events in the late fifth century CE.[60] In any event, for our purposes, it suffices to say that Rav did not share the old, enthusiastic, Palestinian hope for the downfall of Rome.

9.8 Conclusion

The biblical prophecy of Isaiah on the defeat of the Assyrians, symbolized by the vision of Lebanon falling into the hands of "a mighty one," was interpreted in multiple ways by Jews under Roman rule. When Rome took over Judaea in the first century BCE, the prophecy was understood by various Jewish circles as relating to the fall of Rome by a mighty one, namely, God or his messiah. In a series of sectarian works, this Roman defeat was to be brought about by the Sons of Light in an eschatological war that would take place in a messianic era.

This same homiletic tradition was probably used to motivate the rebellion against Roman occupation over a century later, during the First Jewish Revolt, albeit not as a vague vision of the distant future, but rather as divine assurance of an immediate victory over the Romans. However, those opposed to the revolt manipulated the very same verse to mean the opposite: rather than have Rome fall before the Jews, the temple would fall at the hands of the mighty Roman legions led by Vespasian. After the failure of the uprising and the destruction of the temple, we can observe the metamorphosis of this prophecy once again, both in the apocryphal 2 Baruch and in rabbinic liturgy, where it is turned into a vision of heavenly acts against Rome that take place in the distant, messianic future.

After the Bar Kokhba revolt in the first half of the second century CE, the rabbis portrayed the messianic event of the Roman downfall as a truth beyond human ability to predict or effect and warned their audience to

---

[58] Widengren 1963: 128.   [59] Rosenthal 1982: 63–4.   [60] Kalmin 2008: 98.

steer clear of messianic dreams. Interestingly, the wording of this anti-messianic source still echoes that of the ancient Second Temple homiletic interpretation of Isaiah 10.

During the turbulent wars between Rome and Persia in the Talmudic period, we witness a sudden revival of hope for the downfall of Rome. Much like their predecessors during the First Jewish Revolt, the third-century Palestinian rabbis harbored actual and concrete expectations implanted in the current political reality. Unlike them, however, these sages did not imagine that Jews would perpetrate any anti-Roman act, but rather assumed that Roman rule would collapse as a result of the political and military actions of universal powers. Their expectations hinged, as always, on biblical exegesis, this time of Jeremiah and Daniel, as well as on pseudo-historical calculations that predicted victory for nations favorably disposed to Israel. This approach was much more typical of Palestinian rabbis, as Babylonian rabbis occasionally predicted that the Romans would prevail.

In the following centuries, the pendulum swayed again, and concrete hopes for the fall of Rome faded. Late midrashim explicitly declare that this should not be expected to happen until the arrival of the messiah:

> Do not engage them [=the sons of Esau] in battle; for I will not give you enough of their land for [even] the sole of a foot to tread on' (Deut. 2:5). R. Meir says: until his feet stand "on that day" (Zac. 14:4). R. Samuel says: until that one comes, of whom it is written "a star shall come out of Jacob" (Num. 24:17) – this refers to the King Messiah.[61]

The opinions presented here point to an unspecified time in the distant future, in which the land of the sons of Esau – a metonym for Rome – will be given back to Israel. According to the eschatological prophecies of Balaam or Zachariah, this will happen only when the messiah appears. Indeed, this midrash reflects the same idea as the one in the source with which we opened. The eventual punishment of Rome is in divine hands alone and will take place in an unknown future. God's determination, however, should grant comfort to Israel: "therefore fear not, O Jacob my servant – even if you see him rise to the skies, I will bring him down!"

---

[61] Townsend 2003: 279. One of the homilies here is attributed to the second century sage R. Meir, but there is no early source to support this late attribution.

CHAPTER 10

The Sibylline Oracles and Resistance to Rome

Erich S. Gruen

The fall of Jerusalem in 70 CE left a nation shattered, its memories bitter and agonizing. The trauma afflicted the Jews for many generations thereafter. In some ways the shadow of that event still hovers now. Military confrontation with Roman power proved altogether fruitless, as would be demonstrated once again by the failed Bar-Kochba revolt in the 130s, with its painful consequences. Physical resistance was no longer realistic. Could there be a different kind of resistance? Did the people of the book in Palestine or the diaspora engage in a form of textual resistance? Could apocalyptic literature serve as "hidden transcript" to convey disguised and indirect critique of overweening power, a subtle undermining of authority that could restore a sense of self-esteem or an internal recompense for loss?[1] Could oracular pronouncements about the fiery end of Rome provide a means to steel Jewish resolve in the face of otherwise intolerable tragedy?[2]

That is how scholarship on the whole has read Jewish texts in the aftermath of that calamity. Much scholarly work has devoted itself to two major texts composed in the years after the destruction of the Temple: Fourth Ezra and Second Baruch. Both do represent a complex of Jewish reactions to the fall of the Temple, although the ostensible setting in each is the capture of Jerusalem by the Babylonians in the sixth century BCE. That Babylon is a surrogate for Rome has long been recognized. But the principal concern of each of these apocalypses with their visions, interpretations, and dialogues between human and divine is theodicy. They explore the harrowing question of why God permitted this tragedy to fall upon his chosen people. The texts pay little heed to

---

[1] The notion of the "hidden transcript," a concept of considerable influence, was acutely developed by Scott 1990; see also 1985. For the application of this idea to Jewish apocalyptic literature, see the fine work of Portier-Young 2011: esp. 31–45, although she focuses on earlier works, Daniel and the Enochic literature of the Hellenistic period. Cf. also A. Y. Collins 2010: 115–29; J. J. Collins 2011: 1–19; Portier-Young 2014: 145–62.
[2] See the analysis of Hadas-Lebel 2006: 111–26.

Rome (Babylon) as such, and surprisingly little indeed even to the destruction of the Temple.[3] The issue at stake is divine judgment and the relationship between the nation of Israel and its God.[4]

10.1 The Nature of the Sybilline Oracles

By contrast, scholarship has been far less assiduous in exploring another set of texts in this connection, i.e. the Sibylline Oracles. The Sibyllines, though frequently allusive and elusive, do speak more directly to the Jewish experience in the period of the Roman empire, make reference explicitly to Rome and the Romans, and contain material that pertains to Jewish thinking in the decades after the destruction of the Temple. Here, if anywhere, we should find intimations of the "hidden transcript," of subversive writings cloaked in apocalyptic garb that predicted the dismal future of Rome, and that gave voice to Jewish aspirations, framing, at least in verbal form, its opposition to the regime.

The Sibylline Oracles constitute a highly complex collection of texts that span a vast chronological range from the mid second century BCE to the seventh century CE. They were pagan in inspiration but largely Jewish and Christian in composition. They differ widely in date, objective, and organization (insofar as there is organization). Diverse layers of writing exist even within each of the Sibyllines, thereby perplexing and frustrating researchers. The variegated corpus cannot possibly be investigated here.[5] But certain portions, predicting a fateful future for Rome after the catastrophic conquest of Judaea, do possess relevance for this issue.

The Sibyl herself, a famed Greek prophetess of mythical or semi-mythical origins, goes back at least to Archaic Greece, first mentioned by Heraclitus. She was a single figure initially, raving mad but divinely inspired, her voice resonating through a thousand years.[6] In time, however,

---

[3] An exception, with regard to Rome, exists in 4 Ezra, 11, the vision of the fearsome eagle, which presumably represents the Roman empire, and also the image of the cedar in 2 Baruch, 36–40.

[4] The scholarship on 4 Ezra is large. See, in particular, the commentary by Stone 1990. A concise and useful summary in J. J. Collins 1984: 156–69; Schürer 1986: III.1, 294–306. A good discussion with up to date bibliography can be found in Jones 2011: 39–77. Note, in particular, Esler 1994: 99–123. See further Naijman 2014. For 2 Baruch, one should consult Bogaert 1969; Collins 1984: 170–80; Murphy 1985; Schürer 1987: III.2, 750–6; Jones 2011: 79–109; Henze 2011, with additional bibliography.

[5] Only a few of the most important contributions to the subject of the Sibyllines can be registered here. Geffcken 1902 holds its place after more than a century as the most reliable edition. Citations from the text will be drawn from that edition. Among the most useful general discussions of the Sibylline Oracles, see Collins 1974a: 1–19; *i* 1983: 317–24; Schürer 1986: III.1, 618–54; Parke 1988: 1–50; Potter 1990: 95–140; Lightfoot 2007: 3–23.

[6] Heraclitus, in Plut. *Mor.*397A.

the Sibyls multiplied, each attached to a particular site, their forecasts traditionally gloomy and foreboding but eerily reliable.[7] In Ovid's vivid description, the Cumaean Sibyl, when Apollo sought her favors, asked for reward a life with as many years as the grains of sand in a large pile, but forgot to ask for continued youth; she could thus look forward only to endless shriveling until shrunk to nothing but a voice – which would keep on prophesying.[8] Tales about the Sibyls proliferated. And the oracular sayings were collected and duly reshaped by Roman priests who employed them for consultation when serious matters of state or religion needed divine authority.[9] None of those texts (if indeed they were more than fabrication by Roman officials) survives. But inventive Jewish and Christian authors transformed the pagan Sibyl into an authoritative seer whose pronouncements foretold (often *ex eventu*) the fortunes, usually the dire fortunes, of various peoples of the Mediterranean, occasionally accompanied by reference to the eschaton that would bring a brighter future. The extant texts possess that character, and the Sibyl, at least as portrayed in the earliest collection, the Third Sibylline Oracle, is no longer just a Greek prophetess. She is the daughter-in-law of Noah, dating back to the most distant antiquity, a purveyor of both biblical and near eastern traditions, her memory and her prophecies infallible.[10] The Jewish cooptation of this pagan image usurped Greek and Roman authority and turned it to Jewish ends.[11]

Did the Sibylline Oracles, with their forebodings of doom for Rome represent a form of Jewish resistance? They have been described as embodying "a tradition by which both Jews and Christians worked out through an ecstasy of revenge their hatred of the Roman state."[12] Two of the Sibylline texts in particular, the Fourth and the Fifth Sibyl, stem, at least primarily, from the decades that followed the fall of Jerusalem; and the first half of the Eighth Sibyl also appears to belong in that category. How far do they reflect Jewish resentment of the Roman empire or a project for the new order?

10.2 The Fourth Sibyl

The Fourth Sibyl distinguishes herself at the outset from the pagan incarnation of Apollo's seer. She is the spokesperson of the great God

---

[7] The most important testimony comes from Varro, in Lact. *Div Inst* 1.6.8–12, and Pausanias, 10.12.
[8] Ovid, *Met.* 14.130–153.   [9] See Parke 1988: 1–50.   [10] 3 Sib. 809–829.
[11] Cf. Gruen 1998: 15–36.   [12] MacMullen 1976: 9. Cf. Stemberger 1983: 58.

whom no human hands have fashioned, a common Jewish formula for Yahweh.[13] She proceeds to delineate the blessed people as those who are followers of the great God, reject idols and idolators, and scorn the immorality and shamelessness of the gentile. The pious will prosper in a last judgment, while the others will end in a fiery darkness.[14] The Sibyl then moves from eschatology to history, outlining the succession of four empires, which, in diverse forms, was conveyed long before by Herodotus, Daniel, and a range of other authors. In her formulation, the sequence passed through Assyrians, Medes, Persians, and Macedonians.[15] Rome then emerged as a fifth, in a class on its own, its devastation, plundering, and murders to encompass the burning of the Temple itself.[16] Natural disasters extending through much of the world will herald an end time in which the angry god destroys the whole of humankind.[17] He leaves room, however, for repentance, and the text closes with a promise of redemption and resurrection for the pious in a last judgment.[18] Such, in brief, is the outline of the text.

The Fourth Sibyl, amidst predictions of general calamity and disaster, points with some clarity and specificity to a dramatic historical event. She singles out the Romans as villains in the destruction of the Temple. The relevant passage obviously dates to some time after the fall of Jerusalem to Rome in 70 CE. The Sibyl makes a clear reference to that cataclysm. She forecasts an evil tempest of war from Italy that will fall upon Jerusalem and will plunder the great Temple of God.[19] A few lines later, the text speaks of a foremost figure of Rome who will set the Temple of Jerusalem afire, will massacre many, and will destroy the city of wide streets.[20] How long after the event this passage was composed is beyond our grasp. The Sibyl follows these lines with a vivid description of a natural calamity in Italy, replete with fiery ashes that light up the sky and showers from heaven in the form of red earth which will destroy men and cities.[21] The statement almost unmistakably denotes the eruption of Vesuvius in 79 CE. Hence commentators put the text not long after that memorable episode.[22] But there is

---

[13] 4 Sib. 4–7.   [14] 4 Sib. 24–48.   [15] 4 Sib. 49–101.   [16] 4 Sib. 102–129.
[17] 4 Sib. 130–161, 171–178.   [18] 4 Sib. 162–170, 179–191.
[19] 4 Sib. 115–116: ἥξει καὶ Σολύμοισι κακὴ πολέμοιο θύελλα/ Ἰταλόθεν, νηὸν δὲ θεοῦ μέγαν ἐξαλαπάξει.
[20] 4 Sib. 125–127: εἰς Συρίην δ' ἥξει Ῥώμης πρόμος ὅς πύρι νηὸν/ συμφλέξας Σολύμων, πολλοὺς δ' ἅμα ἀνδροφονήσας/ Ἰουδαίων ὀλέσει μεγάλην χθόνα εὐρυάγυιαν. Jones 2011: 191–4, distinguishes between the two passages with regard to the events referred to, and has the first allude to Pompey's seizure of the Temple in 63 BCE. That is possible, although Josephus' evidence that the Temple was not plundered by Pompey stands against it; Jos. *BJ*, 1.152–153; *Ant.* 14.71–73.
[21] 4 Sib. 130–134.   [22] Collins 1983: 381–2; Schürer 1986: III.1, 641–3; Jones 2011: 178–80.

10. The Sibylline Oracles and Resistance to Rome

no compelling reason to do so. Vividness of description (especially of destruction) is the stock-in-trade of Sibylline Oracles. The segments of the Fourth Sibyl dealing with Rome could have come any time after the capture of Jerusalem.[23] The issue at stake for us is whether these lines, the most explicit that we have in the Sibyllines on the subject, constitute a message to the victims of that disaster and a recipe for responding to it.

On the face of it, oracular pronouncements, looking ahead to the eschaton, possess a character quite different from a summons to action. Certainly the Fourth Sibyl contains no clarion call for uprising. Yet it also does not rely upon a distant End of Time. The oracle contains an immediacy and an explicitness that draws the reader back to historical circumstances. Are the circumstances, however, those of Jews laboring under the weight of a recent calamity that put their homeland at the mercy of Roman power?

The ferocity of Rome stands out in the text. But it is one of long standing. The author or redactor of the lines in question has expanded upon a Hellenistic substratum that recounted the traditional sequence of empires, each bringing dire destruction upon its predecessor.[24] The emergence of Rome is outside and subsequent to that scheme, evidently the work of a later redactor. Rome's entrance, to be sure, brings widespread devastation. But the victims long precede any Jewish involvement. The Sibyl proclaims the termination of Macedonian power to come through a great Italian war from the west, one that will bring the whole world to serve under the Italian yoke of slavery. And she proceeds to note nations and peoples as far as Armenia who will endure the necessity of enslavement.[25] Among those who receive explicit mention are Corinth and Carthage, a transparent reference to the nearly simultaneous destruction of those cities at the hands of Rome in the mid second century BCE. And the more general allusion to the end of Macedonian hegemony evokes three wars of Rome against Macedon that established Roman superiority in unequivocal fashion. All of this underlines the ruthlessness and destructiveness of Rome. The author has a clear historical sense.

---

[23] In addition to the Sibyl's references to the destruction of the Temple and to the eruption of Vesuvius, she also speaks of the flight and return of Nero (119–124, 137–139) which most scholars have taken as further grounds for dating the oracle to the aftermath of the Great Revolt; Charles 1913: 373; Collins 1974b: 367; 1983: 382; Jones 2011: 178–80. But references to Nero occur with frequency and variety in the Sibyllines, and cannot serve to pin down dates of composition. No need here to delve into the thorny issue of what parts of the Fourth Sibyl represent an earlier Hellenistic (perhaps pagan) oracle and what parts a Jewish redaction in the Roman period. See Flusser 1972: 148–53; Collins 1974b: 370–6.

[24] 4 Sib. 40–101.   [25] 4 Sib. 102–114.

None of it, however, has any direct connection with the fall of Jerusalem two centuries later. Nor does the author draw any direct connection. The lines that recount the sacking of the Temple through the storm of war that descended from Italy follow upon this. Whether they refer to Pompey's attack on Jerusalem or Titus' assault or both makes little difference. The point is that the episode is part of Rome's long and broad record of devastation which extends from Corinth to Jerusalem and from the Macedonian wars to the capture of the Temple.

What deserves emphasis here is that the Jews are not portrayed as the sole victim or even the prime target. Nor is there any sense in which Jews take part in projected vengeance upon Rome, either on their own hook or as instruments of God. That has often been inferred but has no basis in the text. In the very midst of the lines that twice allude to the Roman assault(s) on the Temple, the author inserts his account of the flight of Nero from Rome to the east.[26] And when he does speak of the vengeance of the Lord as retaliation for the destruction of the pious, the agent is none other than Nero himself, fugitive and matricide though he be. Nero will bring hordes of easterners across the Euphrates and wreak devastation upon the west, crushing various places, like Antioch, Cyprus, and Caria, along the way.[27] Such is the unsavory agent of God's vengeance. Nero's actions hardly seem like something that Jews could contemplate with much pleasure as compensation for the loss of their city and Temple.

Further, the Fourth Sibyl drew extensively on material much earlier than the Flavian era. The oracle delineates the retribution that Rome will suffer in telling terms. Vast wealth will be extracted from the western power and returned to Asia in more than twice the quantity that Rome once plundered from the east.[28] Those words did not arise directly from any Jewish sensitivities in the wake of the Temple's destruction. In fact, they closely echo sentiments expressed in the Third Sibylline Oracle, much of which was composed in the second and first centuries BCE. The author of that text represents the laments of Asia generally, groaning under the burden of Roman taxation after the western Republic had extended its authority over the eastern Mediterranean. The Third Sibyl had warned that whatever wealth Rome has extracted from the east, Asia will seize back three times the

---

[26] 4 Sib. 119–124.   [27] 4 Sib. 135–151.
[28] 4 Sib. 145–148: ἥξει δ' εἰς Ἀσίην πλοῦτος μέγας, ὅν ποτε Ῥώμη/ αὐτὴ συλήσασα πολυκτέανον κατὰ δῶμα/ θήκατο. καὶ δὶς ἔπειτα τοσαῦτα καὶ ἄλλ' ἀποδώσει/ εἰς Ἀσίην, τότε δ' ἔσται ὑπέρκτησις πολέμοιο.

10. The Sibylline Oracles and Resistance to Rome 195

amount and avenge the destructive arrogance of that nation.[29] The author of the Fourth Sibyl has simply reached back to a convention sparked by the circumstances of Rome's much earlier expansionism into the east, and does not owe its formulation to Jewish experience after the fall of Jerusalem.

A healthy portion of the earlier Third Sibyl in fact vents its spleen upon Roman imperialism in the Republican period. The text, for instance, blasts Roman rule over Egypt, seeing it as precursor to a divine judgment that will level the empire, rain destruction on Rome, and slaughter Latin men through a torrent of fire from heaven.[30] In this text's list of imperial powers that follow one another, Rome is the successor of Macedon, "the many-headed from the western sea" (a reference to the Roman senate, by contrast with the eastern monarchies). The Third Sibyl describes Rome as spreading fear among all kings, plundering widely, and oppressing humankind.[31] In another oracle, the one noted above which forecasts Rome's triple repayment to Asia, the author also describes the future humbling of Rome as the enslavement of Italians twenty times the number of those whom Rome had reduced to servitude and ten thousandfold repayment of what had been plundered from Asia. This is a substantial upping of the ante. Numerous places will be reduced to obscurity, and Rome will become a mere street.[32] An equally dire prediction occurs later in the text. It portends a civil war in Italy, with native blood endlessly spilled and self-destruction in prospect. The Sibyl declares Rome not a mother of good men but a nurse of beasts.[33] And further, Romans are depicted as a barbarian people, destroying the leadership of Greece, ravaging flocks and herds, recklessly burning houses, enslaving men, women, and children alike, until God unleashes his terrible fire, leaving just one third of humanity alive.[34]

As is clear, the animosity toward Rome that manifests itself in the Fourth Sibyl, following the Roman conquest of Judaea, had its models in much earlier forecasts. The Third Sibyl, with its references to the spread of Roman power to the east in the Macedonian and Mithridatic wars and to the ferocious civil conflicts in the time of Marius and Sulla, Pompey and

---

[29] 3 Sib. 350–355: ὁππόσα δασμοφόρου Ἀσίης ὑπεδέξατο Ῥώμη,/ χρήματά κεν τρὶς τόσσα δεδέξεται ἔμπαλιν Ἀσίς/ ἐκ Ῥώμης, ὀλοὴν δ' ἀποτίσεται ὕβριν ἐς αὐτήν.

[30] 3 Sib. 46–56. The reference to "the three" who will wreak devastation upon Rome is usually taken to mean the triumvirate of Antony, Lepidus, and Octavian. But that would not fit historical circumstances, and "the three" are more likely the instruments of God; see Gruen 1998: 24–25.

[31] 3 Sib. 175–182.

[32] 3 Sib. 350–364. There is no good reason to see an allusion to Cleopatra here; see Gruen 1998: 26–27.

[33] 3 Sib. 464–471.   [34] 3 Sib. 520–544.

Caesar, set this form of oracular animosity and savage depiction of Rome in a context well outside the consequences of the Temple's destruction. Those who were writing under the shadow of that horrific event had themes and motifs at hand that were already a longstanding part of Sibylline tradition.

10.3 The Fifth Sibyl

Rome comes in for still harsher treatment in the Fifth Sibyl. This text, like the other Sibyllines, is a composite one, not to be pinned down to a specific date. But much of it certainly comes after the Roman conquest and subjugation of Judaea. The Sibyl provides a roll call of Roman rulers, heralded by Aeneas and Romulus and then listed from Caesar through Marcus Aurelius, each identified, in good oracular fashion, by epithets, deeds, or initials rather than name, but nonetheless unmistakable.[35] It does not follow that the Fifth Sibyl as a whole was composed at or after the time of Marcus Aurelius. A reference to Hadrian describes him as a most excellent man and one knowledgeable about everything.[36] A Jewish author would not likely pen such a description after the Jewish revolt of 130 CE. But that does not give a *terminus ante quem* for the entire work which contains more than one layer.[37] In any case, the repeated references to Nero and the forecasts of his deeds after his alleged flight from Rome locates the bulk of the text at least to the years after the destruction of the Temple.[38]

The text of the Fifth Sibylline Oracle falls into various parts, with no clear unity or consistent thread. It opens with an ominous call to hear the woeful history of the Latins. This prompts the historical précis that runs through the Roman rulers from Aeneas through Marcus Aurelius.[39] The Sibyl then switches gears, delivers dire warnings to Egypt, mentions a mysterious Persian marauder, and forecasts evils to befall a whole range of eastern places and peoples.[40] Rome once again enters into the Sibyl's presentation at this point, a connection made between Nero and the burning of the Temple, a deploring of Roman misdeeds and immorality, and an oracular pronouncement on Rome's demise.[41] Then another switch of gears. The prophetess foresees doom for a considerable number of peoples, east and west, from Egypt to Britain, reverts once more to the transgressions of Nero, and then turns suddenly to an apocalyptic vision

---

[35] 5 Sib. 8–50.   [36] 5 Sib. 46–48.
[37] For an effort to reconstruct the strata, see Felder 2002: 373–80.
[38] For discussion and speculations on the date of the Fifth Sibyl, see Collins 1974a: 71–75; 1984: 390; Schürer 1986: III.1, 643–645; Felder 2002: 367–72; Jones 2011: 213–15.
[39] 5 Sib. 1–51.   [40] 5 Sib. 52–136.   [41] 5 Sib. 137–178.

10. The Sibylline Oracles and Resistance to Rome

with rewards for the devout and misery for the wicked.[42] Logical transitions are not part of the Sibyl's *modus operandi*. The text returns to grim forebodings delivered to a diverse collection of cities and nations in the eastern and western Mediterranean.[43] Nero pops in once again, this time in even more baffling fashion as a bringer of both war and peace, Roman immoral misbehavior comes in for another blast, the Temple's destruction receives yet an additional mention, and an eschatological scene concludes the section.[44] The final part of the Fifth Sibyl has a similarly miscellaneous combination: a further denunciation of Rome (as Babylon), more apocalyptic visions, a clash between Egyptians and Ethiopians, and a contest in heaven among the stars that ends in a blaze of fire throughout the earth.[45]

This hodge-podge does not pretend to offer a smooth narrative or a uniform picture. But fierce hostility to Rome plays a major and recurrent role through most of the text, and that is what concerns us here. The Sibyl denounces the "city of the Latin land" for numerous vices and transgressions, brands it as possessing a murderous heart and an impious spirit, and predicts its destruction by fire at the hands of God, with relegation to Hades.[46] In a subsequent oracle she excoriates Rome as "thrice-wretched Italy," everywhere deserted and unwept, awaiting destruction.[47] Yet another passage evidently refers to dire events in store for Rome. The warning actually directs itself to Babylon, but "Babylon," as is well known, is often a stand-in for Rome. The description of the nation as sole kingdom in command of the world for many years, once great and universal, must evoke Rome. And the Sibyl predicts a bitter reckoning for the great power to its enemies as retaliation for its crooked words.[48] The prevailing tone of the work is sharp animus to Rome.

Does this animus, however, stem from the actions of the western power in leveling the Temple, thus generating Jewish reaction to the catastrophe? Only a single passage in the Fifth Sibyl suggests this connection. The author speaks of a great star whose glow will destroy the whole earth, will set alight the deep sea, burning up Babylon and the land of Italy because of which many holy and faithful Hebrews and a true people perished.[49] These lines can certainly be taken to indicate that the anticipated destruction for

---

[42] 5 Sib. 179–285. [43] 5 Sib. 286–360. [44] 5 Sib. 361–433. [45] 5 Sib. 434–531.
[46] 5 Sib. 162–178. [47] 5 Sib. 342–343.
[48] 5 Sib. 434–446: πουλυετὴς βασίλεια μόνη κόσμοιο κρατοῦσα/ ἡ τὸ πάλαι μεγάλη καὶ πάμπολις. So, rightly, Jones 2011: 238–9. A problem lies with the reference to that great power sending hostages to Rome (442–443). But this could allude to captives, prisoners, or slaves taken in Rome's eastern wars.
[49] 5 Sib. 155–61: ἥξει δ᾽ οὐρανόθεν ἀστὴρ μέγας εἰς ἅλα δῖαν/ καὶ φλέξει πόντον βαθὺν αὐτήν τε Βαβυλῶνα/ Ἰταλίης γαῖάν θ᾽, ἧς εἵνεκα πολλοὶ ὄλοντο/ Ἑβραίων ἅγιοι πιστοὶ καὶ λαὸς ἀληθής.

Rome serves as recompense for the fall of Jerusalem and the loss of numerous Jewish lives.[50] Yet the passage may not have so precise a reference. The mention of both "Babylon" and "the land of Italy" may indicate that "Babylon" here is no mere equivalent of Rome, and that the Sibyl alludes to the destruction of both the First and the Second Temple. Indeed she reaches back well beyond the immediacy of her own day. The text mocks Rome for reckoning itself as standing all alone and indestructible; God, in fact, will destroy the nation together with all its people.[51] Those verses resonate very closely with Isaiah's challenge to Babylon, representing the city as claiming to be alone with no competition, while the prophet promises divine retribution and unforeseen calamity.[52] The parallel is notable. The Fifth Sibyl paints on a broad canvas. Motivation does not spring from a single event. Rome stands for a long history of oppressive conquerors.

Vengeance will come. But nowhere in the fifth Sibylline Oracle is there suggestion that the Jews will be the instrument of retaliation – or indeed even a direct beneficiary. The Sibyl mourns the loss of holy and faithful Hebrews and projects the destruction of their oppressors by God who will send them unceremoniously to the netherworld. But the outcome for a Jewish future goes curiously unmentioned.[53] On another occasion, when the text outlines the desolation of Italy to be wrought by the Lord, Italians are not alone as victims. God will bring a vast darkness that encompasses every race of men and shameless tribe.[54] That presumably includes the Jews who receive no exemption. And the forecast of the humbling of "Babylon" (or, rather, Rome) envisions it flattened by an earthquake.[55] The narrative of that harsh fate expresses no sense of direct benefit to the Jews.

10.4 Nero in the Sibyllines

Insofar as an instrument of the Lord surfaces to apply vengeance and retribution, he takes the form of a most unexpected avenger: none other than Nero himself. The figure of Nero moves in and out of the text of the Fifth Sibyl with frequency, and usually amidst a host of negative comments. The emperor is introduced as slayer of his own family, an athlete, charioteer, and murderer, bold and reckless, prepared to cut through

---

[50] So Collins 1974a: 79.
[51] 5 Sib. 173–174: μόνη εἰμὶ καὶ οὐδείς μ' ἐξαλαπάξει/ νῦν δὲ σὲ καὶ σοὺς πάντας ὀλεῖ θεὸς εὕρατο τιμάς.
[52] Isaiah, 47.8–11. See the acute discussion of Jones 2011: 225–7.   [53] 5 Sib. 155–178.
[54] 5 Sib. 342–359.   [55] 5 Sib. 434–446.

10. The Sibylline Oracles and Resistance to Rome

a mountain, and potentially destructive even when he disappears. And, worse still, he reckoned himself equal to God – a claim that God himself will demolish.[56] His next appearance in the text is hardly any more appealing. Nero devotes himself to warbling and acting on the stage, but finds time to murder his mother and many men in addition, until he flees Rome, and takes refuge in the east, an enemy to the "true race," and one who would reappear. In the course of this lengthy rampage, Nero, according to the Fifth Sibyl, captured the Temple and burned those who entered it, thus responsible for the annihilation of a great city and a righteous people.[57] The return of Nero from eastern lands, in the Sibyl's presentation, brought destruction in his wake, including the endeavor to cut a canal through the Isthmus of Corinth, accompanied by the ravaging of land, widespread killings, and terror.[58] And there was still more. Nero is represented as the matricide who fled abroad determined to wage war everywhere, to bring devastation to all lands and people, and to set the world afire as none before him ever did.[59]

The grim portrait prevails. Yet Nero is no one-dimensional character. The Fifth Sibyl, in depicting the Roman ruler as engaging in a wide swath of destruction and setting everything ablaze, adds that he will ponder these matters more wisely than all men.[60] And the oracle concludes with a moving portrayal of the outcome of all the fire and brimstone: war will ultimately come to a close, iron and weaponry will be cast aside, and the wise people who are left, having experienced evil, will enjoy peace.[61] Nero therefore, despite all the destructiveness, heralds a glorious era of concord and joy. And, most notably, he serves as an instrument of the Lord to shatter the Roman empire. What does one make of that?

Nero's role is not altogether incongruous. As we know from other sources, various rumors and tales circulated about the emperor, associating his deposition from the throne with a new career as ruler of the east, his departure as prelude to arrival in the Parthian kingdom, the prime foe of Rome.[62] Word spread indeed that Nero had not, after all, committed suicide as most believed, but remained alive, a report that to many in the east was welcome and desirable.[63] His popularity in the east does have some historical basis and rationale. We are told by Tacitus and Dio Cassius that

---

[56] 5 Sib. 28–34.   [57] 5 Sib. 137–154.   [58] 5 Sib. 214–227.
[59] 5 Sib. 361–370. It is by no means clear that the "Persian" who will spread slaughter everywhere he goes (93–110) is also Nero, as is claimed by Collins 1983: 395; so also Stemberger 1983: 56. See the doubts of Jones 2011: 220–3, although his own suggestion of Antiochus IV is equally hypothetical.
[60] 5 Sib. 366: πάντων τ' ἀνθρώπων φρονιμώτερα πάντα νοήσει.   [61] 5 Sib. 381–385.
[62] Tac. Hist. 2.8.1; Suet. Nero, 40.1, 47.2.   [63] Dio of Prusa, Or. 21.9–10.

Nero had presided over a diplomatic compromise that created a mutually agreeable settlement between Rome and Parthia culminated even by a grand procession in Rome honoring the ruler of Armenia, the brother of the Parthian king, and concluding with the presentation of his diadem by Nero himself.[64] The settlement endured through the next generation, and plainly enhanced Nero's reputation in the eastern Mediterranean and the lands of the Parthian empire. It is no accident that three separate persons impersonated Nero in the two decades after his death, each of them generating considerable enthusiasm in the eastern Mediterranean before his demise.[65] In short, the image of Nero was an appropriate one as champion of the east against the imperial power.[66]

That image takes on special clarity in the Eighth Sibyl. The Jewish portions of that work, essentially its first half, pay particular attention to Nero. References to Hadrian and Marcus Aurelius in the text place it in the later second century CE, thus long after the loss of the Temple. But the appearances of Nero in the oracles show that the author was acquainted with and drew consciously upon the traditions found in the Fifth Sibyl. Nero appears first in familiar form: the fiery matricidal exile now returned from distant parts to supply great wealth to Asia.[67] The Sibyl then immediately delivers dire prophecies to Rome: the Latin city, puffed up with pride, will suffer humiliation, the glory of the eagle-bearing legions will decline, a bloodthirsty time will fall upon the Italian land, that great barbarian nation will disappear amidst the burning dust, with nothing left but cries and moans from its new lodging place in Hades.[68] Rome will not again set others under its yoke of slavery but will itself repay all the injuries and become a spectacle to the world and a reproach to all.[69] These verses do not themselves single out Nero as the agent of destruction. But the following passages leave no doubt. The man who bears carnage and annihilation for the overweening Romans comes from Asia and will cut through the isthmus in bloody pursuit.[70]

---

[64] Dio Cass. 63.1–6; cf. Tac. *Ann.* 16.23–24; Suet. *Nero*, 13, 30, 57.
[65] Tac. *Hist.* 2.8–9; Suet. Nero, 57.2; Dio Cass. 64.9.3, 66.19.3b-c; Zon. 11.15; Joann. Antioch. Fr. 104 M; see, especially, Tuplin 1989: 364–404; cf. also Lawrence 1978: 54–66; Champlin 2003: 10–12; Gruen 2014: 89–92.
[66] It is possible that the mysterious reference in the Fifth Sibyl to a Roman king and dynasts of the west who will put an end to the mad war that has covered the world with blood and dust may allude to Nero; 462–463: κοσμομανὴς πόλεμος πολυαίματος ἐν κονίησιν/ ὃν παύσει Ῥώμης βασιλεὺς δυσμῶν τε δυνάσται.
[67] 8 Sib. 70–72.   [68] 8 Sib. 73–109.   [69] 8 Sib. 124–130.
[70] 8 Sib. 140–157. The same motif is picked up in the Twelfth Sibyl, 12.78–85.

The same motif appears again in the Twelfth Sibyl which dates to the third century CE. Nero, the athlete, charioteer, and murderer who cleaves the mountain and fills it with gore, will be, even when vanished, destructive to the Italians.[71] The repeated theme brings home a striking feature. Nero, a despicable character in almost every regard, nevertheless carries out the will of God in wreaking devastation upon Rome, in humbling the haughty power, and in sending it unceremoniously into the depths of Hell.

How does one account for this? Do the Sibyllines represent the voice of despondent but defiant Jews living in the generation after the fall of their city and loss of their Temple, forecasting the calamitous fate of Rome through a fanciful retaliation, whether as desperate hope or a grasping after some inner consolation? If so, why fasten upon the detestable Nero to exact punishment upon Rome and to carry out the will of God in avenging his people? To be sure, the Hebrew Bible is full of wicked nations carrying out the divine plan by punishing the Israelites themselves for their sins and recalling them to righteousness. And the wicked avenger is avenged in turn when the Israelites return to God's favor. That is a central theme of the Deuteronomistic history. But it is hard to find a character who possesses the baggage that Nero carried. And the oracular pronouncements of the Sibyls lambaste Nero for his plethora of vices and his ruthless destructiveness in the very same verses that record his purported actions in toppling Rome from its lofty position to catastrophic doom.[72]

We need to shift the perspective and ask a more fundamental question. Did these representations of Rome really arise from the lamentable conditions in which Jews found themselves after the fall of Jerusalem? It is well to remember that the composition of the Sibylline Oracles in general did not occur within the short and circumscribed period in which the pain of losing the Temple was fresh and acute. Only the Fourth and the Fifth Sibyllines seem to belong to that era, at least in large part. And each of those texts, like the others, is a composite, with superimposed layers and redactions. One might, for example, find Nero even in the Third Sibylline Oracle, although the bulk of that text was certainly composed much earlier than his day.[73] The consequences of the Great Revolt and the Roman oppression that followed do not explain the impetus behind the Sibylline Oracles or any significant portion of them.

---

[71] 12 Sib. 78–94: ἀλλ' ἔσται καὶ ἄιστος ὀλοίιος Ἰταλίδαισιν.

[72] 8 Sib. 70–80, 124–130, 140–157; 12 Sib. 78–94.

[73] This holds if "Beliar of the Sebastenoi" (3 Sib. 63) is Nero; so, Collins 1974a: 80–87. But see Nikiprowetzky 1970: 138–43.

In fact, the consequences of the Jewish Revolt and the Roman oppression that followed find surprisingly little mention in the Sibyllines at all. They appear most explicitly in the Fourth Sibyl. In that concentrated passage, as noted earlier, the text twice refers to the assault on the Temple by Rome, once as an evil tempest of war from Italy, and second in the form of a Roman leader who will burn the Temple of Jerusalem and bring devastation and massacre upon the land of the Jews.[74] It is noteworthy, however, that between these verses the Sibyl makes equally explicit reference to Nero (without, of course, actually giving the name). The text speaks of a great king from Italy, polluted by the murder of his mother, in flight like a slave, unseen and unheard, across the strait of the Euphrates and beyond the land of Parthia.[75] That of course is Nero, but he is not immediately identified as an avenger of the Jews. Vengeance comes in other forms: earthquake, fire, the eruption of Vesuvius. But Nero's return is not far behind. The fugitive from Rome will recross the Euphrates, holding a great spear, accompanied by multitudes, and spreading war to the west.[76] One might observe that the passage makes direct reference here to the wrath of the God of heaven administered because Romans will destroy the blameless clan of the pious.[77] This constitutes the most unequivocal expression of divine retaliation for the fall of Jerusalem. It will take the form of natural disasters, but also the human revenge represented by the exile Nero at the head of eastern hordes.

The Lord, to be sure, works in mysterious ways. But it is clear that there is not much in the Fourth Sibyl for Jews to take any pride in. Nero bears the weapon of vengeance. And Rome is far from the sole target. The oracle proclaims disasters that will fall upon Cyprus and Antioch as well, upon Carian cities, and wherever the Maeander river flows.[78] The passage itself, even with its explicitness about requital for the loss of the Temple, includes a range of victims of God's fury, well beyond Rome. The Sibyl hardly served as vehicle for Jewish response, let alone resistance, to Roman authority. If Vesuvius and Nero were the instruments of divine wrath, they had already done their worst in the past. The future apocalypse will burn the entire earth and destroy the whole of mankind.[79] This is no mere clash of Rome and Jerusalem.

---

[74] 4 Sib. 115–118, 125–127. See nn. 19–20.

[75] 4 Sib. 119–123: καὶ τότ' ἀπ' Ἰταλίης βασιλεὺς μέγας οἷά τε δράστης/ φεύξετ' ἄφαντος ἄπυστος ὑπὲρ πόρον Εὐφρήταο/ ὁππότε δὴ μητρῷον ἄγος στυγεροῖο φόνοιο/... κείνου ἀποδρήσαντος ὑπὲρ Παρθηΐδα γαῖαν.

[76] 4 Sib. 137–139: ἐς δὲ δύσιν τότε νεῖκος ἐγειρομένου πολέμοιο/ ἥξει καὶ Ῥώμης ὁ φυγάς, μέγα ἔγχος ἀείρας,/ Εὐφρήτην διαβὰς πολλαῖς ἅμα μυριάδεσσιν.

[77] 4 Sib. 135–136: γινώσκειν τότε μῆνιν ἐπουρανίοι θεοῖο/ εὐσεβέων ὅτι φῦλον ἀναίτιον ἐξολέσουσιν.

[78] 4 Sib. 140–151.   [79] 4 Sib. 171–178.

The Fifth Sibyl too offers a jumbled combination of oracles. She does excoriate Rome and deliver harsh predictions of doom.[80] And she does rant against Nero for his sins, his power and ruthlessness, and his pretensions to divinity.[81] Yet the fate of Rome is commingled with that of other nations, not singled out for special vendetta.[82] And Nero's destructiveness encompasses a broad range of humanity.[83] The demolition of the Temple does not play a conspicuous role – and barely any role at all.

10.5 The Temple

That calamitous event appears just twice in the text. First, the Sibyl castigates Romans for that dreadful deed, deploring the image of the Second Temple going up in flames set by an unholy hand, dismaying the pious souls who had expected the Temple of God to be eternal.[84] Apart from a brief allusion to the eventual death of the conqueror Titus brought about by the divinity, the passage gives no sense of any retaliatory consequences of this catastrophe.

Second, a different account elsewhere in the Fifth Sibyl has a surprising twist. The text conveys the conventional invective against Nero, singer and actor, murderer of many including his mother, his claims on divinity, allegedly son of Zeus and Hera, an exile in flight from Rome, and a fugitive in the lands of the Medes and Persians (Parthia).[85] But it then adds a statement unique to these texts: Nero seized the Temple built by God and burned the citizens who entered into it; his appearance shook all creation to its foundation and caused kings to perish; those who remained destroyed a great city and a righteous people.[86] The passage is not easy to interpret. No other text, Jewish or pagan, has Nero seize the Temple and burn its inhabitants, or indeed have anything whatever to do with the fall of Jerusalem.[87] And, of course, he died two years before that event. It is conceivable that Nero was held responsible for the conflagration on the

---

[80] 5 Sib. 162–177, 342–345, 386–396, 434–446.   [81] 5 Sib. 28–34, 137–144, 214–224, 363–385.
[82] 5 Sib. 286–360.
[83] 5 Sib. 152–153, 214–224, 363–374. Note also the extensive destructiveness of the ("Persian"; 93–110. But whether he is Nero remains quite uncertain.
[84] 5 Sib. 397–410.   [85] 5 Sib. 137–148.
[86] 5 Sib. 150–154: ὃ πᾶσαν θεότευκτον ἔλεω καὶ ἔφλεξε πολίτας/ λαοὺς εἰσανιόντας, ὅσους ὕμνησα δικαίως/ τούτου γὰρ φανέντος ὅλη κτίσις ἐξετινάχθη/ καὶ βασιλεῖς ὄλοντο, καί ἐν τοῖσιν μένεν ἀρχή/ ἐξόλεσαν μεγάλην τε πόλιν λαόν τε δίκαιον.
[87] See, however, 8 Sib. 140–141, which has Nero ravage various peoples and tribes, including the nation of the Hebrews. The import of this remains quite obscure, particularly so because it comes in the context of Nero humbling the Roman Empire; 143–150.

grounds that he was still alive at the time of the outbreak of the revolt and that he appointed Vespasian to command the Roman forces who eventually did bring about the calamity. Specific chronology could readily have faded from memory by the time that the Fifth Sibyl was composed. And the fiery destruction may also have triggered recollection of the blaze that Nero had indeed ordered in 64 CE to punish Christians – one in which numerous Jews must have perished.[88] Whatever the grounds for this remarkable and unparalleled statement, however, it is important to stress that it stands essentially alone in the Sibylline corpus. Moreover, even that text makes no direct connection with sufferings that Rome will endure as a consequence.

10.6 Conclusion

The very scarcity of references in the Sibyllines to the Temple's demise stands out and requires emphasis. Even those texts which were produced in the aftermath of the destruction or in subsequent generations give it little play. The sharp criticisms of Rome relate largely to earlier periods of Roman expansionism. The characterization seems more conventional than fresh. The allusions to Nero are repetitious, often confused, and incoherent, and only one associates him with the fall of the Temple. Further, the apocalyptic visions go far beyond the fate of Rome. They proclaim disasters also for Egyptians, Ethiopians, Macedonians, a plethora of Greek cities, Persians, Asians generally, and even Britons and Gauls – very few of whom had ever done any harm to Jews.

The Sibyllines, in short, do not readily qualify as targeted resistance literature. Nor do they serve as expression of Jewish riposte simply or chiefly to the loss of the Temple. The oracles look ahead to a distant divine intervention, but not one triggered by a particular event or by a single deed that sealed the future of Rome. It is time that we stop seizing upon a very few individual allusions in the apocalyptic texts that have generated the modern scenario of political resistance triggered by a specific act of Roman wickedness. The language belongs to the genre rather than to any special historical circumstances. Sibylline verses reflect a much broader experience of long-term perseverance under imperial power. And much as we might like to see a noble, or perhaps a desperate, Jewish resistance to Roman oppression, or an outcry through a "hidden transcript" that might serve as consolation for loss of Temple and homeland at Rome's hands, such an

---

[88] Cf. Gruen 2014: 94–6.

interpretation misses the deeper significance of the apocalypic genre, the promise of eventual redemption by divine power and retaliation against the forces of evil everywhere, no mere summons to subversion against a specific foe. Apocalyptic literature has a momentum of its own, independent of particular events, no matter how cataclysmic.

CHAPTER 11

Revelation 17.1–19.10: A Prophetic Vision of the Destruction of Rome

Peter Oakes

11.1 Introduction

At the end of the sets of seven visions in the Book of Revelation – the seven seals, seven trumpets and seven bowls – John sees a further vision in which a figure identified as 'Babylon' is destroyed. In this article we will show that this figure represents Rome, then discuss why Rome is destroyed and how this happens. In doing this, we will draw a contrast with the conclusions of Erich Gruen's contribution to this volume (Chapter 10). He argues that the Jewish Sibylline Oracles draw predominantly from non-Jewish Sibylline representations of Rome's downfall. We will argue that, in contrast, Revelation 17.1–19.10 is primarily a complex interweaving of motifs from scriptural prophetic texts about various wicked cities and their fates. We will begin by outlining Revelation 17.1–19.10 then consider each of the issues.

11.2 Outline of Revelation 17.1–19.10

In Revelation 16, seven angels pour out, in succession, the 'seven last plagues' that 'complete' 'the wrath of God' (15.1). When the seventh angel pours the seventh plague from its bowl (16.17) various catastrophic consequences occur, especially an unprecedentedly large earthquake (16.18), which splits 'the great city' in three. The 'cities of the nations/ gentiles (ἐθνῶν)' also fall. Moreover, 'Babylon the great was remembered before God, to give her the cup of the wine of the wrath of his anger' (16.19)[1]. Islands flee and hills disappear (16.20). A plague of hailstones torments people, who respond by blaspheming God (16.21).

The 'remembering' of Babylon sets the scene for the subsequent chapters. One of the angels who had the bowls of plagues approaches John and calls him

---

[1] All translations are by the author, unless otherwise stated.

to come and see 'the judgement of the great harlot who sits on many waters, with whom the kings of the earth have committed fornication and the inhabitants of the earth have become drunk with the wine of her fornication' (17.1–2). John is taken, in the spirit, into a desert (17.3). There he sees the luxuriously, gaudily dressed figure, seated on a seven-headed, ten-horned scarlet beast (17.3–4). The harlot is (literally) labelled, 'Babylon the great'. She is 'drunk on the blood of the holy ones and the blood of the witnesses of Jesus' (17.5–6).

Now the angel offers to explain the mystery of the woman and the beast (17.7). The beast's seven heads are explained first as seven hills, then as kings, who are variously assigned to past, present and future (17.9–10). The horns are also kings, who will wage war, alongside the beast, against 'the lamb' and be defeated (7.12–14). The waters on which the harlot sits (17.1) are explained as peoples (17.15). The horns and beast will attack, strip, eat and burn the harlot (17.16).

Chapter 18 opens with another angel announcing that Babylon has fallen (18.1–2, echoing 14.8) and will be abandoned. A further voice from heaven calls God's people to leave Babylon so as not to share in her sins or plagues, because her sins have come up to heaven and the city will be judged in a single day (18.3–8). There is then a succession of laments over Babylon's fate: first by 'the kings of the earth' (18.9–10); then by 'the merchants of the earth' (18.11–17); then by ship-owners and sailors (18.17–19). There is then a call for heaven, the holy ones, the apostles and the prophets, to rejoice in this judgement (18.20). A strong angel throws a great mill-stone into the sea and either laments or gloats over the desolation of Babylon (18.21–24).

John then hears a great crowd in heaven calling out praise to God for the judgement of the harlot and the avenging of the blood of God's servants (19.1–2). A second call praises God as 'her smoke goes up for ever and ever' (19.3). Further rejoicing in heaven culminates in announcement of the wedding of 'the lamb' to a woman clothed in 'bright, pure linen' (19.8). John is told (by the angel of 17.1?) to write that those invited to the wedding feast are blessed and that 'the words are genuine words of God' (19.9). At the end of the vision, John falls down to worship the angel. He is rebuked and directed to worship God, 'for the testimony of Jesus is the spirit of prophecy' (19.10).

11.3 Identifying 'Babylon'

And on her forehead was written a name, a mystery, Babylon the great (17.5)

Attempts have been made to identify the harlot on the beast as Jerusalem, for instance, by Margaret Barker[2]. Some scholars, such as G. K. Beale, have seen the harlot as symbolising all oppressive world powers, with Rome being the most prominent[3]. However, there are many points in the text that suggest that John specifically has Rome in mind.

11.3.1 On Seven Hills

The most specific evidence is in the angel's first explanation of the seven heads of the beast: 'The seven heads are seven hills (ἑπτὰ ὄρη) upon which the woman sits' (17.9). Barker argues that Jerusalem could be described as sitting on seven mountains. She cites the ἑπτὰ ὄρη of precious stones in the vision of *1 Enoch* 18.6, 24.2. She argues that, when Enoch presents the central one of the mountains as carrying God's throne (18.8, 25.3), this implies that the 'mythical geography' of the Jerusalem Temple must have included seven mountains, three on either side of the one with the throne on it[4]. However, this is an extremely tenuous argument for seeing Jerusalem as being reputed to sit on seven mountains or hills. It is particularly difficult to map features of Enoch's vision of the heavens onto the topography of earthly Jerusalem. Even if this were correct, it seems so obscure that the probability of John's hearers understanding 'seven hills/mountains' in this way appears very remote. There is also a reference to Jerusalem as standing on seven hills in *Pirqei deRabbi Eliezer* 71. However, as Caroline Vout notes, this is late, very unusual, and may itself be based on the Rome tradition[5].

Beale seeks to defend an identity wider than Rome for the figure on the ἑπτὰ ὄρη, which he, like Barker reads as 'seven mountains'. He sees this expression as being linked figuratively to strength and, beyond this, to kingdoms (citing Isa. 2.2; Ezek. 35.3; Dan. 2.35, 45 and others)[6]. A point in favour of Beale's argument is that Rev. 17.9 continues with a second explanation of the heads, 'and they are seven kings'. Beale's case makes this second explanation synonymous with the first, rather than being considerably different from it.

However, as Beale himself argues, it was a first-century commonplace to refer to Rome as being on seven hills[7]. Vout documents and explores this at length[8]. It is unclear quite how far back the tradition goes historically, but key extant examples are Varro, *De lingua Latina* 5.41–54, Juvenal, *Satires*

---

[2] Barker 2000: 282–4. [3] Beale 1999: 755. [4] Barker 2000: 285. [5] Vout 2012: 25.
[6] Beale 1999: 868. [7] Beale 1999: 870. [8] Vout 2012: 18–80.

11. Revelation 17.1–19.10: A Prophetic Vision

9.130, and Pliny, *Hist. nat.* 3.66–67[9]. The point can also be well illustrated from the Sibylline Oracles. Book 11 predicts a range of conquests. One of these begins,

> But when Italian soil will generate great wonder unto mortals, there will be moans of children by a fountain pure. In shady cavern, offspring of wild beast that feeds on sheep who, unto manhood grown, will upon seven strong hills (ἐφ ἑπτὰ λόφοισι[10] κραταιοῖς) with reckless soul hurl many headlong down. ... and they will build upon the seven hills strong walls and wage around them grievous war. (11.109–116. Trans. C. Evans [corrected])[11]

Book 2, in a passage with similarities to Rev. 17–18 and with clear Christian elements (especially references to Christ and martyrs in 2.45–47), speaks of a time

> ... when the earth-shaking lightning-giver will break the zeal for idols and will shake the people of seven-hilled Rome (Ῥώμης ἑπταλόφοιο), and riches great will perish, burned by Vulcan's fiery flame (2.16–19).

The composite expression Ῥώμη ἑπτάλοφος occurs in 13.45, in a list of various events not immediately connected with destruction of the city. The same is true of 14.107–108, which speaks of acts carried out 'on behalf of the seven-hilled city of Rome' (ὑπὲρ ἄστεος ... Ῥώμης ἑπταλόφου, my trans.).

In the face of the great weight of evidence of the common designation of Rome as being on seven hills, it is extremely hard to avoid the conclusion that John and his readers would hear 17.9 as a reference to Rome, even if there were not the supporting evidence from other texts in the book.

11.3.2 The Great City

At the conclusion of the explanation of the vision in Revelation 17, the angel explicitly describes 'the woman whom you see', as 'the great city that has kingship over the kings of the earth' (17.17). In a first-century (or early second-century) context, in a book written for the province of Asia (Rev. 1.4; 2.1–3.22), this can only refer to Rome.

---

[9] See also the references and discussion in Aune 1997: 944.
[10] In relation to the lexical point that Rome is typically described as on ἑπτὰ λόφοι rather than on ἑπτὰ ὄρη, Giancarlo Riguzzi 2006: 371–386; here 384, offers a number of instances of examples of ὄρος being used of one or more of the seven hills of Rome (Strabo 5.3.7; Dion. Hal. 2.50.1; Dio Cassius 44.25.3; 53.27.5, etc). The article argues that the Rome is a more likely option than Jerusalem in more-or-less all of the relevant texts in Revelation.
[11] Evans 2016.

The expression, 'the great city', is used in 16.19 and repeated at 18.10, 16, 18, 19. This might evoke ideas of Nineveh (Jonah 1.2; 3.2; 4.11; Judith 1.1; cf. Gen. 10.12) and, indeed, we will see use of ideas relating to prophecy about Nineveh. However, in Revelation, the expression is repeatedly tied to Babylon: indirectly in 16.19, 'the great city was split ... and Babylon the great was remembered ... ', then in various formulations including direct linkages in 18.10, 'the great city, Babylon the strong city' and 18.21, 'Babylon the great city'. We will explore the links to Babylon, further in this chapter.

The political domination described in 17.17 is reinforced by the depiction of economic domination in chapter 18. 'Babylon' is the place to which all trade goods are taken (18.12–13). After its fall, the merchants wail, 'because no one any longer buys their cargo' (18.11). Rome was particularly known as the destination for much of the Mediterranean's traded wheat (18.13). It was also the main destination of trade in luxury goods such as those listed in 18.12–13, 'gold, silver, jewels and pearls, fine linen, purple, silk and scarlet, ... scented wood, ivory ... marble'[12]. More specifically, Rome or its citizens around the empire were the main purchasers of 'bodies and souls of people' (18.13), which must convey some reference to the slave trade. When we consider the scriptural background of the clause, 'with whom the kings of the earth committed fornication' (17.2), we will see further allusion to Rome's economic relationships.

11.3.3 Bloodshed and Babylon

After John was shown the luxurious state of the harlot on the beast, he 'saw that the woman was drunk with the blood of the holy ones and (καί) with the blood of the witnesses (μαρτύρων) of Jesus' (17.6). Is this one group or two? Beale argues that καί 'is best taken as explanatory ("even")'[13], so that the whole reference is to persecution of Christians. For Beale, this 'took the form of ostracism from trade', although in some cases the persecution could involve 'capital punishment'[14]. If, on the other hand, καί is taken as coordinating, 'and', there could be reference to two distinct groups. In 18.24, the fallen city is blamed because 'in her was found the blood of prophets and of holy ones, and of all those on earth who have been slaughtered'. The reference here goes beyond Christians. Aune sees a possible reference to the Jewish dead of the war of 66–73 CE[15]. If that is

---

[12] New Revised Standard Version (NRSV) translation. [13] Beale 1999: 860. [14] Ibid.
[15] Aune 1997: 1009.

11. Revelation 17.1–19.10: A Prophetic Vision

the case, there could also be an allusion to this in 'the blood of the holy ones' in 17.6. However, the expression ἅγιοι, 'saints', 'holy ones' in Revelation generally refers to Christians (e.g. 13.10).

A reference to persecution of Christians fits with a wide range of evidence in Revelation: the possible reference to the author's exile on Patmos (1.9); the specific mention of the killing of Antipas (2.13); then many references to those who have suffered, such as 'those who are coming out of the great tribulation and who washed their robes and whitened them in the blood of the lamb' (7.14). Since Irenaeus, this has frequently been linked to placing Revelation during the reign of Domitian[16], seen as a persecutor of Christians and Jews. Contemporary evidence of some trouble for Christians in Rome during his reign is probably provided by *1 Clement* 1.1; 6.1–3, which compare 'calamities' and torture in Clement's time (probably the 90s CE) with the earlier killing of Peter and Paul (*1 Clem.* 5).

It is difficult to reach overall conclusions about the extent to which Rome, in some general sense, persecuted Christians at any period prior to the Decian persecution of 250 CE. However, there are quite a number of striking specific incidents of Christians suffering at the hands of Roman authority figures ranging from Nero to the governors cited in texts such as the *Passion of Perpetua and Felicitas*. Conversely, there are no strong candidates other than Rome for a figure who could be depicted as 'drunk on the blood of the holy ones'. When Margaret Barker makes her case for the harlot being identified as Jerusalem, Barker virtually skips over 17.6, not attempting to build a case for Jerusalem being responsible for substantial persecution of Christians[17].

In 18.24, there is probably some allusion to Jeremiah 51.49, 'Babylon must fall for the slain of Israel, as the slain of all the earth have fallen because of Babylon' (New Revised Standard Version (NRSV)). This links us back to Rev. 17.5, and elsewhere in these chapters, where the harlot and city are repeatedly called, 'Babylon'. This, paradoxically, further supports a link between Revelation 17–19 and Rome because there appears to have been a broad Jewish literary tradition of representing Rome by using the name, Babylon. Second Baruch and 4 Ezra are both generally viewed as reflecting on 70 CE by the vehicle of discussion of the capture of Jerusalem by Babylon. Gruen argues that *Sib. Or.* 5.434–46 also intends Rome in its reference to destruction of Babylon (although noting the oddity of the mention of Rome itself, in another connection, in the text)[18]. Another early

---

[16] Irenaeus as reported in Eusebius, *H.E.* 3.18.3; 5.8.6. [17] Barker 2000: 280, 283.
[18] Gruen, Chapter 10 n. 48 in this volume.

Christian text that probably uses 'Babylon' as a term for Rome is 1 Peter 5.13, which sends greetings from 'the co-elect woman in Babylon', probably referring to the church in Rome[19].

The name Babylon, the ascription of violence, the identification as the great city that controls the politics and trade of its day and the location on seven hills, mean that the discourse of Rev. 17.1–19.10, even on its own, would evidently be referring to Rome. Taken together with evidence from elsewhere in Revelation, especially the note about the beast's number being 666, which is almost certainly a coded reference to Nero[20], there appears little doubt that Rome is, at least predominantly, in mind in the chapters that are our focus.

11.4 Why Rome Falls

> Fallen, fallen is Babylon the great ... because ... (18.2–3)

A long string of misdeeds are attributed to Rome in Rev. 17–19. Several of these are explicitly indicated as reasons for the city's destruction. The others presumably add to the case against it.

11.4.1 God's Judgement

The whole piece fits within a general perspective that Rome falls because God judges the city. In 16.17–21, the catastrophes unleashed by the pouring out of the seventh bowl are being enumerated in a manner similar to previous such catalogues in Revelation, but there is then an intrusion of a statement about judgement: 'and Babylon the great was remembered before God to give her the cup of the wine of the fury of his wrath' (16.19). What John is then called to see is, 'the judgement of the great harlot' (17.1). Surprisingly, judgement as such is not then mentioned again until 18.8 where John notes, 'strong is the Lord God who judges her'. In 18.20, judgement comes in something like *lex talionis* form, 'God judged (ἔκρινεν) the condemnation (κρίμα) of you by her'. Finally, 19.2 provides an *inclusio* with 17.1 in announcing that God 'judged the great harlot'. For John, every aspect of the downfall of Rome that he sees is a judgement by God. Whatever the mode of destruction, the origin is in God's decision. Any human malevolence or 'natural' catastrophe that might be involved in it is ultimately serving God's decision against Rome. Even in 17.16, when

---

[19] Achtemeier 1996: 348.   [20] See discussion in Aune 1997: 770.

11. Revelation 17.1–19.10: A Prophetic Vision

the harlot is destroyed by the beast and ten kings, John adds the note, 'for God put into their hearts to do his purpose' (17.17).

As a judgement, the downfall of Rome is produced by something like a divine lawsuit, a key topic in recent studies of the prophets. It may be reasonable to follow Alan S. Bandy in seeing an element of the structure of Revelation as being similar to that of major scriptural prophetic oracles of judgement. Bandy's scheme is, broadly, that the letters to the seven churches in Rev. 2–3 correspond to prophetic oracles of judgement on Judah and Jerusalem, followed in Rev. 4–21.8 with oracles of judgement on the nations, then ended in 21.9–22.5 by promises of salvation for God's people in the renewed Jerusalem. For scriptural parallels, Bandy follows scholars such as Jacques Vermeylen by offering sequences such as Isaiah 1–12 (Judah and Jerusalem); 13–27 (the nations); 28–35 (deliverance for God's people)[21]. There are many complications that make such a match far from straightforward. However, there are, of course, also complexities in the prophetic texts that are taken as a model for the lawsuit form.

What is worth noting here is that the lawsuit aspect of Rev. 17.1–19.10 provides a macro-structural paradigm within which John's microstructural use (as we shall see) of prophetic material makes some kind of sense, especially since that material is drawn especially from oracles against the nations in Isaiah, Jeremiah and Ezekiel. In genre terms, the link is not straightforward: Rev. 17–19 is cast in the form of vision (in which the Danielic material of Rev. 17 sits more comfortably) and draws on other genres such as lament. However, even these genres are not entirely alien to scriptural prophetic law-suits.

11.4.2 Rome's Violence

The recapitulating note that God 'judged the great harlot who corrupted the earth with her fornication' (on the latter part of which, see §11.4.4,) is coupled with a direct explanation of God's action, 'and he avenged the blood of his servants, [shed] at her hand (ἐξεδίκησεν τὸ αἷμα τῶν δούλων αὐτοῦ ἐκ χειρὸς αὐτῆς) (19.2). This is an allusion to the Septuagint text of 4 Kgdms 9.7, καὶ ἐκδικήσεις τὰ αἵματα τῶν δούλων μου τῶν προφητῶν καὶ τὰ αἵματα πάντων τῶν δούλων κυρίου ἐκ χειρὸς Ιεζαβελ. This extends the range of intertextuality beyond John's favoured sources in Isaiah, Jeremiah, Ezekiel and Daniel, but it does handle the text in a similar way. There is strong overlap in elements of the vocabulary and in some thematic aspects,

---

[21] Bandy 2009: 469–99, here 485–7, citing Vermeylen 1989.

but there is considerable adaptation and no direct signalling of the source or how it is being used. One move that is consistent in John's approach is that he re-appropriates texts about Israelites, applying them to Christian martyrs. The notion of God's avenging of persecuted Christians is one also found strikingly in 2 Thessalonians 1.5–9, which depicts God violently repaying those who afflict the Thessalonian Christians.

The motive of vengeance in 19.2 fits with 18.20, discussed in §11.4.1, in which an angel calls on 'heaven, and the holy ones, and the apostles, and the prophets' to rejoice 'because God judged (ἔκρινεν) the condemnation (κρίμα) of you by her'. It also fits with both 17.6, where the harlot is 'drunk with blood of the holy ones and with the blood of the witnesses of Jesus' and 18.24a where blood comes at the culmination of a list of reasons for the downfall of Babylon, 'in her the blood of prophets and holy ones was found'. The reference to blood casts God in the role of 'avenger of blood', גֹּאֵל הַדָּם, seen in many texts such as Numbers 35.19 and applied to God in Pss. 9.12; 79.10; Jer. 51.35 (against Babylon); Joel 3.21. In Rev. 6.10, the martyrs cry out for God to act in this way, avenging their blood on 'those inhabiting the earth'.

Rev. 18.24 then concludes with, 'and [the blood] of all those who have been slain on the earth'. This relates to Jer. 51.49, 'Babylon must fall for the slain of Israel, as the slain of all the earth have fallen because of Babylon' (NRSV). However, unlike Rev. 19.2, the link is not with the Septuagint. Rev. 18.24b reads, καὶ πάντων τῶν ἐσφαγμένων ἐπὶ τῆς γῆς. LXX Jer. 28.49, the equivalent of Masoretic Text (MT) Jer. 51.49, reads, καὶ ἐν Βαβυλῶνι πεσοῦνται τραυματίαι πάσης τῆς γῆς. There is hardly any lexical overlap.

For Beale, the broadening to encompass 'all those who have been slain on the earth' supports his 'conclusion that the Apocalypse's Babylon is not just one Satanic nation but a corporate, depraved worldwide system spanning the ages from the cross to the final parousia'[22]. Beale is clearly operating with a particular view of Christian prophecy here. However, he is also implying that John's reference to 'all the earth' is designed to widen the scope beyond Rome's deeds. A different interpretative route is taken by David DeSilva. Although, like Beale, he is willing to discuss what he sees as proper modern Christian re-appropriations of Revelation, DeSilva sees 18.24b not as broadening John's target beyond Rome but as broadening Rome's guilt beyond the persecution of Christians.

---

[22] Beale 1999: 924.

Rome is guilty of 'the blood of prophets and saints ... and all the slain upon the earth', naming not only the violence targeting Christian dissenters but also the violence of conquest and suppression of revolt upon which empire is ultimately founded[23].

This is part of DeSilva's general view that John attacks the violence of Rome in Revelation as a whole. DeSilva sees John as, 'rewriting the myth of peace' (alluding to the *pax Romana*)[24]. In this he is drawing on the work of writers such as J. Nelson Kraybill who argues that in 18.24 we see that, 'John stands in solidarity with all victims of imperial oppression – including, perhaps, the thousands who died in the Colosseum'[25].

The present article is not intending to comment on modern Christian use of Revelation. However, the question of John's intention in referring in 18.24 to the slain of all the earth is of interest to us. Thinking of both Jeremiah and John, there is probably an element of prophetic hyperbole at work. Prophets repeatedly cast events in absolute, sometimes cosmos-wide terms. God is presented as acting because there is some absolute horror at work in the deeds of the oppressing power. We can also probably say that there is what one might call the eschatology of prophecy at work in both cases. God's decisive intervention at the turn of the ages renders account for all past violence, seeing it as somehow summed up in the power that has recently attacked God's people. However, there is also an extent to which DeSilva is probably right. As well this reference to the slain of all the earth, features such as the depiction of Rome's economic activity, especially in trading for 'bodies and souls of people' (18.13), suggest that John has in view a wider idea of Rome's oppressive activity than just their causing trouble to Christians. John may not be going as far as DeSilva thinks in arguing that John is subverting the idea of the *pax Romana* as such, but John certainly thinks that Rome is a source of general suffering.

11.4.3 Rome's Arrogance and Luxury

A less obvious reason for God's judgement of Rome echoes Isaiah's depiction of Babylon. John writes,

> As much as she glorified herself and lived in luxury, give to her so much torment and mourning, because she says in her heart, 'I sit as a queen, and I am not a widow, and I shall certainly not see mourning'. Therefore her plagues will come upon her in one day: death and mourning and famine,

---

[23] DeSilva 2009: 209.   [24] DeSilva 2009: 106–8, 207.   [25] Kraybill 2010: 143–4.

and she shall be burned with fire, because mighty is the Lord God who judges her (Rev. 18.7–8).

Isaiah reads,

> Now therefore hear this, you lover of pleasures, who sit securely, who say in your heart, 'I am, and there is no one besides me; I shall not sit as a widow or know the loss of children' – both these things shall come upon you in a moment, in one day (Isa. 47.8–9, NRSV).

The conceptual links are strong, especially in the flow from luxurious living, to boasting, to destruction in a single day. Verbally, the links are more slender: saying in the heart; sitting; widow; coming upon; in one day. The relationship is more like Rev. 18.24 cf. Jer. 51.49 than the lexically closer one between Rev. 19.2 and LXX 4 Kgdms 9.7.

The charge of luxurious living is probably also implied by the initial description of the harlot as 'clothed in purple and scarlet, and adorned with gold and precious stone and pearls, and holding a golden cup' (17.4). The long list of expensive imports in 18:12–13 also adds to this impression. Of the twenty-seven imports listed here, thirteen feature in a description in Ezek. 27:12–24 of the trading of the city of Tyre. Six further items could be instantiated ('costly wood') or encompassed ('all kinds of spices') in the list in Ezekiel. Again, features such as word-order do not match but, like the depiction of Rome as Babylon, the links with Tyre are part of a pattern running across Rev. 17–18, drawing upon ideas from the depiction of Tyre and its downfall both in Isaiah 23 (Rev. 17.2; 18.3, 23 and generally the lament material in ch. 18) and Ezekiel 26–28 (Rev. 17.4; 18.9–22).

Both arrogance and luxury are offences to God at various points in both the Hebrew Bible and the New Testament. Amos rails against not only violence and social injustice but against arrogance and luxury,

> Alas for those who are at ease in Zion,
> and for those who feel secure on Mount Samaria . . .
> Alas for those who lie on beds of ivory,
> and lounge on their couches . . .
> who drink wine from bowls,
> and anoint themselves with the finest oils,
> but are not grieved over the ruin of Joseph! (Amos 6.1, 4, 6 NRSV)

Acts 12 narrates and explains the grisly death of Herod Agrippa I, killed by God for arrogance in what he allows people to say.

The people were calling out, 'The voice of a god and not a man'. Immediately an angel of the Lord struck him down because he did not give glory to God, and being eaten by worms, he died. (Acts 12.22–23)

Arrogance and luxury were, of course, also charges that would bring criticism across the ancient world, for instance in most strands of Greek and Roman philosophical and dramatic traditions. Hubris, in particular, was regularly presented as the antecedent of downfall.

11.4.4 Rome's Influence

The third type of accusation against Rome is harder to decode than the others. It is couched in terms of a moral effect of Rome on the nations of the world. It is actually the first issue raised. John is invited to see,

> ... the judgement of the great harlot who is sitting on many waters, with whom the kings of the earth committed fornication, and the inhabitants of the earth became drunk on the wine of her fornication (17.1–2).

What is in view here?

J. C. Thomas and F. D. Macchia use scriptural precedents (e.g. Hos. 5.3) to argue that fornication here is a metaphor for idolatry. Rome is guilty of 'seduction of others in her idolatrous activity'[26]. Aune, on the other hand, sees an allusion to the MT of Isa. 23.17 (LXX omits the sexual reference), where the trade of Tyre with 'the kingdoms of the earth' is described as Tyre's fornication. Aune does go on to link this with spread of religious practices but his more prominent conclusion is that we can suppose that, in using the metaphor of sexual immorality, John:

> is denouncing the *political* alliances between Babylon and her client kingdoms ... Such alliances inevitably had significant economic, social, and religious implications and usually worked to the detriment of the kingdoms involved. ... it is reasonable to suppose that he shares the hostility that many Jews from Palestine had toward the Romans and the various rulers of Judea that the Romans manipulated from 63 BC on to the first Jewish revolt of AD 66–73.[27]

The religious and political interpretations of the fornication in 17.2 do probably have some truth in them. However, the recurrence of the fornication terminology in 18.3, 9 and 19.2, wrapped into passages about merchants and trade, suggests that the predominant idea here is the

---

[26] Thomas and Macchia 2016: 292.   [27] Aune 1997: 931.

economic one. Rev. 18.9 is particularly pointed: 'the kings of the earth' have been 'living luxuriously' in their fornication with Rome. As Beale argues, 'The nations' loyalty to Babylon was brought on by her ability to provide economic prosperity'[28]. The economic incentive is the sensual weapon sustaining the violent empire.

One surprising further charge is that Rome's 'sorcery' (φαρμακεία) deceived all the nations (18.23). There is maybe something of the characterisation of Nineveh in Nahum 3.4, where the city is seen as a prostitute who enslaves through sorcery. The Romans put their world domination down to the favour of the gods. Many of their subject people must have attributed it to more malign forces. One might conceivably see such a supernatural alliance as being evoked in Mark 5.9 in the set of demons in the possessed man from Gerasa (or Gadara) who name themselves as 'Legion'.

Violence, especially towards Christians, luxury and an arrogance that, in effect, defies God, a malign influence which centres on economic relations – all these result in God's judgement which brings about the downfall of Rome.

11.5 How Rome Falls

Broadly, there are two main accounts of the destruction of Rome in Rev. 17–19. In the first, the harlot is devoured and burned by the beast on which she rides (17.6). In the second, which occupies most of ch. 18 and parts of chs 17 and 19, 'Babylon' is destroyed by God in ways that evoke scriptural judgements of both that city and Tyre. A third, briefer strand of thought appears to call on God's people both to 'come out' of Babylon and to repay her for her works (18.4–7). The time references of all this are deeply unclear. The actions of the beast are in the future, according to an elaborate, highly symbolic time scheme. God's judgement of Babylon is spoken of both as past (18.2) and future (18.8). The possible actions of God's people are something to which they are currently being called.

11.5.1 Devoured by the Defeated Beast

The harlot Babylon sits on the fourth beast of Daniel 7. The beast in Rev. 17 is introduced as having ten horns (κέρατα δέκα, 17.3), as in Dan. 7.8, although the beast in Rev. 17 differs from the Danielic one by also having

---

[28] Beale 1999: 849.

11. Revelation 17.1–19.10: A Prophetic Vision

seven heads. This is presumably primarily an adaptation to fit it to Rome, since the first interpretation given of the seven heads is as seven hills (17.9). The beast's link to Daniel 7 is made firmer by the interpretation that 'the ten horns that you see are ten kings' (Rev. 7.12), corresponding to the interpretation of the horns in Dan. 7.24.

The surprising end of the harlot's ride on the beast is narrated in 17.16:

> And the ten horns that you saw and the beast, they will hate the harlot and will make her desolate and naked, and will eat her flesh, and burn her with fire.

The beast 'was and is not and will rise from the abyss and goes to destruction' (17.8). As well as being seven hills, the beast's seven heads 'are seven kings: five fell; one is; the other has not yet come, and when he comes he must remain for a little time' (17.9–10). Paradoxically, 'the beast, who was and is not, he too is an eighth, and he is of the seven, and he goes to destruction' (17.11). The ten horns 'are ten kings which have not yet received a kingdom but receive authority as kings for one hour with the beast' (17.12). They and the beast will wage war against the lamb, which is Jesus, and the lamb will defeat them (17.14).

Attempts to unscramble this have been endless. The beast here is linked to 'the beast from the sea' of Rev. 13.1, which is an amalgamation of the Danielic 'beasts from the sea' (Dan. 7.3), mixing parts from a leopard, a bear and a lion (Rev. 13.2 cf. Dan 7.4, 5, 6) and having ten horns (Rev. 13:1 cf. Dan. 7.7) and seven heads (Rev. 13.1). The beast is given authority by a figure called 'the dragon' (13.2) which has featured in Revelation 12. One of the heads of the beast appears to have received a fatal blow, but recovers and 'the whole earth' follows and worships the beast in amazement (13.3–4). The beast is given authority 'for forty-two months' (13.5). A second beast 'ascending from the earth' arises (13.11) and causes people to worship the beast from the sea (13.12). The number of the beast is 666 (13.18).

Among the more historically oriented suggested identifications of the beasts of Revelation 13 are that the beast from the sea is either the Roman governor, arriving in the province of Asia by boat, or more broadly the Roman state. The beast from the earth is most commonly seen as representing the imperial cult although other suggestions include, again, the provincial governors[29]. However, the healed wound and link to the number 666 suggest to most commentators that there is a reference to Nero

---

[29] Aune 1997: 731, 755.

somewhere here (as Beale argues, Rev. 15.2 implies that 666 is the number of the first beast, not the second[30]). In particular, the healed wound and the descriptions, in 17.8, 11, of the beast as having been, not currently being (how does current absence work in a vision?!), but returning, suggest a link to the *Nero redux* or *Nero redivivus* myths that were well known in the late first and early second centuries (e.g., Tacitus, *Hist.* 2.8): either Nero never died and will return at the head of an army from the East, or Nero did die but will return to life and take revenge on his enemies.

The ten horns who are ten kings are generally taken to be client kings of some sort, a role that would be particularly familiar in Asia Minor, where the eastern parts were frequently under such governance. This offers a fairly straightforward possible interpretation of our key text, Rev. 17.16, in which the ten horns and the beast destroy the harlot. As Aune puts it, 'The ten horns (the nations allied with Rome) and the beast (a Roman emperor, presumably Nero) will turn on the city of Rome and destroy it'[31]. Under this scenario, the description of the event in 17.16 becomes a mixture of the metaphorical and the literal (although see further on in the chapter). To 'make her desolate' is probably literal emptying of the city (cf. 18.2). Nakedness and the eating of flesh metaphorically relate to the harlot. Burning presumably takes us back to the city and literality.

The destruction of Rome at the hands of a returning Nero is, as Gruen points out, implied in *Sib. Or.* 8.140–157 which, in turn, draws on traditions in the earlier *Sib. Or.* 5[32]. That oracle predicts destruction of Italy by fire (5.160) and its eternal desolation (5.162). As Gruen notes, Nero is a destructive force in every direction, from the Temple (5.150) to Rome[33]. It is probable that the vision of Rome's destruction in Rev. 17.16 is, to an extent, drawn from the same Graeco-Roman myths about Nero.

However, in keeping with the rest of these chapters, Rev. 17.6 probably also draws on scriptural prophecy. The editors of the Nestlé-Aland Greek New Testament text see in 17.16 an allusion to Lev. 21.9 in which a priest's daughter who acts as a prostitute shall be burned to death, בָּאֵשׁ תִּשָּׂרֵף. This fits (more closely than LXX) with κατακαύσουσιν ἐν πυρί in Rev. 17.16. However, the link to Leviticus is not strong thematically, since Rev. 17.16 is far from a priestly setting. More thematically, Beate Kowalski notes a number of lexical links to

---

[30] Beale 1999: 718.   [31] Aune 1997: 956.   [32] Gruen, Chapter 10 pp. 200–201 in this volume.
[33] Ibid., p.203.

11. Revelation 17.1–19.10: A Prophetic Vision

Ezekiel in Rev. 17.16: to Ezek. 16.27 (hatred), 39 (naked); 23.25 (consumed by fire), 26 (stripped), 29 (hatred and nakedness); 26.19 (made desolate)[34]. These form part of the evidence for her broader structural argument that, in these chapters, John draws thematic parallels between Rome and both Israel as the unfaithful bride of God in Ezek. 16, 23 and Tyre in Ezek. 26–28[35].

The arguments for each of these thematic parallels are evident to any reader familiar with the Ezekiel text. Kowalski's lexical study offers numerous points of specific evidence that give the parallels very significant support. The link to Israel as the unfaithful bride of God is, of course, a rather strange one to make. Ezekiel is lamenting past sin and effectively calling the nation back to faithfulness, whereas John is portraying a doomed Rome. Kowalski sees John's use of this imagery as being due to a lack, among Christians of the first generations, of their own stock of salvation-historical ideas on which to draw[36].

The links between Rev. 17–18 and Ezekiel's depiction of the fall of Tyre are extremely extensive. In 17.16, we could possibly add to Kowalski's list a broad thematic parallel to Ezek. 28.17–19:

> Your heart was proud because of your beauty;
>   you corrupted your wisdom for the sake of your splendor.
> I cast you to the ground;
>   I exposed you before kings,
>   to feast their eyes on you.
> By the multitude of your iniquities,
>   in the unrighteousness of your trade,
>   you profaned your sanctuaries.
> So I brought out fire from within you;
>   it consumed you,
> and I turned you to ashes on the earth
>   in the sight of all who saw you.
> All who know you among the peoples
>   are appalled at you;
> you have come to a dreadful end
>   and shall be no more forever.   (NRSV)

A final note on Rev. 17.16 is that allusion complicates the issue of metaphorical and literal language. Allusion is a further basis for lexical choice. (We will see in the Conclusion (§11.6), that John may also have unusual strategic reasons for some lexical choices.)

---

[34] Kowalski 2004: 184–5.   [35] Kowalski 2004: 358–78.   [36] Kowalski 2004: 368.

II.5.2 *Destroyed by God as Babylon and Tyre*

The timing of the beast's attack on Rome is future and is specified, although in the usual opaque apocalyptic manner. There are time references that appear to be to the writer's present day (17.8, 10, 11, 12) and signals that events after that will not last long: there is due to be one further, briefly reigning ruler (17.10), then an eighth and presumably last, who appears rapidly to head for destruction (17.11); there are also due to be ten people who are kings 'for one hour' (17.12). The beast's attack on the harlot is the culmination of these events. In contrast, the judgement of Babylon by God is depicted in Rev. 18–19 as both past and future and there is no sequence of events for its arrival. What is said, however, is that it is instant.

An angel uses the words of the horsemen in Isa. 21.9, נָפְלָה נָפְלָה בָּבֶל, 'fallen, fallen is Babylon' (another example where LXX does not match, in this case because it does not reduplicate 'fallen'). However, this past event quickly appears to become a future one when another voice calls God's people to leave Babylon so as not to share in her imminent judgement (18.4). The futurity of judgement is reinforced in 18.8, which speaks of plagues, death, mourning, famine and fire, which are all still to come. However, by the next verse, the city is already on fire. The kings of the earth wail as they watch her burning (18.9). The smoke is then visible in 18.18 and in 19.3, where it 'goes up for ever'.

Such temporal mixing is actually a further link between Rev. 17–19 and the prophets. They too show these kinds of shifts. The text shows strong links to the visions of the fall of Babylon in Isaiah 47–48 and Jeremiah 50–51, and of Tyre in Isaiah 23 and Ezekiel 26–28. Jeremiah 50–51 is particularly indicative of the type of relationship between Rev. 17–19 and these texts, showing a range of links in theme, style and temporal presentation, while also exhibiting considerable lexical difference. In the following excerpts, particular links to Rev. 17–19 are in italics.

> *Flee from Babylon*, and *go out* from the land of the Chaldeans . . . (50.8, cf. Rev. 18.4)
> your mother shall be *utterly shamed*,
> and she who bore you shall be *disgraced*.
> Lo, she shall be the last of the nations,
>   a *wilderness*, dry land, and a desert.
> Because of the wrath of the LORD *she shall not be inhabited*,
>   but shall be *an utter desolation*
> *everyone who passes by Babylon shall be appalled*
>   and hiss because of all her wounds . . . (50.12–13, cf. Rev. 17.6; 18.2, 9, etc.)

11. Revelation 17.1–19.10: A Prophetic Vision

For this is the *vengeance* of the LORD:
take vengeance on her,
do to her as she has done ... (50.15, cf. Rev. 18.6; 19.2)
Repay her according to her deeds; just as she has done, do to her – for *she arrogantly defied* the LORD ... (50.29, cf. Rev. 18.6–7)
Therefore *wild animals shall live with hyenas* in Babylon, and *ostriches shall inhabit her;* she shall *never again be peopled, or inhabited for all generations* ... (50.39, cf. Rev. 18.2)
Flee from the midst of Babylon,
save your lives, each of you!
Do not perish because of her guilt
for this is the time of the LORD's *vengeance;*
he is *repaying* her what is due.
Babylon was a *golden cup* in the LORD's hand,
making all the earth drunken;
the nations drank of her wine,
and so the nations went mad
Suddenly *Babylon has fallen* and is shattered;
wail for her (51.6–8, cf. Rev. 17.2, 4; 18.1, 4)
You who *live by mighty waters* (LXX: ἐφ' ὕδασι πολλοῖς),
rich in treasures,
your end has come (51.13, cf. Rev. 17.2, 4)
... the LORD's purposes against Babylon stand,
to make the land of Babylon *a desolation,*
without inhabitant (51.29, cf. Rev. 18.2)
'*May my blood be avenged*' on the inhabitants of Chaldea',
Jerusalem shall say.
Therefore thus says the LORD:
I am going to defend your cause
and *take vengeance for you* ...
and Babylon shall become a heap of ruins,
a den of jackals,
an object of horror and of hissing,
without inhabitant ... (51.35–37, cf. Rev. 18.2, 20; 19.2)
Come out of her, my people!
Save your lives, each of you,
from the fierce anger of the LORD! ... (51.45, cf. Rev. 18.4)
Then *the heavens and the earth*
and all that is in them
shall shout for joy over Babylon ...
Babylon *must fall for the slain of Israel,*
as the slain of all the earth have fallen because of Babylon ... (51.48–49, cf. Rev. 18.24; 19.1, 4, 6)
For the LORD is *laying Babylon waste,*
and *stilling her loud clamour* ... (51.55, cf. Rev. 18.22–24. NRSV)

And the end of all this is that Jeremiah told Seraiah to read the scroll in Babylon then 'tie a stone to it, and throw it into the middle of the Euphrates, and say, "Thus shall Babylon sink, to rise no more"' (63–64). John, near the end of his vision, writes, 'And a mighty angel took a stone like a great mill-stone and threw it into the sea, saying, "With such violence Babylon the great city will be thrown, and never found again"' (Rev. 18.21).

As indicated above, a similar exercise could be carried out for the vision of Babylon in Isaiah 47–48. A particular parallel there is that judgement for Babylon's arrogant speech comes 'in a moment, in one day' (ἐν μιᾷ ἡμέρᾳ in LXX and Rev. 18.8). The same can be done for the visions of the downfall of Tyre in Isaiah 23 and Ezekiel 26–28, above all in the extensive depictions of the lament of kings, merchants and seamen.

11.5.3 Attacked by God's People?

One unexpected point in Rev. 18 is that, just in verses 6–7, there is what looks like a call to God's people to take vengeance against Babylon into their own hands, 'Repay to her as she has given' (18.6). Is this allusion to Jer. 50.29 a call to revolt? DeSilva denies the possibility, citing the lack of similar calls elsewhere in Revelation. Instead,

> it is consistently God and God's heavenly forces who execute judgement *on behalf of* the faithful disciples, rather than those disciples, themselves. The purpose of this solitary exhortation must, then, not be to call Christians to act in a sub-Christian manner[37].

Aune disagrees. Rejecting alternative suggestions that those addressed are 'angels of punishment', or the beast and kings of 17.16, or no one in particular, he follows the logic of the syntax of 18.4–7 to conclude that the Christians are probably addressed and that non-retaliation 'was in all probability not uniformly espoused in early Christianity'[38].

Although DeSilva's argument, that this cannot be a call to violent action because elsewhere in Revelation God acts, is not in itself persuasive, we would have to say that the Book of Revelation would not appear to be a useful manual for violent revolution. The general stance that John encourages is steadfast faith and witness in the face of suffering. Having said that, Revelation has been a key text for Christian groups in some political resistance movements such as those opposing apartheid in twentieth-century South Africa.

---

[37] DeSilva 2009: 266.   [38] Aune 1997: 993.

11. Revelation 17.1–19.10: A Prophetic Vision

Turning Aune's syntactical argument around, we could say that if we look at the syntactical flow from 18.6–7 into 18.8 it suggests that, effectively, it is God who is being called to act, despite the plural imperatives of 18.6–7. Verse 8 links with διὰ τοῦτο, 'therefore', which leads into a description of God bringing on Babylon the plagues that were signalled in 18.4 and in the note of 18.5 that Babylon's unrighteous deeds had been remembered by God.

11.6 Conclusion: Re-appropriating Prophetic Resources for Displaying the Destruction of Rome

Erich Gruen shows that even the Jewish Sibylline Oracles are framed primarily in terms of their non-Jewish precursors. In Rev. 17–19, John takes a different track. There are overlaps with the Sibyllines, for instance in the role of Nero and in destruction by fire. However, John basically draws on the scriptural prophets. In particular, he draws on the prophetic depictions of cities that are seen as wicked, especially Babylon and Tyre.

The manner in which John uses these resources is strange. The texts are soaked in themes, imagery and, sometimes, vocabulary from the prophets. But almost nothing stays as it was. There is an extent to which this is inevitable, since John is taking texts about the life of Israel and re-appropriating them for the very different life of the early Christian communities. However, this could be done without the pervasive sense that texts have been put through a food processor (although not chopping so finely as to produce a paste: the process leaves recognisable chunks).

One suggestion might be that this is the nature of visions: a visionary soaked in the scriptures sees scenes composed of their ideas, but rather loosely so. However, that is unlikely to explain the construction of Revelation. The Book of Revelation is strongly intentional. It is highly patterned. This is clearest in the use of sevens. The overt structures of sevens are obvious in the letters, scrolls, trumpets and bowls. However, there are numerous patterns of sevens apparently scattered across the book: seven beatitudes; seven alpha/omega/first/last self-declarations; seven references to 'the Lord God the almighty', seven occurrences of 'the one who sits on the throne', seven times 'the witnesses of Jesus', seven other times 'Jesus', seven times 'Christ', seven times 'God' and 'the lamb' together, twenty-eight times altogether 'the lamb'[39]. This is only part of the set of patterns that are spread in very subtle ways across the book.

---

[39] Bauckham 1993: 26, 30, 31, 66.

What this shows is that John has some complex agendas at work in constructing his text. This is true of Rev. 17–19 as of the rest of the book. This means that he will adapt his prophetic precursor texts to these agendas. He can convey that the prophets stand behind the vision of the fall of Rome, but the details of how he shapes his text are part of a larger project which spans the book and reshapes every source that he puts to use.

CHAPTER 12

Cicero and Vergil in the Catacombs: Pagan Messianism and Monarchic Propaganda in Constantine's Oration to the Assembly of Saints

Marko Marinčič

> What has Maro to do
> with the gospels? Or Cicero with the Apostle?   Jerome *Letters* 22.29.7

In the manuscript tradition, the four books of Eusebius's *Life of Constantine* are followed by an appendix containing a speech known by its Latin title, *Oratio ad sanctorum coetum*.[1] Moreover, in some manuscripts, the *Speech of Emperor Constantine written for the Assembly of Saints* (Βασιλέως Κωνσταντίνου λόγος ὃν ἔγραψε τῷ τῶν ἁγίων συλλόγῳ) figures as the fifth book of the *Vita*. In spite of its traditional attribution to Constantine the Great,[2] this curious text has not received much scholarly attention.[3] Yet the speech, which includes a lecture-style commentary on Vergil's *Fourth Eclogue* accompanied by an almost complete translation of the poem into Greek, is an important landmark in the history of the

---

[1] There has been no critical edition since Heikel 1902, whose text is used here.
[2] Photius, *Bibl.* cod. 127, knew of a four-book (τετράβιβλος) *Life of Constantine*, but since our text of the *Life* refers to the speech as an example of Constantine's oratory (4.32; cf. 4.29.1–3 on Constantine as author of speeches), the majority of scholars tend to be favorable to the Constantinian authorship: see recently Edwards 1999 and 2003: XVIII–XXII; Barnes 2011: 113–20 (Latin); Girardet 2013: 36–45. The exact date and place remain in dispute; among those authors cited, Edwards chose Rome and 314, Barnes, Nicomedia and 325, Girardet, Trier and 314. According to a note in the present text of Eusebius's *Vita Constantini* (4.32), the preserved Greek is a translation of a speech originally delivered in Latin. This conveniently explains away the discrepancies between the commentary to Vergil's *Fourth Eclogue*, which in many places follows the Latin original, and the Greek translation, which suppresses pagan references even where the commentary explains them as allegories. On the discrepancies see Pfättisch 1908: 20–40 and 1912–13: 13; Kurfess 1920, 1936a, 1937, 1950; Fisher 1982: 177–82; Edwards 2003: *passim*; and Girardet 2013: *passim*.
[3] The English, Italian, and French translations by Edwards 2003, Cristofoli 2005, and Maraval 2010: 107–55 have notes; apart from the reproduction of Heikel's text, translation into German and notes, Girardet 2013 provides a comprehensive discussion of the speech; see also Girardet 2010: 108–23 and Edwards 1999.

Christian reception of Roman literature. Not only is it the earliest documented instance of the Christian appropriation of Vergil as a pagan herald of Christ's birth,[4] but it is also the first known example of a Christian interpretation of a Latin classic.[5] It is worth noting that Vergil was not unequivocally accepted as a pagan prophet of Christ's coming by Christian writers of Late Antiquity. According to Augustine, the poet (almost incidentally) used Sibylline material in what he intended as a panegyric of a mortal.[6] Although Augustine sees Vergil, the *nobilissimus poeta*, as a reliable source on the Sibylline prophecies, he does not credit him with any autonomous prophetic authority.[7] Jerome, in turn, sarcastically dismisses the idea of Vergil being a Christian without Christ (*Maronem sine Christo ... Christianum*) as a childish fancy of Proba and the authors of Christian *Homerocentones* and *Vergiliocentones*, who paraphrased the Scriptures with scraps of pagan poetry. As a serious scholar and a pupil of Donatus, Jerome accused the centonists of a twofold violation as they had disfigured the meaning of the Bible by manipulating pagan poetic texts contrary to the intentions of their authors.[8]

Among the ancient texts we possess, the *Oratio* is the closest precedent for Dante's idolization of the *altissimo poeta* as a proto-Christian. Ecstatic expressions of praise include "the most eminent of the Italian poets" (ὁ ἐξοχώτατος τῶν κατὰ Ἰταλίαν ποιητῶν, 19.4; ἐξοχώτατος is used for God in 1.4 and 11.15!), "a marvelous man, with all the ornaments of learning" (θαυμαστὸς ἀνὴρ καὶ πάσῃ παιδείᾳ κεκοσμημένος, 20.2), and "o Maro wisest of poets"(ὦ σοφώτατε ποιητὰ Μάρων, 20.6; cf. 20.8: ὦ σοφώτατε ποιητά).[9]

Among other things, the speech is an overt plea for monarchic rule.[10] The idea of using Vergil as a political argument[11] makes the hypothesis that Constantine was its author (or at least the actual speaker) even more attractive. Too attractive, perhaps. It would have been almost too easy for a forger to imagine Constantine, the converted emperor and self-styled

---

[4] Maccormack 1998: 24–7. [5] Wlosok 1983: 68.
[6] *Ep.* 104.3.11: *carmine adulatorio nescio cui nobili*. See also Kurfess 1936b: 16 n. 3; and Schelkle 1938: 17–19.
[7] *C.D.* 10.27; *Ep. Rom. inch.* 3. Cf. Maccormack 1998: 29; if Courcelle 1957: 312–15 is right in believing that Augustine actually drew on the *Oratio* (but see Maccormack 1998: 30, n. 104), then Augustine must have deliberately downplayed the importance of Vergil as the author of the text.
[8] *Ep.* 53.7; see Maccormack 1998: 28 for further literature.
[9] Dante, of course, could not have read the speech in Greek, and it is unlikely (though not impossible) that he knew the Latin original, but he may have received some of its ideas indirectly; see the remarks at the end of the paper.
[10] See Edwards 1999: 270–4; Drake 2000: 296–7.
[11] An *instrumentum regni*, according to Bernardi Perini 1999–2000.

theologian, lecturing on Vergil, the "imperial" poet *par excellence*, as a herald of a Christian empire.[12] In such case, however, one would have to assume that 1) the forgery was composed in Latin, 2) translated into Greek, and 3) appended to Eusebius's *Vita*. Even more unlikely is that any forger would have found it worthwhile to produce a convincing imitation of the clumsy and convoluted language so characteristic of Greek translations of official imperial documents that had originally been written in (bombastic) Latin.[13] In addition, echoes of the political theology of Lactantius, including his idea of divine retribution against the persecuting emperors and use of the *Fourth Eclogue* itself, make it reasonable to accept Constantine's court/chancellery as the text's place of origin and Constantine as its speaker (official "author") without speculating about the extent of his originality.[14] It is for purely practical reasons, however, that I will refer to the authorial instance simply as "Constantine" in what follows in this chapter.

12.1 Lactantius on Cicero and Virgil, the Two Blinded Visionaries

As many true fathers as the speech may have had, it does reveal some points of contact with Lactantius' *De mortibus persecutorum* and *Divinae institutiones*.[15] Not only is Lactantius' intellectual influence on Constantine known and recognized, but the dates agree; the earliest possible date for the speech is 313 while *De mortibus persecutorum* was written between 313 and 316, and the *Divine Institutes* (at least in its original form) between 303 and 310.[16] The very idea of using the Sibylline oracles and Vergil's *Fourth Eclogue* as "foreign" testimony supporting Christianity most probably comes from Lactantius (*Div. inst.* 7.24).[17]

The basic problem can be reduced to two simple questions: How could Lactantius resist the temptation of identifying the Vergilian infant-savior with Christ? Why did this identification come so naturally to Constantine,

---

[12] Hanson 1973 and Geymonat 2001 are among those who argue for a date during or after the reign of Julian the Apostate on grounds of a (supposed) allusion to Apollo's oracle in Daphne near Antiochia (*Or.* 18.2).
[13] On the language of Constantinian documents, see Veyne 2010: 198, n. 9, who discusses a similar document of dubious authorship.
[14] See Barnes 1981: 74.
[15] See Schultze 1894: 541–51, Kurfess 1950, De Decker 1978 (with a list of correspondences on p. 80 n. 25), Pizzani 1993, Edwards 2003: 269–72, and Girardet 2013: 22–5.
[16] Lactantius alludes to Galerius as an active persecutor (*Inst.* 5.11.5–6) and writes about the other persecuting emperors as if they were still alive (5.23.1 ff.); this suggests the death of Maximian ca. July 310 as a *terminus ante quem*; see Barnes 1981: 13, n. 96, with bibliography.
[17] See Kurfess 1936b: 12–13. According to Barnes 1981: 74, "Lactantius persuaded Constantine to peruse the Sibylline oracles for himself."

who was far from being *anima naturaliter Christiana*, "a naturally Christian soul?" I believe this fundamental difference in approach between the prince and the *précepteur* has far more to do with the two texts' respective attitudes to Vergil's Augustan context, Roman history, and contemporary politics than it does with their authors' religious convictions or attitude to Vergil.

Lactantius' apologetic strategy in the *Divine Institutes* is based on insistent appeals to pagan authorities, e.g. the Sibyls, semi-divine teachers of wisdom, such as Hermes Trismegistus, and pagan philosophers and poets. This is not the place to pass judgment on Lactantius' historical contribution to what would later take the form of an intellectual synthesis of pagan culture and Christian religion.[18] As far as the appropriation of such pagan authorities in the *Institutes* is concerned, it is clear that Lactantius is not looking for any kind of ideological conciliation between Christianity and paganism. His extensive use of pagan material is above all a tactical weapon of apology and propaganda.[19] Lactantius explicitly refuses to resort to the authority of Old Testament prophets whom pagan readers cannot be expected to trust.[20] Instead, he uses the works of philosophers and historians as a propaedeutic diet for those who are not yet ready to grasp the message of "divine witnesses" (*diuina testimonia*).[21] Above all, he is careful to attribute "prophetic" gifts not to human authors blinded by false religion but to *imaginary* prophetic beings who are (at least conceptually) prone to irrational impulses. Interestingly, he counts the Sibylline oracles among the divine witnesses.[22] However, it is due only to their high reputation among pagans that pagan religious texts commend themselves as some kind of tactical replacement for the Scriptures; they are to be used in cases where the audience suspects poets of inventing fictions and distrusts philosophers who, as human

---

[18] An important recent work by DePalma Digeser 2000 is dedicated to the political aspect of Lactantius' contribution to the politics of religious toleration and to the ideological foundations of Constantine's Christian empire.

[19] Cf. the following part: *Sed cum defendamus causam ueritatis apud eos qui aberrantes a ueritate falsis religionibus seruiunt, quod genus probationis aduersus eos magis adhibere debemus quam ut eos deorum suorum testimoniis reuincamus?* (1.6.17) ("But since we are defending the cause of truth before people who are astray from it in the service of false religions, what sort of proof could we better use against them than to rebut them with evidence from their own gods?") All translations of Lactantius are by Anthony Bowen (in Bowen and Garnsey, 2003; for an overview of relevant passages, see 15–16).

[20] See, e.g., 7.13.1–2: *Neque nunc prophetas in testimonium uocabo ... sed eos potius, quibus istos qui respuunt ueritatem credere sit necesse.* ("I shall not at this point call in the witness of the prophets ... instead I shall call upon people who simply have to be believed by those who reject the truth.")

[21] Cf. 5.4.6; but here again: *ut suis potissimum refutaretur auctoribus.* "[T]hen he could be refuted as far as possible by authorities which he himself acknowledged.")

[22] The two categories, *humana* and *diuina testimonia*, come from Cicero, *part. or.* 2.6.

12. Cicero and Vergil in the Catacombs

beings, are liable to error.[23] Lactantius is not only being hypocritical when it comes to pagan culture, its gods, oracles, philosophers and poets, but he is also flirting with classical culture, including Cicero as the supreme model of prose style, in a grandiose maneuver intended to deliver the decisive blow to pagans. His ploy recalls Plato's Socrates playing the role of an inspired poet possessed by the divine in *Ion* or *Phaedrus*.

A powerful excuse for taking on the role of Devil's advocate is Lactantius' consistently Euhemeristic view of pagan divinities as human benefactors and kings who have been granted divine honors by humanity.[24] In defending poets against the accusation of falsehood (1.11), Lactantius refers to the *licentia* of figurative language, which, in this case, does not imply in the least that Christian allegories should be read in pagan poetry, but merely that poets should not be blamed for adorning the human (!) careers of pagan "divinities" with the ornaments of poetic language.[25]

In an insightful article on Lactantius' view of Cicero and Vergil, Vinzenz Buchheit persuasively argues that there is no basis whatsoever for the widespread belief that Lactantius, the "Christian Cicero," attributed some kind of proto-Christian inspiration to pagan writers such as Cicero and Vergil.[26] The latter could not have known the divine truth because God had hidden it from humanity and made baptism a precondition of cognition: baptism brings "divine wisdom" in and drives stupidity, the "mother of crime," out of a man's heart, and it does so without any need for expensive books or time-consuming philosophy.[27] Lactantius wrote his work "with God's spirit informing and truth itself assisting him" (*diuino spiritu instruente ac suffragante ipsa ueritate*, 6.1.1), whereas Cicero depicted (*depinxit!*)[28] the "holy, celestial Divine Law" (*dei lex ... illa sancta, illa caelestis*) with an "almost (!) divine voice" (*paene divina voce*; 6.8.6–9). The following passage on this point is revealing:

---

[23] *Superest de responsis carminibusque sacris testimonia, quae sunt multo certiora, proferre. Nam fortasse ii, contra quos agimus, nec poetis putent esse credendum, tamquam vana fingentibus; nec philosophis, quod errare potuerint, quia et ipsi homines fuerint.* (1.6.6) ("It remains to present the much more reliable evidence from oracular responses and sacred songs. Possibly our opponents think that poets are not to be believed because they construct empty fictions, nor are philosophers because they can make mistakes, being human themselves.")

[24] For a general overview of Euhemerism in early Christian literature, see Thraede 1966 and the relevant chapters in Winiarczyk 2002.

[25] E.g. 1.11.24: [C]*um officium poetae in eo sit, ut ea quae uere gesta sunt in alias species obliquis figurationibus cum decore aliquo conuersa traducat* ("since a poet's business lies in transposing reality into something else with metaphor and allusion and in covering up the misrepresentation with charm").

[26] Buchheit 1990: esp. 360–7. [27] 3.26.10–11 and Buchheit 1990: 365–7.

[28] On Plato and Aristoteles: *depingebant uerbis et imaginabantur iustitiam quae in conspectu non erat* (5.17.2–6) ("they drew a picture in words of an imagined justice, one not there to see").

> quis sacramentum dei sciens tam significanter enarrare legem dei posset quam illam homo longe a ueritatis notitia remotus expressit? ego uero eos qui uera inprudentes loquuntur sic habendos puto, tamquam diuinent spiritu aliquo instincti. quodsi ut legis sanctae uim rationemque peruidit, ita illut quoque scisset aut explicasset, in quibus praeceptis lex ipsa consisteret, non philosophi functus fuisset officio, sed prophetae. quod quia facere ille non poterat, nobis faciendum est, quibus ipsa lex tradita est ab illo uno magistro et imperatore omnium deo (6.8.10–12).

> No one with knowledge of God's mystery could possibly set forth God's law as meaningfully as that expressed by a man far from the knowledge of the truth. My view of people who speak the truth unawares is that they divine it by some spiritual instinct. But if Cicero had also known or explained what instructions the holy law itself consists of as clearly as he saw its force and reason, he would have fulfilled the role not of a philosopher but of a prophet. That, however, he could not do, and so we must: it is to us that the law has been given by that one God who is master and commander of us all.[29]

Vergil suspected something about the existence of the One God *nostrorum primus Maro non longe afuit a ueritate* ("Maro, the first of our poets, was not far from the truth," 1.5.11), but was still one of those "poets and philosophers." Lactantius is careful to stress that these authors had no cognition of truth, or if they had caught a glimpse of it, they had done so simply because "nobody [could] be so blind as not to see the splendor of divine truth."[30]

Non longe afuit a ueritate ("he was not far from the truth") is not necessarily a litotes, and it would be a stretch to understand *Maro noster* ("our Maro") as a reference to anything but Vergil's Romanity.[31] As in many other places in the *Institutes*, "almost" (*paene*) implies a serious limitation.[32] As Lactantius knew, Vergil was not a monotheist, and even if he had believed in one God, that one God would not have been Christ. In this sense, *non longe afuit* is rather an expression of pity for a great pagan, who, if only for chronological reasons, had been fatally blind to the splendor of Christian truth.

---

[29] Cf. the comments following another quotation from Cicero: *quodsi hoc illi faciunt quibus non est ueritas cognita, quanto magis nos facere debemus qui a deo eruditi et inluminati possumus uera praecipere.* (6.2.15–16) ("If it is done by people who do not know the truth, however, all the more burden on us to do it, since we have been trained and illuminated by God and we can offer advice which is true.")

[30] [N]on *quod illi habuerint cognitam ueritatem, sed quod ueritatis ipsius tanta uis est, ut nemo possit esse tam caecus, quin uideat ingerentem se oculis diuinam claritatem.* (1.5.2) ("[N]ot because they have a knowledge of the truth, but because the effect of the actual truth is too strong for even a blind man not to see divine brightness when it forces itself on his eyes.")

[31] Maccormack 1998: 25 n. 82.   [32] See Buchheit 1990: *passim*.

One of the reasons why Lactantius did not acknowledge Vergil as a prophet of Christ lies in his own millenarian ideology, the expectation of a thousand years of happiness following the second advent of Christ and an eschatological battle between Good and the Evil that would transform the world and man. Millenarianism was not a specifically Christian doctrine, but Lactantius saw it reflected in the apocalyptic prophecies of the Sibylline oracles, which Christians interpreted as referring to the Second Coming of Christ.[33] The main fault Lactantius found with Vergil and other pagan poets lay in their conviction that the Golden Age had already taken place under the rule of Saturn:

> ... non bestiae per hoc tempus sanguine alentur, non aues praeda, sed quieta et placida erunt omnia. leones et uituli ad praesepe simul stabunt, lupus ouem non rapiet, canis non uenabitur, accipitres et aquilae non nocebunt, infans cum serpentibus ludet.
>
> denique tum fient illa, quae poetae aureis temporibus facta esse iam Saturno regnante dixerunt. quorum error hinc ortus est, quod prophetae futurorum pleraque sic proferunt et enuntiant quasi iam peracta. uisiones enim diuino spiritu offerebantur oculis eorum et uidebant illa in conspectu suo quasi fieri ac terminari. quae uaticinia eorum cum paulatim fama uulgasset, quoniam profani a sacramento ignorabant quatenus dicerentur, completa esse iam ueteribus saeculis illa omnia putauerunt, quae utique fieri complerique non poterant homine regnante.
>
> cum uero deletis religionibus impiis et scelere compresso subiecta erit deo terra,
>
> cedet et ipse mari uector nec nautica pinus ...
>
> quae poeta secundum Cymaeae Sibyllae carmina prolocutus est. (7.24.8–12)

> ... wild beasts will not feed on blood in this period, nor birds on prey; everything will instead be peaceful and quiet. Lions and calves will stand together at the stall, wolf will not seize lamb, dog will not hunt, hawk and eagle will do no harm, and children will play with snakes.
>
> This will be the time for all those things to happen that the poets claimed for the golden age when Saturn was king. The mistake about them arises from the fact that prophets foretelling the future keep putting plenty forward like that, delivering it as if it has taken place. Visions were put before their eyes by the divine spirit, and they saw things in their sight as if in process and completion. Their words of prophecy were slowly spread by rumor, but those outside God's mystery did not know their scope; they thought it was all stuff over and done with long before, because it simply could not take place in the reign of a man.

---

[33] See Courcelle 1957: 295 and Girardet 2013: 104–5, with further bibliography.

When wrong religions have been destroyed, however, and crime has been suppressed, and the earth is subject to God, 'Merchants will leave the sea, ship's timbers will not haggle for bargains . . .'
Vergil follows the Sibyl of Cumae in saying this . . .

In the vein of Euhemeristic rationalism, Lactantius saw Saturn as a good ruler under whose reign the belief in one God had still existed; it was Jupiter who had deposed him and established the aberrant cult of his family and his own person (5.5–6, esp. 5.6.13: *progenies Iouis*). One of the main reasons for Lactantius' resentment against Jupiter was the role that Jupiter and his son Hercules played in the religious ideology of the Tetrarchy, which was ruled by two *Iouii* and two *Herculii*. This, in addition to the millenarian expectations, was why Lactantius did not want to associate the *Fourth Eclogue* with the incarnation of Christ. He had good reasons to be suspicious of the infant, the *Iouis incrementum* (*Ecl.* 4.9), who, as a hypostasis of Hercules, could hope to join the feast of gods on Olympus and marry a goddess (v. 63).[34] Everything in the poem recalls the "theology" of the Tetrarchy. It is almost too easy to see its pandemonium personified in Vergil's *puer*, who is *Iouius* and a *Herculius* at the same time – literally a *quint*essential tetrarch.

The identification of the Vergilian *"Herculius"* as Augustus was probably known to Lactantius.[35] Like Augustine (see n. 6), he read the eclogue as a pagan panegyric and automatically associated it with the pagan Roman empire. This is why he affirmed that a true, chiliastic Golden Age could not take place during the reign of a human (*homine regnante*). At the same time, he regarded the birth of Christ as the beginning of a metaphorical Golden Age, an age of justice in which, however, only a small part of humanity would supposedly participate.[36] The early age of Christianity still belonged to the "reign of Jupiter," which is why he described Christ as a *nuntius Dei* who announced the end of time (5.7.1), that is, the millenarian apocalypse.

---

[34] On the *puer* as a second Hercules, see Marinčič 2001.
[35] Serv. ad *Ecl.* 4.1,11,13; Philargyrius ad *Ecl.* 4.1.
[36] *Sed Deus, ut parens indulgentissimus, appropinquante ultimo tempore, nuntium misit, qui vetus illud saeculum fugatamque iustitiam reduceret; ne humanum genus maximis et perpetuis agitaretur erroribus. Rediit ergo species illius aurei temporis, et reddita quidem terrae, sed paucis assignata iustitia est; quae nihil aliud est, quam Dei unici pia et religiosa cultura.* (5.7.1–2) ("God is like a most indulgent parent, however: when the latter days were approaching, he sent a messenger to restore that time long gone and to bring back justice from exile, so that mankind should be wracked no more by its huge and persistent errors. Back came the golden age in its beauty, and justice – which is nothing other than pious and worshipful attention to the one and only God – was restored to earth, though few were given it.") This is an allusion to the Vergilian *redit uirgo* (*Ecl.* 4.7). Lactantius rightly identifies Virgo

12. Cicero and Vergil in the Catacombs 235

Lactantius' aversion to Vergil's infant-savior can be inferred from the very order of the lines he quotes from the eclogue (7.24.11):

Cedet et ipse mari uector, nec nautica pinus	38
Mutabit merces: omnis feret omnia tellus.	39
Non rastros patietur humus, non uinea falcem.	40
Robustus quoque iam tauris iuga soluet arator.	41
Tunc etiam molli flauescet campus arista;	28
Incultisque rubens pendebit sentibus uua;	29
Et durae quercus sudabunt roscida mella,	30
Nec uarios discet mentiri lana colores.	42
Ipse sed in pratis aries iam suaue rubenti	43
Murice, iam croceo mutabit uellera luto.	44
Sponte sua sandyx pascentes uestiet agnos.	45
Ipsae lacte domum referent distenta capellae	21
Ubera, nec magnos metuent armenta leones.	22

Traders will retire from sea, from the pine-built vessels
they used for commerce: every land will be self-supporting.
The soil will need no harrowing, the vine no pruning-knife;
and the tough ploughman may at last unyoke his oxen.
Then a slow flush of tender gold shall mantle the great plains,
then shall grapes hang wild and reddening on thorn-trees,
and honey sweet like dew from the hard bark of oaks.
We shall stop treating wool with artificial dyes,
tor the ram himself in his pasture will change his fleece's colour,
now to a charming purple, now to a saffron hue,
and grazing lambs will dress themselves in coats of scarlet.
Goats shall walk home, their udders taut with milk, and nobody
herding them: the ox will have no fear of the lion.

(trans. C. Day Lewis; with transposition of lines)

What Constantine does in this "*cento*" is more than simply impose greater order on Vergil's poem by joining lines on agriculture (38–41 + 28–30) and stockbreeding (42–45 + 21–22).[37] The intervention is far less innocent. The rearrangement of lines is ideologically tendentious as it destroys the *curriculum* of the *puer* and conflates the phases of his career into a single prophecy of the *millenium*. This is a millenarian, but certainly not a Christian *cento:* it is the work of a Christian, but it makes a truly

---

as *Parthenos-Iustitia*; in the following chapter, 5.8.2, he even makes fun of those who expect Justice to fall from the sky in the form of a statue.
[37] Courcelle 1957: 295.

Christian allegory of the poem impossible. For Lactantius, as for some modern interpreters of the poem, the infant is not a person but a metaphor.

Lactantius' discomfort is probably rooted in his general aversion to the Empire in the years during and immediately following the Great Persecution. His millenarian beliefs are probably themselves subordinate to his political agenda. At least on the surface, his agenda is clearly anti-Roman; it seems to leave no space for a positive, constructive appropriation of Vergil's Augustanism.[38]

12.2 Two "Christians Without Christ" on a Secret Mission

The only trace of Lactantius' apocalyptic interpretation of Vergil's eclogue in Constantine's *Oration to the Assembly of Saints* lies in the reference to a second coming of the Virgin.[39] In all other respects, Constantine follows his own messianic reading of the poem, one that has no basis in the Sibylline oracles and does not function without Isaiah.[40] Constantine is the first known author to identify the *puer* as Christ, the *Virgo* as the Virgin Mary, and Jupiter as God the Father. Although he follows Lactantius' Euhemeristic view of pagan gods in 4.3, he takes a different approach in his reading of the eclogue. As the author himself states, Vergil expressed himself in a simultaneously clear and cryptic manner, through allegories.[41]

---

[38] As Buchheit 1990: 369–70 has shown, Lactantius (5.5–6) also uses the final passage in Vergil's *Georgics* 1 as a paradigm of the chaotic state of contemporary Rome, thus blurring the contrast between Octavian and Mark Antony. Along similar lines, he denigrates Aeneas as the product of a poet who had erroneous ideas about *pietas* (5.10). See Wlosok 1983: 65–8. DePalma Digeser 2000: 40–5 has detected that behind Lactantius' depiction of Saturnus lies a hidden agenda directed against the dominate and tetrarchy as degenerate forms of rule and in favor of a religiously tolerant, monotheistic monarchy; like Augustus, who refused divine honors, Saturnus is an example of an earthly ruler who did not seek to supplant the True God (*Div. inst.* 5.5.3).

[39] 19.6; see Kurfess 1936b: 16; 1937: 100; 1950: 161; Courcelle 1957: 300. According to Pfättisch 1908: 23–4, Lactantius is the reason for the omission of *Saturnia regna* from the translation. It is not clear, however, whether Constantine meant a *millenarist* version of the second advent of Christ.

[40] Lactantius did not want to recognize the messianic potential of the eclogue, and Vergil probably could not find any messianic prophecies in the Sibylline oracles even if a Judaized version was accessible to him. It is true that *Or. Sib.* 3.785–95 mentions the joy of a "maiden" (κόρη) and the peace between the animals, but the *oracula* in the present form do not contain a single reference to the birth of a child. Nisbet 1978: 66 constructs a connection via *Isaiah* 7, which would require Vergil to have read the *Septuagint*. However, Hellenistic models can account for all of the "messianic" material in the poem; see Marinčič 2001 and 2002. Brian Breed, in this volume, discusses both the "messianic" potential of the text and its complicated vision of the future without positing either a proto-Augustan stance or direct acquaintance with Jewish material.

[41] συνίεμεν δὴ φανερῶς τε ἅμα καὶ ἀποκρύφως δι' ἀλληγοριῶν τα<ῦτα> λεχθέντα, τοῖς μὲν βαθύτερον ἐξετάζουσι τὴν τῶν ἐπῶν δύναμιν ὑπ' ὄψιν ἀγομένης τῆς τοῦ Χριστοῦ θεότητος (19.8). ("Now we understand that these things have been said through allegories, at the same time manifestly and obscurely, the divinity of Christ leading to vision those who examine the force of the words more

12. Cicero and Vergil in the Catacombs

This is much closer to the Neoplatonist *allegoresis* of Homer[42] than to Lactantius' tactical Euhemerism.

But there is another, more substantial reason for Constantine's greater sympathy for a "messianic" interpretation of the eclogue. The position of Christianity in the empire had changed since the victory at the Milvian bridge, and apology could now give place to triumphalistic propaganda. As an aspiring sole Augustus, Constantine had a far more favorable image of Vergil and the Augustan *imperium sine fine* than Lactantius would have had a few years earlier, during the persecutions, and in the years immediately following them.

For Constantine, the early imperial period was above all the time when "the presence of the Savior shone forth, and the mystery of the most holy religion prevailed" (19.3). The translation of *cunabula,* "cradle" (*Ecl.* 4.23) as σπάργανα, "swaddling clothes" (20.2; cf. 20.3: τὰ τοῦ θεοῦ σπάργανα) directs the reader to the Gospel of Luke (2:7: ἐσπαργάνωσεν αὐτόν), which, in addition to its bucolic description of the birth of Christ, provides chronological information about his early career (Lk 3). This is where Vergil comes in:

τοῦτον Τιβέριος διεδέξατο, καθ' ὃν χρόνον ἡ τοῦ σωτῆρος ἐξέλαμψε παρουσία, καὶ τὸ τῆς ἁγιωτάτης θρησκείας ἐπεκράτησε μυστήριον ἥ τε νέα τοῦ δήμου διαδοχὴ συνέστη, περὶ ἧς οἶμαι λέγειν τὸν ἐξοχώτατον τῶν κατὰ Ἰταλίαν ποιητῶν·
Ἔνθεν ἔπειτα νέα πληθὺς ἀνδρῶν ἐφαάνθη (19.3-4)

Tiberius succeeded him, and it was in his time that the presence of the Saviour shone forth, and the mystery of the most holy religion prevailed. Then a new race of people was established, of which I think the most eminent of the Italian poets spoke:
Whence then appeared a novel race of men.[43]

Signficantly, the succession of Tiberius is referred to as διεδέξατο and the "new race" (*noua progenies*) of the eclogue is translated as διαδοχή.[44]

---

deeply.") Heikel corrects τὰ λεχθέντα into τα<ῦτα> λεχθέντα. This seems reasonable as ἀγομένης suggests allegorical expression rather than allegorical interpretation. Since the author imputes Christian messages to Vergil in the following, Vergil is to be taken as a self-conscious allegorist. As for τε ἅμα καὶ, there is no obstacle to understanding the expression in the sense of "in alternation": the poem is a blend of overt and allegorical expression.

[42] The allegorization of Achilles marching against Troy as Christ conquering the universe (20.8) is a spectacular example. Other instances may have been obscured by the over-Christianizing zeal of the eclogue's translator; see n. 2. It would be interesting to discuss this passage in light of the polemic of Didymus the Blind against Porphyry; see Binder 1968 and Sellew 1989. The fundamental work on Neoplatonist allegoresis is Lamberton 1989.

[43] All translations of the *Oratio* are by Edwards 2003.

[44] According to Ison 1984: 38, something like *nouus populi successus* might have stood in the Latin original. I, however, believe that the commentator wanted to create a symbolic correspondence

But Constantine does not stop here. He wants his reader to believe that in the generation prior to Vergil, Cicero had read a Sibylline oracle in the acrostic Ἰησοῦς Χρειστὸς Θεοῦ Υἱὸς Σωτήρ Σταυρός (*Or.* 18).[45] He therefore bluntly asserts that Cicero, "as everybody agrees," knew the passage, understood its meaning, translated it into Latin, but kept it hidden so as not to offend the official religion (19.3).

The point of departure for this bizarre invention is a passage in Book 2 of Cicero's *On Divination* (110–12). The context is Cicero's rationalistic reply to his brother Quintus' defense of divination and augury in Book 1. Marcus describes an instance of the political manipulation of "Sibylline" superstition: Lucius Cotta asked the senate to grant Caesar the regal title because there is a prophecy that the Parthians can only be conquered by a king:[46]

> Sibyllae uersus obseruamus, quos illa furens fudisse dicitur. Quorum interpres nuper falsa quadam hominum fama dicturus in senatu putabatur eum, quem re uera *regem* habebamus, appellandum quoque esse *regem*, si *salui* esse uellemus. *Hoc si est in libris, in quem hominem et in quod tempus est?* Callide enim, qui illa composuit, perfecit, ut, quodcumque accidisset, praedictum uideretur hominum et temporum definitione sublata. Adhibuit etiam latebram obscuritatis, ut eidem uersus alias in aliam rem posse accomodari uiderentur. Non esse autem illud carmen furentis cum ipse poema declarat (est enim magis artis et diligentiae quam incitationis et motus), tum uero ea, quae ἀκροστιχίς dicitur ... (110–11)

> We Romans venerate the verses of the Sibyl who is said to have uttered them while in a frenzy. Recently there was a rumour, which was believed at the time, but turned out to be false, that one of the interpreters of those verses was going to declare in the Senate that, *for our safety*, the man whom we had as *king* in fact should be made *king* also in name. *If this is in the books, to what man and to what time does it refer?* For it was clever in the author to take care that whatever happened should appear foretold because all reference to persons or time had been omitted. He also employed a maze of obscurity so that the same verses might be adapted to different situations at different times. Moreover, that this poem is not the work of frenzy is quite evident

---

between the two "successions" rather than "a pun ... which contrasts the accession of the emperor with the beginning of a new race."

[45] The initial letters of the first five stanzas spell ΙΧΘΥΣ. The fact that the Σωτήρ-stanza does not appear in Augustine's Latin version (*C.D.* 18.23) was taken by Mancini 1894, the editor Heikel 1902: XCI–CII and some other early twentieth century scholars as a signal that the *Oratio* must be later than *De Ciuitate Dei*. A more plausible explanation is proposed by Kurfess 1918: the cross-strophe was added in order to make the *Sibyllinum* fit the occasion of the speech, Good Friday. See also Edwards 1999: 256 and Girardet 2013: 102–3.

[46] The event is well attested; see Cf. Suet. *Jul.* 79.4, Dio Cass. 44.15.3, Appian, *BC* 2.110, and Plut. *Caes.* 60.

from the quality of its composition (for it exhibits artistic care rather than emotional excitement), and is especially evident from the fact that it is written in what are termed "acrostics" . . . (trans. Falconer)

There are four pieces of information in Cicero's account that could stir Constantine's imagination: first, the mention of a king and of "salvation" in the prophecy cited by Cotta (*regem, si salui esse uellemus*); second, Cicero's allowance for the possibility that such a written prophecy actually existed (*hoc si est in libris*); third, his acquaintance with Sibylline acrostics, and fourth, his ironic remarks at the end of the passage:

> Hoc scriptoris est, non furentis, adhibentis diligentiam, non insani. Quam ob rem Sibyllam quidem sepositam et conditam habeamus, ut, id quod proditum est a maioribus, iniussu senatus ne legantur quidem libri ualeantque ad deponendas potius quam ad suscipiendas religiones; cum antistitibus agamus, ut quiduis potius ex illis libris quam regem proferant, quem Romae posthac nec di nec homines esse patientur. (112)

> Such a work comes from a writer who is not frenzied, who is painstaking, not crazy. Therefore, let us keep the Sibyl under lock and key so that in accordance with the ordinances of our forefathers her books may not even be read without permission of the Senate and may be more effective in banishing rather than encouraging superstitious ideas. And let us plead with the priests to bring forth from those books anything rather than a king, whom henceforth neither gods nor men will suffer to exist in Rome.

Sibylline oracles with acrostics circulated at the time of Cicero.[47] Yet it is difficult to accept that Constantine actually believed what he said. Kurfess, who once denied that the emperor had had first-hand knowledge of Cicero,[48] spoke in a later article about a *pia fraus*: "'Sibylline's prophecies announcing a king-savior probably existed at the time, and it was up to the reader to decide whether Cicero had known this particular acrostic."[49]

Constantine could take advantage of the fact that Cicero actually *did not tell us* what the oracle said (according to Cotta).[50] It is quite possible (though far from certain) that Constantine did not catch the irony implied in Cicero's suggestion that the Sibyl should be kept under lock and key.

---

[47] Varro ap. Dion. Hal. *Ant. Rom.* 4.62.6.
[48] Kurfess 1950: 14–15, following Pfättisch 1913: 250 n. 2.
[49] Kurfess 1950: 149–50 points out the fourth line of the σωτήρ-strophe: Ἥξουσιν δ' ἐπὶ βῆμα θεοῦ βασιλῆος ἅπαντες (*Or. Sib.* 8.242), also quoted by Lactantius (*Div. inst.* 7.20.3). Kurfess 1952: 56–7, refers to the last two lines of the σταυρός-strophe, Οὗτος ὁ νῦν προγραφεὶς ἐν ἀκροστιχίοις θεὸς ἡμῶν / Σωτὴρ ἀθάνατος βασιλεύς, ὁ παθὼν ἕνεχ' ἡμῶν (249–40) without proposing speculations about possible pre-Christian versions of the prophecy.
[50] See Pizzani 1993: 806–7.

But he was certainly aware of his own manipulative operation, as he was offering an alternative royal candidate as the solution to the prophecy. In retrospect, and especially if Jewish "Sibylline" oracles circulated in late Republican Rome, Constantine's solution is far more conventional than the one proposed by Cotta. Who in the world was ready to believe that it had been Julius Caesar whose advent the Jewish prophets had foretold? Cotta definitely had it wrong.

But the fundamental question remains: does Constantine want us to believe that Cicero and Vergil were prophetically inspired? At first glance, Constantine is inconsistent on this: Vergil was "not a prophet" (μὴ ὄντι γε προφήτῃ, 20.8), but he "knew (ἠπίστατο) . . . the blessed and laudable end (τελετήν) of the Savior" (19.9).[51] The solution I suggest is this: Constantine, following in the footsteps of Lactantius, wants us to believe that the Sibyllines were divinely inspired (whereas Vergil was not). How, then, could Vergil find out the truth about the coming of Christ? The answer is provided by Cicero, who argues that the origins of ambiguous prophecies that can be adapted to different situations at different times lie in the shrewdness of the human mind rather than in divine frenzy and takes the artifice of the acrostic as a proof. This is not a rationalistic reduction of the phenomenon. The emphasis is on the intellectual effort and political prudence of the *quindecimviri*, who, unlike Cotta, know how to correctly administer the books. Their task is to protect true religion from popular superstition. Consultation of the Sibylline books, despite their "inspired" origin, belonged to the typically Roman inductive, technical (as opposed to ecstatic) category of divination.[52] Constantine was probably unaware of these aspects of Roman religion, but he clearly embraced Cicero's idea that there was something intellectual, if not rational, about the activities of the *quindecimviri* and the actual Sibylline texts. Hence the suggestion that Vergil, though not a prophet, could grasp the meaning of the oracle. Cicero, who was not a prophet or even a poet, perhaps understood still more: he was able to *interpret* the acrostic, that is, the most "rational" element of the Sibylline oracles.

Also, like the *quindecimviri*, who wisely kept the books hidden from the superstitious populace and from political usurpers such as "Caesar the Savior," Cicero and Vergil had to hide the Sibyl's secret message from

---

[51] Scholars tend to choose between the two possibilities: for Schelkle 1938: 20, who insists on the difference between Lactantius and Constantine, Vergil is a prophet in spite of 20.8; Courcelle 1957: 314 and n. 3, who tries to bridge the gap between Constantine and Augustine, denies Constantine's Vergil any prophetic authority.

[52] On this, see Šterbenc Erker 2013: 195–200 with further bibliography.

12. Cicero and Vergil in the Catacombs

the political (and ideological) heirs of Julius Caesar. This implies a latent continuity between the pagan *quindecimviri* and the "proto-Christians" Cicero and Vergil. Even the manipulative "leak" orchestrated by Cotta finds a positive counterpart in the clandestine activities of the two: Cicero translated the *stauros*-prophecy and Vergil published the *Fourth Eclogue* as a cryptic "messianic" prophecy:

> ἠπίστατο γὰρ οἶμαι τὴν μακαρίαν καὶ ἐπώνυμον τοῦ σωτῆρος τελετήν, ἵνα δὲ τὸ ἄγριον τῆς ὠμότητος ἐκκλίνοι, ἤγαγε τὰς διανοίας τῶν ἀκουόντων πρὸς τὴν ἑαυτῶν συνήθειαν, καί φησι χρῆναι βωμοὺς ἱδρύσθαι καὶ νεὼς κατασκευάζειν θυσίας τ' ἐπιτελεῖσθαι τῷ νεωστὶ τεχθέντι. ἀκολούθως δὲ καὶ τὰ λοιπὰ ἐπήγαγε τοῖς φρονοῦσι. (19.9)

> For he knew, as I believe, the blessed and laudable end of the Saviour, but in order to avert the rage of savagery, he directed the mind of his audience towards their own tradition, and says that it is necessary to establish altars, build temples and perform sacrifice to the newborn one. As for intelligent readers the rest of his composition is in keeping with this.

In many ways, Constantine inverts the logic of Lactantius' hermeneutics of pagan literature. For Lactantius, unbaptized pagan authors, even such *coryphées* as Cicero and Vergil, are blinded by ignorance because they follow a false religion, and because God wanted the Divine Truth to remain *hidden* from those who are "alien to the sacrament" (*profani a sacramento*), that is, unbaptized. For Constantine, both Cicero and Vergil have such insight into the divine truth that they have to *hide* it from pagan authorities. At least as far Vergil is concerned, the method of concealment corresponds very closely to the one imputed to the pagan poets by Lactantius. The Christian Euhemerist Lactantius argued that poets had a habit of decorating the mortal careers of pagan "gods" with ornaments of figurative language (see p. 231). Conversely, Vergil used imagery drawn from pagan religion as a means of "encrypting" the divinity of Christ. His motives for doing so were in part opportunistic. As Constantine himself states, Vergil resorted to allegory in order not to overtly offend the beliefs of the heathen. Yet in this, too, the poet remained faithful to tradition. According to Lactantius, other pagan poets too used poetic embellishments because they were afraid to reveal the whole story about the "gods":

> mendacium poetarum non in facto est, sed in nomine. Metuebant enim malum, si contra publicam persuasionem faterentur, quod erat uerum. (*Div. inst.* 1.19.5)

The lie the poets tell is one of category, not fact: they were afraid of bad reactions if they affronted public opinion with admission of the truth.

The heretical insights of Lactantius' poets concern the real (mortal) character of the pagan gods and do not amount to any presentiment of the birth of Christ, let alone of his death on the cross. Still, this passage is probably the point of departure for Constantine's anachronistic confabulation. It may have been the emperor himself who chose Cicero and Vergil as the protagonists of a political thriller of eschatological dimensions. Let us take a closer look at a passage that at least on the surface provides chronological proof that the oracle is not a Christian forgery:

> ἐν προφανεῖ δ' ἀλήθεια, τῆς τῶν ἡμετέρων ἀνδρῶν ἐπὶ μελείας συλλεξάσης τοὺς χρόνους ἀκριβέστερον, ὡς πρὸς τὸ μηδένα τοπάζειν μετὰ τὴν τοῦ Χριστοῦ κάθοδον καὶ κρίσιν γεγενῆσθαι τὸ ποίημα καὶ ὡς πάλαι προλεχθέντων ὑπὸ Σιβύλλης τῶν ἐπῶν ψεῦδος διαφημίζεσθαι. ὡμολόγηται γὰρ Κικέρωνα ἐντετυχηκότα τῷ ποιήματι μετενεγκεῖν τε αὐτὸ εἰς τὴν Ῥωμαίων διάλεκτον καὶ ἐντάξαι αὐτὸ τοῖς ἑαυτοῦ συντάγμασιν, τοῦτον <δ'> ἀνῃρῆσθαι κρατήσαντος Ἀντωνίου· Ἀντωνίου δ' αὖ πάλιν Αὔγουστον περιγεγενῆσθαι, ὃς ἓξ καὶ πεντήκοντα ἔτεσιν ἐβασίλευσε. τοῦτον Τιβέριος διεδέξατο ... (19.2–3, see p. 241 for the rest of the passage)

> But the truth is manifest, since the studies of our own men have calculated the times more accurately, so that no one can hold the wild theory that the poem came into being after the descent and judgment of Christ and that a lie was put about that the words had been spoken long before the Sibyl. It is agreed that Cicero, having encountered the poem, translated it into the Roman tongue and included it among his own compositions, and that this man was destroyed during the ascendancy of Antony. And then Augustus got better of Antony and reigned for fifty-six years. Tiberius succeeded him ...

Constantine could find a similar chronological argument in Lactantius, who, however, simply refers to Cicero and Varro as testimony of the antiquity of the Sibylline oracles[53] and refrains from mentioning the acrostic (which he probably knew because he quotes lines from that part of the text). It is precisely the mystery of the acrostic that makes Constantine's novella about Cicero sound not only like Dante's story of Statius the Christian renegade, but almost like Dan Brown's *Da Vinci Code*. Did Constantine need to provide a chronological calculation in order to prove that Cicero had lived before Tiberius? Who did not know that? I think that between the lines Constantine is suggesting something else.

---

[53] *Div. inst.* 4.15.26–27; see Schultze 1894: 549 and Kurfess 1936b: 12.

In order to see the purpose of this pseudo-historical narrative, it is useful to take a closer look at the broader context of its passages on Cicero and Vergil. The real subject of the *Oration to the Assembly of Saints* is not Good Friday but rather the workings of Divine Providence which has intervened in the earthly battle between the forces of Good and Evil and has decided in favor of the pious Constantine. The passage following the lecture on Vergil is a miniature replica of Lactantius' *De mortibus persecutorum*, a work describing the plagues that befell the persecuting emperors. It starts with threatening apostrophes to Decius, Valerian, and Aurelian, and adduces a number of examples of divine retribution against the persecutors. Within this context, the messianic interpretation of the *Oracula* and Vergil's *Fourth Eclogue* replaces Lactantius' apocalyptic, millenarian reading of the Sibylline oracles. With Constantine's ascension to power, the war against the pagan empire became superfluous, and a Christian empire of peace presented itself as a real possibility. Such a change called for a reevaluation of pagan "visionaries" such as Cicero and Vergil. Lactantius saw the infant of the *Fourth Eclogue* as one of those earthly rulers who could not accomplish the task of redemption. Constantine, in turn, saw him as the Redeemer. The reading of the poem could change this radically because in the eyes of the aspiring monarch, the dissolution of Tetrarchy implied the re-establishment of the Augustan principate. A telling symptom of this interpretative shift is the changing image of Cicero, who had been "almost unaware" of the truth a few years earlier in Lactantius' *Divine institutions*, but was now suddenly informed not only about the precise name of the Savior, but also his death by crucifixion.

Yet there is another way of contextualizing the curious chapters on the two Latin classics. Within the plot of the speech, they are framed between the biblical *exempla* of divine retribution and the passage on the Great Persecution. The sequence is chronologically correct. As transmitters of messianic prophecies, Cicero and Vergil somehow represented a Roman sequel to the Old Testament. But they did so not as prophets but as prefigurative examples, as some kind of clandestine proto-Christian activists, who foreshadowed the destinies of many Christians during the persecutions. They *knew* the true meaning of the Sibylline prophecies, but they were wise (or opportunistic?) enough not to provoke the "savage rage" of the authorities. They thus appear as political rather than spiritual figures.

Perhaps the answer to the question as to why Cicero should have known the fish-acrostic, why a cross-stanza was appended to the *Sibyllinum*, and why Cicero had to spend another exile in the *Catacomba di Sta. Sibilla* lies not so much in Constantine's fanciful superstition but rather in the deliberate construction of Cicero's death as a prefigurative martyrdom. The Stauros-acrostic that Cicero was hiding applied to himself before it could apply to Christ. If considered from this perspective, Constantine's rendering of the *Life of Cicero* seems a tasteless *giallo* unworthy of a pupil of Lactantius, but reveals an important motive for including a section on two Roman classics in a Good Friday sermon. Constantine systematically projects his providential victory over the persecutors back on the "messianic" period of Roman history. In order for the symmetry to work flawlessly, he styles the second Triumvirate to foreshadow the tetrarchy (Mark Antony plays the role of Diocletian and other persecutors), and Octavian prefigures Constantine the vindicator: τοῦτον <δ'> ἀνῃρῆσθαι κρατήσαντος Ἀντωνίου· Ἀντωνίου δ' αὖ πάλιν Αὔγουστον περιγεγενῆσθαι (19.3; "and that this man (i.e. Cicero) was destroyed during the ascendancy of Antony. And then Augustus got better of Antony").

A "pious fraud," indeed, especially as the emperor tactfully refrains from suggesting the obvious: that Apollo (*tuus iam regnat Apollo,* Verg. *Ecl.* 4.10), the patron god of Augustus and his own former protector, was a cipher for Christ, and that Constantine (and not Christ) was the new incarnation of the Vergilian "offspring of Jupiter."[54] In this, at least, the new Augustus was a true heir to the sophisticated language of allusion that his pagan predecessor had cultivated in his own monarchic propaganda.

Acknowledgment

My thanks go to the audiences of the classics departments of Trieste and Milan where earlier versions of this paper were presented, especially to Marco Fernandelli and Massimo Gioseffi. Darja Šterbenc Erker contributed a number of suggestions as a reader of the final draft.

---

[54] An overt appropriation of Augustus is suggested by the orator from Autun, who, in his 310 panegyric describes Constantine's vision of Apollo as an omen announcing a new incarnation of Augustus: *Vidisti enim, credo, Constantine, Apollinem tuum . . . uidisti teque in illius specie recognouisti, cui totius mundi regna deberi uatum carmina diuina cecinerunt* (*Paneg. Lat.* 6.21.4–5). ("For you saw, I believe, O Constantine, your Apollo . . . you *saw* and recognized yourself in the likeness of him to whom the divine songs of the bards had prophesied that rule over the world was due." tr. Nixon and Saylor Rodgers). The main literary reference is the passage in the *Aeneid* in which Vergil retrospectively identifies the *puer* of Eclogue 4 as Augustus: *Aen.* 6.791–94 *hic uir, hic est, tibi quem promitti saepius audis, / Augustus Caesar, diui genus, aurea condet / saecula qui rursus Latio regnata per arua / Saturno quondam . . .* ("Here's the man you've heard promised to you so often, he's here now: / Caesar Augustus, born of a god, who will one day establish / all through the farmlands of Latium once, long ago, ruled by Saturn, / ages of Gold." tr. F. Ahl) Cf. Rodgers 1980: 270–4.

CHAPTER 13

The Future of Rome after 410 CE
The Latin Conceptions (410–480 CE)

Hervé Inglebert

In antiquity, Rome was the City while *imperium Romanum* the power of Rome. However, after the *Constitutio Antoniniana* of 212 CE and the nearly universal extension of Roman citizenship, the legal status of its citizen was accompanied by an adherence to the civic and imperial models set out by Tertullian (*De pallio* IV.1) under the term *Romanitas*. The term *Romania* first came to be used for all Roman territory around 330 CE.[1] This explains why today the word "Rome" is used for both the city and the Empire. Nonetheless, we need to distinguish between the two when discussing its future. In effect, when historians speak about the end of Rome, they are referring mainly to the end of the Roman Empire in the West. However, as John Bury pointed out over a century ago, such a thing did not exist.[2] What existed was only the *pars occidentalis* of the Roman Empire, but when that disappeared at the end of the fifth century, the Roman Empire continued to survive in and around Constantinople.

In the early fifth century CE, there were two ideological concepts of Rome. The first was the old Augustean theory of *Roma Aeterna*, which remained the main political notion among the pagans, who linked it to the *religio* of the gods of Rome whose cult was abolished by Theodosius in 391–394 CE. The concept of *Roma Aeterna* did not mean that Roman decline was impossible, but that a Roman *renovatio* could always be expected. However, an old pagan concept of destiny linked to Etruscan "centuries" claimed that the existence of Rome and the power of the city would last 1200 years. Notwithstanding the various dates proposed for the foundation of Rome, the twelve centuries came to an end around 450 CE. The second concept was a Jewish and Christian one: Rome as the fourth and final terrestrial empire of the Book of Daniel.[3] In such case, the end of

---

[1] Irmscher 1986. [2] Bury 1889.
[3] Inglebert 1996b: 342–64. Cf. the chapters in this volume by Price (Chapter 5), Berthelot (Chapter 6), Noam (Chapter 9) and Gruen (Chapter 10).

Rome would mark the end of the world. For the majority of literate Christians, this was supposed to take place 6000 years after Creation. Most people believed that the Incarnation would occur around 5500 years after the Creation (according to the most common Christian biblical calendar), implying that the world would end around 500 CE. Thus, when faced with the events of the fifth century – from the sack of Rome in 410 to the disappearance of Roman power in the West between 476 and 480 – both pagans and Christians came to envisage a doomsday scenario for the future of Rome even if more optimistic interpretations were possible.

Any analysis of fifth-century Latin texts leads to various methodological challenges. The first of these applies to all ancient texts. Most use ideological or exegetical arguments from which it is impossible to draw firm conclusions about what their writers were actually thinking. An author could evoke old age or the end of the world, for example, in order to justify a choice of lifestyle such as asceticism (Eucherius of Lyon) or a pastoral approach, such as moralizing (Augustine of Hippo). Identical catechetical arguments that emphasize salvation have thus crossed the centuries. In order to reduce this intertextuality, the focus has been on texts with computations of time or explicit demonstrations, or else those linked to their authors' activities.

Another issue relates to subject matter. Between the second century BCE and the third century CE, a number of anti-Roman texts contested the claims of Rome's eternal domination. Composed by Greeks, Celts, and Egyptians, these took the form of oracles and predictions.[4] Jews and Christians often wrote encrypted texts, few of which were as clear as the Sibylline Oracles or the Apocalypse of John. In them, we generally find coded biblical references (Rome as Babylon or Edom), allusions to the empire of Satan or the Antichrist, doomsday computations of time, or descriptions of the Last Judgment (e.g. Tertullian at the end of *De spectaculis*). However, pagan sibylline oracles can be interpreted as being negative towards Christian imperial power, which is why Stilicon had them destroyed in 405. Finally, two trends are specific to the fifth century. First, with the conversion of various populations to Christianity, Christian theories became dominant. Theodosian ideology claimed that God protected the orthodox Roman Empire. In this respect, apart from the Jews and the Manicheans, minority groups included dissident Christian groups, which were deemed heretics, and pessimist orthodox groups (to which

---

[4] MacMullen 1967: 128–62; see also Noam (Chapter 9), Gruen (Chapter 10) and Oakes (Chapter 11) in this volume.

some clerics and ascetics belonged). But orthodox Christian texts from this period are largely allusive. There are two reasons for this. Towards the end of the second century CE and during the struggle against Montanism, bishops began frowning on speculation about the end of the world. It therefore became difficult for clerics to express their fears openly on the matter. Second, the established Theodosian Church could not claim that Roman defeats in the West were punishment for the persecution of the emperors or ascribe them to a lack of faith by orthodox emperors. Their interpretation consequently remained confused. Only Orosius, who defended an imperial Christian optimism, or Augustine, who drew a distinction between the destinies of the Empire and those of Christianity, could produce a well-formed argument. Pessimistic Christians – clerics, ascetics, or laymen – generally voiced their opinion indirectly, through exegetical hypotheses or numerical conjectures.[5]

Finally, in order to understand the future of Rome, it is useful to apply the categories developed by Reinhart Koselleck, who defined the specific historicity of an era through the relation of "the space of experience" (*Erfahrungsraum*, concerning past and present) to "the horizon of expectation" (*Erwartungshorizont*, regarding the future). Koselleck and François Hartog[6] have argued that when combined, these two categories provide insight into specific concepts of history during major eras; antiquity, for example, was dominated by the authoritative tradition of the past, Christian times with eschatological hope or fear, the modern era since 1750 with a rejection of the past and confidence in the future, and the present with distrust of both past and future. But the existence of such general concepts for each era is problematic. Thus it is probably wiser to apply this grid to all literary works, as the historicity of a moment may be experienced in different ways by its contemporaries and be linked to their statutes, ideologies, or circumstances.

This, in fact, is what we have done with different items (the city of Rome, the Empire of Rome, the Christianization of the world) in Tables 1, 2, and 3 in the Appendix. We can thus observe that there were several conceptions of Rome's future in the same period, that these accorded with places and statutes, and that the same author (e.g. Gregory the Great) could express different opinions depending on a variety of things, and thus be pessimistic about the future of the city of Rome but optimistic about the future of the Roman Empire or the diffusion of the Christian faith through the world. It was these speculations about the future of "Rome" that helped

---

[5] Fauvarque 1994. [6] Koselleck 2004; Hartog 2012.

the people of the fifth and sixth centuries endure the present or hope for a better time, and explain an event as being auspicious or inauspicious for Rome.

13.1 The Future of the City of Rome (410–455 CE)

13.1.1 The Sack of Rome in 410 CE and Its Interpretations

Eight centuries after the Celtic raid on Rome, the three-day sack of Rome by Alaric (August 24–27, 410 CE) was an unimaginable event and a major psychological shock. Comparable events in modern history would be the French military disaster of 1940, the fall of the Iron Curtain in 1989 or the Al Qaida attack on New York on September 11, 2001. Alaric's sack of Rome is well documented, so we do not need to go over the events in detail.[7] Pagan Romans had a clear explanation for what they considered to be sacrilege as Rome was not only a city or a city-state, but also a goddess whose temple had stood on the Forum since the time of Hadrian. Their interpretations, as recorded by Augustine from 410 to 412,[8] are also well known. The decline of religious worship, recently reaffirmed by Honorius, they claimed, had unleashed the wrath of the gods,[9] and the *tempora Christiana* had brought about the downfall of Rome. It was therefore crucial to restore the worship of the gods in order to secure the future of Rome. Christians, in turn, believed that the events had been prophesied and insisted on the punishment of either pagans (if they regarded Rome as another Babylon or Sodom), or less than devout Christians (if they regarded Rome as another Jerusalem reviled by the prophets). Some interpreted the calamity as a sure sign of the end of the world or, at the very least, of a decaying world.[10] Others believed that they would have to lead more pious lives to avert the wrath of the Biblical God.[11] Augustine wrote that if Rome had been struck because it had not been sufficiently devout, it had nonetheless been spared as God did not wish its end, but rather its conversion. Thanks to this ascetic or moral awakening,

---

[7] Courcelle 1964; Piganiol 1964; Veyne 2005; Doignon 1990.

[8] Augustine, *Sermo* 81.8–9; 105.12–13; 296.9; Marcellinus, *Ep.* 136.2 to Augustine kept a record of Senator Volusianus' criticisms. *S.* 81 is from 410, *S.* 105 and 296 from 411 and *S.* 397 from 412.

[9] *CTh.* 16.10.19 (November 15, 408). Zosimus, 5.35.5 wrote about it a century later in the East, maintaining that the departure of the gods had left the world at the mercy of demonic forces.

[10] The belief dates back to Cyprian, *Ad Demetrianum* 4, and was later taken up by Augustine, *Sermo* 81.8.

[11] Jerome, *Ep.* 130.6, thus maintained in 414 that Demetrias' vow of chastity was analogous to Rome's rebirth after the sack of the Goths.

a Christian Rome could still hope for a terrestrial future if it aspired to celestial eternity.

13.1.2 Renewed Hope circa 417 CE

The psychological shock of 410 lasted until around 413, with Augustine mentioning the events in the first three books of *De civitate Dei* (413–427). By 417, however, two authors had put forward a far more optimistic view.

Rutilius Namatianus, appointed prefect of the city in 414, returned to his native Gaul in 417. In a poem dedicated to his voyage home (*De redito suo*, circa 418), the pagan aristocrat explained the disaster of 410 as the result of the political activities of Stilicho, son of a Vandal, whom he portrayed as an ally of Alaric. Above all, however, he blamed it on Stilicho's religious activities, as the latter had ordered the destruction of the *Sibylline Oracles*, which were believed to hold the key to Rome's everlasting power. Yet, Rutilius Namatianus remained confident in Rome's future.[12] He used historical arguments (121–128; in the second century BCE, Polybius had already shown that Rome would be able to recover from any defeat), and justifications of a religious-cosmic nature (137–140) to reassert a Roman rebirth and the eternity of Roman power (141–146) in a way that could be linked to Jupiter's prophecy in the *Æneid* (I, 278–279):

> *His ergo nec metas rerum nec tempora pono*
> *Imperium sine fine dedi*
>
> To them no bounds of empire I assign,
> nor term of years to their immortal line.

Thanks to the *ordo renascendi* (140), neither the *fatum* nor the great age of Rome (1168 years, 133–136) were sufficient to destroy Rome. This claim came close to the Augustean theme of *renouatio*. In 417 CE, therefore, the old pagan, romano-centric ideology was still a possibility for thinking about Rome's future.[13]

Orosius was a Spanish priest who took refuge in Africa during the 409 CE invasion of Spain by Vandals, Alans, and Suevi. He settled in Hippo to be near Augustine. The latter asked him to write a book of history recounting the Romans' misfortunes in pagan times in order to

---

[12] *De redito suo* 119–146 (Text 1 in the Appendix). The best edition of *De redito suo* is that of Wolff 2007.
[13] In the East, heathens like Eunapius of Sardes (circa 407) and Zosimus (circa 500), spoke about the events of 402–410, attributing them to the end of the worship of gods.

complement *De civitate Dei*. Orosius strayed from the task and wrote a somewhat different sort of book, in which he described the joyfulness of the Christian era, taking Augustus as his starting point in this respect. He also drew on those of Eusebius of Caesarea's ideas that had helped establish the Theodosian ideology of a Christian Roman Empire. Orosius argued that the barbarians' invasions were God's means of converting them, and that once they embraced Christianity, they would yield to Rome. He also produced his own, original exegesis of the Book of Daniel[14] (Text 2 in the Appendix). In doing so, he first associated the four empires with the four cardinal points: Babylon with the East, Macedonia with the North, Carthage with the South, and Rome with the West. Secondly, he pointed out that both Babylon and Rome had retained their dominance for fourteen centuries, as opposed to Macedonia and Carthage, which had only done so for seven (7.2.9 and 12). Since Rome had been founded in 753 BCE (Orosius used the Livian system of computing time to determine the year *ab Urbe condita*), its dominion would end in 648 CE. Until then, it would continue to rule the world, and the barbarians would convert to Christianity. Thirdly, he claimed that the destinies of Babylon and Rome had been identical until each had reached its 1164th year (in the case of Rome, that year was 410 CE), but differed from that point on because Rome had become Christian (2.3.2). The end of the terrestrial Christian Roman Empire would coincide with the advent of a celestial Jerusalem. Augustine rejected this position several years later in *De civitate Dei* XVI–XVIII, in which he stressed the diverging destinies awaiting the Roman Empire and Christianity, and claimed that the latter would be able to survive autonomously regardless of the terrestrial city's condition.[15]

By 417, the sack of the city was perceived as a secondary incident. The ravages in Rome had been limited, the city had been restored by its governors, and the Empire seemed set to last. According to Orosius, the Goths abandoned the idea of *Gothia* in 415 and instead chose to pledge allegiance to *Romania* (7.43.5). Indeed, it was the agreement reached between the Goths and Honorius in 416 that led Rutilius Namatianus to return to Gaul and Orosius to Spain the following year. Their actions confirm that they really did believe in their optimistic views of Rome's future.[16]

---

[14] *Historiae aduersus paganos* (Text 2 in the Appendix). [15] Inglebert 1996a: 489–94.
[16] In a similar vein, Olympiodorus of Thebes, a pagan scholar who wrote a contemporary history around 425, left an enthusiastic description (Fragments 25 and 43) of the renewal of the city's population and monuments (the Baths of Caracalla and Diocletian).

13.1.3 Debates in Rome circa 450 CE

According to the Roman tradition as recounted by Livy 1.6–7, it was Romulus, not Remus, who had founded Rome, since, when looking for omens, the former had seen twelve vultures from the Palatine Hill, while his brother had spotted only six from the Aventine Hill. In the Empire, the celebration of secular games under Augustus, and later, the anniversary of the founding of Rome observed annually from 48 CE on,[17] led some people to link the number of birds with that of the number of centuries granted by the gods or by destiny to Rome. This was a revised version of an ancient Etruscan belief according to which each individual or group of people has a limited lifespan. Various dates were put forward for the foundation of Rome, but the most common was April 21, 753 BCE, as fixed by Varro at the end of the Republic. According to this calculation, the 1200th year of Rome would end on April 20, 448 CE.

The fatalistic concept that Rome would last twelve centuries was relatively widespread,[18] as we have already seen in Rutilius Namatianus' poem. Some Christians saw it as an argument supporting the end of the world,[19] while some pagans, witnessing the imperial defeats and territorial losses – especially those of Africa, which fell into the hands of the Vandals in 439 – believed that the destiny of Rome was coming to a close. However, some Christians found arguments to prove that the history of Rome depended less on *fatum* than on divine providence.[20]

The other major event of these years was the pillage of Rome by the Vandal King Genseric in 455. Although this appeared to indicate the weakness of imperial power after the death of Valentinian III, Prosper of Aquitaine offered a different interpretation. He described the pillage towards the end of the second extension to his chronicle (edited in 433 and updated first in 444, and again in 455), and concluded with the celebration of the Easter festival by the Roman Bishop Leo. The meaning

---

[17] Benoist 2005. [18] Duval 1980.
[19] In around 430, Eucherius of Lyon decided that Rome had reached its 1185th year, *De contemptu mundi*, PL 50, 721–722. He noted the aging of the world and global Christianization, which he consequently linked to the end of the world. But in around 420 in the East, Palladius, *Lausiac History* 54.7, linked the sack of Rome – the ruin of the city but not the end of the world – to its 1200th year.
[20] In 449, Polemius Silvius, in his *Breviarum temporum* (*Chronica Minora* I = *MGH AA* 9, 547) stressed the fact that Asterius (associated with Protogenes) was made consul the year following the consulate of Postumianus and Zeno, which marked the 1200th year of Rome: *Cuius regni ab urbis exordio mille et ducentis completis annis Postumiano et Zenone consulibus, Asterio consule tanquam primus anus incipit*. The Catholic author of the 463 version of *Liber Genealogus* associated the sack of Rome in 455 with the 1200th year of Rome, though according to his count, the total came to 1207 years.

is clear. Dissociating the destinies of Christianity and the Roman Empire in *De ciuitate Dei*, Augustine could envisage a Christian future even after the eventual demise of the Roman Empire. A good Augustinian disciple, Prosper showed how Rome the spiritual capital (the citadel of Christian faith) had survived the Rome of the Caesars. On the other hand, this scenario did not fit the chronology as the pillage of Rome by Genseric occurred after Easter, from June 2–16, 455.

Finally, the subsequent destiny of the city is rarely mentioned in later texts. Perhaps because it was due to a Roman civil war, the siege of 472 and the third fall of the city had hardly any impact. Rome was taken five more times during the war between Constantinople and the Goths (by Belisarius in 536, by Totila in 546, by Belisarius in 547, by Totila in 549, and by Narses in 552). In 546, Totila made all the city's inhabitants leave, and it remained empty for one month. However, none of these events, or even the sacks of 455 and 472, had the same ideological or psychological impact as the one in 410. It was only in the late sixth century that Pope Gregory I understood the vanished prosperity of the city as the sign of an aging world.[21]

13.2 The End of the Roman Empire and the End of the World circa 420 CE

Christians inherited eschatological concepts that had been developed by Jews between the second century BCE and the second century CE. Yet though rabbis avoided these sorts of speculations after the failed revolt of Bar Kokhba, Christians continued pursuing them and at times also millenarian ideas that saw in the end of Rome the prelude to the end of the world.[22] In the fifth century, the debate drew on four main arguments:

---

[21] *Homily on Ezechiel* II, *hom.* 6.22.

[22] Based on the texts in the Book of Daniel (the seventy weeks and the four empires), the Gospels (with references to the destruction of Jerusalem) and the Apocalypse, some groups, like the Montanists, began preaching an imminent end to the world, which they sometimes justified with computations, after 160. Accordingly, they likened the Roman Empire, which they viewed as a persecutor, to the kingdom of evil that the Parousia would eventually destroy. After 200, however, some Christian authors developed theories that the end of the world, which they estimated to occur after 6000 years, would be delayed until circa 500 CE, thereby making any immediate eschatological expectations futile. In this scenario, the Roman Empire could have either negative (e.g. Hippolytus of Rome, *In Danielem* and *De Christo et Antichristo*, circa 204) or positive connotations (Julius Africanus, *Chronographiae*, circa 220). While the mid-third-century crisis led some (Cyprian, Commodian) to believe in the imminent end of the world, the reestablishment of Rome after 275 undermined such expectations. At the beginning of the fourth century, Eusebius of Caesarea corrected Julius Africanus' chronology by three centuries and postulated a Nativity in 5200, claiming, in other words, that the end of the sixth millennium would fall in 800 CE.

1. The exegesis of certain prophetic texts, particularly the prophecy of seventy weeks in the Book of Daniel (Jerome's *In Danielem* of 407 summarizes and explains its various interpretations) or the Apocalypse of John.
2. Reasoning based on calculations, according to which the birth of Christ occurred 5500 years (Julius Africanus and Hippolytus of Rome), 5200 years (Eusebius of Caesarea), or around four millennia (according to calculations in the Hebrew Bible used by Jerome) from the moment of Creation.[23] However, save in cases of persecuted Christians (such as the Donatists),[24] it is difficult to determine whether calculations based on the belief that the Nativity took place in 5500 reflect expectations or eschatological concerns.[25]
3. Exegesis of prophetic signs of the end of the world: epidemics, famines, invasions, civil wars, heresies, natural catastrophes, or miracles, all of which were widely discussed in order to determine whether or not to link them to the coming of the Antichrist. Such events did occur on a regular basis throughout the imperial era, but the misfortunes of the fifth century, particularly the Roman defeats (sack of Rome in 410, fall of Carthage in 439, Attila's invasion of Italy in 452, sack of Rome in 455) and the victories of homoean Barbarians (Goths, Vandals), who were considered heretics, could easily be linked to the end of the world.
4. The realization of the prophecy of the Gospel as preached across the world. Once this happened, the end of the world would follow. However, beliefs about whether or not the Roman Empire was an approximation of the world generated controversy.

Of course, several conflicting arguments could occur in the same text. Often, lines of reasoning were implicit, offering clues without coming to any clear conclusions.

Some authors also left behind detailed accounts. Thus, around 419, Hesychius of Salona wrote to Augustine asking him what he thought about certain prophetic passages, notably the seventy weeks in Daniel. Augustine wrote a cautious reply, picking up on Jerome's comments about

---

[23] The use of this computation occurs for the first time in the *Expositio temporum a mundi incohatione* (*Chronica minora* III = *MGH AA* 13, 415), which dates to 468, and in which the author cites Jerome and counts 4113 years from the Creation to the Passion, thereby leaving 1449 years to the world before the year 6000.

[24] Perhaps *De duratione mundi* of Q. Julius Hilarianus in 397 as well as the first versions of the *Liber Genealogus* (427 and 438).

[25] Inglebert 1996a: 595–609. In 452, the year of Attila's attack on Italy, the *Computatio a. CCCCLII* counted 5949 years.

Daniel and stressing that any computation of time was unfeasible (*Ep.* 197). For him, the only sure sign of the end of the world would be the propagation of the Gospel to all nations in a virtually impossible-to-calculate time frame. But Augustine did suggest that the conversion of the world could occur within one or two generations.

Hesychius wrote back to Augustine with four arguments.[26] First, according to the Scriptures, it was not necessarily impossible to calculate the end of the world; second, prophetic signs of the end of the world in the form of disasters and signs in heaven had definitely occurred (198.5; perhaps the solar eclipse of July 19, 418, which had been visible in Constantinople); third, the Gospel had already been preached across the world, first by the apostles and later by the conversion of the emperors to Christianity (198.6); and finally, the exegesis of Daniel, if applied to the Parousia, could provide a possible basis for calculation.

Augustine responded with a very long letter,[27] which he later entitled "*De fine saeculi*" (*De civitate Dei* XX.5.4). First, he disputed the scriptural possibility of calculating the end of the world. With regard to the weeks mentioned in Daniel, he pointed out that while they referred to the Parousia (which he did not believe), there were another seventy to one hundred years to go (199.20). In terms of signs of the end of the world, Augustine argued that there had been miracles throughout history, and that those of the past had sometimes been even more extraordinary (199.34). Similarly, the present invasions were no worse than those of the third century in the time of Gallienus (199.35). Finally, the apostles had not finished their missionary work, so their successors needed to continue spreading the Word. If the Gospel was known in the westernmost island of the ocean (199.47, possibly an allusion to Ireland), it was not yet being preached everywhere, as the example of African tribes beyond the confines of Roman power demonstrated (199.46). Therefore, it was not possible to predict the end of the world (199.51).

The argument of Christianity's propagation across nations was the only one that Augustine was willing to concede in *Letters* 197 and 199. However, the dialectic between the universal empire of the Caesars and the even more universal empire of Christ, which dated back to 200, varied according to authors. It could be applied solely to the Roman world, traditionally considered an image of the whole world,[28] or to the Roman Empire and

---

[26] *Ep.* 198 (Text 3 in the Appendix).   [27] *Ep.* 199 (Text 4 in the Appendix).

[28] This was the case of Eucherius of Lyon (see n. 20); cf. Prococo 1990. In around 430, Eucherius, like Origen and Eusebius and unlike Augustine, linked the Nativity to the reign of Octavian Augustus and the Christianization of the Roman Empire. As Christianity was being preached in each of the

all the nations outside its confines that had become Christian in the fourth century,[29] or to all peoples across the globe. Similarly, while Orosius justified the invasions of the barbarians in 417 by their eventual outcome – Christianization[30] – Augustine rejected this model of centripetal conversion in 419, as he believed that the Gospel should be brought to the barbarians, who would then worship God in their own country.[31] However, he did not think it was necessary to send missionaries to the Moorish tribes beyond the defensive *limes*.

13.3 The Future of the Roman Empire in the West (450–470 CE)

Despite the predictions about Rome lasting 1200 years, or the world 6000 years, we should not believe that the Romans of the Western world stood by helplessly wringing their hands when faced with the destruction of imperial Rome. Not everyone saw the plundering of Rome, the capture of Carthage, and the attacks by the Huns as signs of the end of the world, even if some people understood that the loss of Africa irremediably weakened the Western portion of the Empire.[32] The emperors continued to rule and the generals to fight, and coins were minted with the motto *Victoria Augusti* or *Augustorum* until the time of Julius Nepos and Romulus Augustus.[33] By appointing his nephew, Valentinian III, as emperor of the West in place of the usurper Joannes (423–425) after the death of Honorius, Theodosius II demonstrated his ambition to consolidate imperial rule. He followed up by authorizing the compilation of the *Theodosian Code*, which was published in 438, and by sending reinforcements to fight the Vandal

---

four cardinal directions and had reached peoples as varied as the Thracians in the North, the Libyans in the South, the Syrians in the East, and the Hispanics in the West, Eucherius deduced that the end of the world was near. However, all these peoples lived within the Roman Empire. As the latter had been considered equivalent to the world (with the link between *Urbs* and *orbis*) since the time of Pompeius, some Christians believed that the Gospel had been preached everywhere and that the end of the world was nigh, based on the fact that all peoples in the Empire had converted to Christianity.

[29] In his section of the *Ecclesiastical History*, which he wrote in 401–402 and which covered the years 325–395, Rufinus of Aquilaea described the conversions of the Aksumites, the Iberians (Georgians) and some Arab tribes (the Saracens). These peoples from outside the Empire joined the empire of Christ thanks to Christians of Roman origin, thereby guaranteeing the Christian empire a central place in the history of salvation. Rufinus did not mention the conversion of the Germanic peoples to the homoean Christianity of Constantius II and Valens, emperors whom he considered heretics. See Thélamon 1981.

[30] *Historiae* 7.41.8. [31] *Ep.* 199.47.

[32] In *De gubernatione Dei* 6.68, written around 440, Salvian noted that the fall of Carthage signified the end of the Roman Empire, but did not link it to the end of the world.

[33] However, *Romae Aeternae*, attested since Augustus, disappeared from coins after the Tetrarchs. Later, one finds it only in 318–320 (*RIC* VII, 314 and 317) and 348–350 (*RIC* VIII, 258).

invasion in 439. After the loss of Carthage in 439, the Western part of the Empire, despite its weakened state, managed to fight Attila in 451 and prepare an expedition against the Vandals in 460. Even after the Theodosian dynasty (in 450 in the East and 455 in the West) the emperors of the East continued helping those of the West by appointing new emperors and organizing a new expedition against the Vandals in 468. It was only after this point in time that all hope of a recovery was lost and the end of the Western Roman Empire appeared likely.

We offer two examples of pessimistic episcopal discourse. The first is by Quodvultdeus, bishop of Carthage during its capture by the Vandals in 439, after which he was exiled to Campania. Prior to his banishment, he had corresponded with Augustine. Later, in his *Liber promissionum et praedictorum Dei* of around 450, he defended the idea that the end of the world was imminent and apparently expected it to occur circa 510 or 540.[34] The second is by Hydatius of Chaves, who had met Jerome in his youth and witnessed the victory of the homoean Goths and Suevi over the orthodox Romans of Spain. In around 468 he wrote a *Chronicle*, in which, towards the end, he described a series of miracles, in which he seemed to indicate that he expected the world to end around 482.[35] In their writings, both bishops associated Roman defeats, miracles, and the spread of homoean Christianity, which they deemed heretic, while presenting a pessimistic argument. For them, the disastrous present of Western Rome condemned its future, and the destruction of the Theodosian, Roman, and Orthodox Empire truly signaled the end of the world.[36]

An excellent witness of the final defenders of the Roman order in the West was Sidonius Apollinaris, a great Gallo-Roman aristocrat, son-in-law of the Emperor Avitus (455–456), and prefect of the city of Rome in 468, before becoming the Catholic bishop of Clermont-Ferrand in 470, and defending his see from the homoean Visigoths in 475. From 455 to 468, he was constantly reaffirming his hopes of a *renovatio* of Rome in the West. Thus, in 456, the panegyric of Avitus[37] referred to the omen of twelve vultures, signifying the 1200 years of Rome (51–56), and linked it to the events of 454–455 (v. 357–361: death of Aetius, of Valentinian III, of Petronius, and sack of Rome by Genseric in 455), but this *fatum* was deemed void as the advent of Avitus, which breathed new life into

---

[34] Inglebert 1996a 618–22.   [35] Burgess 1993.
[36] The *Computatio anni CDLII* could also be read in this way.
[37] *Carmen* 7 (Text 5 in the Appendix).

Rome, heralded a revival (v. 127–135, 552–564 and 595–598) and a new golden century worthy of Trajan.

Similarly, in 458, the panegyric of Majorian[38] postulated that the 455 sack of Rome was of secondary importance as Rome fought better after a defeat (61–87), as Rutilius Namatianus had already observed; Majorian, therefore, would be victorious (586–602). Finally, in 468, the panegyric of Anthemius again claimed that the new emperor would lead to a *renovatio* of Rome.[39] This echoed the most traditional official Roman discourse, without Christianizing the subject matter.

Yet Sidonius was not merely expressing an official point of view. Due to his unswerving fidelity to Rome, he always hoped that his son would be able to carve out a career for himself in the imperial administration and would one day gain the consulate that Sidonius himself had never had.[40] And in 478, when Roman rule finally disappeared in the West, and with it all hope of gaining access to *dignitates*, which were henceforth reserved solely for Italian aristocrats, Sidonius redefined Roman civilization as a Latin culture with Catholic faith.[41] The Romans would indeed survive Rome.

13.4 Conclusion

Chronologies of the future of Rome differed according to whether they referred to the city or the Empire. After 410, the future of the city of Rome was variously conceived in three phases. First, the sack of Rome in 410 was seen either as a warning of the re-creation of a future pagan state, or as an invitation to a more Christian future. Then, in around 417, pagans and Christians alike believed that the power of Rome had reasserted itself after the crises of the years 407–413. Finally, in around 448, pagans feared that the twelve centuries of Rome were coming to an end, while Christians believed in a new future for the city, henceforth bound to the role of the Bishop of Rome, Leo I, defender of orthodoxy in Chalcedon (451), and negotiator with Attila in 452 and with Genseric in 455. Rome was thus redefined as the citadel of faith and the center of the universal and spiritual empire of Christ. The future of the Roman Empire in the West thus unfolded in three stages. After the crisis of the early fifth century, imperial optimism revived from 415 to 429. The Vandals' conquest of Africa, the

---

[38] *Carmen* 2 (Text 5). [39] *Carmen* 2.132.
[40] Sidonius Apollinaris, *Ep.* V.16.4: . . . *ut sicut nos utramque familiam nostram praefectoriam nancti etiam patriciam divino favore reddidimus, ita ipsi quam suscipiunt patriciam faciant consularem.*
[41] *Ep.* VIII. 2.

richest region in the Western world, meant a real decline in imperial power from 429 to 439, with the consequence that some Romans opted to pledge allegiance to barbarian kings after 450. However, it was not until 468 that the last glimmer of hope for an imperial recovery finally vanished. Nevertheless, the cultural and Catholic rites and customs of Rome survived the fall of its power in the West, which greatly benefited Justinian (I) fifty years later.

Appendix

Table 1 *The regimes of historicity in relation to the city of Rome during the fifth century CE*

Authors	Space of experience	Horizon of expectation	Regime of historicity
Sack of Rome by the Goths in 410			
410–412: Some pagans (Augustine, *Sermones* 81 and 105) and Volusianus (Marcellinus in Augustine, *Ep.* 136.2)	Eternal power of the pagan *Urbs* and Sack of 410 during the *tempora Christiana*	Waiting for the restoration of pagan cults	Pagan reaction in favor of *Roma Aeterna*
410–411: Augustine *Sermones* 81 and 105	Power of the pagan *Urbs* and Sack of 410	Waiting for the religious and moral conversion of the Romans	Ecclesiastical Christian hope and future eschatology
414: Jerome *Ep.* 130 to Demetrias	Power of the pagan *Urbs* and Sack of 410	Waiting for the Romans' ascetic conversion	Terrestrial Christian hope and future eschatology
417: Rutilius Namatianus *De redito suo*	Eternal power of the pagan *Urbs* and Sack of 410	Hope for *renovatio* even after 1200 years of Rome	Cosmic hope for perpetuity and a glorious Roman destiny
417: Orosius *Historiae contra paganos*	Sack of 410. But pagan era was worse for the *Urbs*, while Christian era is better	Christian time will be better for the *Urbs*	Terrestrial Christian triumphalism and future eschatology

(*cont.*)

Table 1 (cont.)

Authors	Space of experience	Horizon of expectation	Regime of historicity
Circa 448: some pagans	End of the power of the *Urbs*	The end of Rome's 1200-year existence	Pagan pessimism in relation to *Fatum*
Sack of Rome by the Vandals in 455			
455: Prosper of Aquitaine: *Chronicon (455)*	End of the terrestrial power of the Caesars' *Urbs*	The Church will be the new universal terrestrial structure with Rome as its spiritual head	Ecclesiastical optimism and future eschatology
End of the *pars occidentalis* in 476/480			
Circa 500: Zosimus *Nea Historia* 5.35.5	Lost power of the *Urbs* due to the end of pagan cults from Constantine to Theodosius	The world is no longer ruled by gods, but by a *daimon*	Pagan pessimism
Sacks of Rome in 536, 546, 547, 549, 552			
Circa 590: Gregory the Great *Homily on Ezechiel* II.6.22–23	Lost power and glory of the *Urbs*	Waiting for a true Christian society	Christian patience and future eschatology

Table 2 *The regimes of historicity in relation to the Roman Empire during the fifth century CE*

Authors	Space of experience	Horizon of expectation	Regime of historicity
	Sack of Rome in 410 by the Goths		
417: Orosius *Historiae contra paganos*	Greatness of the Roman Empire	End of the Roman Empire circa 648 and end of the terrestrial world	Terrestrial Christian triumphalism and future eschatology
Circa 419: Hesychius of Salone (Augustine, *Ep.* 198)	End of the Roman Empire	Waiting for the imminent end of the world	Imminent eschatology
Circa 419: Augustine of Hippo *Ep.* 199	The military situation is not as bad as under Gallian	The Roman Empire could survive	Future eschatology
Theodosian dynasty	Greatness of the Roman Christian Empire	Perpetuation of the Roman Empire (425: Valentinian III; 438: Theodosian Code)	Christian imperial optimism (Theodosian ideology)
Circa 430: Eucherius of Lyon *De contemptu mundi*	The world is old and dying	Waiting for the imminent end of the world	Ascetic pessimism and imminent eschatology
	439: Fall of Carthago by the Vandals		
Circa 440: Salvianus of Marseille *De gubernatione Dei*	Destruction of the Roman Empire by pagan or heretical, but morally superior barbarians	End of the Roman Empire	Ascetic pessimism
Circa 450: Quodvultdeus of Carthago *Liber promissionum et praedictorum Dei*	Destruction of the Roman Empire by heretical barbarians	Waiting for the imminent end of the world	Future eschatology (less than one century)
456–468: Sidonius Apollinaris *Carmina* 2, 5, 7	Greatness of the Roman Empire	*Renovatio* of Rome by a new emperor	Imperial optimism
Circa 468: Hydatius of Chaves	Destruction of the Roman		Imminent eschatology

(*cont.*)

Table 2 (cont.)

Authors	Space of experience	Horizon of expectation	Regime of historicity
Cronica	Empire by heretical barbarians	Waiting for the imminent end of the world	
Circa 474: Sidonius Apollinaris *Ep.* V, 16.4	Greatness of the Roman Empire	Hope for the consulate for his son	Imperial optimism
End of the *pars occidentalis* in 476/480			
Barbarian kings 476–533	The Roman Empire (*Romania*) still exists in the East	Good relations with the Roman Empire	Caution and fear of the Roman Empire
Romans of Constantinople (480–552)	The Roman Empire (*Romania*) still exists in the East and is going to reconquer the West	Rebirth of a unified Christian orthodox Roman Empire	Christian imperial optimism (Theodosian ideology)

Table 3 *The regimes of historicity in relation to the Christianization of the world (linked to Rome or to Roman Empire) during the fifth century CE*

Authors	Space of experience	Horizon of expectation	Regime of historicity
401–402: Rufinus of Aquileia *Historia ecclesiastica*	Some foreign peoples are converted to Christianity by Romans	Christianization of other foreign peoples	Theodosian Christian and imperial optimism
417: Orosius *Historiae contra paganos* 7.41.8	Foreign invaders are converted to Christianity	Coexistence of Roman and barbarian Christians in the Theodosian Empire	Theodosian Christian and Roman imperial optimism
Circa 417: Augustine of Hippo *Ep.* 197	Christianity is not known everywhere	Possible Christianization of foreign peoples in one or two generations	Future eschatology
Circa 419: Hesychius of Salone (Augustine, *Ep.* 198.6)	Christianity is known everywhere	Waiting for an imminent end of the world	Imminent eschatology
Circa 419: Augustine of Hippo *Ep.* 199.46	Christianity is not known everywhere outside the Roman Empire (e.g. African tribes)	Christianization of foreign peoples	Future eschatology
Circa 430: Eucherius of Lyon *De contemptu mundi*	Christianity is known everywhere in the Roman Empire	Waiting for an imminent end of the world	Ascetic pessimism and imminent eschatology
Circa 450: Prosper of Aquitaine *De uocatione omnium gentium*	End of the terrestrial greatness of the imperial *Urbs*, but spiritual greatness of the See of St Peter	Hope for the Christianization of foreign peoples	Christian pontifical optimism Future eschatology

(*cont.*)

Table 3 (cont.)

Authors	Space of experience	Horizon of expectation	Regime of historicity
	End of the *pars occidenta lis* in 476/480		
	Justinianic wars in the West (533–552)		
Gregory the Great (590–604)	Destruction or conversion of the Homean barbarian kingdoms of Africa, Italy, and Spain	Christianization of foreign peoples (like the Anglos in 598)	Christian pontifical optimism Future eschatology

Text 1 *Rutilius Namatianus*, De redito suo (On his return, 417–418 CE); Translation by J. Wight Duff and Arnold M. Duff (1935)

119–146

Abscondat tristem deleta iniuria casum;
contemptus solidet uulnera clausa dolor.
Aduersis solemne tuis sperare secunda;
exemplo caeli ditia damna subis.
Astrorum flammae renouant occisabus ortus;
lunam finiri cernis ut incipiat.
Victoris Brenni non distulit Allia poenam;
Samnis seruitio foedera saeua luit.
Post multas Pyrrhum clades superata fugasti;
fleuit successus Hannibal ipse suos.
Quae mergi nequeunt, nisu maiore resurgunt
exiliuntque imis altius acta uadis.
Vtque nouas uires fax inclinata resumit,
clarior ex humili sorte superna petis.
Porrige uicturas Romana in saecula leges
solaque fatales non uereare colos,
quamuis sedecies denis et mille peractis
annus praeterea iam tibi nonus eat.
Quae restant nullis obnoxia tempora metis,
dum stabunt terrae, dum polus astra feret.
Illud te reparat quod cetera regna resoluit:
ordo renascendi est crescere posse malis.
Ergo age, sacrilegae tandem cadat hostia gentis:
summittant trepidi perfida colla Getae.
Ditia pacatae dent uectigalia terrae;
impleat augustos barbara praeda sinus.
Aeternum tibi Rhenus aret, tibi Nilus inundet,
Altricemque suam fertilis orbis alat.

Let forgetfulness of thy wrongs bury the sadness of misfortune;
let pain disregarded close and heal thy wounds.
Admist failure it is thy way to hope for prosperity:
after the pattern of the heavens losses undergone enrich thee.
For flaming stars set only to renew their rising
thou seest the moon wane to wax afresh.
The Allia did not hinder Brennus' penalty;
The Samnit paid for a cruel treaty by slavery
after many disasters, though defeated, thou didst put Pyrrhus to flight
Hannibal himself was the mourner of his own successes.
Things which cannot be sunk rise again with greater energy,
sped higher in their rebound from lowest depths
and, as the torch held downward regains fresh strenght,
So from lowly fortune thou dost soar more radiant aloft.
Spread forth the laws that are to last througough the ages of Rome;
Alone you needst not dread the distaffs of the Fates,
though with a thousand years and sixteen decades overpast,
thou hast besides a ninth year in its course.
The span which doth remain is subject to non bounds,
so long as earth shall stand firm and heaven uphold the stars!
That same thing builds the up which wrecks all other realms:
the law of thy new birth is the power to thrive upon thine ills.
Come, then, let an impious race fall in sacrifice at last:
let the Goths in panic abase their forsworn necks.
Get land reduced to peace pay rich tribute
and barbarian booty fill the majestic lap.
Evermore let the Rhineland plough for thee, for thee the Nile overflow
and let a teeming world give nurture to its nurse.

Text 2 *Orosius*, Historiae adversus paganos (Histories against pagans, 417–418 CE); Translation by A. T. Fear (2010)

2.3.2. Ita Babylon, post annos MCLX et propemodum quattuor quam condida erat, a Medis et Arbato, rege eorum, praefecto autem suo, spoliata opibus et regno atque ipso rege priuata est; ipsa tamen posteo aliquamdiu mansit incolumis.

2.3.3. Similiter et Roma post annos totidem, hoc est MCLX et fere quattuor, a Gothis et Alarico rege eorum, comite autem suo, inrupta et opibus spoliata non regno, manet adhuc et regnat incolumis.

2.3.4. quamvis in tantum arcanis statutis inter utramque urbem conuenientiae totius ordo seruatus sit ut et ibi praefestus eius Arbatus regnum inuaserit, et hic praefectus eius Attalus regnare temptarit, tametsi apud hanc solam merito Christiani imperatoris ademptatio prafana uacuata sit. [. . .]

6. Ecce similis Babyloniae ortus et Romae, similis potentia, similis magnitudo, similia tempora, similia bona, similia mala, tamen non similis exitus similisue defectus. Illa enim regnum amisit, haec retinet; illa interfectione regis orbata, haec incolumi imperatore, secura est.

7.2.9. Regnum Cartaginiense a conditione usque ad euersionem eius, paulo amplius quam septingentis annis stetit, aeque regnum Macedonicum a Carano usque ad Persem paulo minus quam settingentis. [. . .]

2.3.2. Almost 1164 years after its foundation, Babylon was stripped of its wealth, and had its kingdom and its own king taken from it by the Medes and Arbatus, who was king of the Medes and also gouvernor of Babylon. Nevertheless, the city itself remained unscathed for sometimes after this.

2.3.3. Similarly, Rome after the same number of years, namely almost 1164, was stormed by the Goths and Alaric, who was their king and a Count of the City. She was stripped of her wealth, but not her kingdom, for she still remains and rules in safety.

2.3.4. Nevertheless, the order of all these parallels between the two cities, which was brought about by mystic decree, has been kept to this degree: that there the prefect Arbatus invaded the kingdom, and here the City's prefect, Attalus, tried to become its ruler, but here, unlike at Babylon, because of the merits of our Christian ruler, Attalus's attempt was made in vain and came to nothing. [. . .]

6. Behold, how Babylon and Rome had a similar beginning, similar power, a similar size, a similar age, similar goods and similar evils, but their ends and decline are not similar. Babylon lost her kingdom, Rome retains hers. Babylon was left an orphan on the death of her king, Rome is secure and her emperor safe.

7.2.9. The kingdom of Carthage stood a little over 700 years from its foundation to its destruction. Equally, the kingdom of Macedon lasted a little less than 700 years from the reign of Caranus to that of Perseus. [. . .]

7.2.12. Poteram quoque ostendere eundem duplicatum numerum mansisse Babyloniae quae post mille quadragentos et quod excurrit annos ultime a Cyro rege capta est, nisi praesentium contemplatione reuocarer.

7.43.5. Se inprimis ardenter inhiasse, ut, oblitterato Romano nomine, Romanum omne solum Gotthorum imperium et faceret et uocaret, essetque, ut uulgariter loquar, Gothia quod Romania fuisset. [...]

7.43.6. elegisse saltim ut gloriam sibi de restituendo in integrum augendoque Romano nomine Gothorum uiribus quaereret habareturque apud posteros Romanae restitutionis auctor, postquam esse non putuerat immutator.

7.2.12. Were I not recalled by consideration of the present, I could demonstrate that Babylon lasted for twice this number of years, when she was finally captured by Cyrus, after existing a little more than 1400 years.

7.43.5. At first, he (*Athaulf*) earnestly had wanted to obliterate the name of Rome and makes the Romans' land the Goths' empire in both word and deed, so that there would have been, to put it in everyday speech, a Gothia where there had once been Romania. [...]

7.43.6. He chose at least the seek fot himself the glory of having restored and extended the Roman empire by the might of his Goths and, since he could not be her suppplanter, to be remembered by posterity as the author of Rome' renewal.

Appendix

Text 3 *Hesychius of Salona, Letter 198 to Augustine (c. 419 CE); Translation by Roland Teske (2004)*

5. Quod autem nemo possit temporum mensuras colligere manifestum est. Euangelium quidem dixit: *De die et hora nemo scit*, ego autem pro impossibilitate intellectus mei dico neque diem neque mensem neque annum aduentus ipsius sciri posse; sed signa quae sunt aduentus uiuendo et credendo et expectare me conuenit et credentibus escam hanc retribuere, ut expectantes diligant aduentum eius, qui dixit: *Hae omnia cum uideritis, scitote, quoniam prope est inianuis*. Signa ergo euangelica et prophetica, quae in nobis completa sunt, aduentum domini manifestant. Nam frustra, aut qui quaerunt aut qui calumniantur, dies et annos in computo comprehendere quaerunt, cum scriptum sit, quia: *Et nisi adbreuiati fuissent dies illi, non fieret salua omnis caro; sed propter electos breuiabuntur dies illi*. Certum est tempus carere computum, quod breuiandum est a domino, qui tempora constituit; adpropinquasse autem aduentum, cuius signa aduentus aliqua uidimus ex his, quae facta sunt, esse completa. Et iterum dicit: *His autem fieri incipientibus respirabitis et leuabitis capita uestra, quoniam adpropriabit redemptio uestra*. Quae autem signa dixit uiuenda, manifestum in euangelio sancti Lucae: *Et Hierusalem calcabitur a gentibus, donec impleantur tempora gentium*. Hoc factum est et fieri nulli dubium est. Et insequitur: *Et erunt signa in sole, in luna, in stellis et in terra pressura gentium*. Ea, quae patimur, confiteri et poena compellit, si forte non curet uoluntas; nam in uno tempore et signa in caelo et pressuram gentium in terris ab hominibus uideri et sustineri manifestum est. Et insequitur: *Arescentibus hominibus prae timore et expectatione, quae super ueniunt uniuerso orbi*. Nullam patriam, nullum locum nostris temporibus non affligi aut humiliari certum est, sicut dictum est: *prae timore et expectatione, quae super*

5. But it is clear that no one can calculate the periods of times. The Gospel certainly says *No one knows the day or the hour* (Mt 24:36; Mk 13:32). But, taking into account the inability of my intellect, I say that neither the day nor the month nor the year of this coming can be known. But by seeing and believing signs of his coming it is right that I wait for it and distribute this food to believers so that they may await and long for his coming. For he said, *When you see all these things, know that he is near the gates* (Mt 24:33). Hence the signs in the gospel and in the prophets that have been fulfilled among us reveal the coming of the Lord. For in vain do either those who seek them or those who criticize them seek to calculate the days and the tears, because scripture says, *And if thoses days were not cut short, no flesh would be saved, but those days will be shortened on account of the elect* (Mt 24:22; Mk 13:20). It is certain that the time cannot be calculated that the Lord, who has established all times, will shorten, but it is certain his coming has drawn near. For we see from events that have occurred that some signs of his coming have been realised. And again, he says, *But when these events begin to come about, you will take a breath and lift up your heads, because your redemption has drawn near* (Lk 21:28). What signs he said that they would see are clear in the Gospel of Saint Luke, *And Jerusalem will be trod upon by Gentiles until the time of the Gentiles has been completed* (Lk 21:24). This has been done, and no one doubts that it is being done. And there follows, *And there will be signs in the sun and the moon and in the stars, and on earth the consternation of the nations* (Lk 21:25). The sufferings and chastisement that we endure compels us to admit it, even if the will perhaps doe not want to. For it is clear that at the same time people saw signs in the sky and endured

(cont.)

Text 3 (cont.)

ueniunt uniuerso orbi, et omnia signa, quae superius euangelium legentibus manifestat, ex maxima parte completa est.

6. Quod autem dictum est: *Et praedicabitur hoc euangelium in uniuerso mundo et tunc ueniet finis*, prius quod ipsius domini repromissio talis fuit, ut ipsi apostoli eius nomini et resurrectionis textes fierent *in Hierusalem et in Iudaeam et in Samariam et usque ad extremum terrae*, et apostolus hac auctoritate docet: *Sed dico, numquid non audierunt? in omnem terram exiuit sonus eorum et in fines orbis terrae uerba eorum*. Item: *Propter spem, quae reposita est uobis, quam ante audistis in uerbo euangelii, quod aduenit in uos, sicut et in omni mundo est fructificans et crescens*. Sed apostolis initiata fides in gentibus habuit multos persecutores, ut retenda tardius inualesceret, ut illus impleretur: *Ante haec omnia primum in uos manus inmittent suas et persequentur et tradent uos in synagogas et in custodias ducentes ad reges et ad praesides propter nomen meum*, ut illud impleretur, quod scriptum erat: *Et uelociter reaedeficaberis, quibus destructa es*. Nam ex quo clementissimi imperatores Christiani dei uoluntate esse coeperunt, quicquid paulatim fides, causa persecutionis, crescebat in saeculis, factis regibus Christinis ubique in paruo tempore euangelium Christi penetrauit.

the consternation of the nations on earth. And there follows, *As human beings wither away out of fear and in expectation of what is coming upon the whole world* (Lk 21:26). It is certain that no country, no place is not afflicted and brought low in our times, as scripture says, *out of fear and in expectation of what is coming upon the whole world*, and all the signs that the gospel discloses above to the readers have been for the most part realized.

6. But it is said, *And this gospel will be preached in all the world, and then the end will come* (Mt 24:14), first, because it was the promise of the Lord himself that the apostles could be his witnesses *in Jerusalem and in Judea and in Samaria and to the end of the world* (Acts 1:8), and the apostle teaches on the basis of this authority, *But I say, Have they not heard? Their voice has gone out to the whole world and their words to the end of the earth.* (Rom 10:18; Ps 19:5) He likewise teaches, *On account of the hope that has been stored up for you, of which you heard before in the word of the truth, that is, of the gospel that has to come to you, bearing fruit and increasing, as it is in all the world* (Col. 1:5–6). But the faith preached among the nations by the apostles had many persecutors so that it was held back and grew strong slowly; thus the words of scripture were fullfilled, *Before all these things, they will lay hands upon you and persecute you and hand you over to their synagogues and prisons, taking you before kings and gouvernors, on account of my name* (Lk 21:12). Thus were these words also fulfilled, "And you will quickly be rebuilt by those who destroyed you." For from the time when the most merciful emperors became Christian by God's will, however slowly the faith grew in the world on account of persecution, once the emperors became Christians the gospel of Christ spread everywhere in a short time.

Text 4 *Augustine of Hippo to Hesychius, Letter 199 (c. 419 CE); Translation by Roland Teske (2004)*

34. But as for the signs in heaven and on earth, have we seen greater ones than they saw who lived before us? If we read the history of the nations, do we no find that such great wonders were produced in heaven and on earth that some of them are not even believed?

35. When, however, has the earth not been devastated by wars at different times and in different places? For, to pass over the most ancient wars, under the emperor Gallienus, when the barbarians spread everywhere through the Roman provinces, how many of our brothers living in the flesh at that time do we suppose could have believed that the end was near, because that occured long after the ascension of the Lord!

46. I do not know yet whether in regard to this present question we could discern something more certain, if we were able to use reason or ability, than I already quoted in the earlier letter about when the whole world will have the gospel preached to it. For I have established by certain proofs that what Your Reverence thinks was already accomplished by the apostles is not the case. For there are among us, that is, in Africa, countless barbarian nations where the gospel has not yet been preached; it is easy for us to learn this every day from those who are taken captive from them and are now among the slaves of the Romans. Yet it was only a few years ago that certain of them, very exceptional ones and few in number, were pacified and became part of the Roman territories, so that they do not have their own kings but have governors set over them by the Roman empire, and they and their governors began to be Christian. But those who are further inland and are not under Roman power have no contact with the Christian religion in any of their people, and yet, it is by no means correct to say that God's promise does not pertain to them.

34. Signa uero de caelo et terra numquid maiora nos uidimus, quam qui fuerunt ante nos? Nonne, si gentium legatur historia, tanta mira reperiuntur extitisse de caelo terraque, ut aliqua etiam non credantur?

35. Bellis autem per diuersa interualla temporum et locorum quando non terra contrita est? nam, ut nimis antiqua praeteream, sub imperatore Gallieno, cum Romanas prouincias barbaries usque quaque peruaderet, quam multos fratres nostros, qui tunc erant in carne, putamus propinquium finem credere potuisse, quoniam longe post ascensionem domini factum est!

46. Nescio tamen, utrum intueri aliquid certius in hac quaestione possemus, si ulla ratione seu facultate possemus, quam illud, quod in epistula priore iam posui, quando euangelio mundus uniuersus impleatur. Quod enim putat uenerabilitas tua iam hoc per ipsos apostolos factum, non ita esse certis documentis probaui. Sunt enim apud nos, hoc est in Africa barbarae innumerabiles gentes, in quibus nondum esse praedictum euangelium ex his, qui ducuntur inde captiui et Romanorum seruitiis iam miscentur, cotidie nobis addiscere in promptu est. Pauci tamen anni sunt, ex quo quidam eorum rarissimi atque paucissimi, qui pacati Romanis finibus adhaerent, ita ut non habeant reges suos, sed super eos prafecti a Romano constituantur imperio, et illi ipsi eorum praefecti Christiani esse coeperunt. Interiores autem, qui sub nulla sunt potestate Romana, prorsus nec religione Christiana in suorum aliquibus detinentur neque ullo modo recte dici potest istos ad promissionem dei non pertinere.

47. Non enim Romanos sed omnes gentes dominus semini Abrahae media quoque iuratione promisit. Ex qua promissione iam factum est, ut nonnullae gentes, quae non tenentur dicione Romana, reciperent euangelium et adiungerentur ecclesiae, quae fructificat et crescit in uniuerso mundo [...]

Propheta autem dicit: *Et adorabunt eum unusquisque de loco suo, omnes insulae gentium*. Omnes insulae dixit, tanquam diceret etiam omnes insulae hinc ostendens, quam nulla relinquintur insularum, quarum nonnullae etiam in Oceano sunt constitutae et quasdam earum euangelium iam suscepisse didicimus. Atque ita et in insulis singulis quibusque impletur, quod dictum est: *Dominabitur a mari usque ad mare*, quo unaquaeque insula cingitur, sicut in uniuerso orbe terrarum, quae tamquam omnium quodam modo maxima est insula, quia et ipsam cingit Oceanus, ad cuius littora in occidentalibus partibus ecclesiam peruenisse iam nouimus et, quocumque mitrorum eius nondum peruenit, peruentura est utique fructificando atque crescendo.

51. Si ergo latet, quando ecclesia fructificante atque crescente uniuersus omnino *a mari usque ad mare orbis* implebitur, procul dubio latet, quando finis erit; ante, quippe non erit.

47. For, by means of an oath the Lord also promised not the Romans, but all nations of the offspring of Abraham. Because of that promise it has already come about that some nations that are non subject to Roman rule have received the gospel, and have been united to the Church, which is bearing fruit and increases in the whole world. [...]

The prophet, however, says, *And they will worship him, each from his own place, all the islands of the nations* (Zep 2:11). He said "all the islands", as if to say "even all the islands", showing from this that there will be no land left where the Church does not exist, since no island will be left. Some of them are located in the Ocean, and we have learned that some of them have already received the gospel. And so even in each individual island there are being fulfilled the words, *He will have dominion from sea to sea* (Ps. 72:8), the sea by which each island is girt. It is the same way in the whole world, which is in a sense like the largest islands of all because Ocean girds it. And we know that the Church has arrived in the West at its shores, and to whatever shores of it she has not come, she will come as she bears fruit and increases.

51. If, then we do not know when, as the Church bears fruit and increases, the whole world will be absolutely filled *from sea to sea*, we undoubtedly do not know when the end will be; it will, of course, not be before that.

Text 5 *Sidonius Apollinaris*, Carmen 7 *(Panegyric of Avitus, January 1, 456 CE) and* Carmen 5 *(Panegyric of Majorian, December 458 CE); Translation by W. B. Anderson (1936)*

Carmen 7, 51–56
Testor, sancte parens, inquit, te, numen et illud
quiquid Roma fui, summo satis obruta fato
inuideo abiectis: pondus non sustinet ampli
culminis arta domus nec fulmen uallibus instat
Quid, rogo, bis seno mihi uultures Tuscus aruspex
Portendit?

Carmen 7, 357–361
Iam prope fata tui bis sena uulturis alas
Complebant (scis namque tuos, scis Roma, labores)
Aetium Placidus mactauit semiuir amens;
Uixque tuo impositum capiti diadema, Petroni,
ilico barbaries

Carmen 7, 595–598
Laetior at tanto modo principe, prisca deorum,
Roma, parens, attole genas ac turpe ueternum
depone; en princeps faciet iuuenescere maior,
quam pueri fecere senem

Carmen 5, 586–602
Cum uictor scandere currum
incipies crinemque sacrum tibi more priorum
nectet muralis, uallaris, ciuica laurus
et regum aspicient Capitolia fulua catenas,

Poem 7, 51–56
O holy Father, I call thee to witness, thee and the divine power I, Rome, owned: wholly overwhelmed by my exalted fortune, I envy the very outcast: a narrow house has not a spacious roof to support, and the lowly vales are not harassed by the lightning. What, pray, did the Tuscan seer foretell for me from the twelve vultures?

Poem 7, 357–361
Now destiny was well-nigh bringing to fulfilment the sign of the twelve flying vultures (thou knowest, O Rome, thou knowest all thy troubles) Placidus (*Valentinian III*), the mad eunuch, slaughtered Aëtius. Scarce was the diadem set on the head of Petronius when all at once came barbarians

Poem 7, 595–598
But now be of good cheer with such a man for Emperor, O Rome, ancient mother of gods; lift up thine eyes and cast off thine unseemly gloom. Lo! a prince of riper years shall bring back youth to thee, whom child-princes have made old

Poem 5, 586–602
When you shall step into the victor's chariot
and after the manner of our forefathers the mural, castrensian and civic crowns shall entwine thy sacred hair,
and the golden Capitol shall behold kings in chains;

cum uesties Romam spoliis, cum diuite cera
pinges Cyniphii captiua mapalia Bocchi,
ipse per obstantes populos raucosque fragores
praecedam et tenui, sicut nunc, carmine dicam
te geminas Alpes, te Syrtes, te mare magnum,
te freta, te Libycas pariter domuisse cateruas

when thou shalt clothe Rome with spoils and shalt depict in costly wax the
captured huts of some of African Bocchus,
then I myself will walk before thee amid the obstructing throngs and the clamour
of hoarse shouts, and in my puny strain, as now, I will tell how thou hast
subdued two Alpines ranges, the Syrtes, the Great Sea, the narrower waters and
the Libyan hordes

Bibliography

Achard, G. 1981. *Pratique rhétorique et idéologie politique dans les discours "optimates" de Ciceron*. Leiden: Brill.
Achtemeier, P. 1996. *1 Peter*. Minneapolis: Augsburg Fortress.
Alexander, P. S. 2003. "The Evil Empire: The Qumran Eschatological War Cycle and the Origins of Jewish Opposition to Rome," in S. M. Paul et al. (eds.), *Emanuel: Studies in Hebrew Bible, Septuagint, and Dead Sea Scrolls in Honor of Emanuel Tov*. Leiden: Brill. 17–31.
Alon, G. 1977. "Rabban Johanan B. Zakkai's Removal to Jabneh," in *Jews, Judaism and the Classical World: Studies in Jewish history in the Times of the Second Temple and Talmud*, tr. by I. Abrahams. Jerusalem: Hebrew University Magnes Press. 269–313.
Alonso-Núñez, J. M. 1983. "Die Abfolge der Weltreiche bei Polybios und Dionysos von Halikarnassos," *Historia* 32 (4): 411–26.
  1989. "Aemilius Sura," *Latomus* 48 (1): 110–19.
Amusin, J. D. 1977. "The Reflection of Historical Events of the First Century B.C. in Qumran Commentaries (4Q161; 4Q169; 4Q166)," *Hebrew Union College Annual* 48: 123–52.
Ando, C. 2008. *The Matter of the Gods. Religion and the Roman Empire*. Berkeley: University of California Press.
  2010. "The Ontology of Religious Institutions," *History of Religions* 50(1): 54–79.
Astin, A. E. 1967. *Scipio Aemilianus*. Oxford University Press.
Atkins, J. W. 2013. *Cicero on Politics and the Limits of Reason: The Republic and Laws*. Cambridge University Press.
Atkinson, K. M. T. 1959. "The Historical Setting of the Habakkuk Commentary," *Journal of Semitic Studies* 4(3): 238–63.
  1999. "On the Herodian Origin of Militant Davidic Messianism," *Journal of Biblical Literature* 118(3): 435–60.
Aune, D. 1997. *Revelation. Word Biblical Commentary 52A-C*. Nashville: Thomas Nelson.
Babut, D. 1969. *Plutarque et le Stoïcisme*. Paris: PUF.
Baer, Y. 1971. "Jerusalem in the Times of the Great Revolt," *Zion* 36(3/4):127–190 (in Heb.).

Bandy, A. S. 2009. "The Layers of the Apocalypse: An Integrative Approach to Revelation's Macrostructure," *Journal of the Study of the New Testament* 31(4): 469–99.
Barker, M. 2000. *The Revelation of Jesus Christ*. Edinburgh: T&T Clark.
Barnes, T. D. 1981. *Constantine and Eusebius*. Cambridge, Mass.: Harvard University Press.
  2011. *Constantine: Dynasty, Religion and Power in the Later Roman Empire*. Malden, Mass. and Oxford: Wiley-Blackwell.
Baronowski, D. W. 2011. *Polybius and Roman Imperialism*. London: Bristol Classical Press.
Barrett, J. C. 1993. "Chronologies of remembrance: the interpretation of Roman inscriptions," *World Archaeology* 25(2): 236–47.
Barthèlemy, D. and Milik, J. T. 1955. "Livre Des Mistères," in *Discoveries in the Judean Desert, I: Qumran Cave I*. Oxford University Press. 102–7.
Bauckham, R. 1993. *The Theology of the Book of Revelation*. Cambridge University Press.
  1995. "The Messianic Interpretation of Isa. 10:34 in the Dead Sea Scrolls, 2 Baruch and the Preaching of John the Baptist," *Dead Sea Discoveries* 2(2): 202–16.
Beale, G. K. 1999. *The Book of Revelation: A Commentary on the Greek Text*. Grand Rapids: Eerdmans.
Beard, M. 1985. "Writing and Ritual. A Study of Diversity and Expansion in the Arval Acta," *Papers of the British School at Rome* 40: 114–62.
  1986. "Cicero on Divination: The Formation of a Latin Discourse," *Journal of Roman Studies* 76: 33–46.
  1989. "Acca Laurentia Gains a Son. Myths and Priesthood at Rome," in M. M. MacKenzie and C. Roueché (eds.), *Images of Authority. Papers Presented to Joyce Reynolds on the Occasion of her Seventieth Birthday*. Cambridge Philological Society. 41–61.
  1990. "Priesthood in the Roman Republic," in M. Beard and J. North (eds.), *Pagan Priests*. London: Duckworth. 17–48.
  1991. "Writing and Religion: Ancient Literacy and the Function of the Written Word in Roman Religion," in J. H. Humphrey (ed.), *Literacy in the Roman World*. Ann Arbor: University of Michigan Press. 35–58.
  1994. "The Roman and the Foreign. The Cult of the "Great Mother" in Imperial Rome," in N. Thomas and C. Humphrey (eds.), *Shamanism, History and the State*. Ann Arbor: University of Michigan Press. 164–90.
  2007. "Writing and Religion," in S. I. Johnston (ed.), *Ancient Religions*. Cambridge, Mass.: Belknap Press of Harvard University Press. 127–38.
Beck, H. 2011. "Consular Power and the Roman Constitution: The Case of Imperium Reconsidered," in H. Beck et al. (eds.), *Consuls and Res Publica: Holding High Office in the Roman Republic*. Cambridge University Press. 77–96.
Beltrán Lloris, F. 2014. "The 'Epigraphic Habit' in the Roman World," in C. Bruun and J. Edmondson (eds.), *Oxford Handbook of Roman Epigraphy*. Oxford University Press. 131–48.

Ben Shahar, M. 2017. "The Prediction to Vespasian," in T. Ilan and V. Noam (eds.), *Josephus and the Rabbis*. Jerusalem: Ben-Zvi Institute. 604–44.
Bendlin, A. 1997. "Peripheral Centres – Central Peripheries: Religious Communication in the Roman Empire," in H. Cancik and J. Rüpke (eds.), *Römische Reichsreligion und Provinzialreligion*. Tübingen: Mohr Siebeck. 35–68.
Benko, S. 1980. "Virgil's Fourth Eclogue in Christian Interpretation," *Aufstieg und Niedergang der römischen Welt* 2.31.1: 646–705.
Benoist, S. 2005. *Rome, le prince et la cité*. Paris: Presses universitaires de France.
Bernard, J.-E. 2000. "Philosophie politique et antijudaïsme chez Cicéron," *Scripta Classica Israelica* 19: 113–31.
Bernardi Perini, G. 1999–2000. "Virgilio, il Cristo, la Sibilla. Sulla lettura 'messianica' della quarta egloga," *Atti e memorie dell'Accademia Galileiana di Scienze Lettere ed Arti in Padova* 112: 115–24.
Berrin, S. L. 2004. *The Pesher Nahum Scroll from Qumran: An Exegetical Study*. Leiden: Brill.
  2005. "Pesher Nahum, Psalms of Solomon and Pompey," in E. G. Chazon, M. Dimant, and R. A. Clements (eds.), *Reworking the Bible: Apocryphal and Related Texts at Qumran: Proceedings of a Joint Symposium by the Orion Center for the Study of the Dead Sea Scrolls and Associated Literature and the Hebrew University Institute for Advanced Studies Research Group on Qumran, 15–17 January, 2002*. Leiden: Brill. 65–84.
Berthelot, K. 2011. "Philo's Perception of the Roman Empire," *Journal for the Study of Judaism* 42(2): 166–87.
  2016. "*The Rabbis Write Back!* L'enjeu de la 'parenté' entre Israël et Rome–Ésaü–Édom," *Revue de l'Histoire des Religions* 234: 165–92.
  2019. "Philo on the Impermanence of Empires," in K. Berthelot and J. Price (eds.), *The Crucible of Empire, The Impact of Roman Citizenship upon Greeks, Jews and Christians, Interdisciplinary Studies in Ancient Culture and Religion* 21. Leuven: Peeters. 1–17.
Berti, E. 1963. *Il De re publica di Cicerone e il pensiero politico classico*. Padua: CEDAM.
Betz, O., Hengel, M. and Haacker, K. (eds.) 1974. *Josephus-Studien: Untersuchungen zu Josephus, dem antiken Judentum und dem Neuen Testament*. Göttingen: Vandenhoeck und Ruprecht.
  1982. *Biblia Patristica: Supplément Philon d'Alexandrie*. Paris: Editions du CNRS.
Bickerman, E. J. 1952. "Origines Gentium," *Classical Philology* 47(2): 65–81.
Bilde, P. 1988. *Flavius Josephus between Jerusalem and Rome*. Sheffield: JSOT.
  1998. "Josephus and Jewish Apocalypticism," in Mason (ed.), 35–61.
Binder, G. 1968. "Eine Polemik des Porphyrios gegen die allegorische Auslegung des Alten Testaments durch die Christen," *Zeitschrift für Papyrologie und Epigraphik* 3: 81–95.
Birley, A. R. 2000. "Two Unidentified Senators in Josephus, *A. J.* 19," *Classical Quarterly* 50(2): 620–23.

Blenkinsopp, J. 2000. *Isaiah 1–39: A New Translation with Introduction and Commentary.* New York: Doubleday.
Bogaert, P. M. 1969. *L'Apocalypse Syriaque de Baruch.* Paris: Editions du Cerf.
Booth, J. (ed.) 2007. *Cicero on the Attack. Invective and Subversion in the Orations and Beyond.* Swansea: Classical Press of Wales.
Bowen, A. and Garnsey, P. (eds.) 2003. *Lactantius: Divine Institutes.* Liverpool University Press.
Boyer, P. 2001. *Religion Explained. The Human Instincts that Fashion Gods, Spirits and Ancestors.* London: Heinemann.
Breed, B., Damon, C. and Rossi, A. (eds.) 2010. *Citizens of Discord: Rome and its Civil Wars.* Oxford University Press.
Brennan, C. 2000. *The Praetorship in the Roman Republic.* Oxford University Press.
Brooke, G. J. 1991. "The Kittim in the Qumran Pesharim," in L. C. A. Alexander (ed.), *Images of Empire.* Sheffield Academic Press. 135–59.
  2015. "The Kittim and Hints of Hybridity in the Dead Sea Scrolls", in M. Laban and O. Lehtipu (eds.), *People under Power: Early Jewish and Christian Responses to the Roman Empire.* Amsterdam University Press. 17–32.
Brownlee, W. H. 1979. *The Midrash Pesher of Habakkuk.* Missoula: Scholars Press.
Bruce, F. F. 1965. "Josephus and Daniel," *Svenska Teologiska Institutet* 4: 148–62.
Buchheit, V. 1990. "Cicero inspiratus Vergilius propheta? Zur Wertung paganer Autoren bei Laktanz," *Hermes* 118: 357–72.
  2002. "Laktanz und seine testimonia Veritatis," *Hermes* 130: 306–15.
Burgess, R. W. 1993. *The Chronicle of Hydatius and the Consularia Constantinopolitana: Two Contemporary Accounts of the Final Years of the Roman Empire.* Oxford: Clarendon Press.
Burkert, W. 1987. "Die antike Stadt als Festgemeinschaft," in P. Hugger, W. Burkert and E. Lichtenhahn (eds.), *Stadt und Fest. Zu Geschichte und Gegenwart europäischer Festkultur.* Unterägeri: W&H Verlags. 25–44.
Bury, J. 1889. *A History of the Later Roman Empire from Arcadius to Irene (395 AD to 800 AD).* London: Macmillan.
Cagnat, R. et al. (eds.) 1901–1927. *Inscriptiones Graecae ad res Romanas pertinentes.* Paris: Leroux (repr. 1964. Rome: "L'Erma" di Bretschneider).
Candou Morón, J. M. 2005. "Polybius and Plutarch on Roman Ethos," in G. Scheppens and J. Bollansée (eds.), *The Shadow of Polybius: Intertextuality as a Research Tool in Greek Historiography.* Leuven: Peeters. 307–28.
Caquot, A. and Philonenko, M. (eds.) 1971. *Hommages à André Dupont-Sommer.* Paris: Adrien-Maisonneuve.
Carroll, M. 2006. *Spirits of the Dead: Roman Funerary Commemoration in Western Europe.* Oxford University Press.
Champion, C. B. 2004. *Cultural Politics in Polybius's Histories.* Berkeley: University of California Press.
  2010. "Timaios (566)," in I. Worthington et al. (eds.), *Brill's New Jacoby.* Brill Reference Online: http://referenceworks.brillonline.com/entries/brill-s-new-jacoby/timaios-566-a566?s.num=37&s.start=20

Champlin, E. 2003. *Nero*. Cambridge, Mass.: Harvard University Press.
    2008. "Tiberius the Wise," *Historia* 57(4): 408–25.
Chaniotis, A. et al. (eds.) 1923–. *Supplementum epigraphicum Graecum*. Leiden: Brill.
Charles, R. H. 1913. *The Apocrypha and Pseudepigrapha of the Old Testament in English*. Oxford: Clarendon Press.
Charlesworth, J. H. et al. 1995. *The Dead Sea Scrolls: Hebrew, Aramaic, and Greek Texts with English Translations. Vol. 2. Damascus Document, War Scroll, and Related Documents*. Tübingen and Louisville: Mohr Siebeck.
    2002. *The Dead Sea Scrolls: Hebrew, Aramaic, and Greek Texts with English Translations. Vol. 6B. Pesharim, Other Commentaries, and Related Documents*. Tübingen and Louisville: Mohr Siebeck.
Clarke, K. 2008. *Making Time for the Past. Local history and the polis*. Oxford University Press.
Clausen, W. 1994. *A Commentary on Virgil, Eclogues*. Oxford: Clarendon Press.
Cohen, G. 1967. "Esau as Symbol in Early Medieval Thought," in A. Altmann (ed.), *Jewish Medieval and Renaissance Studies*. Cambridge, Mass.: Harvard University Press. 19–48.
Cole, S. 2013. *Cicero and the Rise of Deification at Rome*. Cambridge University Press.
Collins, A. Y. 2010. "The Second Temple and the Arts of Resistance," in P. Walters (ed.), *From Judaism to Christianity*. Leiden: Brill. 115–29.
Collins, J. J. 1974a. *The Sibylline Oracles of Egyptian Judaism*. Missoula: Society of Biblical Literature.
    1974b. "The Place of the Fourth Sibyl in the Development of the Jewish Sibyllina," *Journal of Jewish Studies* 25: 365–80.
    1983. "Sibylline Oracles," in J. H. Charlesworth (ed.), *The Old Testament Pseudepigrapha, Vol. 1*. London: Darton, Longman & Todd. 317–472.
    1984. *The Apocalyptic Imagination*. New York: Crossroad.
    2011. "Apocalypse and Empire," *Svensk Exegetisk Aresbokj* 76: 1–19.
Conington, J. and Nettleship, H. 1898. *The Works of Virgil, Vol I: Eclogues and Georgics*, 5th ed. F. Haverfield (rev.). London: Whittaker.
Connerton, P. 1989. *How Societies Remember, Themes in the Social Sciences*. Cambridge University Press.
Cooley, A. E. (ed.) 2002. *Becoming Roman, Writing Latin? Literacy and epigraphy in the Roman West*. Portsmouth, RI: Journal of Roman Archaeology.
    2012. *Cambridge Manual of Latin Epigraphy*. Cambridge University Press.
Corbell, A. 2002. "Ciceronian Invective," in J. May (ed.), *Brill Companion to Cicero Oratory and Rhetoric*. Leiden: Brill. 197–218.
Corbier, M. 2006. *Donner à Voir, Donner à Lire. Mémoire et communication dans la Rome ancienne*. Paris: CNRS Editions.
Courcelle, P. 1957. "Les exégèses chrétiennes de la quatrième églogue," *Revue des Études Anciennes* 59: 294–319 = 1984. *Opuscula Selecta*. Paris: Études Augustiniennes. 156–81.

1964. *Histoire littéraire des grandes invasions germaniques*. 3rd ed. Paris: Études Augustiniennes.
Cowan, R. 2009. "Scanning Iulus: Prosody, Position and Politics in the *Aeneid*," *Vergilius* 55: 3–12.
Crawford, J. W. 1994. *M. Tullius Cicero. The Fragmentary Speeches*. Atlanta: Scholars Press.
Cristofoli, R. 2005. *Costantino e l'Oratio ad Sanctorum Coetum*. Naples: M. D'Auria.
Cucchiarelli, A. 2012. *Publio Virgilio Marone: Le Bucoliche*. Rome: Carocci.
Dauge, Y. A. 1981. *Le Barbare: Récherche sur la conception romaine de la barbarie et de la civilisation*. Bruxelles: Latomus.
De Decker, D. 1978. "Le Discours à l'Assemblée des Saints attribué à Constantin et l'oeuvre de Lactance," in J. Fontaine and M. Perrin (eds.), *Lactance et son temps: Recherches actuelles*. Paris: Beauchesne. 75–89.
De Jonge, M. 1974. "Josephus und die Zukunftserwartungen seines Volkes," in O. Betz, M. Hengel and K. Haacker (eds.), *Josephus-Studien: Untersuchungen zu Josephus, dem antiken Judentum und dem Neuen Testament*. Göttingen: Vandenhoeck und Ruprecht. 205–19.
Deininger, J. 2013. "Die Tyche in der pragmatischen Geschichtsschreibung des Polybios," in V. Grieb and C. Koehn (eds.), *Polybios und seine Historien*. Stuttgart: Franz Steiner Verlag. 71–111.
DePalma Digeser, E. 2000. *The Making of a Christian Empire: Lactantius and Rome*. Ithaca: Cornell University Press.
DeSilva, D. 2009. *Seeing Things John's Way: The Rhetoric of the Book of Revelation*. Louisville: Westminster John Knox.
Dessau, H. 1892–1916. *Inscriptiones Latinae Selectae*. Berlin.
Dewald, C. 2005. *Thucydides' War Narrative: A Structural Study*. Berkeley: University of California Press.
Dimant, D. 2013. "4th Ezra and 2 Baruch in Light of Qumran Literature," in H. Matthias and B. Gabriele (eds.), *Fourth Ezra and Second Baruch: Reconstruction after the Fall*. Leiden: Brill. 31–61.
Dobbin, R. F. 1995. "Julius Caesar in Jupiter's Prophecy, *Aeneid*, Book 1," *Classical Antiquity* 14(1): 5–40.
Doeve, J. W. 1977. "The Flight of Rabban Yohanan ben Zakkai from Jerusalem: When and Why?" in *Übersetzung und Deutung: Studien zu dem Alten Testament und seiner Umwelt Alexander Reinard Hülst gewidmet von Freunden und Kollegen*. Nijkerk: Callenbach. 50–65.
Doignon, J. 1990. "Oracles, prophéties, 'on-dits' sur la chute de Rome (395–410). Les réactions de Jérôme et d'Augustin," *Revue des Études Augustiniennes* 36: 141–3.
Domaszewski, A. von. 1892. "Dislocation des römischen Heeres im Jahre 66 n. Chr. (Josephus *bell. Jud.* 2, 16, 4)," *Rheinisches Museum für Philologie* 47: 207–18.
Dominik, W. J, Garthwaite, J. and Roche, P. A. (eds.) 2009a. *Writing Politics in Imperial Rome*. Leiden and Boston: Brill.

2009b. "Writing Imperial Politics: The Context," in W. J. Dominik, J. Garthwaite and P. A. Roche (eds.), *Writing Politics in Imperial Rome*. Leiden and Boston: Brill. 1–22.

Douglas, M. 2007. *Thinking in Circles: An Essay on Ring Composition*. New Haven: Yale University Press.

Drake, H. A. 2000. *Constantine and the Bishops: the Politics of Intolerance*. Baltimore and London: Johns Hopkins University Press.

Du Quesnay, I. 1977. "Vergil's Fourth Eclogue," in F. Cairns (ed.), *Papers of the Liverpool Latin Seminar 1976*. University of Liverpool. 25–99.

Dubourdieu, A. 1997. "Les sources du Clitumne. De l'utilisation et du classement des sources littéraires," *Cahiers du Centre Gustave Glotz* 8: 131–49.

Dueck, D. 2000. *Strabo of Amaseia. A Greek Man of Letters in Augustan Rome*. London and New York: Routledge.

Duval, Y.-M. 1980. "Les douze siècles de Rome et la fin de l'Empire romain. Histoire et arithmologie," in *Colloque Histoire et historiographie, Caesarodunum 15 bis*. Paris: Les Belles Lettres. 239–54.

Eckstein, A. M. 1995. *Moral Vision in the Histories of Polybius, Hellenistic Culture and Society* 16. Berkeley: University of California Press.

Edwards, D. R. 1996. *Religion and Power: Pagans, Jews and Christians in the Greek East*. Oxford University Press.

Edwards M. J. 1999. "The Constantinian Circle and the Oration to the Saints," in M. J. Edwards, M. Goodman and S. Price (eds.), *Apologetics in the Roman Empire*. Oxford University Press. 251–75.

2003. *Constantine and Christendom*. Liverpool University Press.

Ehrenkrook, J. von 2008. "Sculpture, Space and the Poetics of Idolatry in Josephus' *bellum Judaicum*," *Journal for the Study of Judaism* 39(2): 170–91.

Elgvin, T. 2003. "Qumran and the Roots of the Rosh Hashanah Liturgy," in E. G. Chazon et al. (eds.), *Liturgical Perspectives: Prayer and Poetry in Light of the Dead Sea Scrolls*. Leiden: Brill. 49–67.

2006. "4QMysteries^c: A New Edition," in F. Garcia Martinez, A. Steudel, and E. Tigchelaar (eds.), *From 4QMMT to Resurrections Melanges Qumraniens en homage à Emile Puech*. Leiden: Brill. 75–85.

Erskine, A. 2013. "How to Rule the World: Polybius Book 6 Reconsidered," in B. Gibson and T. Harrison (eds.), *Polybius and His World: Essays in Memory of F.W. Walbank*. Oxford University Press. 231–45.

Eshel, H. 2001. "The Kittim in the War Scroll and in the Pesharim," in D. Goodblatt, A. Pinnick and D. R. Schwarz (eds.), *Historical Perspectives: From the Hasmoneans to Bar Kokhba in Light of the Dead Sea Scrolls*. Leiden: Brill. 29–44.

2008. *The Dead Sea Scrolls and the Hasmonean State*. Grand Rapids and Jerusalem: Ben-Zvi Institute.

Esler, P. F. 1994. "The Social Function of *4 Ezra*," *Journal for the Study of the New Testament* 53: 99–123.

Evans, C. A. 2016. *Pseudepigrapha (New English)*. accordancebible .com: www.accordancebible.com/store/details/?pid=PSEUD-E

Farrell, J. and Nelis, D. (eds.) 2013. *Augustan Poetry and the Roman Republic*. Oxford University Press.
Fauvarque, B. 1994. *Fin de Rome, fin du monde? L'évolution des conceptions eschatologiques de la fin de Rome de Marc Aurèle à Anastase*. Ph.D. Diss., Paris IV-Sorbonne.
Feeney, D. C. 1984. "The Reconciliations of Juno," *Classical Quarterly* 34 (1): 179–94.
  1991. *The Gods in Epic: Poets and Critics of the Classical Tradition*. Oxford: Clarendon Press.
  1998. *Literature and Religion in Rome*. Cambridge University Press.
  2007. *Caesar's Calendar: Ancient Time and the Beginnings of History*. Berkeley: University of California Press.
Fejfer, J. 2008. *Roman Portraits in Context*. Berlin: De Gruyter.
Felder, S. 2002. "What is the Fifth Sibylline Oracle?" *Journal for the Study of Judaism* 33(4): 363–85.
Feldherr, A. 1995. "Ships of State: *Aeneid* V and Augustan Circus Spectacle," *Classical Antiquity* 14(2): 245–65.
  2010. *Playing Gods: The Politics of Ovid's Metamorphoses*. Princeton University Press.
Feldherr, A. and Hardy, G. (eds.) 2011. *The Oxford History of Historical Writing Vol. 1: Beginnings to AD 600*. Oxford University Press.
Feldman, L. H. 1953. "Asinius Pollio and His Jewish Interests," *Transactions of the American Philological Association* 84: 73–80.
  1992. "Some Observations on Rabbinic Reaction to Roman Rule in Third Century Palestine," *Hebrew Union College Annual* 63: 39–81.
Ferrary, J.-L. 1977. "Le discours de Philus (Cicéron, *De re publica*, III, 8–31) et la philosophie de Carnéade." *Revue des Études Latines* 55: 128–56.
  1984. "L'archéologie du *De re publica* (2.2.4–37.63): Cicéron entre Polybe et Platon," *Journal of Roman Studies* 74: 87–97.
  1988. *Philhellénisme et impérialisme. Aspects idéologiques de la conquête romaine du monde hellénistique, de la seconde guerre de Macédoine à la guerre contre Mithridate*. Ecole Française de Rome.
Festugière, A.-J. 1949. *La révélation d'Hermès Trismégiste. II. Le dieu cosmique*. Paris: J. Gabalda.
Fisher, E. 1982. "Greek Translations of Latin Literature in the Fourth Century A. D.," *Yale Classical Studies* 27: 173–215.
Flower, H. 2006. *The Art of Forgetting: Disgrace and Oblivion in Roman Political Culture*. Chapel Hill, NC: University of North Carolina Press.
Flusser, D. 1972. "The Four Empires in the Fourth Sibyl and in the Book of Daniel," *Israel Oriental Studies* 2: 148–75.
  2007a. "Apocalyptic Elements in the War Scroll," in, *Judaism of the Second Temple Period, Vol. I, Qumran and Apocalypticism*, tr. by A. Yadin. Grand Rapids: Eerdmans. 140–58.
  2007b. "The Death of the Wicked King," in, *Judaism of the Second Temple Period, Vol. I, Qumran and Apocalypticism*, tr. by A. Yadin, Grand Rapids: Eerdmans. 159–69.

2007c. "The 'Book of the Mysteries' and the High Holy Days Liturgy," in *Judaism of the Second Temple Period, Vol. I, Qumran and Apocalypticism*, tr. by A. Yadin. Grand Rapids: Eerdmans. 119–39.

2007d. "4QMMT and the Benediction against the Minim," in *Judaism of the Second Temple Period, Vol. I, Qumran and Apocalypticism*, tr. by A. Yadin. Grand Rapids: Eerdmans. 70–118.

Fortenbaugh, W. W. and Schütrumpf, E. (eds.) 2000. *Demetrius of Phalerum. Text, Translation and Discussion*. New Brunswick and London: Transaction Publishers.

Fowler, D. P. 1989. "First Thoughts on Closure: Problems and Prospects", *Materiali e Discussioni* 22: 75–122.

1997. "Second Thoughts on Closure," in D. H. Roberts, F. M. Dunn, and D. P. Fowler (eds.), *Classical Closure*. Princeton University Press. 3–22.

Frazier, F. 2010. "Introduction," in F. Frazier and D. F. Leão (eds.), *Tychè et Pronoia: la marche du monde selon Plutarque, III–XXIII*. Centro de estudios clássicos e humanísticos da Universidade de Coimbra.

Freudenburg, K. 2014. "*Recusatio* as Political Theater: Horace's Letter to Augustus," *Journal of Roman Studies* 104: 105–32.

Gabba, E. 1976–1977. "L'impero romano nel discorso di Agrippa II (Joseph., B, II, 345–401)," *Rivista storica dell'antichità* 6–7: 189–94.

1991. *Dionysius and the History of Archaic Rome*. Berkeley: University of California Press.

Gafni, I. M. 1990. *The Jews of Babylonia in the Talmudic Era: A Social and Cultural History*. Jerusalem: The Zalman Shazar Center.

Galinsky, K. 1988. "The Anger of Aeneas," *American Journal of Philology* 109(3): 321–48.

1996. *Augustan Culture: An Interpretative Introduction*. Princeton University Press.

Gatz, B. 1967. *Weltalter, goldene Zeit und sinnverwandte Vorstellung*. Hildesheim: Olms.

Geffcken, J. 1902. *Die Oracula Sibyllina*. Leipzig: J. C. Hinrichs.

Gell, A. 1992. *The Anthropology of Time: Cultural Constructions of Temporal Maps and Images*. Oxford: Berg.

1998. *Art and Agency: An Anthropological Theory*. Oxford: Clarendon Press.

Geue, T. 2013. "Princeps 'avant la lettre': The Foundations of Augustus in Pre-Augustan Poetry," in M. Labate and G. Rosati (eds.), *La costruzione del mito augusteo*. Heidelberg: Winter. 49–67.

Geymonat, M. 2001. "Un falso cristiano della seconda metà del IV secolo (sui tempi e le motivazioni della Oratio Constantini ad Sanctorum Coetum," *Aevum Antiquum* 1: 349–66.

Gibson, B. and Harrison, T. (eds.) 2013. *Polybius and His World: Essays in Memory of F. W. Walbank*. Oxford University Press.

Girardet, K. M. 1983. *Die Ordnung der Welt: Ein Beitrag zur Philosophischen und Politischen Interpretation von Ciceros Schrift De Legibus*. Wiesbaden: Steiner.

2010. *Der Kaiser und sein Gott: Das Christentum im Denken und in der Religionspolitik Konstantins des Großen*. Berlin: De Gruyter.

2013. *Konstantin: Oratio ad sanctorum coetum / Rede an die Versammlung der Heiligen*. Freiburg: Herder.
Gladhill, C. W. 2012. "Gods, Caesars, and Fate in *Aeneid 1* and *Metamorphoses 15*," *Dictynna* 9: 1–17.
Goins, S. 1993. "Two Aspects of Virgil's Use of Labor in the *Aeneid*," *Classical Journal* 88(4): 375–84.
Goldschmidt, V. 1969 (1953). *Le système stoïcien et l'idée de temps*. Paris: Librairie philosophique J. Vrin.
Goodman, M. 1987. *The Ruling Class of Roman Judaea: The Origins of the Jewish Revolt against Rome, AD 66–70*. Cambridge University Press.
  2007. *Rome and Jerusalem: The Clash of Ancient Civilizations*. London: Allen Lane.
Gordon, R. P. 1992. "Appendix 2: The Interpretation of 'Lebanon' and 4Q285," in G. Vermes, "Qumran Corner: Qumran Publications," *Journal of Jewish Studies* 43(1): 92–94.
Gradel, I. 2002. *Emperor Worship and Roman Religion*. Oxford University Press.
Graham, E.-J. 2006. *The Burial of the Urban Poor in Italy in the Late Roman Republic and Early Empire*. Oxford: Archeopress.
Grethlein, J. 2013. *Experience and Teleology in Ancient Historiography: 'Futures Past' from Herodotus to Augustine*. Cambridge University Press.
Gros, P. 1976. *Aurea Templa. Recherches sur l'architecture religieuse de Rome à l'époque d'Auguste*. École française de Rome.
Gruen, E. S. 1984. *The Hellenistic World and the Coming of Rome*. Berkeley: University of California Press.
  1998. "Jews, Greeks, and Romans in the Third Sibylline Oracle," in M. Goodman (ed.), *Jews in a Graeco-Roman World*. Oxford: Clarendon Press. 15–36.
  2011. "Polybius and Josephus on Rome," in J. Pastor, P. Stern, and M. Mor (eds.), *Flavius Josephus, Interpretation and History*. Supplements to the Journal for the Study of Judaism 146. Leiden: Brill. 149–62.
  2014. "Nero in the Sibylline Oracles," *Scripta Classica Israelica* 32: 87–98.
Guelfucci, M.-R. 2010. "Polybe, la Τύχη et la marche de l'histoire," in F. Frazier and D. F. Leão (eds.), *Tychè et Pronoia: la marche du monde selon Plutarque*. Centro de estudios clássicos e humanísticos da Universidade de Coimbra. 141–167.
Guillaumont, F. 1984. *Philosophe et augure. Recherches sur la théorie cicéronienne de la divination*. Brussels: Latomus.
  2006. *Le De diuinatione de Cicéron et les théories antiques de la divination*. Brussels: Latomus.
Gurtner, D. M. 2009. *Second Baruch: A Critical Edition of the Syriac Text with Greek and Latin Fragments, English Translation, Introduction, and Concordances*. New York: Bloomsbury.
Habitch, C. 1990. *Cicero the Politician*. Baltimore and London: Johns Hopkins University Press.
Hadas, D. 2013. "Christians, Sibyls, and *Eclogue 4*," *Recherches Augustiniennes et Patristiques* 37: 51–129.
Hadas-Lebel, M. 2006. *Jerusalem Against Rome*, tr. by R. Fréchet. Leuven: Peeters.

2012. *Jérusalem contre Rome*. Paris: Cerf – Editions du CNRS.
Hahn, I. 1962. "Zwei dunkle Stellen in Josephus (*Bellum Judaicum* VI § 311 und II § 142)," *Acta Orientalia Academiae Scientiarum Hungaricae* 14: 131–8.
Hannah, R. 2013. "Time in Written Spaces," in G. Sears, P. Keegan and R. Laurence (eds.), *Written Space in the Latin West 200 BC to AD 300*. London & New York: Bloomsbury 83–102.
Hanson, R. P. C. 1973. "The *Oratio ad Sanctos* Attributed to the Emperor Constantine and the Oracle at Daphne," *Journal of Theological Studies* 24: 505–11.
Hardie, P. 1992. *The Epic Successors of Virgil: A Study in the Dynamics of a Tradition*. Cambridge University Press.
  1994. "Augustan Poets and the Mutability of Rome," in A. Powell (ed.), *Roman Poetry and Propaganda in the Age of Augustus*. London: Bristol Classical Press. 59–82.
  1997. "Closure in Latin Epic," in D. H. Roberts, F. M. Dunn and D. P. Fowler (eds.), *Classical Closure*. Princeton University Press. 139–62.
  2006. "Cultural and Historical Narratives in Virgil's Eclogues and Lucretius," in M. Fantuzzi and T. Papanghelis (eds.), *Brill's Companion to Greek and Latin Pastoral*. Leiden: Brill. 275–300.
  2012. *Rumour and Renown: Representations of Fama in Western Literature*. Cambridge University Press.
  2014. *The Last Trojan Hero: A Cultural History of Virgil's Aeneid*. New York: Tauris.
Harrer, G. A. 1918. "Cicero on Peace and War," *Classical Journal* 14(1): 26–38.
Harrison, S. J. 1990. "Some Views of the Aeneid in the Twentieth Century," in S. J. Harrison (ed.), *Oxford Readings in Vergil's Aeneid*. Oxford University Press. 1–20.
Hartog, F. 2012. *Régimes d'historicité: Présentisme et expériences de temps*. Paris.
Hasel, G. F. 1979. "The Four World Empires of Daniel 2 against its Near Eastern Environment," *Journal for the Study of the Old Testament* 12: 17–30.
Hay, P. J. 2017. *Time, Saecularity, and the First Century BC Roman World*. PhD. Dissertation, University of Texas at Austin.
Heikel, I. A. (ed.) 1902. *Eusebius Pamphili, Werke. Vol. 1*. Leipzig: J. C. Hinrichs.
Hejduk, J. 2009. "Jupiter's *Aeneid*: *Fama* and *Imperium*," *Classical Quarterly* 28(2): 279–327.
Henze, M. 2011. *Jewish Apocalypticism in Late First Century Israel*. Tübingen: Mohr Siebeck.
Herchenroeder, L. 2010. *Hellenistic Historiography and the Sciences: Practices and Concepts in Polybius' Histories*, Ph.D. Diss., University of Southern California.
Hinds, S. 1992. "*Arma* in Ovid's *Fasti* 2: Genre, Romulean Rome, and Augustan Ideology," *Arethusa* 25(1): 113–53.
  1998. *Allusion and Intertext: Dynamics of Appropriation in Roman Poetry*. Cambridge University Press.
Hopkins, K. and Beard, M. 2005. *The Colosseum*. London: Profile Books.

Houghton, L. B. T. 2014. "Renaissance and Golden Age Revisited: Virgil's Fourth *Eclogue* in Medici Florence," *Bibliothèque d'Humanisme et Renaissance* 76: 413–32.
  2015. "The Golden Age Returns: Virgil's Fourth *Eclogue* in the Political Panegyric of the Italian Courts," *Journal of the Warburg and Courtauld Institutes* 78: 71–95.
Hughes, J. 2017. *Votive Body Parts in Greek and Roman Religion.* Cambridge University Press.
Inglebert, H. 1996a. *Les Romains chrétiens face à l'histoire de Rome: histoire, christianisme et romanités en Occident dans l'Antiquité tardive (IIIe–Ve siècles).* Paris: Études Augustiniennes.
  1996b. *Interpretatio Christiana. Les mutations des savoirs (cosmographie, géographie, ethnographie, histoire) dans l'Antiquité chrétienne (30–630 ap. J.-C.).* Paris: Études Augustiniennes.
Irmscher, J. 1986. "Sulle origini del concetto Romania," in Università degli studi La Sapienza (ed.), *Da Roma alla Terza Roma III. Popoli e spazio romano tra dirito et profezia.* Naples: Ed. scientifiche italiane. 421–29.
Isaac, B. 2017. "Roma Aeterna," in *Empire and Ideology in the Graeco-Roman World.* Cambridge University Press. 33–44.
Ison, D. J. 1984. *The Constantinian Oration to the Saints: Authorship and Background.* Ph.D. Diss., University of London.
Jal, P. 1963. *La guerre civile à Rome. Étude littéraire et morale.* Paris: PUF.
Japhet, S. 2003. "'Lebanon' in the Transition from Derash to Peshat: Sources, Etymology and Meaning (with Special Attention to the Song of Songs)," in S. M. Paul et al. (eds.), *Emanuel: Studies in Hebrew Bible, Septuagint, and Dead Sea Scrolls in Honor of Emanuel Tov.* Leiden: Brill. 707–24.
Jenkyns, R. 1998. *Virgil's Experience: Nature and History, Times, Names, and Places.* Oxford University Press.
Jones, K. R. 2011. *Jewish Reactions to the Destruction of Jerusalem in A.D. 70.* Leiden: Brill.
Kaden, D. A. 2011. "Flavius Josephus and the '*gentes devictae*' in Roman Imperial Discourse: Hybridity, Mimicry, and Irony in the Agrippa II Speech (Judean War 2.345–402)," *Journal for the Study of Judaism* 42 (4–5): 481–507.
Kalmin, R. 2008. "Sasanian Persian Persecution of the Jews: A Reconsideration of the Evidence," in S. Shaked and A. Netzer (eds.), *Irano-Judaica: Studies Relating to Jewish Contacts with Persian Culture throughout the Ages,* Vol. VI. Jerusalem: Ben-Zvi Institute. 87–122.
Kalmin, R. and Schwartz, D. R. (eds.) 2003. *Jewish Culture and Society Under the Christian Roman Empire.* Leuven: Peeters.
Kany Turpin, J. 2006. *Cicéron, De la divination.* Paris: Garnier Flammarion.
Keegan, P. 2014. *Roles for Men and Women in Roman Epigraphic Culture and Beyond: Gender, Social Identity and Cultural Practice in Private Latin Inscriptions and the Literary Record.* Oxford: Archeopress.
Kelly, A. 2007. "How to End an Orally-Derived Epic Poem," *Transactions of the American Philological Association* 137(2): 371–402.

Kimelman, R. 2005. "Blessing Formulae and Divine Sovereignty in Rabbinic Liturgy," in R. Langer and S. Fine (ed.), *Liturgy in the Life of the Synagogue: Studies in the History of Jewish Prayer*. Winona Lake: Eisenbrauns.

Kister, M. 1998. "Legends of the Destruction of the Second Temple in Avot De-Rabbi Natan," *Tarbiz* 67(4): 484–529 (in Heb.).

2004. "Wisdom Literature and its Relation to Other Genres: From Ben Sira to Mysteries," in J. J. Collins et al. (eds.), *Sapiential Perspectives: Wisdom Literature in Light of the Dead Sea Scrolls*. Leiden: Brill. 13–47.

2009. "Wisdom Literature at Qumran," in *The Qumran Scrolls and Their World, Vol. I*. Jerusalem: Ben-Zvi Institute, 2009. 299–319.

Klawans, J. 2012. *Josephus and the Theologies of Ancient Judaism*. Oxford University Press.

Koortbojian, M. 2013. *The Divinization of Caesar and Augustus: Precedents, Consequences, Implications*. Cambridge University Press.

Koselleck, R. 2004. *Futures Past: On the Semantics of Historical Time*, tr. K. Tribe. New York: MIT Press.

Kowalski, B. 2004. *Die Rezeption des Propheten Ezekiel in der Offenbarung des Johannes*. Stuttgart: Verlag Katholisches Bibelwerk.

Kraus, C. S. 1994. "'No Second Troy': Topoi and Refoundation in Livy, Book V," *Transactions of the American Philological Association* 124: 267–89.

Krauss, S. 1947. *Persia and Rome in the Talmud and the Midrashim*. Jerusalem: Mosad Harav Kook (in Heb.).

Kraybill, J. N. 2010. *Apocalypse and Allegiance: Worship, Politics, and Devotion in the Book of Revelation*. Grand Rapids: Brazos Press.

Kubitschek, W. and Ritterling. E. 1924. "Legio," in *Pauly-Wissowa, Realencyclopädie der classischen Altertumswissenschaft*, II.2. Stuttgart: J. B. Metzler.

Kurfess, A. 1918. "Das Akrostichon Ἰησοῦς Χρειστὸς Θεοῦ Υἱὸς Σωτήρ Σταυρός," *Sokrates* 6: 99–105.

1920. "Vergils vierte Ekloge in Kaiser Konstantins Rede an die Heilige Versammlung," *Sokrates* 8: 90–96.

1936a. "Der griechische Übersetzer von Vergils vierter Ekloge in Kaiser Konstantins Rede an die Versammlung der Heiligen," *Zeitschrift für die Neutestamentliche Wissenschaft* 35: 97–100.

1936b. "Kaiser Konstantin und die Sibylle," *Theological Quarterly* 117: 11–26.

1937. "Die griechische Übersetzung der vierten Ekloge Vergils," *Mnemosyne*, Ser. 3, (5): 283–88.

1950. "Zu Kaiser Konstantins Rede an die Versammlung der Heiligen," *Theological Quarterly* 130: 145–65.

1952. "Kaiser Konstantin und die Erythraische Sibylle," *Zeitschrift für Religions- und Geistesgeschichte* 4: 42–57.

Lamberton, R. 1989. *Homer the Theologian: Neoplatonist Allegorical Reading and the Growth of the Epic Tradition*. Berkeley: University of California Press.

Langer, R. 2012. *Cursing the Christians?: A History of the Birkat HaMinim.* Oxford University Press.
Lanieri, A. (ed.) 2011. *The Western Time of Ancient History: Historiographical Encounters with the Greek and Roman Pasts.* Cambridge University Press.
  (ed.) 2016. *Knowing Future Time in and Through Greek Historiography.* Berlin: De Gruyter.
Lapin, H. 2012. *Rabbis as Romans: The Rabbinic Movement in Palestine, 100–400 CE.* New York: Oxford University Press.
Laurence, R. and Smith, C. 1995–6. "Ritual, time and power in ancient Rome," *Accordia Research Papers* 6: 133–52.
Lauterbach, J. Z. 2004 (1933–1935). *Mekhilta de-Rabbi Ishmael: A Critical Edition, Based on the Manuscripts and Early Editions with an English Translation, Introduction, and Notes.* 2nd ed. Philadelphia: Jewish Publication Society.
Lawrence, J. 1978. "Nero Redivivus," *Fides et Historia* 11: 54–66.
Levi-Strauss, C. 1972. *The Savage Mind.* London: Weidenfeld and Nicolson.
Levick, B. 1999. *Vespasian.* London and New York: Routledge.
Levine, C. 2015. *Forms: Whole, Rhythm, Hierarchy, Network.* Princeton University Press.
Lévy, C. 1984. "La dialectique de Cicéron dans les livres II et IV du *De finibus*." *Revue des Études Latines* 62: 111–27.
  2007. "De la critique de la sympathie à la volonté: Cicéron, *De fato*, 9–11," *Lexis* 25: 17–35.
  2012. "Philosophical Life versus Political Life: An Impossible Choice for Cicero?," in W. Nicgorski (ed.), *Cicero's Practical Philosophy.* Notre Dame, IN: University of Notre Dame Press. 58–79.
Liénard, P. and Boyer, P. 2006. "Whence Collective Rituals? A Cultural Selection Model of Ritualized Behavior," *American Anthropologist* 108(4): 814–27.
Lightfoot, J. L. 2007. *The Sibylline Oracles. With Introduction, Translation, und Commentary on the First and Second Books.* Oxford University Press.
Lim, T. H. 2000. "Kittim," in L. H. Schiffman, and J. C. VanderKam (eds.), *Encyclopedia of the Dead Sea Scrolls, Vol. 1.* New York: Oxford University Press. 469–71.
Luke, T. 2014. *Ushering in a New Republic: Theologies of Arrival at Rome in the First Century BCE.* Ann Arbor: University of Michigan Press.
MacConnell, S. 2014. *Philosophical Life in Cicero's Letters.* Cambridge University Press.
MacCormack S. 1998. *Shadows of Poetry: Vergil in the Mind of Augustine.* Berkeley: University of California Press.
MacMullen, R. 1967. *Enemies of the Roman Order: Treason, Unrest, and Alienation in the Empire.* Cambridge, MA: Harvard University Press.
  1976. *Roman Government's Response to Crisis, A.D. 235–237.* New Haven: Yale University Press.
  1982. "The Epigraphic Habit in the Roman Empire," *American Journal of Philology* 103: 233–46.

Mancini, A. 1894. "La pretesa Oratio Constantini ad sanctorum coetum." *Studi Storici* 3: 92–117, 207–27.
Mankin, D. 1995. *Horace Epodes*. Cambridge University Press.
Maraval, P. (ed.) 2010. *Constantin le Grand: Lettres et discours*. Paris: Cerf.
Marinčič, M. 2001. "Der Weltaltermythos in Catulls Peleus-Epos (c. 64, der kleine Herakles Theokrit id. 24 und der römische 'Messianismus' Vergils)," *Hermes* 129(4): 484–504.
  2002. "Roman Archaeology in Vergil's Arcadia (Vergil Eclogue 4; Aeneid 8; Livy 1.7)," in D. S. Levene and D. P. Nelis (eds.), *Clio and the Poets: Augustan Poetry and the Traditions of Ancient Historiography*. Leiden and Boston: Brill. 143–61.
Marincola, J. 1997. *Authority and Tradition in Ancient Historiography*. Cambridge University Press.
  2001. *Greek Historians*. Oxford University Press.
Mason, S. 1994. "Josephus, Daniel and the Flavian House," in F. Parente and J. Sievers (eds.), *Josephus and the History of the Greco-Roman Period: Essays in Memory of Morton Smith*. Leiden, New York and Köln: Brill. 161–91.
  1998. *Understanding Josephus: Seven Perspectives*. Sheffield Academic Press.
Masters, J. 1992. *Poetry and Civil War in Lucan's Bellum Civile*. Cambridge University Press.
May, J. M. 2002. *Brill's Companion to Cicero: Oratory and Rhetoric*. Leiden.
Meijer, F. 2004. *Emperors Don't Die in Bed*. London: Routledge.
Mendels, D. 1981. "The Five Empires: A Note on a Propagandistic Topos," *The American Journal of Philology* 102(3): 330–7.
Meyer, E. A. 1990. "Explaining the Epigraphic Habit in the Roman Empire: The Evidence of Epitaphs," *Journal of Roman Studies* 80: 74–96.
Michel, A. 1960. *Rhétorique et philosophie chez Cicéron. Essai sur les fondements philosophiques de l'art de persuader*. Paris: Presses Universitaires.
Miles, G. B. 1995. *Livy. Reconstruction Early Rome*. Ithaca: Cornell University Press.
Miller, J. F. 2009. *Apollo, Augustus, and the Poets*. Cambridge University Press.
Miltsios, N. 2013. *The Shaping of Narrative in Polybius*. Berlin: De Gruyter.
Mitchell, T. N. 1991. *Cicero the Senior Statesman*. New Haven: Yale University Press.
Mitchell-Boyask, R. 1996. "*Sine Fine*: Vergil's Masterplot," *American Journal of Philology* 117(2): 289–307.
Moatti, C. 1997. *La raison de Rome*. Paris: Seuil.
  1998. *La mémoire perdue: recherches sur l'administration romaine*. École française de Rome.
Moehring, H. R. 1984. "Joseph ben Matthia and Flavius Josephus: The Jewish Prophet and Roman Historian," in W. Haase (ed.), *Aufstieg und Niedergang der römischen Welt, Vol. II, 21.2*. Berlin and New York: De Gruyter. 864–944.
Momigliano, A. 1977a. "Athens in the Third Century BC and the Discovery of Rome in the Histories of Timaeus of Tauromenium," in *Essays in Ancient and Modern Historiography*. Middletown, CT: Wesleyan University Press. 37–66.

1977b. "Time in Ancient Historiography," in *Essays in Ancient and Modern Historiography*. Middletown, CT: Wesleyan University Press. 179–204.

1980. "Daniele e la teoria greca della successione degli imperi," *Atti della Accademia Nazionale dei Lincei, Classe di Scienze morali, storiche e filologiche. Rendiconti XXXV: 157–62 = 1984. Settimo contributo alla storia degli studi classici e del mondo antico*. Rome: Edizioni di Storia e letteratura. 297–304.

1982. "The Origins of Universal History," *Annali della Scuola Normale Superiore di Pisa. Classe di Lettere e Filosofia*, 12(2): 533–60.

1984. "The Origins of Universal History," in *Settimo contributo alla storia degli studi classici e del mondo antico*. Rome: Edizioni di Storia e letteratura. 77–103.

Mommsen, T. et al. (eds.) 1853–. *Corpus Inscriptionum Latinarum*. Deutsche Akademie der Wissenschaften zu Berlin.

Mouritsen, H. 2005. "Freedmen and Decurions: Epitaphs and Social History in Imperial Italy," *Journal of Roman Studies* 95: 38–63.

Munnich, O. 2011. "La fugacité de la vie humaine (De Josepho §127–147): la place des motifs traditionnels dans l'élaboration de la pensée philonienne," in S. Inowlocki and B. Decharneux (eds.), *Philon d'Alexandrie: un penseur à l'intersection des cultures gréco-romaine, orientale, juive et chrétienne*. Turnhout: Brepols. 163–83.

Muntz, C. E. 2017. *Diodorus Siculus and the World of the Late Roman Republic*. Oxford University Press.

Murphy, F. J. 1985. *The Structure and Meaning of Second Baruch*. Atlanta: Scholars Press.

Naijman, H. 2014. *Losing the Temple and Recovering the Future: An Analysis of 4 Ezra*. Cambridge University Press.

Naiweld, R. 2016. "The Use of Rabbinic Traditions about Rome in the Babylonian Talmud," *Revue de l'Histoire des Religions*, 233 (2): 255–85.

Narducci, E. 2009. *Cicerone, la parola e la politica*. Bari: Laterza.

Ndiaye, E. 2005. "L'étranger barbare à Rome: essai d'analyse sémique." *L'Antiquité classique* 74: 119–35.

Neusner, J. 2008. *Persia and Rome in Classical Judaism*. Lanham, MD: University Press of America.

Newlands, C. E. 1995. *Playing with Time: Ovid and the Fasti*. Ithaca, NY and London: Cornell University Press.

Nicgorski, W. 2016. *Cicero's Skepticism and His Recovery of Political Philosophy*. New York: Palgrave Macmillan.

Nicolet, C. 1988. *L'inventaire du monde. Géographie et politique aux origins de l'Empire*. Paris: Fayard.

Niehoff, M. 2001. *Philo on Jewish Identity and Culture*. Tübingen: Mohr Siebeck.

Nikiprowetzky, V. 1970. *La Troisième Sibylle*. Paris: Mouton.

1971. "La mort d'Éleazar fils de Jaïre et les courant apologétiques dans le De Bello Judaico de Flavius Josèphe," in A. Caquot and M. Philonenko (eds.), *Hommages à André Dupont-Sommer*. Paris: Adrien-Maisonneuve. 461–90.

Nisbet, R. G. M. 1978. "Virgil's Fourth Eclogue: Easterners and Westerners," *Bulletin of the Institute of Classical Studies* 25(1): 59–78. = 1995. in S. J. Harrison (ed.), *Collected Papers on Latin Literature*. Oxford: Clarendon Press. 47–75.

Nitzan, B. 1986. *Pesher Habakkuk: A Scroll from the Wilderness of Judaea (1QpHab)*. Jerusalem: Bialik Institute (in Heb.).

Ogilvie, R. M. 1970. *A Commentary on Livy Books 1–5*. Oxford University Press.

O'Hara, J. 1990. *Death and Optimistic Prophecy in Vergil's Aeneid*. Princeton University Press.

  1996. *True Names: Vergil and the Alexandrian Tradition of Etymological Wordplay*. Ann Arbor: University of Michigan Press.

Oliver, J. H. 1953. *The Ruling Power: A Study of the Roman Empire in the Second Century after Christ through the Roman Oration of Aelius Aristides*. Philadelphia: American Philosophical Society.

Osgood, J. 2006. *Caesar's Legacy: Civil War and the Emergence of the Roman Empire*. Cambridge University Press.

  2015. "Breviarium Totius Imperii: the background of Appian's Roman History," in K. Welch (ed.), *Appian's Roman History: Empire and Civil War*. Swansea: Classical Press of Wales. 23–44.

Oswalt, J. N. 1986. *The Book of Isaiah: 1–39*. Grand Rapids: Eerdmans.

Pagán, V. E. 2005. *Conspiracy Narratives in Roman History*. Austin: University of Texas Press.

Pandey, N. 2017. "Sowing the Seeds of War: The *Aeneid*'s Prehistory of Interpretive Contestation and Appropriation," *Classical World* 111(1): 7–25.

Parente, F. and Sievers, J. (eds.) 1994. *Josephus and the History of the Greco-Roman Period: Essays in Memory of Morton Smith*. Leiden, New York and Köln: Brill.

Parke, H. W. 1988. *Sibyls and Sibylline Prophecy in Classical Antiquity*. London: Routledge.

Pearson, L. 1987. *The Greek Historians of the West: Timaeus and His Predecessors*. Atlanta: Scholars Press.

Pédech, P. 1964. *La méthode historique de Polybe*. Paris: Les Belles Lettres.

Peirano, I. 2010. "Hellenized Romans and Barbarized Greeks. Reading the End of Dionysius of Halicarnassus, *Antiquitates Romanae*," *Journal of Roman Studies* 100: 32–53.

Pelling, C. 2010. "'Learning from that violent schoolmaster': Thucydidean Intertextuality and Some Greek Views of Roman Civil War," in B. Breed, C. Damon and A. Rossi (eds.), *Citizens of Discord: Rome and its Civil Wars*. Oxford University Press. 105–18.

  2016. "Preparing for Posterity: Dionysius and Polybius," in A. Lanieri (ed.), *The Western Time of Ancient History: Historiographical Encounters with the Greek and Roman Pasts*. Cambridge University Press. 155–73.

Perkell, C. 2002. "The Golden Age and its Contradictions in the Poetry of Vergil," *Vergilius* 48: 3–39.

Perkins, D. 1992. *Is Literary History Possible?* Baltimore: Johns Hopkins University Press.

Petzold, K.-E. 1969. *Studien zur Methode des Polybios und zu ihrer historischen Auswertung*. Munich: Beck.
Pfättisch, J. M. 1908. *Die Rede Konstantins des Grossen an die Versammlung der Heiligen auf ihre Echtheit untersucht*. Freiburg: Herder.
  1912–13. *Die vierte Ekloge Vergils in der Rede Konstantins an die Versammlung der Heiligen*. Programm des Kgl. Gymnasiums im Benediktinerkloster Ettal.
  1913. "Die Rede an die Versammlung der Heiligen," in *Des Eusebius von Cäsarea ausgewählte Schriften*. Munich: Kösel. 191–272.
Picard, C. 1956. "Néron et le blé d'Afrique", *Les Cahiers de Tunisie* 4: 163–73. = *Comptes rendus des séances de l'Académie des Inscriptions et Belles-Lettres* 100–10: 68–71.
Piganiol, A. 1964. *Le sac de Rome*. Paris: Albin Michel.
Pitcher, L. 2016. "Future's Bright? Looking Forward in Appian," in A. Lanieri (ed.), *The Western Time of Ancient History: Historiographical Encounters with the Greek and Roman Pasts*. Cambridge University Press. 281–92.
Pizzani, U. 1993. "Costantino e l'Oratio ad Sanctorum Coetum," in G. Bonamente and F. Fusco (eds.), *Costantino il Grande dall'Antichità all'Umanesimo, Vol. 2*. Università degli studi di Macerata. 791–822.
Portier-Young, A. E. 2011. *Apocalypse Against Empire: Theologies of Resistance in Early Judaism*. Grand Rapids: Eerdmans.
  2014. "Jewish Apocalyptic Literature as Resistance Literature," in J. J. Collins (ed.), *The Oxford Handbook of Apocalyptic Literature*. Oxford University Press. 145–62.
Potter, D. S. 1990. *Prophecy and History in the Crisis of the Roman Empire: A Historical Commentary on the Thirteenth Sibylline Oracle*. Oxford: Clarendon Press.
Powell, J. G. F. 1994. "The Rector *rei publicae* of Cicero's *De re publica*," *Scripta Classica Israelica* 13: 19–29.
Price, J. J. 2001. *Thucydides and the Internal War*. Cambridge University Press.
  2005. "The Provincial Historian in Rome," in J. Sievers and G. Lembi (eds.), *Josephus and Jewish History in Flavian Rome and Beyond*. Leiden: Brill. 101–18.
  2011. "Josephus," in A. Feldherr and G. Hardy (eds.), *The Oxford History of Historical Writing Vol. 1: Beginnings to AD 600*. Oxford University Press. 219–43.
  2015. "Thucydidean Stasis and Roman Empire in Appian's Interpretation of History," in K. Welch (ed.), *Appian's Roman History: Empire and Civil War*. Swansea: Classical Press of Wales. 45–63.
Prococo, S. (ed.) 1990. *Eucherio di Lione, Il rifiuto del mondo*. Florence: Nardini.
Quint, D. 1993. *Epic and Empire*. Princeton University Press.
Rajak, T. 1983. *Josephus, the Historian and his Society*. London: Duckworth.
  1991. "Friends, Romans, Subjects: Agrippa II's Speech in Josephus's Jewish War," in L. Alexander (ed.), *Images of Empire*. Sheffield Academic Press. 122–34.
Rawson, E. 1985. *Intellectual Life in the Late Roman Republic*. Baltimore: Johns Hopkins University Press.
Richardson, J. 2008. *The Language of Empire: Rome and the Idea of Empire from the Third Century BC to the Second Century AD*. Cambridge University Press.

Riguzzi, G. 2006. "Is the Babylon of Revelation Rome or Jerusalem?" *Biblica* 87: 371–386.
Roberts, D. H., Dunn, F. M. and Fowler, D. P. (eds.) 1997. *Classical Closure*. Princeton University Press.
Rodgers, B. S. 1980. "Constantine's Pagan Vision," *Byzantion* 50: 259–78.
Roduit, A. 2003. "Le discours d'Agrippa II dans La Guerre Juive de Flavius Josèphe," *Revue des Études Juives* 162(3–4): 365–402.
Rosenthal, E. S. 1982. "La-Milon ha-Talmudi," in S. Shaked (ed.), *Irano-Judaica: Studies Relating to Jewish Contacts with Persian Culture throughout the Ages, Vol. I*. Jerusalem: Ben-Zvi Institute. 38–134.
   1987. "The History of the Text and Problems of Redaction in the Study of the Babylonian Talmud," *Tarbiz* 57: 1–36 (in Heb.).
Rosen-Zvi, I. 2017. "Is the Mishnah a Roman Composition?" in Ch. Hayes, Z. Novick and M. Bar-Asher Segal (eds.), *The Faces of Torah. Studies in the Texts and Contexts of Ancient Judaism in Honor of Steven Fraade*. Göttingen: Vandenhoeck & Ruprecht. 487–508.
Rossi, A. F. 2000. "The Tears of Marcellus: History of a Literary Motif in Livy," *Greece & Rome* 47(2): 56–66.
Rostovtzeff, M. 1904. "Geschichte der Staatspacht in der römischen Kaiserzeit bis Diokletian," *Philologus. Supplement* 9: 329–512.
Runnalls, D. 1997. "The Rhetoric of Josephus," in S. E. Porter (ed.), *Handbook of Classical Rhetoric in the Hellenistic Period, 30 B.C.–A.D. 400*. Leiden: Brill. 737–54.
Rüpke, J. 1995. *Kalender und Öffentlichkeit. Die Geschichte der Repräsentation und religiösen Qualifikation von Zeit in Rom*. Berlin: De Gruyter.
   2004. "Acta aut agenda. Relations of Script and Performance," in A. Barchiesi, J. Rüpke and S. Stephens (eds.), *Rituals in Ink: A Conference on Religion and Literary Production in Ancient Rome held at Stanford University in February 2002*. Stuttgart: F. Steiner. 23–43.
   2005. *Fasti Sacerdotum: Die Mitglieder der Priesterschaften und das sakrale Funktionspersonal römischer, griechischer und jüdisch-christlicher Kulte in der Stadt Rom von 300 v. Chr. bis 499 n. Chr.* 3 Vols. Stuttgart: Steiner.
Sanders, E. P. 1992. *Judaism: Practice and Belief, 63 BCE – 66 CE*. London and Philadelphia: Trinity Press.
Santangelo, F. 2013. *Divination, Prediction and the End of the Roman Republic*, Cambridge University Press.
Saulnier, C. 1991. "Flavius Josèphe et la propagande flavienne II," *Revue biblique* 98: 199–221.
Sayler, G. B. 1984. *Have the Promises Failed? A Literary Analysis of 2 Baruch*. Chico, CA: Society of Biblical Literature.
Schäfer, P. 1979. "Die Flucht Johanan b. Zakkais aus Jerusalem und die Gründung des 'Lehrhauses' Jabne," in W. Haase (ed.), *Aufstieg und Niedergang der römischen Welt, Vol. 2*, 19.2. Berlin: De Gruyter. 43–101.
Schalit, A. 1975. "Nevuoteihem shel Yosef Ben Matityahu ve-Rabban Yohanan ben Zakkai Al Aliyat Aspasianus la-Shilton," in S. Lieberman and A. Hyman

(eds.), *Salo Wittmayer Baron Jubilee Volume: On the Occasion of His Eightieth Birthday*. Jerusalem: American Academy of Jewish Research. 397–432 (in Heb.).
Scheid, J. 1975. *Les frères Arvales: Recrutement et origine sociale sous les empereurs julio-claudiens*. Paris: Presse Universitaires de la France.
  1985. "Sacrifice et banquet à Rome," *Melanges de l'École française à Rome* 97 (1): 193–206.
  1990. *Romulus et ses frères: le collège des frères arvales, modèle du culte public dans la Rome des empereurs*. École française de Rome.
  1995. "Graeco ritu: A Typically Roman Way of Honoring the Gods," *Harvard Studies in Classical Philology* 97: 15–21.
  1996. "Pline le jeune et les sanctuaires d'Italie," in A. Chastagnol, S. Demougin and C. Lepelley (eds.), *Splendidissima Civitas. Études d'histoire romaine en hommage à François Jacques*. Paris: Publications de la Sorbonne. 241–58.
  1998. *Recherches archéologiques à la Magliana. Commentarii fratrum arvalium qui supersunt. Les copies épigraphiques des protocoles annuels de la confrérie arvale (21 av.-304 ap. J.-C.)*. École française de Rome / Soprintendenza archeologia di Roma.
  2003. "Hierarchy and Structure in Roman Polytheism: Roman Methods of Conceiving Action," in C. Ando (ed.), *Roman Religion*. Edinburgh University Press. 164–89 = Original, 1999. "Hiérarchie et structure dans le polythéisme romain: façons romaines de penser l'action," *Archiv für Religionsgeschichte* 1: 184–203.
  2005. *Quand croire, c'est faire: Les rites sacrificiels des Romains*. Paris: Aubier.
Schelkle, K. H. 1938. *Virgil in der Deutung Augustins*. Stuttgart and Berlin: Kohlhammer.
Schiffman, L. 1997. "301. 4Qmysteries^c?" in *Discoveries in the Judean Desert, Vol. 20: Qumran Cave 4 XV: Sapiential Texts, Pt. I*, 113–23. Oxford University Press.
Schnegg-Köhler, B. 2002. *Die augusteischen Säkularspiele, vol. 4*. Munich & Leipzig: K. G. Saur.
Schneider, M. 2013. *Cicero Haruspex*. Piscataway, NJ: Gorgias Press.
Schofield, M. 1986. "Cicero for and against Divination," *Journal of Roman Studies* 76: 47–65.
  1995. "Cicero's Definition of Res Publica", in J. Powell (ed.), *Cicero the Philosopher: Twelve Papers*. Oxford University Press.
Schremer, A. 2010. *Brothers Estranged: Heresy, Christianity, and Jewish Identity in Late Antiquity*. Oxford University Press.
Schultz, B. 2009. *Conquering the World: The War Scroll (1QM) Reconsidered*. Leiden: Brill.
Schultze, C. 1986. "Dionysius of Halicarnassus and his Audience," in I. S. Moxon, J. D. Smart and A. J. Woodman (eds.), *Past Perspectives: Studies in Greek and Roman Historical Writing*, Cambridge University Press. 121–41.
Schultze, V. 1894. "Quellenuntersuchungen zur *Vita Constantini* des Eusebius," *Zeitschrift für Kirchengeschichte* 14: 503–55.

Schürer, E. 1986. *The History of the Jewish People in the Age of Jesus Christ, Vol. III.1*. Edinburgh: Clark.

1987. *The History of the Jewish People in the Age of Jesus Christ, Vol. III.2*. Edinburgh: Clark.

Schwartz, S. 2001. *Imperialism and Jewish Society, 200 BCE to 640 CE*. Princeton University Press.

Scott, J. C. 1985. *Weapons of the Weak: Everyday Forms of Peasant Resistance*. New Haven: Yale University Press.

1990. *Domination and the Arts of Resistance: Hidden Transcripts*. New Haven: Yale University Press.

Scullard, H. H. 1960. "Scipio Aemilianus and Roman Politics," *Journal of Roman Studies* 50: 59–74.

Seager, R. 2013. "Polybius' distortions of the Roman "constitution": a simpl(istic) explanation," in B. Gibson and T. Harrison (eds.). *Polybius and His World: Essays in Memory of F. W. Walbank*. Oxford University Press. 247–54.

Sears, G., Keegan, P. and Laurence, R. (eds.) 2013. *Written Space in the Latin West 200 BC to AD 300*. London & New York: Bloomsbury.

Sellew, P. 1989. "Achilles or Christ? Porphyry and Didymus in Debate over Allegorical Interpretation," *Harvard Theological Review* 82(1): 79–100.

Shackleton Bailey, D. R. 1977. *Cicero Epistulae ad Familiares*. Cambridge University Press.

Sharon, N. 2016. "The Kittim and the Roman Conquest in the Qumran Scrolls," *Meghillot* 11: 357–388 (in Heb.).

Sharples, R. 1986. "Cicero's *Republic* and Greek Political Theory", *Polis* 5(2): 30–50.

Sievers, J. and Lembi, G. (eds.) 2005. *Josephus and Jewish History in Flavian Rome and Beyond*. Leiden: Brill.

Smith, R. R. R. 1988. "*Simulacra Gentium*: The Ethne from the Sebasteion at Aphrodisias," *Journal of Roman Studies* 78: 50–77.

Spilsbury, P. 2002. "Josephus on the Burning of the Temple, the Flavian Triumph, and the Providence of God," *Society of Biblical Literature Seminar Papers* 41: 306–27.

2003. "Flavius Josephus on the Rise and Fall of the Roman Empire," *Journal of Theological Studies* 54: 1–24.

2005. "Reading the Bible in Rome: Josephus and the Constraints of Empire," in J. Sievers and G. Lembi (eds.), *Josephus and Jewish History in Flavian Rome and Beyond*. Leiden: Brill. 209–27.

Starr, R. 2009. "*Annos undeviginti natus*: Augustus and Romulus in Res Gestae 1.1," *Historia* 58(3): 367–69.

Stegemann, H. 1998. *The Library of Qumran: On the Essenes Qumran, John the Baptist, and Jesus*. Grand Rapids: Eerdmans.

Stemberger, G. 1983. *Die römische Herrschaft im Urteil der Juden*. Darmstadt: Wissenschaftliche Buchgesellschaft.

Šterbenc Erker, D. 2013. *Religiöse Rollen römischer Frauen in "griechischen" Ritualen*. Stuttgart: Steiner.

Sterling, G. E. 1992. *Historiography and Self-Definition: Josephos, Luke-Acts, and Apologetic Historiography.* Leiden: Brill.
Stern, M. 1980. *Greek and Latin Authors on Jews and Judaism. Vol. 2.* Jerusalem: Israel Academy of Sciences and Humanities.
Stone, M. E. 1990. *Fourth Ezra: A Commentary on the Fourth Book of Ezra.* Minneapolis: Fortress Press.
Sullivan, F. A. 1941. "Cicero and *Gloria*," *Transactions of the American Philological Association* 72: 382–91.
Swain, J. W. 1940. "The Theory of the Four Monarchies: Opposition History under the Roman Empire," *Classical Philology* 35: 1–21.
Swain, S. 1989. "Plutarch: Chance, Providence, and History," *American Journal of Philology* 110(2): 272–302.
Syme, R. 1980. *Some Arval Brethren.* Oxford: Clarendon Press.
Teeter, A. 2012. "Isaiah and the King of As/Syria in Daniel's Final Vision: On the Rhetoric of Inner-Scriptural Allusion and the Hermeneutics of 'Mantological Exegesis'," in E. F. Mason et al. (eds.), *A Teacher for All Generations: Essays in Honor of James C. VanderKam, Vol. 1.* Leiden: Brill. 169–99.
Thélamon, F. 1981. *Païens et chrétiens au IVe siècle: l'apport de l'Histoire ecclésiastique de Rufin d'Aquilée.* Paris: Études Augustiniennes.
Thérond, B. 1981. "Les Flaviens dans la Guerre Juifs de Flavius Josèphe." *Dialogues d'Histoire Ancienne* 7: 235–45.
Thomas, J. C. and Macchia, F. D. 2016. *Revelation.* Grand Rapids: Eerdmans.
Thomas, R. F. 2001. *Virgil and the Augustan Reception.* Cambridge University Press.
Thraede, K. 1966. "Euhemerismus," *Reallexikon für Antike und Christentum* 6: 877–89.
Tigchelaar, E. 2003. "Notes on the Reading of the DJD Editions of 1Q and 4QMysteries," *Revue de Qumrân* 21(1): 99–107.
Townsend, J. T. 2003. "Midrash Tanhuma." S. Buber Recension (ed. and tr.), *Vol. 3. Numbers and Deuteronomy.* Jersey City, NJ: Ktav.
Trimble, G. 2013. "Catullus 64 and the Prophetic Voice in Virgil's Fourth Eclogue," in J. Farrell and D. Nelis (eds.), *Augustan Poetry and the Roman Republic.* Oxford University Press. 263–77.
Tuplin, C. 1989. "The False Neros of the First Century," in C. Deroux (ed.), *Studies in Latin Literature and History* V. Bruxelles: Latomus. 364–404.
Urbach, E. E. 1964. "The Laws Regarding Slavery as a Source for Social History of the Period of the Second Temple, the Mishnah and Talmud," in J. G. Weiss (ed.), *Papers of the Institute of Jewish Studies London, Vol. 1.* Jerusalem: The Magnes Press. 1–94.
Vermès, G. 1973. *Scripture and Tradition in Judaism: Haggadic Studies.* Leiden: Brill.
  1992. "The Qumran Corner: Qumran Publications," *Journal of Jewish Studies* 43 (1): 85–90.
  2007. "Historiographical Elements in the Qumran Writings: A Synopsis of the Textual Evidence," *Journal of Jewish Studies* 58(1): 121–39.

Vermeylen, J. 1989. "L'unité du livre d'Isaïe," in J. Vermeylen (ed.), *Le livre d'Isaïe: Les oracles et leurs relecteurs unité et complexité de l'ouvrage*. Leuven University Press.

Veyne, P. 1983. "'Titulus Praelatus': offrande, solemnisation et publicité dans les ex-voto greco-romains," *Revue Archéologique*: 281–300.

2005. "La prise de Rome en 410 et les grandes invasions," in *L'empire gréco-romain*. Paris: Seuil. 713–47.

2010. *When Our World Became Christian, 312–394*. tr. by J. Lloyd. Cambridge: Polity.

Vout, C. 2012. *The Hills of Rome: Signature of an Eternal City*. Cambridge University Press.

Walbank, F. W. 1957–79. *A Historical Commentary on Polybius*, 3 Vols. Oxford: Clarendon Press.

1972. *Polybius*. Berkeley: University of California Press.

1974. "Polybius between Greece and Rome," in E. Gabba (ed.), *Polybe: Entretiens sur l'Antiquité Classique Entretiens sur l'Antiquité classique de la Fondation Hardt* 20. Geneva: Librairie Droz. 1–38.

1998. "A Greek Looks at Rome: Polybius VI Revisited," *Scripta Classica Israelica* 17: 45–59. = 2002. in *Polybius, Rome and the Hellenistic World*. 277–92.

2002. *Polybius, Rome and the Hellenistic World: Essays and Reflections*. Cambridge University Press.

Wallace-Hadrill, A. 1982. "The Golden Age and Sin in Augustan Ideology," *Past & Present* 95: 19–36.

1987. "Time for Augustus: Ovid, Augustus and the Fasti," in M. Whitby, P. Hardie and Mary Whitby (eds.), *Homo Viator: Classical Essays for John Bramble*. Bristol Classical Press. 221–30.

Waterfield, R. (tr.) 2010. *Polybius, The Histories*. Oxford University Press.

Watson, L. 2003. *A Commentary on Horace's Epodes*. Oxford University Press.

Weinfeld, M. 1997. "Publications", *Shnaton: An Annual for Biblical and Ancient Near Eastern Studies* 11: 349–60.

Weinstock, S. 1971. *Divus Julius*. Oxford University Press.

Weissenberger, M. 2002. "Das Imperium Romanum in den Proömien dreier Griechischer Historiker: Polybios, Dionysios von Halikarnassos und Appian," *Rheinisches Museum für Philologie* 145(3–4): 262–81.

Widengren, G. 1963. "The Status of the Jews in the Sassanian Empire," *Iranica Antiqua* 1: 117–62.

Wiesehöfer, J. 2013. "Polybios und die Entstehung des römischen Weltreichschemas," in V. Grieb and C. Koehn (eds.), *Polybios und seine Historien*. Stuttgart: Franz Steiner Verlag. 59–69.

Wilkinson, S. 2005. *Caligula*. London: Routledge.

Winiarczyk, M. 2002. *Euhemeros von Messene: Leben, Werk und Nachwirkung*. Munich and Leipzig: K. G. Saur.

Wiseman, T. P. 1974. "Legendary Genealogies in Late Republican Rome," *Greece & Rome* 21(2): 153–64.

1991. *Death of an Emperor: Flavius Josephus*. University of Exeter Press.

1995. *Remus: A Roman Myth*. Cambridge University Press.
Wistrand, M. 1979. *Cicero Imperator*. Göteborg: Acta Universitatis Gothoburgensis.
Wlosok, A. 1983. "Zwei Beispiele frühchristlicher Vergilrezeption: Polemik (Lact. Div. inst. 5.10) und Usurpation (Or. Const. 1931)," in V. Pöschl (ed.), *2000 Jahre Vergil: Ein Symposium*. Wiesbaden: Harrassowitz. 63–86.
Wolf, R. 2015. *The Philosophy of a Roman Sceptic*. London and New York: Routledge.
Wolff, S. 2007. *Rutilius Numantianus: sur son retour*. Paris: Les Belles Lettres.
Woolf, G. 1996. "Monumental Writing and the Expansion of Roman Society," *Journal of Roman Studies* 86: 22–39.
  2001. "Inventing Empire in Ancient Rome," in S. E. Alcock et al. (eds.), *Empires: Perspectives from Archaeology and History*. Cambridge University Press. 311–22.
  2006. *Et tu, Brute?: the Murder of Caesar and Political Assassination*. London: Profile Books.
Yadin, Y. 1962. *The Scroll of the War of the Sons of Light against the Sons of Darkness*. London: Oxford University Press.
Yerushalmi, Y. H. 1989. *Zakhor: Jewish History and Jewish Memory*. New York: University of Washington Press.
Zago, G. 2012. *Sapienza filosofica e cultura materiale: Posidonio e le altre fonti dell' Epistola 90 di Seneca*. Bologna: Il Mulino.
Ziolkowski, J. M. and Putnam, M. C. J. (eds.) 2008. *The Virgilian Tradition: The First Fifteen Hundred Years*. New Haven: Yale University Press.

Index Locorum

Classical Literature
Aelius Aristides
  Pan. Or.
    (234(183–4)), 8, 110
  Rom. Or.
    (26), 144
    (28), 117
    (29), 117
    (36), 117
    (91), 114, 117
    (106), 118
    (108), 117
Appian
  B.C.
    (2.110), 238
  Praef.
    (1.32–37), 148
    (8), 113, 117
    (26), 108
    (29–42), 107
    (35–6), 108
    (38), 108
    (42), 108
    (43), 108
    (44), 108
    (46), 107
    (48–9), 107
  Pun.
    (628–30, [132]), 87–8
Aristotle
  Ath. Pol.
    (20–21), 136
  Pol.
    (3.1285a), 136
Calpurnius Siculus
  (1.33–88), 32
Cato the Elder
  Agr.
    (139–141), 74
Censorinus
  D.N.
    17.6, 42

Cicero
  Att.
    (11.9.2), 22
    (14.9.2), 22
  Cael.
    (26), 67
  Div.
    (1.72), 18
    (1.84), 28
    (2.110–111), 238–9
    (2.110–112), 238–9
  Fam.
    (6.2), 22
    (6.6), 18
    (6.6.3–4), 19
    (6.6.8), 20
    (6.6.11), 20
  Flac.
    (24), 29
    (69), 29
  Inv.
    (1.35), 28
    (1.103), 28
  N.D.
    (2.41), 35
    (2.118), 35
  Part. Or.
    (2.6), 230
  Phil.
    (8.13), 30
  Rab. Per.
    (10.30), 23
  Rep.
    (1.38), 25
    (1.45), 21–2
    (1.47), 30
    (1.58), 28
    (1.65), 21
    (2.2), 26
    (2.3), 26
    (2.10), 26
    (2.30), 26

(2.57), 27
(3.23), 30
(3.34), 25
(5.2), 30
(6.24), 35
Sch. Bob.
  (172.4), 24
Sest.
  (50), 3, 24
  (137), 24
Verr.
  (2.5.147), 28
Claudianus
  Ruf.
    (1), 32
Codex Theodosianus
  (16.10.19), 248
Dio Cassius
  (44.15.3), 238
  (44.25.3), 209
  (53.27.5), 209
  (56.34.1–3), 143
  (60.15.1), 161
  (63.1–6), 200
  (64.9.3), 200
  (66.19.3b-c), 200
  (66.33.2), 141
Dio Chrysostomus
  Or.
    (21.9–10), 199
Diodorus Siculus
  (2.1–34), 86
  (31.10), 120
  (32.24), 88
Dionysius of Halicarnassus
  A.R.
    (1.2.1), 100–1, 116–17
    (1.2.1–4), 113
    (1.2.1–6), 148
    (1.2.2–3), 101
    (1.3.1–2), 113
    (1.3.3–5), 117
    (1.4.2), 103, 104, 121
    (1.5.3), 102, 103
    (1.6.4), 102
    (1.7.2), 105
    (1.31.3), 8, 102
    (1.85.4–5), 106
    (2.50.1), 209
    (2.71), 67
    (4.62.6), 239
    (7.54–6), 105
    (7.66), 105
    (14.6.5), 103
    (19.14.1), 104
    (19.14–18), 104
    (20.6.1), 104
Gellius
  N.A.
    (3.16.9–11), 36
    (7.7.8), 67
Herodotus
  (1.5.4), 60
  (1.95), 86
  (1.130), 86
  (6.131), 136
Homer
  Il.
    (6.448–9), 88
    (9.410–16), 52
Horace
  Carm.
    (1.12), 53
    (3.30–6-9), 4, 66
  Carm. Saec.
    (53–57), 32
    (57–60), 32
  Epod.
    (1.17–18), 44
    (16.10), 42
    (16.11), 44
    (16.11–14), 42
    (16.25–34), 44
    (16.32–33), 41
    (16.35–41), 44
    (16.39), 43
    (16.41), 40, 44
    (16.41–62), 40
    (16.53), 44
    (16.63), 43
    (16.63–66), 40
    (16.65–66), 43
    (17.81), 60
Isocrates
  Panath.
    (3.24), 136
John of Antioch
  (fr. 104 M), 200
Josephus
  A.J.
    (1.14), 164
    (1.23), 164
    (1.128), 171
    (4.112–125), 158
    (4.112–128), 150
    (4.127–128), 149
    (10.203–210), 149, 157
    (10.210), 11, 157
    (10.276), 158
    (13.288–298), 147

Josephus (cont.)
   (13.301–319), 135
   (13.320–404), 135
   (13.405–432), 135
   (14.71–73), 192
   (18), 129
   (18.12–15), 147
   (18.55–88), 166
   (18.211–214), 160, 163
   (18.222), 160
   (18.259–260), 160
   (18.261–309), 160
   (18.281–285), 160
   (18.309), 160
   (19.1–15), 165
   (19.15–16), 161
   (19.29), 161
   (19.37), 161
   (19.40–43), 165
   (19.42), 165
   (19.60–61), 161
   (19.69), 163
   (19.78–83), 165
   (19.87), 161
   (19.94–95), 161
   (19.167–273), 163
   (19.201–211), 165
   (20.6–10), 166
   (20.17–96), 163
   (20.103–127), 166
   (20.173–178), 139
   (20.182), 166
   (20.182–184), 139
Ap.
   (2.127), 150
   (2.165–166), 137
B.J.
   (1.70–84), 135
   (1.85–106), 135
   (1.107–119), 135
   (1.152–153), 192
   (1.223–245), 166
   (2.16.4), 11
   (2.117–308), 139
   (2.162–166), 147
   (2.266–270), 139
   (2.284–292), 139
   (2.308), 139
   (2.333–341), 166
   (2.342–404), 130
   (2.345–347), 132, 133
   (2.345–401), 168
   (2.348–350), 132
   (2.348–357), 132
   (2.348–361), 132, 133
   (2.350–354), 132
   (2.351), 139
   (2.353), 139
   (2.355), 134
   (2.355–361), 132, 134
   (2.356–357), 134
   (2.358), 134, 136, 144
   (2.358–387), 132, 142
   (2.359), 136
   (2.360), 136, 146
   (2.361), 140
   (2.361–362), 132, 140
   (2.361–387), 140
   (2.361–395), 132, 140
   (2.363–387), 132, 141
   (2.365), 137
   (2.366), 137
   (2.367–368), 137
   (2.369), 138
   (2.372), 144
   (2.372–374), 138
   (2.373), 144, 146
   (2.375–376), 138
   (2.378), 138
   (2.379), 138
   (2.381), 138
   (2.382–383), 144
   (2.388–389), 132, 140
   (2.388–401), 132
   (2.390), 141, 145, 146, 150
   (2.390–395), 132, 141
   (2.391–393), 141, 146
   (2.391–395), 151
   (2.394), 141
   (2.396–400), 133, 147
   (2.397), 133, 147
   (2.398), 133
   (2.398–399), 147
   (2.399), 132
   (2.400), 133, 147
   (2.401–404), 133, 147
   (2.402), 139
   (3.351–354), 146
   (3.391–408), 178
   (4.224–353), 152
   (4.622), 146
   (5.367), 148, 156
   (5.367–368), 146
   (5.381), 151
   (5.412), 146
   (6.312–313), 164, 179
   (7.437–453), 168
Vita
   (1), 135

Index Locorum

Juvenal
  Sat.
    (9.130), 209
Livy
  (1.1.2), 47
  (1.4.1), 122
  (1.6), 62
  (1.6–7), 251
  (3.1), 62
  (5.7.10), 31, 86
  (21.1), 61
  (22.53.8), 51
Lucan
  B.C.
    (1.72–80), 35
Lucian
  Macr.
    (22), 95
Matial
  (5.19), 32
Olympiodorus of Thebes
  (fr. 25), 250
  (fr. 43), 250
Ovid
  Fast.
    (2.684), 119
    (3.72), 5
    (5.550–564), 147
  Met.
    (1.1–2), 61
    (14.130–153), 191
    (14.136–51), 55
    (15.418–37), 58–9
    (15.420), 61
    (15.420–22), 60
    (15.421), 60
    (15.431), 62
    (15.431–5), 60
    (15.434), 61
    (15.439–49), 60
    (15.447–9), 62
    (15.449), 59
    (15.871–79), 60
Panegyrici Latini
  (6.21.4–5), 244
Pausanias
  (10.12), 191
Philargyrius
  ad Ecl.
    (4.1), 234
Philo
  Deus
    (140), 124
    (140–182), 152
    (171–176), 124
    (173), 115, 149
    (173–176), 152
    (174), 114, 138
    (175), 114
    (176), 123, 125, 127
    (177–178), 126
    (180), 125
  Flac.
    (114–115), 140
    (162–191), 140
  Ios.
    (134), 126
    (134–136), 114, 115, 125–6, 149
    (135), 126
    (136), 114, 126
    (140), 126
    (144), 126
  Leg.
    (1–2), 129
    (3–4), 129
    (8), 118
    (8–10), 126
    (10), 118, 144
    (13), 119
    (114), 119
    (140), 129
    (143–147), 118, 144
    (148–151), 144
    (152–160), 145
    (256), 120
    (284), 123
    (309), 118, 145
    (346), 140
  Quaest. Gen.
    (4.43), 115, 126–7, 149, 152
  Spec.
    (2.231), 123, 147
    (3.137), 128
    (3.137–140), 128, 140
Plato
  Rep.
    (546a), 25
Pliny the Elder
  N.H.
    (1.2b.11.197), 18
    (3.66–67), 209
    (4.10), 166
    (7.45), 166
    (11.143), 166
    (13.83), 166
    (35.18), 166
    (36.39), 143
    (36.74), 166
    (36.111), 166

Pliny the Younger
  Ep.
    (8.8), 76
Plutarch
  Caes.
    (60), 238
  Cat. Mai.
    (20.5), 38
  Fort. Rom.
    (1), 118, 122
    (2), 119, 122
    (4), 122–3
  Lyc.
    (5–7), 136
    (28–29), 136
  Mor.
    (397A), 190
Polybius
  (1.1.4–6), 94
  (1.1.5), 89–90, 92
  (1.2.1–6), 113
  (1.2.1–7), 90, 116
  (1.2.2–4), 146
  (1.2.4–7), 148
  (1.2.7–8), 146
  (1.3.7–10), 146
  (1.4.1), 90, 91
  (1.4.1–5), 146
  (1.4.4), 91
  (2.21.2), 146
  (3.1.4), 90
  (3.2.6), 90
  (3.4.7–8), 93
  (3.4.12–13), 93–8
  (3.14), 146
  (3.90–118.9), 90
  (5.102), 146
  (6.1–18), 136, 137
  (6.2.3), 92
  (6.2.3–7), 96
  (6.3.3), 96
  (6.5.1), 97
  (6.5–7), 155
  (6.5–9), 96
  (6.9.10), 97
  (6.9.12–13), 97
  (6.11.11–18.8), 97
  (6.18.1–7), 97
  (6.18.8), 97
  (6.19–42), 92
  (6.25.11), 92
  (6.26.12), 92
  (6.39.11), 92
  (6.42.1), 92
  (6.51.4), 98
  (6.57.1–2), 98
  (6.57.5–9), 98
  (7.2–7), 146
  (8.2.3–6), 146
  (8.2.21), 146
  (8.2.32), 90
  (8.24.10), 146
  (15.20.4–6), 146
  (16.8), 146
  (18.28.5), 146
  (18.35.1), 96
  (29.21), 89, 120, 157
  (29.21.3–5), 146
  (31.25.5), 96
  (36.17.2), 146
  (38.7.11), 146
  (38.8.8), 146
  (38.21), 87, 88, 89
  (38.21–22), 148
  (38.22), 62, 87
  (39.8.1–2), 146
Propertius
  (2.30.19–22), 41
Rutilius Namantianus
  (119–146), 249, 265
  (121–128), 249
  (133–136), 249
  (137–140), 249
  (140), 249
  (141–146), 249
Seneca the Younger
  Dial.
    (6.26.6–7), 35
  Ep.
    (90), 20
  N.Q.
    (2.49), 18
    (2.56.1), 18
Serv. Dan.
  (9.46), 43
Servius
  ad Aen.
    (8.721), 143
  ad Ecl.
    (4.1), 234
    (4.4), 35
    (4.10), 35
    (4.13), 234
Sibylline Oracles
  2 Sib.
    (16–19), 209
    (45–47), 209
  3 *Sib.*
    (46–56), 195
    (63), 201

Index Locorum 303

(175–182), 195
(188–235), 41
(350–355), 195
(350–364), 195
(399–412), 41
(434–456), 41
(464–471), 195
(520–544), 195
(785–795), 236
(809–829), 191
(928–947), 41
(954–988), 41
4 *Sib.*
(4–7), 192
(24–48), 192
(40–101), 193
(47), 42
(49–101), 192
(102–114), 193
(102–129), 192
(115–116), 192
(115–118), 202
(119–123), 202
(119–124), 193, 194
(125–127), 192, 202
(130–134), 192
(130–161), 192
(135–136), 202
(135–151), 194
(137–139), 193, 202
(140–151), 202
(145–148), 194
(162–170), 192
(171–178), 192, 202
(179–191), 192
5 *Sib.*
(1–51), 196
(8–50), 196
(28–34), 199, 203
(46–48), 196
(52–136), 196
(93–110), 203
(137–144), 203
(137–148), 203
(137–154), 199
(137–178), 196
(150), 220
(150–154), 203
(152–153), 203
(155–161), 197
(155–178), 198
(160), 220
(162), 220
(162–177), 203
(162–178), 197

(173–174), 198
(179–285), 197
(214–224), 203
(214–227), 199
(286–360), 197, 203
(342–343), 197
(342–345), 203
(342–359), 198
(361–370), 199
(361–433), 197
(363–374), 203
(363–385), 203
(366), 199
(381–385), 199
(386–396), 203
(397–410), 203
(434–446), 197, 198, 203, 211
(434–531), 197
(462–463), 200
8 *Sib.*
(70–72), 200
(70–80), 201
(73–109), 200
(124–130), 200, 201
(140–141), 203
(140–157), 200, 201, 220
(143–150), 203
(199), 42
(242), 239
(249–250), 239
11 Sib.
(109–116), 209
12 Sib.
(78–85), 200
(78–94), 201
13 Sib.
(45), 209
14 Sib.
(107–108), 209
Strabo
Geog.
(5.3.7), 209
(6.4.1), 145
Suetonius
Aug.
(101.6–7), 141
Cal.
(56.2), 161
Iul.
(75.5), 18
(79.3), 42
(79.4), 238
Nero
(13), 200
(30), 200

Suetonius (cont.)
   (40.1), 199
   (46.1), 143
   (47.2), 199
   (57), 200
   (57.2), 200
  Vesp.
   (4.5), 179
Tacitus
  Agr.
   (29–38), 134
  Ann.
   (1.11.7), 141
   (6.9), 161
   (16.23–24), 200
  Hist.
   (2.8.1), 199
   (2.8–9), 200
   (2.8), 220
   (5.8.1), 86
   (5.13.2), 179
Thucydides
  (1.1), 61
  (1.10.2), 60
  (1.22.2), 131
Tibullus
  (1.3.35–44), 39
  (2.5.23), 5, 31
Varro
  Ling.
   (5.15), 67
   (5.41–54), 208
Velleius Paterculus
  (1.6.6), 86
  (2.39.2), 143
Virgil
  Aen.
   (1.6), 53
   (1.6–7), 58
   (1.10), 58
   (1.33), 47
   (1.199), 47
   (1.205), 48
   (1.223), 47, 54
   (1.241), 47, 54
   (1.249), 47
   (1.264), 57
   (1.267), 56
   (1.267–88), 49, 56
   (1.268), 56, 57
   (1.268–74), 56
   (1.270), 57,
   (1.272), 57
   (1.273), 57
   (1.274), 56
   (1.276), 57
   (1.276–7), 57
   (1.277), 57
   (1.278), 57
   (1.278–279), 42, 49, 249
   (1.279), 86
   (1.281–2), 55
   (1.286–7), 55
   (1.288), 56
   (1.294–6), 56
   (1.437), 47
   (4.265–7), 47
   (6.781–97), 57
   (6.791–794), 244
   (6.791–795), 32–3
   (6.791–95), 42
   (6.801–803), 32
   (8.11–12), 53
   (8.722–728), 143
   (12.793), 54
   (12.826–8), 54
   (12.880–1), 55
  Ecl.
   (1.4), 44
   (1.6), 44
   (1.6–8), 53
   (1.9–10), 44
   (1.11–12), 44
   (1.19–25), 40
   (1.27–35), 44
   (1.42–43), 44
   (1.44–45), 44
   (1.46), 43, 44
   (1.46–58), 43
   (1.51), 43
   (1.53), 43
   (1.58), 43
   (1.64), 43
   (1.64–66), 43
   (1.64–78), 43
   (1.67), 43
   (1.69), 43, 44
   (1.70), 43
   (1.70–71), 43
   (1.71), 43
   (1.72), 43
   (1.73), 43
   (4.4–5), 35
   (4.4–7), 32, 36
   (4.5), 37
   (4.6), 33
   (4.7), 234
   (4.8–9), 36
   (4.9), 42, 234
   (4.10), 33, 244

(4.11), 35
(4.11–12), 38–9
(4.13), 36
(4.15), 43
(4.17), 33, 42
(4.21–22), 235
(4.21–30), 42
(4.23), 237
(4.26–27), 38
(4.28), 38
(4.28–30), 235
(4.31), 36
(4.31–36), 36
(4.35–36), 41
(4.37), 43
(4.38–41), 235
(4.39), 42
(4.42–45), 42, 235
(4.46–47), 36, 38
(4.48), 36
(4.52), 36, 42
(4.53), 36
(4.61), 35
(9.46–50), 43
G.
  (1), 236
  (1.125–27), 39
  (2.458–540), 42
  (3.25–33), 143
Xenophon
  Lac.
    (30), 136
Zonaras
  (11.15), 200

Bible
Hebrew Bible
Amos
  (6:1), 216
  (6:4), 216
  (6:6), 216
Daniel
  (2:31–35), 112, 149
  (2:31–45), 157
  (2:35), 208
  (2:39–43), 112
  (2:45), 208
  (7), 218
  (7:3), 219
  (7:4), 219
  (7:5), 219
  (7:6), 219
  (7:7), 219
  (7:8), 218
  (7:24), 219
  (8:20), 185
  (8:21), 185
  (11:29–30), 171
  (11:40ff), 175
Deuteronomy
  (2:5), 188
  (3:25), 178
Exodus
  (21:20–21), 128
Ezekiel
  (16), 221
  (16:27), 221
  (16:39), 221
  (23), 221
  (23:25), 221
  (23:26), 221
  (23:29), 221
  (26:19), 221
  (26–28), 216, 221, 222, 224
  (27:12–24), 216
  (28:17–19), 221
  (35:3), 208
Genesis
  (6:12), 124
  (10:2), 185
  (10:4), 171
  (10:12), 210
  (28:12), 169
  (28:12–13), 152
Habakkuk
  (1:6), 177
  (1:12), 172
Hosea
  (5:3), 217
Isaiah
  (2:2), 208
  (6:3), 12, 164
  (7), 236
  (10:33–11:5), 177
  (10:33–34), 12, 174
  (10:34), 177, 178–80
  (10–11), 173, 176
  (13–27), 213
  (21:9), 222
  (23), 216, 222, 224
  (23:17), 217
  (28–35), 213
  (47:8–9), 216
  (47:8–11), 198
  (47–48), 222, 224
Jeremiah
  (30.10), 13, 169
  (30:21), 178
  (49:20), 184
  (50:8), 222

Jeremiah (cont.)
 (50:12–13), 222
 (50:15), 223
 (50:29), 223, 224
 (50:39), 223
 (50–51), 222–3
 (51:6–8), 223
 (51:13), 223
 (51:29), 223
 (51:35), 214
 (51:35–37), 223
 (51:45), 223
 (51:48–49), 223
 (51:49), 211, 214, 216
 (51:55), 223
 (51:63–64), 224
Joel
 (3:21), 214
Jonah
 (1:2), 210
 (3:2), 210
 (4:11), 210
Leviticus
 (21:9), 220
Micah
 (5:2), 186
Nahum
 (1:4), 172
 (3:4), 218
Numbers
 (22–24), 158
 (23:24), 158
 (24:17), 188
 (24:17–24), 158
 (24:24), 171
 (35:19), 214
Obadiah
 (1:4), 169
Psalms
 (9:12), 214
 (19:5), 269
 (72:8), 271
 (79:10), 214
Zechariah
 (12:9), 168
 (14:4), 188
Zephaniah
 (2:11), 271

New Testament
Acts
 (1:8), 269
 (12:22–23), 216–17
Colossians
 (1:5–6), 269
Luke
 (2:7), 237
 (3), 237
 (21:12), 269
 (21:24), 268
 (21:25), 268
 (21:26), 269
 (21:28), 268
Mark
 (5:9), 218
 (13:20), 268
 (13:32), 268
Matthew
 (24:14), 269
 (24:22), 268
 (24:33), 268
 (24:36), 268
1 *Peter*
 (5:13), 212
Revelation
 (1:4), 209
 (1:9), 211
 (2:1–3:22), 209
 (2:13), 211
 (2–3), 213
 (4–21:8), 213
 (6:10), 214
 (7:12), 219
 (7:14), 211
 (12), 219
 (13:1), 219,
 (13:2), 219
 (13:3–4), 219
 (13:5), 219
 (13:10), 211
 (13:11), 219
 (13:12), 219
 (13:18), 219
 (14:8), 207
 (15:1), 206
 (15:2), 220
 (16:17), 206
 (16:17–21), 212
 (16:18), 206
 (16:19), 206, 210, 212
 (16:20), 206
 (17:1), 207, 212
 (17:1–2), 207, 217
 (17:1–19:10), 206–26
 (17:2), 210, 216, 217, 223
 (17:3), 207, 218
 (17:3–4), 207
 (17:4), 216, 223
 (17:5), 208, 211
 (17:5–6), 207

Index Locorum 307

(17:6), 210, 211, 214, 218, 222
(17:7), 207
(17:8), 219, 220, 222
(17:9), 208, 209, 219
(17:9–10), 207, 219
(17:10), 222
(17:11), 219, 220, 222
(17:12), 219, 222
(17:12–14), 207
(17:14), 219
(17:15), 207
(17:16), 207, 212, 219–21, 224
(17:17), 209, 210, 213
(17–18), 209
(18:1), 223
(18:1–2), 207
(18:2), 218, 220, 222–3
(18:2–3), 212
(18:3), 216, 217
(18:3–8), 207
(18:4), 222, 223, 225
(18:4–7), 218, 224
(18:5), 225
(18:6), 223, 224
(18:6–7), 223, 224–5
(18:7–8), 215–16
(18:8), 212, 218, 222, 224, 225
(18:9), 217, 218, 222
(18:9–10), 207
(18:9–22), 216
(18:10), 210
(18:11), 210
(18:11–17), 207
(18:12–13), 210, 216
(18:13), 210, 215
(18:16), 210
(18:17–19), 207
(18:18), 210, 222
(18:19), 210
(18:20), 207, 212, 214, 223
(18:21), 210, 224
(18:21–24), 207
(18:22–24), 223
(18:23), 216, 218
(18:24), 210, 211, 214–16, 223
(18:24a), 214
(18:24b), 214
(19:1), 223
(19:1–2), 207
(19:2), 212, 213, 214, 216, 217, 223
(19:3), 207, 222
(19:4), 223
(19:6), 223

(19:8), 207
(19:9), 207
(19:10), 207
(21:9–22:5), 213
Romans
(10:18), 269
2 Thessalonians
(1:5–9), 214

Rabbinic Literature
Avodah Zarah
(18a), 152
Avot de-Rabbi Natan
(A, 4), 178
(B, 6), 178
Genesis Rabbah
(68:14), 152
Gittin
(56a-b), 178
Lamentations Rabba
(1:5), 178
Leviticus Rabbah
(29:2), 152, 169
Mechilta de-RY
  Vayassa (1:248), 184
Pesahim
(54b), 184
Pirqei deRabbi Eliezer
(35), 152
(71), 208
Yoma
(10a), 184–6

Christian Literature
Augustine
  C.D.
    (10.27), 228
    (16–18), 250
    (18.23), 238
    (20.5.4), 254
  Ep.
    (104.3.11), 228
    (136.2), 248, 259
    (197), 254
    (198), 254
    (198.5), 254
    (198.5–6), 268–9
    (198.6), 254, 263
    (199), 254
    (199.20), 254
    (199.34), 254, 270
    (199.35), 254, 270
    (199.46), 254, 263, 270
    (199.47), 254, 255, 271

Augustine (cont.)
  (199.51), 254, 271
  Ep. Rom. inch.
    (3), 228
  Serm.
    (81.8), 248
    (81.8–9), 248
    (105.12–13), 248
    (296.9), 248
Chronica Minora
  (1), 251
  (3), 253
Constantine
  Or.
    (1.4), 228
    (4.3), 236
    (11.15), 228
    (18), 238
    (18.2), 229
    (19.2–3), 242
    (19.3), 237, 238, 244
    (19.3–4), 237
    (19.4), 228
    (19.6), 236
    (19.8), 236
    (19.9), 240, 241
    (20.2), 228, 237
    (20.3), 237
    (20.6), 228
    (20.8), 228, 237, 240
Cyprian
  ad Dem.
    (4), 248
Eucherius of Lyon
  De Cont. Mund.
    (*PL* 50, 721–722), 251
Eusebius
  Constantine's Speech to the Assembly of the Saints. See Constantine, Or.
  H.E.
    (3.18.3), 211
    (5.8.6), 211
  Vit. Const.
    (4.29.1–3), 227
    (4.32), 227
Gregory the Great
  Hom. Ezec.
    (2.6.22), 252
    (2.6.22–23), 260
Jerome
  Ep.
    (22.29.7), 227
    (53.7), 228
    (130.6), 248
Lactantius
  Div. Inst.
    (1.5.2), 232
    (1.5.11), 232
    (1.6.6), 231
    (1.6.8–12), 191
    (1.6.17), 230
    (1.11), 231
    (1.11.24), 231
    (1.19.5), 242
    (3.26.10–11), 231
    (4.15.26–27), 242
    (5.4.6), 230
    (5.5.3), 236
    (5.5–6), 234, 236
    (5.6.13), 234
    (5.7.1), 234
    (5.7.1–2), 234
    (5.8.2), 234
    (5.10), 236
    (5.11.5–6), 229
    (5.23.1), 229
    (6.1.1), 231
    (6.2.15–16), 232
    (6.8.6–9), 231
    (6.8.10–12), 232
    (7.13.1–2), 230
    (7.20.3), 239
    (7.24), 229
    (7.24.8–12), 233–4
    (7.24.11), 235
MGH
  AA (9.547), 251
  AA (13.415), 253
Orosius
  (2.3.2), 250
  (2.3.2–4), 266
  (2.3.6), 266
  (7.2.9), 250, 266
  (7.2.12), 250, 267
  (7.41.8), 255, 263
  (7.43.5), 250, 267
  (7.43.6), 267
Palladius
  Laus. Hist.
    (54.7), 251
Photius
  Bibl. cod.
    (127), 227
Salvian
  G.D.
    (6.68), 255
Sidonius Apollinaris
  Carm.

Index Locorum 309

(2.61–87), 257
(2.132), 257
(2.586–602), 257
(5), 257
(5.586–602), 272–3
(7), 256
(7.51–56), 256, 272
(7.127–135), 257
(7.357–361), 256, 272
(7.552–564), 257
(7.595–598), 257, 272
Ep.
  (5.16.4), 257, 262
  (8.2), 257
Tertullian
  De Pal.
    (4.1), 245
Zosimus
  (5.35.5), 248, 260

Judaean Desert Documents
Cairo Genizah copy of the *Damascus Document* (CD)
  (4:15), 178
1Q *Mysteries* 27
  (5–7) = 4Q *Mysteries*[b] 300
  (3), 180
1Q *Pesher Habakkuk*
  (II:10–17), 172
  (III), 172
  (III:5), 172
  (III:12–13), 172
  (IV), 172
  (IV:10–13), 172
  (IV:16-V:1ff.), 172
  (V:3–4), 172
  (V:14–15), 172
  (VI:1–12), 172
  (IX:4–7), 172
4Q *Pesher Habakkuk*
  (III:1–2), 177
  (VI:12), 177
4Q *Pesher Isaiah*[a] 161
  (III:6–21), 173
4Q *Pesher Nahum*
  (1–2 II:3–4), 172
  (3–4 I:3), 172
  (3–4 II:3–6), 172
  (3–4 IV:1–4), 172
1Q *Thanksgiving Hymns*[a]
  (11:27), 178
4Q *Time of Righteousness* 215a
  (1 II), 181
1Q *War Scroll*
  (1:4–5), 173

(1:6), 171
(1:9:6), 173
(15:2–3), 173
(16:3), 173
(16:6), 173
(16:8), 173
(16:9), 173
(19:9–13), 173
(19:10), 173
1Q *War Scroll* 33
  (1:4–6), 181-2
4Q *War Scroll* 491
  (10 II), 173
  (11 II), 173
  (13), 173
4Q *War Scroll* 492
  (1:9), 173
  (1:12), 173
4Q *War Scroll* 496
  (3:6), 171, 173

Apocrypha and Pseudepigrapha
2 *Baruch*
  (36:7–10), 176–7
  (36:8), 177–8
  (36–40), 176, 190
  (39:5–7), 177
1 *Clement*
  (1:1), 211
  (5), 211
  (6:1–3), 211
1 *Enoch*
  (18:6), 208
  (18:8), 208
  (24:2), 208
  (25:3), 208
4 *Ezra*
  (4:13–19), 177
  (5:1), 177
  (5:23–24), 177
  (11), 190
  (11:38–12:3), 177
  (12:4–35), 177
  (12:13), 177
  (14:18), 177
Jubilees
  (24:28–29), 171
  (37:10), 171
Judith
  (1:1), 210
1 *Maccabees*
  (1:1), 171
  (8:5), 171
Septuagint
  4 Kingdoms

Septuagint (cont.)
    (9:7), 213, 216
  Jeremiah.
    (28:49), 214

Inscriptions
CIL
  (6.930), 165
  (6.2107), 70
  (6.31207), 165
I. Salamine
  (138), 9
IGRR
  (4.661), 9
ILS
  (244), 165
  (5037), 78
  (5048), 70, 81

RG
  (3.1), 119
  (6.1), 119
  (8.5), 119
  (26.3–4), 119
  (26–33), 141
  (32.2), 119
  (34.1), 105, 119
RIC
  (II, 265a-d), 5
  (VII, 314), 255
  (VII, 317), 255
  (VIII, 258), 255
SEG
  (17.750), 9
  (18.578), 9
  (49.1488), 9
  (59.278), 9

Index of Names and Places

Abraham, 271
Achilles, 52
Actium, 37
Adiabene, 163
Adolenda, 71
Adriatic, 90, 116
Aelius Aristides, 8, 109, 112–13, 117–18, 119, 143
Aemilius Regulus, 161
Aemilius Sura, 8, 85–6
Aeneas, 47–8, 50–2, 53–4, 57–60, 62, 196
Aetius, 256, 272
Africa, 249, 251, 255, 257, 264, 270
Agrippa I, 135, 160, 163, 216
Agrippa II, 11–12, 130–54
Akmonia, 9
Alaric, 248–9, 266
Alba Longa, 48, 57
Alexander Jannaeus, 134
Alexander the Great, 86, 91, 101, 108, 113, 122, 125, 136, 157
Alexandria, 9, 41–2, 128, 140, 144, 149
Alpines, 273
Amos, 216
Anchises, 32
Ando, Clifford, 70
Anilaeus, 163
Annius Minucianus, 161
Antenor, 47
Anthemius, 257
Antioch, 194, 202
Antonius, M., 23, 32, 242, 244
Apennines, 59
Apion, 160
Apollo, 33, 59, 191, 244
Appian, 7–8, 87–9, 99–100, 107–11, 112–13, 117
Aquila, Caligula's assassin, 162
Arbatus, 266
Arete, 121–3
Argos, 55
Aristobulus IV, son of Herod, 135
Aristotle, 19, 136

Armenia, 193, 200
Artabanus V, 185
Ascanius. *See* Iulus
Asclepius, 68
Asia, 90–1, 107, 116, 124, 194–5, 200, 209, 219
Asia Minor, 68, 82, 220
Asinaeus, 163
Asinius Pollio, C., 35, 38, 39, 40
Asshur. *See* Assyria
Assyria, 171–6
Athens, 59–61, 113, 136–7
Attila, 253, 256, 257
Auden, Wystan H., 58
Augustine, 29, 228, 234, 246–7, 248–52, 253–6, 259, 261, 263
Augustus, 15, 32–3, 49, 53, 56, 60, 66–7, 68, 74, 105–6, 111, 116, 118, 119, 141, 144, 147, 153, 234, 242, 244, 250–1
Aune, David E., 210, 217, 220, 224–5
Aurelian, 243
Aurelius Cotta, L., 238–41
Aventine Hill, 251
Avilius Flaccus, A., 128, 140
Avitus, 256

Babylon, 14, 149, 152, 163, 168, 169, 184, 186, 189–90, 197–8, 206–7, 210–12, 214, 215–16, 217–18, 222–5, 246, 248, 250, 266–7
Balaam, 149, 158, 168, 171, 188
Balak, 158
Bandy, Alan S., 213
Bar Kochba, 13, 252
Barker, Margaret, 208, 211
Barrett, John, 76–7, 78
Bauckham, Richard, 177
Beale, Gregory K., 208, 210, 214, 218, 220
Beard, Mary, 75
Belisarius, 252
Ben Mattatihu, Joseph. *See* Josephus
Berthelot, Katell, 151
Bethel, 170

311

Index of Names and Places

Bhabha, Homi, 143
Bithynia, 138
Bocchus, 273
Boyer, Pascal, 64, 74, 79
Britain, 108, 141, 196
Brooke, George, 175
Brown, Dan, 242
Buchheit, Vinzenz, 231
Bury, John, 245

Caecina Severus, Aulus, 18, 21–2
Caesarea, 139
Calgacus, 134
Caligula. *See* Gaius Caligula
Camillus, 5, 51–2
Campania, 256
Cannae, 51
Capitol. *See* Capitoline
Capitoline Hill, 66
Cappadocia, 138
Caracalla, 184
Caranus, king of Macedonia, 266
Caria, 194
Carthage, 47, 52, 62, 87–9, 95, 114–15, 124, 138, 148, 193, 250, 253, 255–6, 261, 266
Cassius Chaerea, 161–2, 164–5
Cato. *See* Porcius Cato
Catullus, 37
Catullus, governor of Cyrene, 168
Chalcedon, 257
Chaldea, 223
Christ. *See* Jesus Christ
Cicero. *See* Tullius Cicero
Cilicia, 138
Claudius, 163
Claudius Marcellus, M., 58
Clermont-Ferrand, 256
Clitumnus, 76
Coinquenda, 71
Constantine, 14–15, 227–30, 235–44, 260
Constantinople, 245, 252, 254, 262
Corinth, 95, 193–4, 199
Cornelius Scipio Aemilianus Africanus, P. (Numantinus), 21, 25–6, 28, 62, 87–9, 100, 148
Cornelius Scipio Africanus, P. (the elder), 51
Cornelius Sulla, L., 37, 195
Cotta. *See* Aurelius Cotta
Ctesias, 86
Cyprus, 9, 194, 202
Cyrene, 168
Cyrus, 86, 186, 267

Daniel, 149, 152, 157–8, 168, 188, 192
Dante Alighieri, 228, 242
Danube, 90, 116
David, king of Israel, 184
Dea Dia, 64, 68–9, 71, 76, 79, 83, 84
Decius, 243
Demetrius of Phalerum, 112, 120, 126, 157
Democritus, 122
Descartes, René, 3, 30
DeSilva, David, 214–15, 224
Dido, 52
Diocletian, 244
Diodorus Siculus, 88
Dionysius of Halicarnassus, 7–8, 85, 87, 99–111
Domitian, 78, 211
Donatus, Aelius, 228

Eber, 171
Eckstein, Arthur M., 145
Edom, 124, 125, 169, 184–5, 246
Egeria, 68
Egypt, 91, 100, 107, 114–15, 122, 124, 125–6, 142, 163, 173, 195, 196
Elagabalus, 83
Elgvin, Torleif, 182
Enoch, 208
Epidaurus, 68
Esau, 125, 188
Eshel, Hanan, 171
Ethiopia, 115
Eucherius of Lyon, 246, 261, 263
Euphrates, 118–19, 194, 202, 224
Europe, 90–1, 101, 116, 124, 126
Eusebius of Caesarea, 250, 253
Ezekiel, 221

Fabricius Luscinus, C., 104
Feeney, Denis, 42
Festugière, André-Jean, 126
Flaccus, prefect of Egypt. *See* Avilius Flaccus
Flavius Stilicho, 246, 249
Flora, 71
Flusser, David, 175, 180, 182
Fons, 71
Fortune, goddess. *See* Tyche

Gabba, Emilio, 105–7, 151
Gadara, 218
Gaius Caligula, 11–12, 118–19, 123, 128–9, 140, 144, 156, 159–67
Galinsky, Karl, 153
Gallienus, 254, 261, 270
Gaul, 249, 250
Gell, Alfred, 76
Genseric, 251–2, 256–7
Gerasa, 218
Girardet, Klaus M., 17

Index of Names and Places

Gomer, 185
Goodman, Martin, 131
Gracchus. *See* Sempronius Gracchus
Greece, 68, 113, 116, 124, 152, 169, 185, 190, 195
Gregory the Great, 247, 252, 260, 264
Grethlein, Jonas, 1, 2, 5
Gruen, Erich, 148–51, 206, 211, 220, 225

Hadas-Lebel, Mireille, 144
Hades, 197, 200
Hadrian, 196, 200, 248
Hannibal, 138, 265
Hardie, Philip, 5
Hartog, François, 2, 247
Helenus, 6, 59–60, 62
Hera, 203
Heraclitus, 190
Hercules, 71, 234
Hermes Trismegistus, 230
Herod Antipas, 211
Herod the Great, 135
Herodotus, 7, 60–1, 86, 113, 114, 192
Hesiod, 36
Hesychius of Salona, 253–4, 261, 263
Hippo, 249
Hippolytus of Rome, 253
Homer, 62, 88, 237
Honorius, 248, 250, 255
Horace, 39–44, 51, 66, 75
Hydatius of Chaves, 256, 261

Ilia, 48, 56–7
Ilium. *See* Troy
Irenaeus, 211
Isaiah, 176, 187, 198, 215, 236
Isles of the Blest, 51
Israel, Biblical figure. *See* Jacob
Isthmus, 199
Italy, 53–4, 62, 72–3, 82, 105, 146, 148, 157, 192–4, 197–8, 202, 220, 253, 264
Iulus, 5, 48–9, 55–8, 59–60, 62

Jacob, 124, 152, 169–70, 188
Janus, 5, 71
Japheth, 171, 185
Javan, 171, 185
Jeremiah, 188, 215, 224
Jerome, 228, 253, 256, 259
Jerusalem, 11, 29, 130–1, 153, 156, 168, 172, 178–9, 186, 189, 191–5, 198, 201–3, 208, 211, 213, 223, 248, 250, 268, 269
Jesus Christ, 14–15, 207, 210, 214, 219, 225, 228–9, 232–7, 240–4, 253, 254, 257, 269
Joannes, 255
John, 206–26

Joseph, 125, 216
Josephus, 9–12, 114, 130–54, 155–68, 179
Judaea, 11, 131–5, 139, 143, 147, 155, 158, 161–3, 166–7, 170, 174, 179, 187, 190, 195–6, 213, 217, 269
Judah. *See* Judaea
Judah Aristobulus I, 135
Julius Africanus, 253
Julius Caesar, C., 6, 18–20, 23–4, 26, 29, 37, 41, 53, 55–6, 60, 62, 196, 238, 240
Julius Nepos, 255
Juno, 48, 54–5, 68, 71
Jupiter, 5, 14, 40, 42, 47–8, 49–51, 53–5, 57–8, 63, 70–1, 234, 236, 244, 249
Justinian I, 15, 258
Juturna, 55

Kaden, David A., 139–40, 142–3, 145, 147
Kerdir, Mazdaic priest, 187
Kister, Menahem, 179, 181
Kittim, 171–6, 182
Koselleck, Reinhart, 247
Kowalski, Beate, 220–1
Kraybill, J. Nelson, 215
Kurfess, Alfons, 239

La Magliana, 69
Lactantius, 14–15, 229–37, 240–4
Laelius, C. (Sapiens), 28
Latium, 33, 48, 53–4, 58
Lavinium, 48
Lebanon, 12, 173–9, 187
Leo I, 251, 257
Levine, Caroline, 37–8
Lévi-Strauss, Claude, 64
Libya, 90, 115, 116, 124
Livy, 31, 51, 62
Lucan, 53
Lucceius, L., 21
Lucretius, 25, 37
Lycia, 138

Macchia, Frank D., 217
Macedonia, 124, 136–7, 149, 193, 195, 250, 266
Madai, 185
Maeander river, 202
Magna Mater Deorum, 68
Magog, 185
Majorian, 257
Manlius Torquatus, L., 22
Marcellinus, 259
Marcellus. *See* Claudius Marcellus, M.
Marcus Aurelius, 196, 200
Mariamne I, Hasmonean, 135
Marius, C., 23, 195

Mark Antony. *See* Antonius, M.
Mars, 48, 71
Mary, Mother of Jesus, 14, 236
Mason, Steve, 158
Massilia, 29
Media, 149, 185
Mediterranean, 108, 111, 115, 171, 191, 194, 197, 200, 210
Meliboeus, 40, 43–5
Meotis, 137
Mercury, 47, 71
Meshech, 185
Meyer, Fik, 83
Middle East, 157
Minerva, 71
Moatti, Claudia, 19
Momigliano, Arnaldo, 2
Moses, 151
Mussolini, Benito, 16
Mycenae, 48, 55, 59, 61

Nahum, 172
Naiweld, Ron, 185
Narses, 252
Nebuchadnezzar, 149, 157–8
Nero, 13, 130, 139, 141–2, 194, 196–204, 211–12, 219–20, 225
New York, 248
Nicolet, Claude, 141–2
Nile, 265
Nineveh, 210, 218
Noah, 125, 191
North Africa, 126
Numa, 67

Obadiah, 170
Octavian. *See* Augustus
Olympus, 234
Orosius, 247, 249–50, 255, 259, 261, 263
Ovid, 4–6, 53, 60–3, 191

Padua, 47–8, 56
Palatine Hill, 122, 161, 251
Palestine, 170, 184, 186, 189, 217
Palladium, 53
Pamphylia, 138
Parcae, 36, 38
Parthia, 41, 184–6, 200, 202, 203
Patmos, 211
Paul, 211
Pédech, Paul, 145
Peirano, Irene, 104
Pericles, 24
Perseus, king of Macedonia, 120, 266
Persia, 13, 91, 115, 149, 152, 184–8

Pessinus, 68
Peter, 211
Petronius Maximus, 256, 272
Petronius, P., 160–2, 164–6
Philip II, king of Macedonia, 136
Philo, 9–10, 112–15, 118–20, 123–9, 138–40, 144, 149, 151–2, 160, 162
Phoebus. *See* Apollo
Phthia, 48, 52, 55
Pillars of Hercules, 101, 117
Placidus. *See* Valentinian III
Plato, 19, 25–6, 122, 136, 231
Pliny, the Elder, 18, 67, 71
Pliny, the Younger, 76
Plutarch, 8, 110, 112, 121–3, 136
Polybius, 7–9, 19, 23, 62, 85–103, 105, 107, 110–11, 112–13, 115–16, 120, 136–8, 143, 145–8, 151–2, 155, 168, 249
Pompeius Magnus, Cn., 19, 134, 194, 195
Pompeius Trogus, 8, 85, 86
Pompey. *See* Pompeius Magnus
Pontus, 115, 124, 137
Porcius Cato, M. (the Elder), 74
Priam, 59, 88
Price, Jonathan, 150
Priscus Attalus, 266
Prosper of Aquitaine, 251–2, 260, 263
Ptolemais, 160
Pydna, 7, 86, 92, 96, 120
Pyrrhus, 104, 265
Pythagoras, 6, 50, 58, 60–3

Quint, David, 52
Quodvultdeus, 256, 261

Rabbah b. 'Ullah, 185
Rabbah b. Bar Hana, 186
Rabbi Akiva, 13
Rabbi Assi, 186, 187
Rabbi Habiba b. Surmaki, 185
Rabbi Johanan, 186
Rabbi Joseph, 185
Rabbi Joshua b. Levi, 184
Rabbi Judah, 186
Rabbi Judah b. Illai, 186
Rabbi Judah the Prince, 184–5
Rabbi Kahana, 186, 187
Rabbi Meir, 188
Rabbi Samuel, 188
Rabbi Samuel b. Nachman, 169–70
Rabbi Yohanan b. Zakkai, 178–9
Rabbi Yose ben Kisma, 152
Rabirius, C., 23
Rajak, Tessa, 131, 134, 139, 142–4, 151–2
Rav, 186–7

Rav Nachman, 169–70
Remus, 57, 251
Rhine, 118–19
Rhineland, 265
Roduit, Alexandre, 131, 139, 140–2
Romulus, 28, 31, 48, 56–7, 69, 106, 111, 196, 251
Romulus Augustus, 255
Rostovtzeff, Michael, 130
Rufinus of Aquileia, 263
Runnals, Donna, 132
Rutilius Namatianus, 249, 250–1, 257, 259

Salome Alexandra, 134, 135
Salvianus of Marseille, 261
Samaria, 269
Samaria, mountain, 216
Sardinia, 90, 116
Saturn, 33, 36, 71, 119, 153, 233–4
Saulnier, Christiane, 141–2
Scheid, John, 69, 80
Schneider, Maridien, 21
Scipio. *See* Cornelius Scipio
Sempronius Gracchus, C., 106
Sempronius Gracchus, Ti., 37
Seneca the Younger, 139
Seneca, the Younger, 18, 29
Seraiah, 224
Severus Alexander, 83
Sharon, Nadav, 175
Shem, 186
Sicily, 18, 90, 116
Sidonius Apollinaris, 256–7, 261, 262
Simon Thassi, 134
Socrates, 231
Sodom, 248
Solomon, king of Israel, 186
South Africa, 14, 224
Spain, 249–50, 256, 264
Sparta, 59–61, 91, 113, 136–7
Spilsbury, Paul, 149
Stilico. *See* Flavius Stilicho
Suetonius, 161
Sulla. *See* Cornelius Sulla
Summanus, 71
Syria, 17, 122, 166

Teman, 184
Terentius Varro, M. (Reatinus), 67, 71, 251
Tertullian, 245, 246
Thebes, 59, 61, 113
Theodosius I, 245, 260
Theodosius II, 255
Thomas, John C., 217

Thucydides, 8, 24, 60–1, 66, 90, 100, 106, 109, 130
Tiber, 59, 68, 122
Tiberias, 160
Tiberius, 9, 118, 160, 162, 237, 242
Tiberius Gemellus, 160, 162
Tibullus, 31
Tiras, 185
Titus, 74, 146, 179, 194
Tityrus, 39–40, 43–5
Totila, 252,
Trajan, 186, 257
Troy, 5, 41–2, 47, 48, 51–2, 53–5, 56–7, 59, 62, 87–8
Tubal, 185
Tullius Cicero, M., 2–3, 14, 17–31, 227, 231–2, 238–44
Tullius Cicero, Q., 28, 238
Turnus, 5, 51, 54–5
Tyche, 10, 91, 104, 120–4, 128–9, 138, 140, 144–7, 148, 151–2, 156
Tyre, 216–18, 221–2, 224–5

Valentinian III, 251, 255, 256, 261, 272
Valerian, 243
Valerius Maximus, M., 105
van Gennep, Arnold, 75
Varro. *See* Terentius Varro
Veii, 5, 51, 68
Velleius Paterculus, 86
Venus, 5, 47–8, 49–51, 54–6, 63, 71
Vermeylen, Jacques, 213
Verres, C., 28
Vespasian, 130, 135, 146, 178–9, 187, 204
Vesta, 70–1
Vesuvius, 192, 202
Virgil, 3–5, 15, 32–43, 46, 50–1, 53, 58, 142, 153, 227–44
Virtue, goddess. *See* Arete
Volaterrae, 18
Vout, Caroline, 208
Vulcan, 71

Walbank, Frank W., 88, 98, 145
Wallace-Hadrill, Andrew, 33
Western Europe, 90, 116
Wiseman, Timothy P., 106, 162

Yahweh, 192

Zechariah, 168, 188
Zeus, 203
Zion, 216
Zosimus, 260

CPSIA information can be obtained
at www.ICGtesting.com
Printed in the USA
LVHW011049030821
694401LV00005B/334